Using WordStar 7.0

KATHERINE MURRAY

Publisher: Lloyd J. Short

Associate Publisher: Rick Ranucci

Product Development Manager: Thomas H. Bennett

Book Designer: Scott Cook

Production Team: Jeff Baker, Michelle Cleary, Terri Edwards, Mark Enochs, Denny Hager, Carrie Keesling, Phil Kitchel, Loren C. Malloy, Cindy L. Phipps, Linda Seifert, Sandra Shay, Mae Louise Shinault, Kevin Spear, Tina Trettin, Angie Trzepacz, Mary Beth Wakefield, Julie Walker, Kelli Widdifield, Lisa Wilson, Allan Wimmer, Christine Young

To Kelly and Christopher,

    Because too often "in a minute" becomes "later,"

    and "just a second" means "after I finish this chapter."

The book's done, kids—

Now we can play.

love, Mom

CREDITS

Product Director
Brenda Carmichael

Senior Editor
Jeannine Freudenberger

Editors
Louise Lambert
Susan S. Shaw

Acquisitions Editor
Chris Katsaropoulos

Technical Editor and Final Review
Tamra Senior Wallace

Composed in Cheltenham and MCPdigital by Que Corporation

Katherine Murray is the president of reVisions Plus, Inc., a writing and desktop publishing company that deals primarily with the development and production of microcomputer-related materials. She is the author of *Using Microsoft Publisher, Que's PS/1 Book, Introduction to Personal Computers, Using Publish It!, Using PFS:First Publisher, Using Professional Write, Using PFS: First Choice*, and other computer titles.

TRADEMARK ACKNOWLEDGMENTS

ACKNOWLEDGMENTS

The publication of any book is the result of efforts from many people. I would like to thank the following people who contributed to the publishing of *Using WordStar 7.0*:

Chris Katsaropoulos, Acquisitions Editor, who is always surprisingly helpful, encouraging, and even-tempered.

Brenda Carmichael, Product Development Specialist, who met the challenge of shepherding me through this project with undying optimism (thanks, Brenda. . .).

Tamra Wallace, Technical Editor, for netting out any stubborn bugs in this manuscript and making sure all the examples worked the way I reported them, and helping with a final review of the edited manuscript.

Jeannine Freudenbeger, Senior Editor, for pushing the project through a hectic schedule, ensuring that editorial accuracy standards were being met.

Susan Shaw and Louise Lambert, Copy Editors, who were responsible for up-holding those editorial standards (and did a fine job).

Doug, Kelly, and Christopher, as always, for keeping me sane in the midst of insane deadlines.

CONTENTS AT A GLANCE

TABLE OF CONTENTS

Introduction

Think about your word processor for a minute. Can you use your mouse to open menus, choose commands, and position the cursor? Are all your text options, such as font, style, alignment, and spacing, placed on the edit screen waiting to be selected? Can you use paragraph styles, powerful macros, and graphics to streamline and enhance your work? Do you have an automatic indexer? A table of contents generator? If not, you're going to love WordStar 7.0.

If you're not using a word processor now, the time and trouble you'll save producing documents you previously typed on a typewriter may astound you. Whether you type memos, correspondence, reports, or other materials, you'll find in WordStar 7.0 special features that can help you learn comfortably all the basics of word processing, cutting an incredible amount of time from routine typing tasks and giving you the option of using powerful features not available on even the most sophisticated typewriters.

This newest version of WordStar includes all the basic word processing features—and much more. With WordStar 7.0, you can do the following:

- Create professional-looking memos and correspondence
- Compose sophisticated reports complete with integrated graphics, headers and footers, and note boxes
- Use paragraph styles to apply to paragraphs formats you use often
- Create publications with multiple text columns
- Merge print letters and mailing labels for large-volume printing
- Generate an index and a table of contents for your document
- Communicate your WordStar data by using a modem or fax machine

- Convert WordStar files to and from other word processing formats by using Star Exchange, a conversion utility

- Print your document on one of more than 200 supported printers

These tasks are just a few that you can perform with WordStar 7.0.

Without sacrificing any of the power or speed of the program, the makers of WordStar 7.0 have made the program incredibly easier to use. Now users can use the mouse to navigate around the edit screen, select commands, and position the cursor. Enhanced macro capabilities also make automating work sessions easier than ever before.

Additional features significantly lessen the amount of time you'll spend creating and fine-tuning your documents. WordStar helps you streamline your word processing tasks by enabling you to do the following:

- Open menus and easily make selections by using your mouse

- Change text font, style, and alignment from the edit screen without using the menus

- Customize the menus and help screens to display only the information you need

- Use paragraph styles to apply formats you use often

- Check the accuracy of your work with the spelling checker and thesaurus

If you are new to WordStar—or to word processing in general—you should find the menus systems easy to understand and use. The always-available help system also is a big benefit to users who find themselves stuck in the middle of an operation. And because you can perform many tasks with the simple click of a mouse button, the program is user-friendly.

If you are an experienced WordStar user, the reorganized menus should please you: new menus and restructured existing menus make the locations of commands more logical. Similar commands are grouped together so that you can find and use them more easily. And those of you who want to keep the edit screen as open as possible still can choose from different menu levels, displaying in the work area only the amount of help you need. A new macro utility also has increased the program's power and replaces the old Shorthand macros with more sophisticated programmable macro capabilities.

Whether you are a new WordStar user or an experienced WordStar enthusiast, you'll find out about the basic and more specialized features of WordStar 7.0 in this book. With simple step-by-step instructions, numerous examples and illustrations, and a variety of tips and checklists, *Using WordStar 7.0* helps you get up to speed with this powerful new program no matter what your level of experience.

What Is WordStar 7.0?

WordStar has been around forever, so it seems. WordStar was peeking into the PC market at the time when the original IBM PC was just being introduced. For the first time, the original WordStar offered users the sparkling benefits of word processing: no more correction fluid, no more carbon paper, and no more retyping documents that contain "typos" or bad margins. With the introduction of word processing, typists could reduce dramatically the amount of time they spent typing and retyping documents.

Since that early release of WordStar more than a decade ago, the program has gone through numerous revisions and enhancements. Different menu systems have been added. Merge-print capabilities appeared, enabling users to print large volumes of materials with names and addresses inserted for them. Macros helped users carry out—at the press of a key—complex series of keystrokes needed for tasks they performed often.

WordStar also was so flexible that users could work with the program in the manner most comfortable for them: they could choose menu levels to display the amount of help needed on-screen, embed dot commands and special format codes in text to control the layout of text, and use multiple windows to compare and contrast documents.

Although WordStar 7.0 is many generations from its earliest ancestor, the makers of WordStar have never lost sight of the most important aspects of the program: speed, flexibility, and power.

In WordStar 7.0, you control how much information you want displayed. If you are a new user, you should use help level 4, which causes the full pull-down menu system to be displayed at all times; if you are an experienced user, you may want to choose a help level (such as 3, 2, 1, or 0) that suppresses the display of menus so that you have more room to work on-screen.

The add-on features of the program enhance the power WordStar offers you by giving you the option of generating indexes and tables of contents, producing mailing lists and labels, sending data via fax or modem, or integrating graphics into your documents.

Since its introduction, WordStar has become an industry standard. Popular all over the world, WordStar continues to meet the needs of users by adding new features, streamlining old ones, and increasing the performance of the software to rival and surpass competing programs. In this book, you find out how WordStar 7.0 brings you the best word processing developments of the last decade, enabling you to create professional-quality documents more easily than ever before.

Advantages of WordStar 7.0

Before looking at specific benefits of WordStar 7.0, consider the advantages of word processing in general. When the first word processing programs were being developed, users were looking for programs that would enable them to create documents easily. In a typical small business, a variety of documents are needed, from memos to reports to invoices and press releases. Typing definitely had its bad points: if you noticed a typographical error after you typed a letter, you had to retype it (or use correction fluid). Then, if you wanted to use the same letter again later, you had to retype it again.

Word processing took the repetition out of typing. Never again do you have to type the same letter twice: the document is saved on disk, ready to be reused. If you want to change a name and address, or a few sentences, you can open the file, press a few keys, print, and have a new letter. Word processing programs also ease the task of formatting the text the way you want it to look.

The original benefits of word processing are, of course, alive and well in WordStar 7.0. The program also includes many other features that take WordStar up a few notches from competing word processing programs. Here are a few of the highlights:

- In WordStar 7.0, the menus have been rearranged from previous versions so that similar commands and procedures are grouped together.
- WordStar now provides mouse capability, which means that you can use a mouse to open and close menus, select commands, highlight text, and place the cursor.
- On-screen help is always available in the Help menu.
- Fax support enables you to send WordStar data through fax machines.
- The macro capabilities have been enhanced dramatically, enabling you to create and store sophisticated macros to increase your WordStar productivity.
- MailList is a utility WordStar users can rely on for creating mailing lists and printing mailing labels.
- TelMerge, a utility present with WordStar 7.0, enables you to send WordStar data through a modem.
- Automatic index and table of contents generators enable you to add special elements to your documents.

- Inset, a text and graphics integration utility, enables you to add graphics to your WordStar documents.

- The edit screen has been rearranged (from previous versions) so that you now can make all text style selections, such as font, size, style, and alignment, on-screen.

This book takes you through all the basics—and then some—that you need to create documents with WordStar 7.0. Whether you've used WordStar for years and are getting acquainted with this new version or this is your first experience with word processing of any kind, you'll find out how to use these WordStar 7.0 benefits to your advantage.

Why Do You Need a Book on WordStar?

Learning anything new involves some kind of learning curve, whether you're building on experience or starting from scratch. Although most users prefer being able to sit down with a new computer program and be productive immediately without even opening the documentation, this scenario rarely happens.

The problem with truly powerful programs is that you may find them somewhat difficult to learn. Although the procedures themselves may not be complicated, you have so many different things to explore that you may miss out on some important features. Likewise, sometimes when you try out a procedure that just doesn't work the way you think it should, having a step-by-step tutorial book at your side is a great advantage.

Using WordStar 7.0 is meant to help you learn the basics of WordStar without suffering through the headaches of trial and error. By providing clear, step-by-step instructions, examples, and illustrations, *Using WordStar 7.0* helps you get up to speed quickly and points you in the direction of features you may not discover on your own.

Whether you use *Using WordStar 7.0* as a tutorial guide, a reference, or a place to turn when you're stuck and don't know what else to do, you'll find troubleshooting tips, design suggestions, and other hints that help you use the many features of WordStar in a way that best suits your publications.

Who Should Read This Book?

If you currently work with a word processing program or suspect that you soon will inherit WordStar responsibilities, you'll find information in this book that tells you what all this WordStar fuss is about. Specifically, if you are now the proud new owner of WordStar 7.0 and are eager to get started using the program, you'll find in *Using WordStar 7.0* examples and instructions that help you become productive quickly, whether you currently are using WordStar or are trying out word processing for the first time.

This book explains the feature-laden WordStar 7.0 to readers of various skill and experience levels, including the following:

- Professionals who need to publish high-quality documents quickly

- Support staff personnel who are responsible for doing corporate reports

- Public relations people who need professional, attention-getting press releases

- Business owners who need a variety of documents, including mailing lists and labels, reports, memos, and business correspondence

- Corporate personnel who publish newsletters and other documents

Whether you're new to computers or have used a computer for years, you'll find that the features in WordStar 7.0—and the examples in this book—enable you to produce effective documents quickly. With just a small time investment, you'll find yourself cranking out high-quality, professional-looking documents and tapping into the additional features of the program.

What Is in This Book?

This section explains what you'll find in the various parts of *Using WordStar 7.0*. The text starts with the basics and moves gradually into more advanced techniques and features. You can read the book straight through, or you can turn to the chapter or section that explains what you need to know at the moment.

Part I

Part I, "Introducing WordStar 7.0," consists of Chapters 1 through 4. These chapters explain all the basics of word processing in general and WordStar in particular. You learn about the new features of WordStar 7.0 and find out how to begin working with the program, using keyboard and mouse techniques to perform simple operations. Part I also includes a tutorial quick-start chapter, which includes simple procedures for all the basic tasks involved in creating and printing a short document.

Chapter 1, "Getting Started," acquaints you with this newest version of WordStar. From an introduction to the keyboard and mouse techniques you use to navigate around the program to a tutorial section on starting and exiting WordStar, this chapter sets the foundation for the procedures used throughout the rest of the book. This chapter also provides an overview of WordStar evolution and discusses the new features in WordStar 7.0.

Chapter 2, "Learning WordStar Basics," explains the different menus, commands, and procedures to use as you begin creating documents. Specifically, this chapter includes sections on understanding the WordStar opening menu, learning to open and close menus, and understanding dialog boxes; an introduction to commands and quick-key combinations; and a discussion of the edit screen. You also find out about the help screens and the different help levels available to you at any time during your WordStar work session.

Chapter 3, "A WordStar Quick Start," takes you on a whirlwind tour through the basic features of WordStar 7.0. You learn to start WordStar, open a new document, enter text, choose text styles, select text alignment, use the spelling checker, perform simple keyboard editing techniques, and save and print your document.

Chapter 4, "Working with WordStar Files," takes Chapter 3 one step further by explaining more fully how to save WordStar files. You also learn how to retrieve files you've already saved, change the logged drive and directory, and create backup and template files.

Part II

Part II, "Creating and Printing WordStar Documents," consists of Chapters 5 through 11. These chapters cover all the procedures you need to use to enter, edit, enhance, format, view, and print text in your WordStar documents.

Chapter 5, "Designing the Document," helps you plan the type of document you want. Are you adding special design features such as boxes or notes? Do you need to add headers and footers? Should your text be one column wide, or do you need to use more than one column? This chapter encourages you to consider the overall design of your publication before you begin creating it. Design tips and checklists help you decide which features you want to include in your document.

In Chapter 6, "Entering and Importing Text," you learn how to get the text into your WordStar document. This chapter includes basic typing techniques and editing keys, as well as simple step-by-step examples you can use to try out different procedures. Chapter 6 also explains how to bring already entered text into your WordStar document and provides an overview of Star Exchange, a conversion utility that converts text files created in other word processing programs to a format compatible with WordStar 7.0. This chapter also introduces you to paragraph styles, which are built-in formats you can assign to individual paragraphs in your document. (Chapter 8 includes more about paragraph styles.)

Chapter 7, "Editing Text," concentrates on one of the biggest benefits of any word processing program: the capability to edit text you've entered. In this chapter, you learn about basic keyboard editing; marking text as a block; copying, moving, deleting, and pasting blocks of text; using the find-and-replace feature; and using various Go To commands to move around in the document. You also learn how to use the spelling checker and the thesaurus included with WordStar 7.0.

Chapter 8, "Enhancing Text Styles," explains how you can modify the look of your text. From a basic discussion of changing the selected font to choosing text size; working with boldfaced, italic, and underlined type; and choosing text alignment, this chapter progresses into more specialized WordStar techniques such as setting up, using, and modifying paragraph styles in WordStar 7.0.

Chapter 9, "Viewing the Document," shows you your options for displaying the document you're working with. WordStar 7.0 enables you to display a variety of different help menus and control display options, such as command tags, highlighting, prompts, and other optional screen items. You learn how to preview a page and work with WordStar windows. This chapter also shows you how to check the status of your document so that you can find out how much memory your document is using and how much memory is still available.

Chapter 10, "Finishing Page Layout," helps you fine-tune the document you are creating. You learn to control the appearance of your document by using the Alignment and Spacing options, adjust the spacing of individual characters by using the kerning feature, and work with and adjust multiple columns. This chapter also shows you how to add a few special touches to your document by inserting notes, adding headers and footers, and adding page numbers.

Chapter 11, "Printing Your Documents," includes all the basics you need to know about printing your document. From a basic section on making sure that your printer is set up and ready, to step-by-step instructions for starting the print routine and using the printing options, this chapter helps you get your document down in black and white. This chapter also includes troubleshooting tips for printing.

Part III

Part III, "WordStar's Special Features," looks at WordStar 7.0's additional features. The features covered in Chapters 12 through 16 include Inset, which enables you to integrate graphics into your text documents; macros, which are specialized, high-powered command sequences you can use to automate your work sessions; MailList, a mailing label utility that helps you create mailing lists and labels without the usual headaches; and TelMerge, WordStar's communications utility, which enables you to send WordStar data through a modem to remote computers or to a fax machine. Part III ends with Chapter 17, which provides a set of WordStar examples, using the different features of the program in various types of documents.

Chapter 12, "Adding Graphics," explains how to use Inset, a special add-on utility that enables you to incorporate graphics into your WordStar documents. Basic procedures for loading and using Inset graphics are explained, as are practical tips for printing documents that use Inset graphics.

Chapter 13, "Creating and Using WordStar Macros," concentrates on one of the most powerful new enhancements of WordStar 7.0: the macro features. You learn to create a simple macro, using the recording and playback routines. You also find out how to edit the macros you create and set up a file to store your macros. A number of troubleshooting tips help you get unstuck when your macros don't work the way you envisioned them. This chapter also includes several macros you can use as you create your own WordStar documents.

Chapter 14, "Creating Form Letters and Labels," teaches you how to use MailList to create form letters, mailing lists, and labels. Instructions for setting up and using lists and printing labels are included, as are tips for selecting and printing mailing labels. A troubleshooting section also helps you eliminate printing problems.

Chapter 15, "Using WordStar's Communication Features," introduces you to TelMerge, a communications utility that enables you to send WordStar files through a modem or fax. (Using a fax is new with WordStar 7.0.) A hardware primer teaches you the basics about using communications, and a sample communications session helps you see how you can use TelMerge to transmit WordStar data.

Chapter 16, "Using the Index and TOC Features," shows you how to use WordStar to create an index and a table of contents for your publication. You learn to create a file for index entries, mark entries in your documents, and compile the index. For the table of contents, you find out how to select entries and compile the list.

Chapter 17, "A WordStar Sampler," provides you with several examples of different WordStar documents, each created with different formats, margins, text fonts and styles, column configurations, and special features. You can use these samples to pick and choose the features you want to incorporate into your own WordStar documents.

The book is rounded out by six appendixes and a glossary. Appendix A explains how to install and set up WordStar 7.0; Appendix B lists troubleshooting tips you may need as you experiment with your new program; Appendix C lists design ideas you may want to use in your own documents; and Appendix D lists the various quick-key combinations and special dot commands used in WordStar 7.0. Appendix E gives you tips for working with professional printing shops, and Appendix F tells you how you can customize WordStar. Finally, the glossary brings commonly used WordStar and word processing terms to your fingertips.

As you can tell from the number of features this book covers, learning WordStar 7.0 is no small feat. Although this newest version of the program is easier to master than its predecessors and the mouse capabilities make the program more fun to use, you've still got quite a learning curve ahead of you. So, now that you know the overall game plan for the book, get started.

Conventions Used in This Book

The conventions in this book have been established to help you learn to use WordStar 7.0 as quickly as possible.

1. Information you are to type (usually found in examples with numbered steps) is indicated by italic type (such as "Type *cd*") or is indented and set on a line by itself.

2. Names of menus (such as Format or Options menu) and dialog boxes are shown with the initial letter capitalized. Options on the menus are also capitalized (for example, Define Paragraph Style).

3. Messages and prompts that appear on-screen are shown in a special typeface, such as LPT1.

4. Special tips are highlighted by a special design box.

In addition to these conventions, figures are used liberally throughout the book to illustrate the examples in various stages of completion.

Introducing WordStar 7.0

PART

1

OUTLINE

Getting Started

Welcome to WordStar 7.0. When you finish this book, you will have learned a great deal about word processing in general and about WordStar in particular. You will be able to create, edit, format, and print basic documents, such as memos, reports, and other similar documents. You'll also understand WordStar 7.0's special features: MailList, TelMerge, and Inset, and more.

Three special add-on features—MailList, TelMerge, and Inset—were available in earlier versions of WordStar but have even more power and flexibility in WordStar 7.0. With MailList, you can create a database (a file that stores data). You can have WordStar insert automatically into your printed document items of data from this database, enabling you to create mailing labels and form letters easily. TelMerge is a communications program with which you send and receive files by using a modem and your phone line. Inset is a program that "takes a picture" of images on your computer screen; then you can integrate those graphics into your printed document.

Before beginning the journey through WordStar 7.0's many powerful features, however, you first learn a few basics: What *is* word processing? How will word processing benefit you? What types of word processing programs are in the market today? After an initial overview of word processing software, this chapter introduces you to WordStar and, specifically, to the new features in WordStar 7.0. This chapter concludes with tutorial sections on using the keyboard and the mouse and starting and exiting WordStar.

What Is Word Processing?

If you are new to computers but have researched different types of software, you know that word processing programs enable you to use your personal computer to work with words. Not a difficult concept. The capabilities of different word processors vary, however; so let's start with the basic concept of word processing and work from there.

Word processing is the electronic replacement for that Smith Corona typewriter collecting dust in the corner of your office. Anything you previously created on the typewriter—or with a pen and paper, for that matter—you can now do with word processing. And more.

Think about the kinds of things you do with your typewriter: you set margins and tabs, type text, press the carriage return to move to the next line, and so on. These tasks can be done easily—even automatically—by a word processing program.

And what types of documents did you create on the typewriter? You created letters, memos, reports, perhaps even newsletters and advertising fliers. Your choices were limited, however, when it came to choosing the way your text would look, the way it was formatted, and the quality of the printed page.

Thankfully, the evolution of the personal computer brought with it a number of timesaving options for the wordsmith. The benefits of word processing are discussed in the next section.

The Advantages of Word Processing

When given a choice, many people hesitate to make the change from typewriter to word processor because the leap in technology is just plain intimidating. Once typists become familiar with the advantages of word processing, however—benefits such as reusable data, capability to add art work, easy editing, and high-quality printouts—the risk doesn't seem nearly as great.

The following paragraphs explain the major advantages of word processing.

Reusable data. For many people, the greatest benefit of word processing is reusable data. Suppose, for example, that you create a report for one department in your company; this report contains an overall review of the past year, some department-specific information about new employees, and a projection of events for the next quarter. Now suppose that you've just completed that report and an order comes from another department for a second report—this one with the same year review and projections but different new-employee information.

What are your options? With a typewriter, you have only one option: retype the report. Oh, sure, you could copy the parts of the report you want to keep, type only the new section, and then manually paste the new section in place in the report, but you would wind up with a pretty shoddy-looking report. In this case, the only way to get a professional-looking report is to retype the entire document—even though you've already typed most of it once. If you are using a word processor, however, the report you typed is saved in a file ready to be used again and again. You can simply open the file, delete the names of the employees in the first report and type the correct names for the second report, save the document, and print. No matter how many times you need to change the file, it is saved on disk ready to be used at any time.

Variable type size. If you used your typewriter to type a title page for a report, you were limited to using characters that were all the same size. Depending on the capabilities of your typewriter, you may have been able to make the title boldface to make the type stand out, but you didn't have the choice of making the title text larger than the text on the rest of the page. Word processing provides that option.

Capability to add art work. If you had graphics, such as a picture or a logo, to worry about adding to a document, you had to type the text (perfectly, with no typos), leaving a blank space where the picture or logo could be manually pasted in. With WordStar 7.0 and many other word processors, the program inserts the picture or logo for you and automatically reformats the text to allow space for the graphic element.

Ensured accuracy. Even the best typists make typing errors. When you made a mistake on a typewriter, your options were limited to pressing the delete key (and that's only if you had a modern typewriter) while hoping the correction ribbon was still functional. Or you could use some kind of correction fluid, which left a white blotch on the page and called unwanted attention to your error. Word processing, on the other hand, gives you effortless editing. You can use the Backspace key or other editing keys to make sure that your document is correct *before* you print it, so you never again have to open that bottle of correction fluid. Additionally, most word processing programs (and WordStar is one) include a spelling checker, so that spelling errors don't slip unnoticed into your printed document, and a thesaurus, so that you can be sure of using words correctly.

Control over print quality. With a typewriter, the quality of your document was pretty much written in stone (or at least in metal). The quality of your typed output was limited to the quality your typewriter was capable of producing. Even if you had a typewriter with changeable type, the formation of the letters was still typewriter quality. Most popular word processors, however, print on the highest quality printers available, including laser printers, PostScript printers, and even imagesetters, a form of typesetting machine. These upper-level printers create crisp, clear letters and well-formed graphics at such a high quality that readers usually cannot make out the individual dots that comprise the letters.

The benefits of word processing mentioned in this section are the obvious ones. Undoubtedly, you will discover others as you begin to work with WordStar 7.0. All these benefits are built into the word processing concept; however, some benefits are more specialized and depend on the specific word processing program you purchase. The next section explains the types of word processing programs currently available.

Types of Word Processing Programs

Like other computer software programs—and, in fact, like computers themselves—word processing software comes in a variety of packages. It can be easy to use and not so easy to use, powerful and not so powerful. Ideally, you have the time—and the option—to explore the variety of word processors available on the market before making a decision about the one you will use. Because you are reading this chapter, you probably have explored the various software options and have chosen WordStar 7.0 (a good choice, by the way), or you still are researching software options. Perhaps, however, your boss has appeared at your desk with WordStar 7.0 and a simple statement: "Learn this." In any case, knowing how word processing programs differ and how WordStar stands in relation to its main competitors may prove helpful.

If you have the luxury of thinking about the software you want before purchasing it, ask yourself what types of documents you will be producing on your personal computer. Will you create simple letters once or twice a month? Will you produce daily reports, memos, or client correspondence? Will you need a word processor that helps automate many of the routine tasks and makes editing a breeze?

The range of capabilities available in different word processors is as diverse as the programs themselves. Some programs have menu systems that appear on-screen while you work. The menus take up quite a bit of screen space and can become a nuisance once you are familiar with the program. Other programs display a blank screen, which can intimidate new users, and show the menu only when you press a certain key combination. WordStar offers several different menu levels, so you can display on-screen only the amount of help you need.

Some word processors have become pseudo-desktop publishers by integrating desktop publishing capabilities into their features. WordStar contains some desktop publishing features, but its primary focus is— and has always been—word processing. Other word processors include a wealth of add-on features in addition to the standard spelling checker. Depending on the program, you may find a thesaurus (which WordStar has), a grammar checker, several different libraries for spelling and the-saurus use, indexing capabilities, table of contents generation, outlining capabilities, and draw features. A few high-end programs, like WordStar 7.0, enable you to import graphics into your printed documents.

On the low end, you will find word processors that do little more than enable you to enter, edit, and format text. These word processors come with a lower price tag than the more powerful word processing programs, but have dramatically fewer capabilities. Low-end word processors lack special add-on features like indexing and table of con-tents generation, previewing capabilities, and a method of integrating graphics.

These less powerful word processing programs also are unable to rival the speed of WordStar and other high-end programs. In addition, the low-end programs may not be as compatible with other programs. If programs are compatible, you can create a document or picture in a different program and use that document or picture in your program. WordStar, for example, can use files from a variety of other programs, but programs with fewer capabilities may be capable of using only files created in that program.

Like everything else in the computer world, you get what you pay for. In the long run, purchasing a program that offers too much power is better than purchasing a program you will outgrow. With a word processing program like WordStar 7.0, you have a program that is powerful enough to keep you satisfied for a long, long time.

Getting To Know WordStar

In the last section, you learned a bit about word processing in general. You learned about the overall benefits you will discover by working with a word processing program, and you found out where WordStar fits among other popular programs. This section teaches you about your word processor of choice, WordStar 7.0, by taking a look back through WordStar history and seeing how the program evolved through its many generations into the powerful yet user-friendly program we have today.

A Little WordStar History

As mentioned in the Introduction, WordStar has been an industry stan-dard for a long, long time. Before personal computers had truly become personal and were more apt to be toys of computer techies, WordStar was available on CP/M machines. (CP/M is a type of operating system used on non-IBM computers.)

Soon after the IBM PC was introduced, WordStar for DOS was made available. (DOS, which stands for Disk Operating System, was—and is—the operating system used with IBM and IBM-compatible computers.) This new word processing program was by far the most sophisticated word cruncher available: you could enter, edit, and format text as well as control line spacing, set alignment, and add special text enhancements such as boldface, italic, underline, superscript, and subscript text styles. You could choose how much of the menu you wanted to display on the screen by choosing a menu level of 3, 2, or 1. (Level 3 displayed the entire menu on the screen at all times).

This early WordStar, even though it was the first in its class, took some heat because of what some users saw as the complexity of the program. Users selected commands by pressing key combinations. To move the cursor to the next word in a paragraph, for example, you pressed Ctrl-F (shown on the menu as ^F). Figure 1.1 shows an example of an early WordStar menu.

Key combinations to display additional menus

Ctrl-F key combination

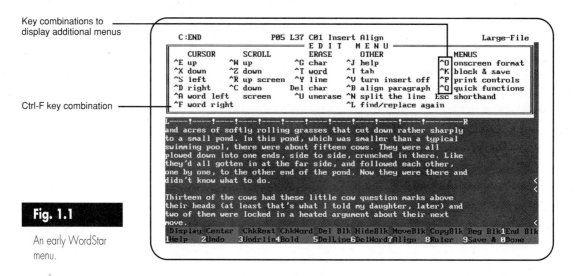

Fig. 1.1

An early WordStar menu.

Early WordStar users either fell in love with the program and learned the keystrokes easily or had a difficult time finding their way through the key combinations and looked for another word processing program. Critics claimed that beginning users had too many keystrokes to remember and use; others said too many features in the product would go unused in normal, everyday operations.

Things have changed a great deal since those days. Today, virtually every program has key combinations—sometimes known as quick keys or speed keys—that enable you to move through the program more quickly than you can move using menu-based selections. In some of today's popular programs, for example, you select an option from a menu by highlighting it (using the arrow keys or the mouse) and pressing Enter (or clicking the mouse button). Experienced users often prefer to press a simple key combination, such as Ctrl-S, to save a file instead of opening a menu, choosing a command, and pressing Enter. Now the keyboard seems faster. (For a complete list of WordStar quick key combinations, see the tear-out command card in the back of this book.)

As a result of the criticism and suggestions made by users, the makers of WordStar renovated it, and it continued to become more user friendly and more powerful. With WordStar 5.0 came the introduction of pull-down menus, originating with Macintosh software and popular in many other programs. *Pull-down menus* are menus that open over the work-space when you need them and tuck neatly away in a menu bar at the top of the screen when you've finished selecting the command you want. In addition, WordStar 5.0 included dialog boxes, little windows that popped up on-screen when the user was being prompted to supply information for a particular operation. Accordingly, WordStar 5.0 added another help level, level 4, to enable users to choose for themselves whether they wanted to use the new pull-down menus or the classic WordStar menus available in levels 1 through 3.

Another feature added to WordStar 5.0 was the advanced page preview. Now you could display on-screen exactly what you would see in print. This feature was a great benefit to WordStar users: WYSIWYG (what you see is what you get) programs were becoming popular in the word processing niche. You couldn't edit the document in preview mode, but you could, at least, see how the different type and formats affected the printed document.

WordStar 6.0 brought with it scalable fonts (type that can be scaled to any size—an important addition for PostScript laser printer users) and a wealth of additional features: column layout capabilities, paragraph styles, automatic leading (spacing) in documents, the new Star Exchange conversion program, the Inset graphics integration program, and the capability to preview graphics in documents. Again, the new features increased the speed and performance of the program while still giving users the choice of selecting pull-down menus or the classic control-key menus.

The fact that WordStar has stuck with its original idea—offering a key-based word processing program that gives both new and experienced users the flexibility to use the program in the way that best suits them—keeps a large, happy user base flourishing throughout the world. WordStar is still one of the fastest word processors around. It can take on any other popular word processor in a search-and-replace operation and, depending on the speed of your coprocessor, come out the winner. In addition, the logical selection of the keys used to select commands (such as Ctrl-U for Unerase) makes the keys easy to remember and use whether you're a beginning typist or a keyboard expert.

Are you wondering what specific new features are available in WordStar 7.0? That's the topic of the next section.

New Features in WordStar 7.0

As contradictory as the statement sounds, the makers of WordStar 7.0 have actually made the program *easier* to use while also making it *more powerful*. The new menus in help level 4 and the addition of mouse capabilities make the program easier to remember and use (especially for new users); and new enhancements, like the revised macro language and fax support, add another dimension for experienced users. The following paragraphs describe the new or enhanced features of WordStar 7.0.

New menu organization. If you are an experienced WordStar user, the new look of the program may fool you. Version 7.0 looks like a complete overhaul. When you start the program for the first time, you see pull-down menus similar to the menus introduced in WordStar 5.0. If you look closely, however, you see that the menus have been reorganized so that similar commands and functions are grouped together, making the commands easier to remember and use.

Full mouse support. Aside from the basic reorganization of the menus, WordStar has added full mouse support. Now you can use your mouse to select commands, choose options, make selections in dialog boxes, and position the cursor. If you've previously used a mouse, you'll be glad to find this new addition in WordStar 7.0. The capability to use the mouse gives you greater flexibility in the way you interact with the program.

Dialog boxes and on-screen instructions. The overall look of the program is friendlier. The dialog boxes have been revamped to be understood more easily by beginning users. Instructions have been added to clarify procedures. And the edit screen, where you do most of your work, has been changed. You can select the font, size, style, alignment, and spacing for your text by using the mouse to click buttons right there on the screen.

Powerful new macro language. More specialized enhancements include the new macro language, which replaces the Shorthand macros available in earlier versions of WordStar. (A *macro* is a string of commands that can be carried out by pressing a simple key combination.) Now you can record, edit, and play back macros by working interactively with WordStar or by creating the macros in a macro file. Additionally, WordStar 7.0 includes over 40 predesigned macros, which you can use to automate your word processing tasks or modify to suit your needs. (Chapter 13 explains how to create and use WordStar macros.)

WordStar 7.0 also offers fax support that enables you to create a file saved in one of 23 fax formats ready for transmission. In creating a fax file, WordStar 7.0 creates a PCX file (a type of graphics file) that can be read by most fax machines. You then can use your own fax software to send the fax information to the desired location without first having to print the file.

Additional enhancements include expanded graphics file support (WordStar now supports 27 types of graphics files), speed enhancement through use of EMS (Expanded Memory Support), the capability to copy text to and from documents running in Microsoft Windows by using the Windows Clipboard, specialized printing enhancements, additional communication protocols added to TelMerge (WordStar's communication utility), and more file formats for Star Exchange (WordStar's file conversion utility).

Getting Around in WordStar

Now that you've learned about the benefits of word processing and the specific features of WordStar 7.0, you're ready to get some hands-on experience with the program. In this section, you first learn to start WordStar; then you find out how to use both the keyboard and the mouse to move around in the program.

Assuming that you've already installed WordStar (if you haven't, see Appendix A), starting WordStar requires just a few simple keystrokes:

1. Start your computer. (Use your DOS disk, if necessary.)

2. Make sure that the DOS prompt (C>) is displayed.

3. Change to the directory in which you've installed WordStar 7.0 by typing *CD*, a space, and the directory name, such as

   CD WS

   (WS is the default directory created by the installation program. If you changed the name of your WordStar 7.0 directory to, say, WS7, type that name after the CD command.) You can type either capital or lowercase letters.

4. Press Enter. You are now in the WordStar 7.0 directory.

5. Type *WS* and press Enter.

After a moment, a screen appears telling you about the various copyrights of the programs used along with WordStar. In a moment, that screen is automatically replaced with the WordStar 7.0 opening screen (see fig. 1.2).

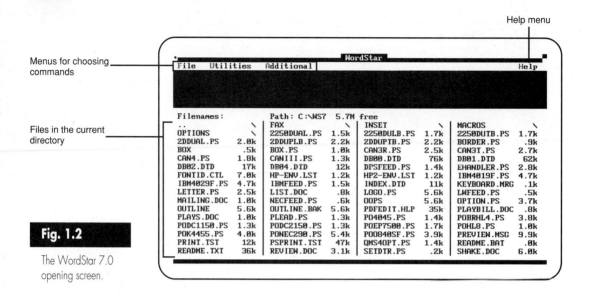

Help menu

Menus for choosing commands

Files in the current directory

| WordStar |
| File   Utilities   Additional | Help |

Filenames: Path: C:\WS7   5.7M free

..	\	FAX	\	INSET	\	MACROS	\
OPTIONS	\	2250DUAL.PS	1.5k	2250DULB.PS	1.7k	2250DUTB.PS	1.7k
2DDUAL.PS	2.0k	2DDUPLB.PS	2.2k	2DDUPTB.PS	2.2k	BORDER.PS	.9k
BOX	.5k	BOX.PS	1.0k	CAN3R.PS	2.5k	CAN3T.PS	2.7k
CAN4.PS	1.8k	CANIII.PS	1.3k	DB00.DTD	76k	DB01.DTD	62k
DB02.DTD	17k	DB04.DTD	12k	DPSFEED.PS	1.4k	EHANDLER.PS	2.8k
FONTID.CTL	7.0k	HP-ENV.LST	1.2k	HP2-ENV.LST	1.2k	IBM4019F.PS	4.7k
IBM4029F.PS	4.7k	IBMFEED.PS	1.5k	INDEX.DTD	11k	KEYBOARD.MRG	.1k
LETTER.PS	2.5k	LIST.DOC	.8k	LOGO.PS	5.6k	LWFEED.PS	.5k
MAILING.DOC	1.0k	NECFEED.PS	.6k	OOPS	5.6k	OPTION.PS	3.7k
OUTLINE	5.6k	OUTLINE.BAK	5.6k	PDFEDIT.HLP	35k	PLAYBILL.DOC	.8k
PLAYS.DOC	1.0k	PLEAD.PS	1.3k	PO4045.PS	1.4k	POBRHL4.PS	3.8k
PODC1150.PS	1.3k	PODC2150.PS	1.3k	POEP7500.PS	1.7k	POHL8.PS	1.0k
POK4455.PS	4.0k	PONEC290.PS	5.4k	PO0840SF.PS	3.9k	PREVIEW.MSG	9.9k
PRINT.TST	12k	PSPRINT.TST	47k	QMS40PT.PS	1.4k	README.BAT	.0k
README.TXT	36k	REVIEW.DOC	3.1k	SETDTR.PS	.2k	SHAKE.DOC	6.0k

Fig. 1.2

The WordStar 7.0 opening screen.

Now that you've started the program successfully, what can you do with it? First, you need to learn to use the keyboard and the mouse to get around in WordStar 7.0. The next two sections explain how.

A Keyboard Primer

A computer wouldn't do you much good without a keyboard. While you are using WordStar 7.0, you will find that you use some keys frequently and other keys rarely. This section helps familiarize you with the keys and keystroke procedures you use frequently as you create documents in WordStar.

Introducing the Keyboard

The locations of specific keys on your keyboard depend on the type of keyboard you are using. Generally, important keys—such as Ctrl, Alt, Tab, and Enter—are in the same places on every keyboard. The standard layout of the alphanumeric keys—the keys you actually use to type characters and numbers—are identical no matter what keyboard you are using. Several popular computer keyboards are currently available; most are left over from standards set by early IBM computers. Table 1.1 gives an overview of the different kinds of keys on your standard keyboard.

Table 1.1 Keys on Standard Keyboards

Keys	Location and Use
QWERTY keys	The basic keys you use to type documents; including all alphabetic keys, numeric keys, and punctuation keys. These keys are named the QWERTY keys for the first six characters on the left side of the top row of the alphanumeric section of the keyboard. This portion of the keyboard also includes other special keys you use in your operations with WordStar. Among these keys are Ctrl, Alt, Enter, Backspace, Tab, Shift, and the space bar.
Function keys	Depending on the keyboard you are using, the function keys may be found along the left side of the keyboard or across the top of the keyboard. Function keys are programmable keys you use to carry out certain operations quickly; for example, pressing F1 displays a help screen, pressing F2 unerases the last item you erased, and so on. Your particular keyboard may have 10 or 12 function keys.
Numeric keypad	A set of numeric keys long the right side of your keyboard. On some computer keyboards, this keypad is separate from the standard alphanumeric (or QWERTY) keys. On others, these keys are found just to the right of the Enter key. In early keyboards, the numeric keypad was also used to move the cursor.
Cursor-control	The IBM Enhanced Keyboard, the latest in the line of IBM keyboards, includes a separate keypad for cursor-control keys. This keypad includes four keys: an up-arrow key, a down-arrow key, a right-arrow key, and a left-arrow key. You use these keys to move the cursor on the screen. (*Note:* If you do not have a separate cursor-control keypad, you can use the arrow keys on the numeric keypad to move the cursor.)
Special keys	The last group of keys on your keyboard includes the Insert, Home, Page Up, Page Down, Delete, and End keys. You use these keys to move the cursor around on the screen (Page Up, Page Down, Home, and End) and to insert and delete text. If you are using the IBM Enhanced Keyboard, these keys are set off in a group to the left of the numeric keypad. If you are using an earlier model keyboard, you find these keys a part of the numeric keypad.
Esc key	The Esc (Escape) key is usually set off by itself, either in the upper left corner of the keyboard (IBM Enhanced Keyboard) or in the top left corner of the numeric keypad (earlier models). You use the Esc key to cancel operations in WordStar.

You can use figures 1.3, 1.4, and 1.5 to locate the various keys on your type of keyboard. Figure 1.3 shows the earliest IBM PC keyboard. Notice that the numeric keypad includes the cursor- control keys and that the function keys are placed along the left edge of the keyboard.

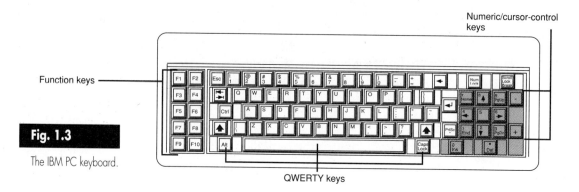

Fig. 1.3

The IBM PC keyboard.

Figure 1.4 shows the IBM PC AT keyboard, a revised keyboard introduced after the early IBM PC. On the IBM PC AT keyboard, the numeric keypad (still with cursor-control keys) has been separated from the rest of the keyboard. The function keys are still positioned on the left.

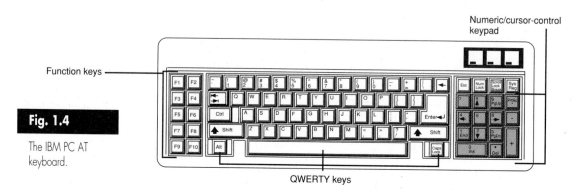

Fig. 1.4

The IBM PC AT keyboard.

The final revision of the IBM keyboard, the IBM Enhanced Keyboard, is shown in figure 1.5. Notice that this keyboard brought with it a complete overhaul; now the function keys are aligned across the top of the keyboard, a separate cursor-control keypad has been added, and special keys (such as Insert, Delete, Home, End) have been given their own keypad to the right of the numeric keypad.

You use the keyboard, of course, to enter and edit text. You also can use the keyboard to open menus and select commands. Now that the program supports the use of the mouse, however, you may prefer to select commands by using mouse procedures.

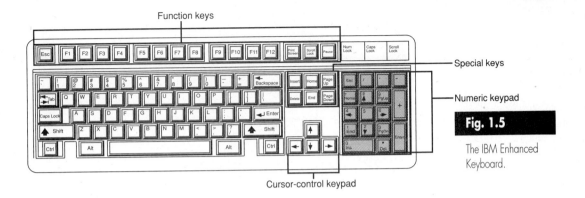

Function keys

Special keys

Numeric keypad

Fig. 1.5

The IBM Enhanced Keyboard.

Cursor-control keypad

Using the Keyboard

If you prefer not to use the mouse to open menus and select commands, you will rely pretty heavily on a few special keys and key combinations. The term *key combination* means two or more keys you press simultaneously to carry out a particular task. When the opening screen is displayed, for example, you can display the Print dialog box by pressing the key combination Ctrl-P.

WordStar makes things even easier by enabling you to open menus and choose commands with a single key press. Once you've started WordStar and the opening screen is displayed, for example, you can open the File menu by simply pressing F. You can tell which key to press to open a menu by the character displayed in a different color or, on monochrome monitors, the character displayed in a lighter shade of gray.

Even before you get your finger off the F key, WordStar displays the File menu (see fig. 1.6). On this menu, you see a great deal of information: the names of commands you can choose (New, Open Document, Open Nondocument, and so on), and additional keys you can press to carry out the commands of your choice.

Selecting Commands Quickly

As you become more comfortable with WordStar, you'll start to remember which keys you use to select which commands. Before long, you'll know that you can open a new document by simply pressing S, for example, or you can retrieve a document you've already created by pressing D. When the opening screen is displayed, you can press these keys to move directly to the edit screen without opening the File menu. (You learn more about this topic in Chapter 2.)

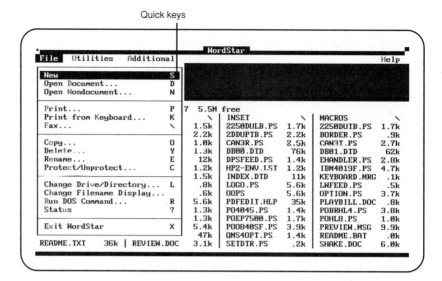

Fig. 1.6

Opening the File menu.

Once the menu is displayed, you can use the keyboard in two different ways to issue the command you want. You can type the letter or character listed to the right of the command (such as S for New or O for Copy), or you can use the arrow keys on your keyboard to highlight the command you want and then press Enter.

Play around with the keyboard for a minute. Start with the File menu. (If the menu isn't open, press F to open the menu.)

1. Press the down-arrow key four times. The highlight should now be positioned on the Print from Keyboard command.

2. Press the up-arrow twice. The highlight moves to Open Nondocument. If you wanted to choose this command, you would press Enter now.

3. Press O. This letter selects the Copy command and displays the Copy dialog box in the upper portion of your screen.

4. Press Esc. The dialog box is removed from the screen, but so is the File menu. Press F to reopen the File menu.

5. Press the right-arrow key. WordStar opens the next menu to the right, Utilities. If you press the right-arrow key a second time, you open the Additional menu.

6. Press the left-arrow key to move back to the File menu.

7. Press Esc to close the menu.

Opening Menus on the Edit Screen

When you move to the edit screen after you start a new document or open an existing document, you use *key combinations* instead of single keys to open menus if you do not use the mouse. On the edit screen, for example, you open the File menu by pressing Alt-F, which means that you press and hold the Alt key while pressing the F key. When you release both keys, the edit screen's File menu appears.

As you progress through this book, you'll learn more about different ways you can enter commands and choose options. For now, you know how to find and use the necessary keys for performing basic WordStar operations.

A Mouse Primer

If you are at all familiar with computers, chances are that you've seen a mouse. A mouse is a hand-held *pointing device* with which you select menus and commands and other on-screen items by simply rolling the mouse on the desktop and clicking a mouse button.

Figure 1.7 shows an example of the IBM mouse. As you can see, the mouse is small, shaped to fit under the palm of your hand, and has two buttons. (Some mice have three.) Underneath the mouse is a small pressure-sensitive roller ball; when you roll the mouse, the roller ball moves, touching small electronic sensors inside the mouse. These sensors send information to your computer, enabling the system and the software to keep track of the location of the mouse as you roll it across your desktop. On the screen, the mouse cursor—the small highlighted rectangle—follows the exact movement of the mouse under your hand, enabling you to select items on-screen as easily as you could if you were simply pointing to them with your finger.

When mice first entered the computer market, they appeared only with Apple Macintosh computers. Users soon became attached to their mice—the mouse capabilities made programs easier to understand and use. The pointing concept made selecting menus and commands more intuitive for users. And because people spent so much time at their computer keyboards, the mouse provided them with a nice break for performing commands that didn't require data entry.

The mouse was particularly helpful in programs that used graphics, giving users on-screen control for where they placed pictures, lines, boxes, and other graphics items. As the mouse became more popular, software programs were changed so that users could work with the mouse in a variety of other programs. Spreadsheets, databases, and word processing programs that let you use the mouse to open menus, choose commands, position the cursor, and select other on-screen items began appearing on the market.

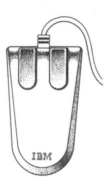

Fig. 1.7

The IBM mouse.

If you've used a computer before, you can get an idea of the amount of time using a mouse can save you when you think about the amount of time needed to move the cursor from one end of the screen to the other by pressing the arrow keys. Now consider how quickly you can reach up and point to the place you want the cursor. That's how long you take to move the cursor by using the mouse. Just point to the spot you want and click the mouse button.

In WordStar 7.0, you use the mouse to choose and open menus, select commands, choose settings in dialog boxes, and select text settings (on the edit screen). Before you start using the mouse, however, you need to understand the basic mouse procedures you use with WordStar 7.0, summarized in table 1.2.

Table 1.2 Basic Mouse Operations

Task	Definition
Point	Move the mouse so that the on-screen mouse pointer points to the item you want to select
Click	Press and release the mouse button
Double-click	Press and release the mouse button twice quickly
Drag	Press and hold the mouse button while dragging the mouse to another location on the screen

Mouse Accessories

As the mouse has gained in popularity, add-on products have been created to help you make the most of your mouse. Some people complain about the long cord that attaches the mouse to the system unit of the computer—they say the cord gets in the way as they work and generally clutters up their desks. The solution? A mouse house, that is, a small pocket that attaches to the side of your computer, where you "house" your mouse when it is not in use. The cord and the body of the mouse tuck neatly away, uncluttering your desktop.

Another accessory that is more like a necessity is the mouse pad. (Sounds like a '70's version of a mouse house . . .) A mouse pad is a thick, cushionlike surface (roughly 10 by 12 inches) that sits beneath your mouse. This cushiony pad helps you move the mouse more accurately. The roller ball inside the mouse can be more accurate on this surface than on the slippery surface of the desktop. Additionally, the mouse pad can keep your mouse from accumulating the ordinary office hazards—dust, dirt, and crumbs—that can eventually affect your mouse's performance.

Suppose that you try a few exercises using the mouse:

1. Move the mouse so that the mouse cursor is positioned on the word *File* in the menu bar.

2. Click the left mouse button. The File menu opens.

3. Move the mouse cursor to the Copy command.

4. Click the left mouse button. The Copy dialog box is displayed (see fig. 1.8).

5. Move the mouse cursor to the Cancel button.

6. Click the left mouse button. You are returned to the opening screen.

After you begin opening and working with existing files, you can use the mouse to select the file you want to open. You can choose a file from the Filenames list, for example, in the bottom half of your opening screen by simply moving the mouse cursor to the file name you want and double-clicking the left mouse button.

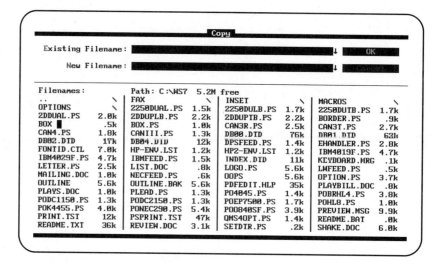

Exiting WordStar

When you're ready to end your WordStar session, you can do so in one of two ways:

To use the keyboard to exit WordStar, follow these steps:

1. Press Alt-F. The File menu opens.

2. You then have two options:

   You can press the down-arrow key until the highlight is positioned on Exit WordStar, and then press Enter.

   You can press X.

You are then returned to the DOS prompt in the directory where you first started WordStar 7.0.

Exiting Fast: Keyboard Method

The fastest way to exit WordStar (why, you may ask, would you use any other way?) is to press X when the opening screen is displayed. (If you are working in any other area of WordStar, such as on the edit screen, or using MailList or TelMerge, you need to save your file before you exit. More about this subject in subsequent chapters.)

To use the mouse to exit WordStar, follow these steps:

1. Move the mouse cursor to the word *File* in the menu bar.

2. Click the left mouse button. The File menu opens.

3. Move the mouse cursor to Exit WordStar.

4. Click the left mouse button.

You are returned to the DOS prompt, in the directory from which you started WordStar.

Exiting Fast: Mouse Method

You can exit quickly using the mouse by moving the mouse cursor up to the close box in the upper left corner of the screen (see Chapter 2) and double-clicking the mouse button.

Chapter Summary

In this chapter, you've learned about word processing in general and about WordStar—how it has evolved from the early days of word processing into the powerful, feature-laden WordStar 7.0. Additionally, this chapter has explained how to start and exit WordStar and has provided sections on using the keyboard and the mouse to find your way around in WordStar. The next chapter introduces you to all the menus, commands, and basic procedures you use as you begin your WordStar documents.

Learning WordStar Basics

In the last chapter, you learned how to start and exit WordStar. You also found out how to use keyboard and mouse techniques to move around in the program. In this chapter, you use those skills as you explore the basics of the program by working with the opening and edit screens in WordStar 7.0. Specifically, this chapter helps you do the following:

- Understand the opening screen
- Explore the opening screen menus
- Select a file
- Scroll through displayed files
- Change the displayed menu level
- Use the help system
- Work with menus
- Choose commands
- Use dialog boxes
- Use the edit screen
- Examine each edit screen menu

The first step, of course, is to start WordStar 7.0, if you haven't done so already. Chapter 1 explains the procedure more fully, but here are the steps if you need a review:

1. Start your computer.

2. Change to the directory in which your WordStar files are stored by
    typing *CD*, pressing the space bar, and typing the name of the direc-
    tory. (For example, to change to the WordStar directory, the com-
    mand is CD C:\WS.) Press Enter.

3. Type *WS* and press Enter.

After a moment, WordStar displays the copyright screen. Then, without
any interaction from you, the WordStar opening screen appears (see
fig. 2.1).

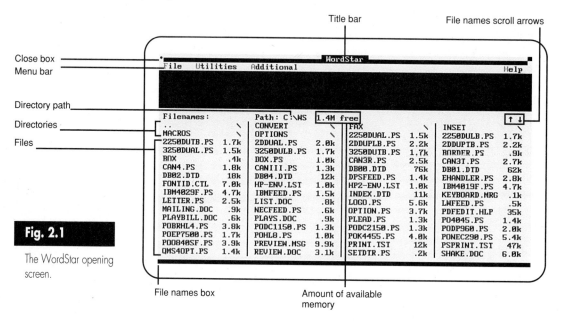

Fig. 2.1

The WordStar opening
screen.

Exploring the Opening Screen

Assuming that you are working with an unmodified version of WordStar
7.0, the screen you see when you first start WordStar closely resembles
figure 2.1. The list of files you see in the lower two-thirds of your screen
may not include the same files as the ones shown in the figure. That's
nothing major—your system may not be set up to work with a laser
printer or may have drives or directories different from those on the
system used in these examples. These minor differences do not affect
the way you work with WordStar.

At the top of the opening screen, you see the *title bar* with the title of the
program, and in the far left corner of the title bar is a small rectangle
with a black dot in the center. This rectangle is the *close box*. You can

use this close box to exit WordStar quickly if you are using the mouse; simply position the mouse cursor on the box and double-click the mouse button. You then return to the DOS prompt.

That's Not What *I* See . . .

If the menus on your screen are different from the ones shown in figure 2.1, you can assume that someone has modified your version of WordStar to display different menus. To reset your menu level so that it matches the examples in this chapter and those throughout the first section of this book, press H to open the Help menu; then select Change Help Level by pressing the down-arrow key and pressing Enter. When the Help Level dialog box appears, select level 4, Pull-Down Menus. Press Enter. Your opening screen should now resemble figure 2.1. (You learn more about setting help levels later in this chapter.)

Understanding Opening Screen Menus

Beneath the title bar, you see an all-important line that houses the commands you use during your WordStar experience. In this line, known as the *menu bar*, you see four words, each naming a different menu. Table 2.1 briefly describes these menus.

Table 2.1 WordStar Opening Menus

Menu	Description
File	Contains commands for opening new and existing files; printing, faxing, copying, deleting, and renaming files; protecting files; changing directories; running DOS commands; displaying the file status; and exiting WordStar
Utilities	Stores the commands you use for working with the add-on features of the program, specifically the index and table of contents generator and the macro language
Additional	Lists a group of specialized programs that work with WordStar to provide database and merge print capabilities (MailList), telecommunications capabilities (TelMerge), and file conversion utilities (Star Exchange)
Help	Enables you to access immediate on-line help for your current operation and to change the help level, which alters the menu system displayed as you work with WordStar

In the sections that follow, you get acquainted with each of the menus available on WordStar's opening screen.

The File Menu

The File menu contains all the commands you use to work with your WordStar files. With the commands on the File menu, you can perform the following tasks:

- Start a new document (with New)
- Open an existing document (with Open Document or Open Nondocument)
- Print a file (with Print)
- Print characters you type (with Print from Keyboard)
- Prepare a file in fax format (with Fax)
- Copy a file (with Copy)
- Delete a file (with Delete)
- Rename a file (with Rename)
- Protect a file so that it cannot be edited (with Protect/Unprotect)
- Display files on a different drive or directory (with Change Drive/Directory)
- Display specific groups of files in the Filenames list (with Change Filename Display)
- Perform DOS operations (with Run DOS Command)
- Check the amount of memory used and the amount available for a selected file (with Status)
- Return to the DOS prompt (with Exit WordStar)

You'll See These Commands Again . . .

Many of the commands available for working with files—such as Print, Fax, Copy, Delete, Rename, and others—are also available in the File menu on the edit screen. As you are working on a file, therefore, you can perform many operations without saving and closing the file you're working on.

To open the File menu, press F or position the mouse pointer on File and click the mouse button. Figure 2.2 shows the File menu available in the opening screen.

```
File
┌─────────────────────────────────┐
│ New                          S  │
│ Open Document...             D  │
│ Open Nondocument...          N  │
│                                 │
│ Print...                     P  │
│ Print from Keyboard...       K  │
│ Fax...                       \  │
│                                 │
│ Copy...                      O  │
│ Delete...                    Y  │
│ Rename...                    E  │
│ Protect/Unprotect...         C  │
│                                 │
│ Change Drive/Directory...    L  │
│ Change Filename Display...       │
│ Run DOS Command...           R  │
│ Status                       ?  │
│                                 │
│ Exit WordStar                X  │
└─────────────────────────────────┘
```

Fig. 2.2

The opening screen
File menu.

As you can see, quite a few commands are available on this menu. The keys listed at the right of the menu show you which keys you can press to carry out the command of your choice. Each command also has a highlighted letter, such as the *F* in Fax; you can also press that letter to choose that command. (In some cases, the key shown at the right of the command and the key highlighted within the command are different characters. You can press either character to select the command.) The dots following some commands (such as Open Document) tell you that a dialog box asking for more information is displayed when you select that command. Table 2.2 summarizes the function of each File menu command.

The Utilities Menu

If the File menu is still open, you can display the Utilities menu simply by pressing the right-arrow key. If you have already closed the File menu, open the Utilities menu by pressing U or by positioning the mouse cursor on the word *Utilities* and clicking the mouse button.

You use the commands in the Utilities menu to perform operations above and beyond the call of duty of most word processors. As you learned in Chapter 1, WordStar 7.0 includes some specialized features that help you create professional documents of any length. The commands on the Utilities menu help you. Specifically, you use these commands to do the following:

■ Create an index for your document. You can choose to index every word or enter index codes in the document before you put it all together. How much or how little you index is up to you.

Table 2.2 The File Menu (Opening Screen)

Command	Description
New	Opens a new file
Open Document	Enables you to choose an existing (non-ASCII) file to open
Open Nondocument	Opens a nondocument (ASCII) file
Print	Displays the Print dialog box; used for printing a file
Print from Keyboard	Enables you to type characters that are printed on your printer as soon as you press Enter
Fax	Creates a file in a format that can be sent via fax
Copy	Makes a copy of a specified file
Delete	Deletes a file you specify
Rename	Renames the file of your choosing
Protect/Unprotect	Protects a file so that it cannot be edited; unprotects already protected files
Change Drive/ Directory	Displays files on a different disk drive or in a different directory you specify
Change Filename Display	Changes the display of files in the Filenames portion of your screen
Run DOS Command	Enables you to enter and run a DOS command without leaving WordStar
Status	Displays the file name, printer, and other vital information (such as memory used and memory available) about the file you choose
Exit WordStar	Leaves WordStar and takes you to the DOS prompt

■ Generate a table of contents for your document. WordStar reads the headings you enter in your document file and compiles the table of contents for you, adding page numbers automatically.

■ Record and work with macros. A *macro* is a string of commands that you record and then carry out with the simple press of a key.

Figure 2.3 shows the commands available on the Utilities menu. Again, you see the familiar keys at the right side of the commands, and the highlighted letters in the commands themselves indicating which letter to press to select the command—in this case the letters match. The last command, Macros, shows you something you probably haven't seen before. A triangle appears at the right side of the command, indicating that when you select that command, a pop-up box appears, offering you another list of options. Try that. Press M to see the pop-up box available when you select Macros (see fig. 2.4).

Press Esc to back out of the displayed pop-up box, and press U again to open the Utilities menu. Now you're ready to take a closer look at the Utilities menu. Table 2.3 introduces you to the commands and their functions.

Table 2.3 The Utilities Menu (Opening Screen)

Command	Description
Index	Creates an index for an existing document
TOC	Creates a table of contents for the document you select (You must first enter headings in the document so that WordStar has something to work with. More about this in Chapter 16.)
Macros	Enables you to record, edit, play, rename, copy, or delete macros you create to automate your WordStar procedures (More about this in Chapter 13)

The Additional Menu

Again, if the Utilities menu is still open, you can press the right-arrow key to open the Additional menu. If not, press A or use the mouse to open the menu. In this menu, you find more features of WordStar not available in other word processing programs. With the commands on the Additional menu, you can perform the following tasks:

- Create a mailing list to merge print documents and envelopes (using MailList)

- Send or receive files via modem (with TelMerge, the telecommunications utility)

- Convert files from other word processors so that you can use them with WordStar or vice versa (using Star Exchange)

Figure 2.5 shows the commands on the Additional menu. Here is something different: the characters shown on the right side of the command menu are different from the highlighted characters. Do you need to press AM to choose MailList? No, pressing M will do. If you want to start MailList without first opening the Additional menu, you can press AM (or AT for TelMerge, or AS for Star Exchange).

Fig. 2.5

The Additional menu.

When you choose any of these commands, WordStar takes you into what looks like a completely different program: MailList, TelMerge, and Star Exchange all have their own menu systems and commands. (Don't panic— we'll get to them in Part III.)

Table 2.4 summarizes the features on the Additional menu.

Table 2.4 The Additional Menu (Opening Screen)

Command	Description
MailList	Takes you to the MailList utility, which enables you to enter data on a data entry form similar to a database. You can later use the data in printing form letters and mailing labels.
TelMerge	Starts a telecommunications program you can use to send and receive files via modem, connect to information services, or link with other computers
Star Exchange	Enables you to convert documents created in other word processors to a format usable with WordStar 7.0. You can also change WordStar 7.0 documents into other formats.

The Help Menu

The Help menu is the last menu on the opening screen. You also see this menu available on the edit screen when you begin working with documents. Located way off by itself on the far right side of the menu bar, the Help menu gives you the option of choosing context-sensitive help, which means that the program displays a help screen related to the operation you were performing when you selected help, and setting different help levels, which control the menu system displayed as you work. Figure 2.6 shows the Help menu.

Fig. 2.6

The Help menu.

Table 2.5 summarizes the commands available on the Help menu.

Table 2.5 The Help Menu (Opening Screen)

Command	Description
Help	Displays a pop-up screen of help for the currently highlighted command or option
Change Help Level	Enables you to modify the way menus are displayed on the screen

Getting Help

As you can see from the Help menu, you have two basic options for the way you ask for and receive help in WordStar 7.0. The first, *context-sensitive help*, does just what it sounds like—it brings up a help screen based on where you are in the program. If you are trying to figure out how to copy a file, for example, you can highlight the Copy command (in the File menu) and press F1 (the Help quick key). A screen of help information appears, telling you more about the Copy command. The second choice you have in asking for help concerns the amount of information displayed in the menus.

Using Context-Sensitive Help

First, try an example using context-sensitive help. Suppose that the Print from Keyboard command, available in the File menu, stumps you. What, exactly, is that command used for? You can use WordStar's Help command to find out:

1. Open the File menu by pressing F.

2. Press the down-arrow key four times to move the highlight to the Print from Keyboard command.

3. Press F1. A help screen appears telling you more about the highlighted command (see fig. 2.7).

4. After you've read through the help screen, press Esc to close the help window.

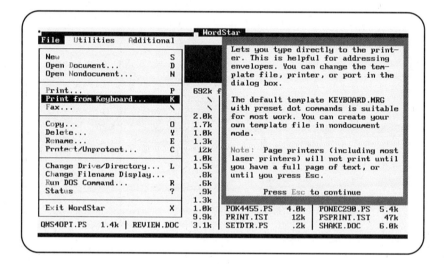

Fig. 2.7

Context-sensitive help for the Print from Keyboard command.

Changing the Help Level Display

Your second option for the way in which WordStar helps you concerns the amount of information displayed on the menus. When you first started WordStar, if you were using an unmodified version, you saw the menus shown throughout this chapter, complete with pull-down menus and the Filename screen. This display is known as help level 4. You also have the choice of selecting the classic WordStar menus (levels 3 and 2), all menus off (level 1), and all menus off with hidden block changes allowed (level 0).

To change the display of the menus, open the Help menu and choose the Change Help Level command. The screen shown in figure 2.8 appears.

As you can see, help level 4, which is the default, is selected. You can change the help level either by typing the number that corresponds to

the level you want, by clicking the circle to the left of the level, or by
using the arrow keys to change your selection. If you want to select help
level 3, for example, click the circle to the left of the level 3 line. The
circle turns into a black diamond, indicating that level 3 is now the selected level. Click OK or press Enter to finalize the change. Figure 2.9
shows the screen as it appears if you select help level 3, Classic Menus.
(If you've used WordStar before, you may recognize these menus.)

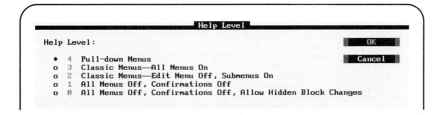

Fig. 2.8

Changing the help
level.

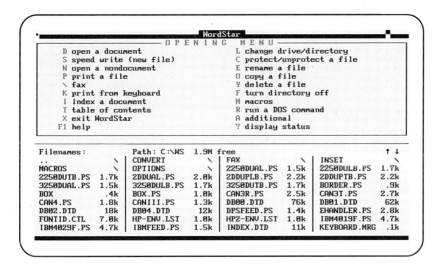

Fig. 2.9

The opening menu in
help level 3.

Wandering Mouse

Although you will still see the mouse cursor in level 3 or 2, you
won't be able to select commands by clicking the mouse button.
You can, however, open a file by double-clicking the file name.

As you can see, this menu is much different from the help level 4 menu,
which uses the mouse or the keyboard in whichever method is most
comfortable for you. For this reason, help level 4 is by far the friendliest

method for new users. If you have past experience with WordStar and prefer to use the other help levels, choose the menu display that works best for you. If you are a new user, you are better off learning the program with level 4, until you are comfortable enough to remove some of the on-screen help constantly available to you.

The other help levels—levels 2 through 0—won't make any drastic changes to the opening screen. You will see changes, however, when you begin working with the edit screen. Figure 2.10 shows the edit screen in help level 4, figure 2.11 shows the edit screen in help level 3, and figure 2.12 shows the edit screen in help level 2.

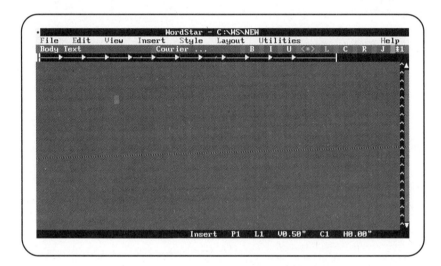

Fig. 2.10

The edit screen in help level 4.

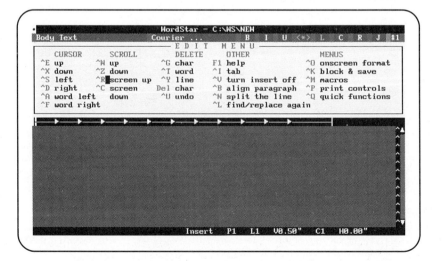

Fig. 2.11

The edit screen in help level 3.

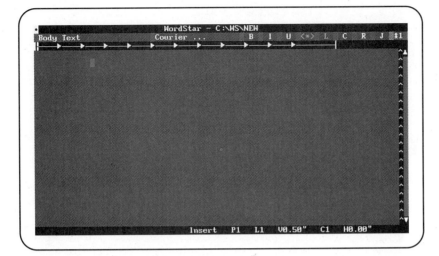

Fig. 2.12

The edit screen in help level 2.

How Do I Get Back?

If you've been experimenting with the menu displays and you want to return to a higher help level, you can press Ctrl-JJ to display the Help Level screen. Then type the level you want and press Enter. The menus will be restored.

Working with the Filenames List

As mentioned earlier in this chapter, the Filenames list, which may occupy more than half of your opening screen, contains all the files in the current directory. In the example shown in figure 2.13, you can see several different items of information in the Filenames list.

In the top line of the Filenames list, you see the current directory (here shown as C:\WS). DOS—and computers in general— calls this information the *path* because it is the path the computer follows to locate the files in that directory. Beside the path, you see the amount of available disk storage, which varies according to the amount of memory you have in your computer. At the far right side of the top line, you see two *scroll arrows*: one pointing up and one pointing down. You can use your mouse to click these arrows to display additional files that cannot be seen on the first screen of files in the Filenames list.

The files are displayed in four columns, each with its file size displayed to the right of the file name. At the top of the file columns are subdirectory names, indicated by the backslash (\).

Available disk storage space

Scroll arrows

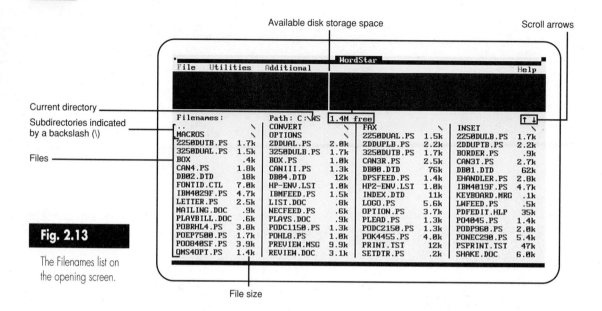

Current directory

Subdirectories indicated
by a backslash (\)

Files

Fig. 2.13

The Filenames list on
the opening screen.

File size

You can move directly from one directory to another from the Filenames
box by clicking the name of the directory you want to move to. Additionally, you can open files without going through normal menu selections
by simply double-clicking the name of the file you want. (Chapter 4 explains more about working with files and directories in WordStar.)

Using Menus

At various points in this chapter, you have learned how to open the
menus on the opening screen. Because this information is scattered
throughout the chapter, important basic procedures are recapped for
you in this tutorial section. In this section, you review how to perform
the following tasks:

- Open a menu
- Close a menu
- Select a command
- Use a dialog box
- Close a dialog box

Opening a Menu

When you are working with the opening screen, you open a menu by simply pressing the first letter of the name of the menu you want. For example, to open the File menu, press F. To open the Utilities menu, press U. To open the Additional menu—you guessed it—press A.

When you get to the edit screen, however, you see that the rules have changed slightly. In the edit screen, if you press A, guess what happens . . . you type an *A* in the work area. For this reason, you open menus on the edit screen by pressing and holding the Alt key while you press the first letter of the menu you want. Table 2.6 shows you the keys you can use to open the menus on the edit screen.

Table 2.6 Keys for Opening Menus on the Edit Screen

Key Combination	Opens This Menu
Alt-F	File menu
Alt-E	Edit menu
Alt-V	View menu
Alt-I	Insert menu
Alt-S	Style menu
Alt-L	Layout menu
Alt-U	Utilities menu
Alt-H	Help menu

Closing a Menu

When you're ready to close a menu, you can do so easily whether you're using the mouse or the keyboard. First, you should know that whenever you select a command from a menu, the menu closes automatically. But what about the times when you open a menu and then decide you don't want to use it?

You can close a menu in one of two ways:

- If you are using the keyboard, you can close the menu by pressing Esc.

- If you are using the mouse, close the menu by moving the mouse off the menu and clicking the mouse button.

This procedure isn't affected by where you are in the program; in other words, use the same steps to close a menu whether you are using the opening screen or the edit screen.

Selecting a Command

If you are using the mouse, the procedure you use to choose a command is the same all the way through WordStar—as long as you're using help level 4. (If you're not using help level 4, you can't use your mouse!)

If you are using the keyboard, the way in which you select a command varies slightly, depending on which screen you are using. As you learned, if you are working with the opening screen, you select commands by simply pressing one character. When the opening screen is displayed, for example, you can select the Copy command by pressing O, the Delete command by pressing Y, the Rename command by pressing E, and so on.

When you are using the edit screen, however, you have additional key combinations to worry about when you're selecting commands. To choose Copy, Delete, or Rename from the edit screen's File menu, you need to press Ctrl-KO; Ctrl-KY; or Ctrl-KE, respectively. As these key combinations become familiar, you won't even think about the extra keystrokes; but for now, remember to keep your help level set to 4 so that you have on-screen reminders of which keys to press to activate the commands.

Working with Dialog Boxes

Some commands display dialog boxes, which ask you for more information before the command is carried out. You can tell which commands display dialog boxes by the ellipsis (. . .) that follows the command. Figure 2.14 shows an example of the Print dialog box, which is displayed when you choose the Print command from the File menu.

Although the Print dialog box contains more information than most others in WordStar, this box is being used for a reason. In figure 2.14, you can see the many different ways you provide information in a dialog box. In some places, you enter information into a text box (the Filename box), select options from a list of radio buttons (Pages) or check boxes (the group of options in the lower right corner of the box), or click command buttons (OK or Cancel). Table 2.7 provides a few guidelines for dealing with dialog boxes.

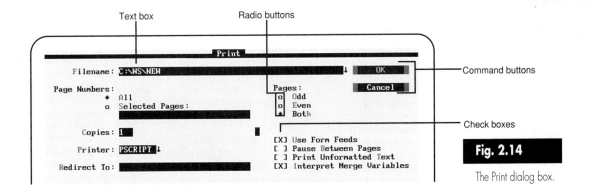

Fig. 2.14

The Print dialog box.

Table 2.7 Guidelines for Working in Dialog Boxes

When You See This	Do This
Text box	Type the requested information
Radio button	Click the option you want or press the highlighted letter of the option you want
Check box	Click the option or press the highlighted letter
Command button	Click the button or press Enter (for OK) or Esc (for Cancel)

When you are finished entering information in the dialog box, close the box by pressing Enter, the F10 function key, or Esc. (If you're using the mouse, you can click OK or Cancel to produce the same effect.) After the dialog box closes, you are returned to the place you were on-screen before the dialog box appeared.

Understanding the Edit Screen

You do all your work with documents in the edit screen. This screen, as you'll soon see, is much different from the opening screen, although you can use many of the same procedures for working with menus and commands.

To get to the edit screen, you must first start a new document or open an existing one. For now, start with a new document. When the opening screen is displayed, press S. The edit screen appears, as shown in figure 2.15.

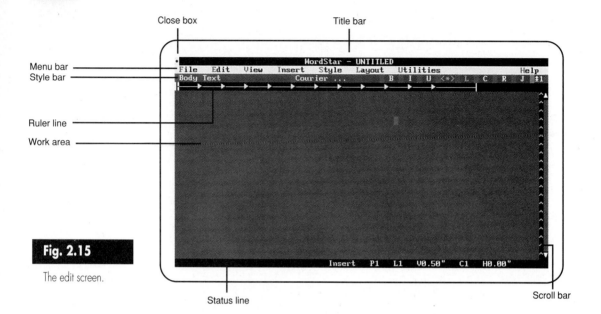

Close box

Title bar

Menu bar

Style bar

Ruler line

Work area

Fig. 2.15

The edit screen.

Status line

Scroll bar

The Title Bar

Across the top of the screen, you see the edit screen's *title bar*. Like the opening screen, the edit screen shows you the name of the program you're using and the name of the current document. If you are working on a new file that you haven't saved, the name in the title bar is UN-TITLED, as it is in figure 2.15. After you save the file, or if you retrieve another file that has already been saved, the name of the file appears in place of UNTITLED. In the far left corner of the title bar, you see the *close box*. As you may recall, if you double-click this box when the opening screen is displayed, you are taken to the DOS prompt. If you double-click the close box when the edit screen is displayed, WordStar closes your document and displays the opening screen.

Beneath the title bar, you see the familiar menu bar. The sections that follow introduce you to each menu in the row.

The Menu Bar

As you can see, the menu bar in the edit screen includes many more menus than the opening screen menu bar offers. The edit screen divides its commands into eight different menus, summarized in table 2.8.

In the sections that follow, you get a closer look at each of these menus.

Table 2.8 WordStar Editing Menus

Menu	Description
File	Contains many of the same commands as the opening screen File menu; also includes commands for opening and switching between windows, saving files, and closing files
Edit	Stores the commands you use for marking blocks of text; moving, copying, or deleting text; finding specified text; moving the cursor to a desired location; or adding notes and note options; also contains the Undo command.
View	Controls the way items are displayed on-screen; includes the Preview command, commands for working with multiple windows, and screen settings
Insert	Enables you to insert page and column breaks, add date and other variable information, insert text and graphics files, add index and table of contents entries, and specify outline codes
Style	Controls the way your text looks; you can choose from a variety of type styles, choose to add paragraph styles to your text, or further control text settings.
Layout	Enables you to fine-tune the layout of your document by adding and aligning lines, controlling page and column layout, adding headers and footers, adjusting spacing, adding page and line numbers, and adding special effects
Utilities	Contains commands for using add-on features, such as the spelling checker, thesaurus, calculator, macros, merge-print commands, graphics integration, and others
Help	The same Help menu as the one in the opening screen, this menu enables you to select context-sensitive help or change the help level.

The File Menu

Similar to the File menu in the opening screen, the edit screen's File menu enables you to work with files you create or bring into WordStar. To open the File menu, press Alt-F or position the mouse cursor on the word *File* in the menu bar and click the mouse button. The menu appears, as shown in figure 2.16.

Notice the additional characters on the right side of the menu; these are the *quick keys* you can use to bypass the menu selections. If you want to select the Save command, for example, you can do it in one of four ways:

■ You can press S (the highlighted letter).

Highlighted command ————————— 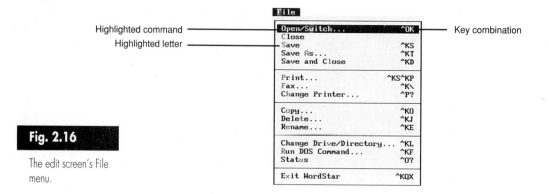 ————— Key combination

Highlighted letter —————————

The edit screen's File menu.

■ You can press the down-arrow key twice, so that the command, is highlighted and then press Enter.

■ You can move the mouse cursor to the Save command and click the mouse button.

■ Before you open the File menu, you can press the Ctrl-KS key combination.

If you want to bypass the menu selections, you can press Ctrl-KS without opening the File menu. This quick key automatically brings up the Save dialog box (if this is the first time you've saved the file) or updates the existing file (if you've saved the file before).

Table 2.9 provides an overview of the commands on the File menu.

Table 2.9 The File Menu (Edit Screen)

Command	Description
Open/Switch	Creates a second window in which you can view another part of the same document or open another document; switches between windows
Close	Closes the current file
Save	Displays the Save dialog box so that you can save the current file
Save As	Saves the file under a different name
Save and Close	Saves the current document and closes it, returning you to the opening screen
Print	Displays the Print dialog box so that you can print a document

Command	Description
Fax	Creates a file in a format that can be transmitted by fax
Change Printer	Enables you to choose a printer other than the default
Copy	Copies a file of your choice
Delete	Deletes the file you specify
Rename	Renames the file you specify
Change Drive/ Directory	Enables you to display files in a different drive or directory
Run DOS Command	Enables you to perform a DOS operation without leaving WordStar (or your current document)
Status	Displays the amount of memory used in the current work session and tells you how much memory is still available
Exit WordStar	Leaves WordStar

The Edit Menu

In the Edit menu, you find the commands you need to perform operations on blocks of text. Specifically, these commands enable you to mark blocks; copy, move, and delete blocks of text; find and replace text strings; move the cursor to a specific location in the document; and add and edit notes. To open the Edit menu, press Alt-E or click the menu name. Figure 2.17 shows the Edit menu.

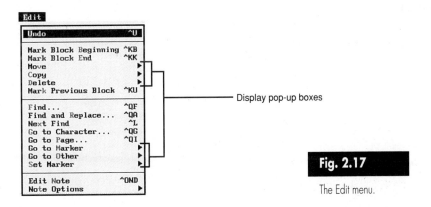

Display pop-up boxes

Fig. 2.17

The Edit menu.

On the Edit menu, you see the familiar quick key combinations, and something else: small triangles to the right of several of the commands (such as Move and Delete) tell you that another pop-up option box is displayed when you choose those commands. Additionally, you see after some commands the familiar ellipsis (. . .), indicating that dialog boxes appear when you choose those commands. Table 2.10 summarizes the commands in the Edit menu.

Table 2.10 The Edit Menu (Edit Screen)

Command	Description
Undo	Cancels your last delete operation, placing the deleted text back in the document
Mark Block Beginning	Specifies the beginning of a block of text you want to mark
Mark Block End	Specifies the end of the marked block
Move	Moves the marked block to a different place in your document
Copy	Copies the marked block and places the copy at the cursor position
Delete	Deletes the marked block
Mark Previous Block	Rehighlights the previously marked block
Find	Searches your document for text you specify
Find and Replace	Finds text you specify and replaces that text with information you provide
Next Find	Positions the cursor at the next occurrence of the word or text you entered for the Find operation
Go to Character	Moves the cursor to a specific character
Go to Page	Moves the cursor to a page you specify
Go to Marker	Finds a marker you've entered previously
Go to Other	Positions the cursor at another specified point in the document
Set Marker	Sets a nonprinting marker in the document
Edit Note	Enables you to edit a note you've entered
Note Options	Displays your options for adding notes to your document
Editing Settings	Enables you to enter additional settings for blocks of text, such as columnar settings, word wrap, and so on

The View Menu

As you might expect, the View menu controls the way you see your document. In this menu, you find commands for previewing the document as it will appear in print, hiding the display of command tags and block markers, opening and changing the display of windows, and customizing the elements displayed on-screen. You open the View menu by pressing Alt-V or clicking View. Figure 2.18 shows the View menu.

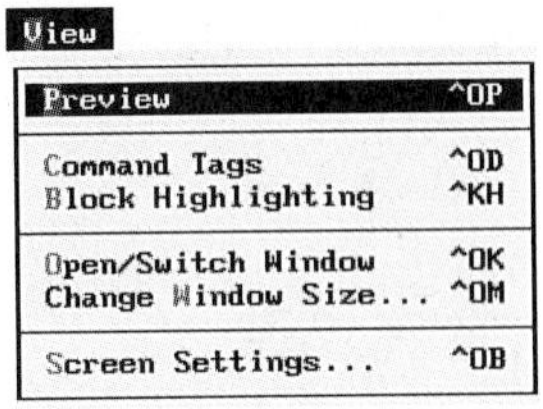

Fig. 2.18

The View menu.

Table 2.11 introduces you to the various commands on the View menu.

Table 2.11 The View Menu (Edit Screen)

Command	Description
Preview	Enables you to see the open document exactly as it will appear in print
Command Tags	Hides or displays command tags and dot commands you place in your document
Block Highlighting	Displays or hides the block markers you set in your document
Open/Switch Window	Opens another document window for the same document or for another document; also used to move between windows
Change Window Size	Changes the number of lines displayed in the windows
Screen Settings	Enables you to choose whether to display menus, the status line, ruler line, style bar, and so on

The Insert Menu

The next menu on the edit screen's menu bar is the Insert menu. As you can tell from the name, the Insert menu contains all the commands you use to insert into your document various items—such as page and column breaks, printing codes, and index entries. To open the Insert menu, press Alt-I or click Insert with the mouse. Figure 2.19 shows the Insert menu.

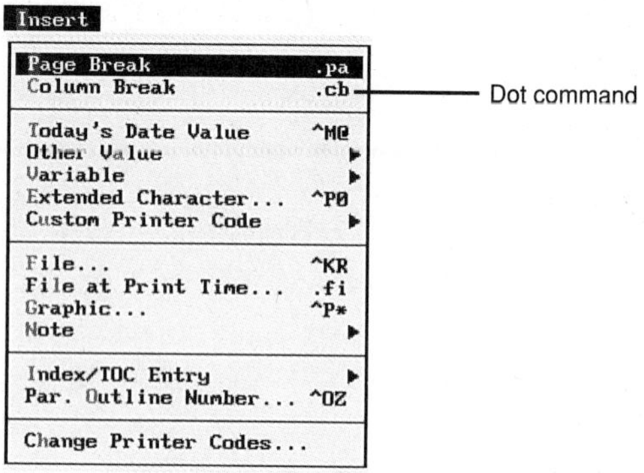

Insert	
Page Break	.pa
Column Break	.cb
Today's Date Value	^M@
Other Value	▶
Variable	▶
Extended Character...	^P0
Custom Printer Code	▶
File...	^KR
File at Print Time...	.fi
Graphic...	^P*
Note	▶
Index/TOC Entry	▶
Par. Outline Number...	^OZ
Change Printer Codes...	

Dot command

Fig. 2.19

The Insert menu.

In this menu, you see something new. Across from the Page Break command, you see something other than a simple quick key: you see the characters .pa. This command is a *dot command* (named for the period that precedes the characters) When you choose this command, WordStar places the command directly into your document. WordStar has many different dot commands for various alignment, layout, and printing tasks. In the Insert menu, you see three dot commands:

Page Break	.pa
Column Break	.cb
File at Print Time	.fi

The dot commands do not print; WordStar does not print any line that begins with a period. Chapter 10 explains more about dot commands.

Table 2.12 summarizes the commands available on the Insert menu.

The Style Menu

In the Style menu, you find the commands that change the look of your text. Want to choose a different font? Need to make a title stand out in boldfaced type? You find the necessary commands in the Style menu. To open the Style menu, press Alt-S or click the Style menu name. Figure 2.20 shows the Style menu.

Table 2.12 The Insert Menu (Edit Screen)

Command	Description
Page Break	Adds a page break at the cursor location by inserting .pa into your document
Column Break	Inserts a column break at the cursor position by adding .cb to the document
Today's Date Value	Inserts the current date at the cursor position
Other Value	Enables you to insert other information at the cursor position
Variable	Enables you to choose from different variables that can be inserted when you print the document
Extended Character	Inserts an extended character (a character not available on the standard keyboard) at the cursor position
Custom Printer Code	Enables you to customize printing codes for your printer
File	Adds a file at the cursor position
File at Print Time	Merge prints by inserting a file at the marked position at print time
Graphic	Places a graphic at the cursor position
Note	Inserts a footnote, endnote, comment, or annotation at the cursor position
Index/TOC Entry	Marks the text you'll use to generate the index or table of contents
Par. Outline Number	Numbers paragraphs in outline format
Change Printer Codes	Enables you to modify printing codes for your printer (for the current work session only)

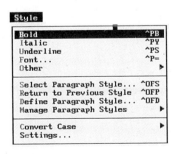

Fig. 2.20

The Style menu.

You also find in this menu commands for working with *paragraph styles*, that is, preset formats you can apply to your paragraphs. Paragraph styles can save you a considerable amount of time when you're working with items that require special formats—such as bulleted lists and numbered steps. Paragraph styles are presented in more detail in Chapter 6.

Table 2.13 explains the commands in the Style menu.

Table 2.13 The Style Menu (Edit Screen)

Command	Description
Bold	Inserts a bold code into the text so that text following the code is printed in boldface. You must add a second code to turn off boldface.
Italic	Inserts an italic code into the text so that text following the code is italicized. You must insert a second italic code to turn off italic.
Underline	Inserts an underline code at the cursor position and underlines all text following the code. You must add another underline code to turn off underlining.
Font	Changes the font for all text entered after the cursor position
Other	Enables you to choose from other text attributes including subscript, superscript, double-strike, or strikeout
Select Paragraph Style	Enables you to choose a paragraph style for existing text or text entered after the cursor position
Return to Previous Style	Reverts to the paragraph style used before the current one
Define Paragraph Style	Enables you to define your own paragraph style
Manage Paragraph Styles	Renames, deletes, or copies existing paragraph styles
Convert Case	Converts lowercase to uppercase (or vice versa) for selected text
Settings	Modifies underline and strikeout settings

The Layout Menu

The Layout menu, as you might expect, contains the commands you use to fine-tune the layout of your text. With these commands, you work with the way text is positioned on the page, add headers and footers, control page and line numbering, and make adjustments to spacing. To open the Layout menu, press Alt-L or click the Layout menu name. Figure 2.21 shows the Layout menu. Table 2.14 explains each command on the menu.

```
Layout
Center Line              ^OC
Right Align Line         ^OJ

Ruler Line...            ^OL
Columns...               ^OU
Page...                  ^OY
Headers/Footers            ▶
Page Numbering...        ^O#
Line Numbering...        .1#
Alignment and Spacing... ^OS
Special Effects            ▶
```

Fig. 2.21

The Layout menu.

Table 2.14 The Layout Menu (Edit Screen)

Command	Description
Center Line	Centers the text on the current line
Right Align Line	Aligns the text on the current line along the right margin
Ruler Line	Modifies margin and tab settings
Columns	Lays out the document in columns. You specify the number of columns and space between columns, and WordStar does the rest.
Page	Enables you to enter the margins for your document and select the orientation: portrait or landscape. (See Chapter 10 for more information about selecting the orientation of your page.)
Headers/Footers	Creates a header or footer for your document
Page Numbering	Enables you to position the page number and choose the first page number for your document
Line Numbering	Aligns the line numbers for your document and turns line numbering on and off
Alignment and Spacing	Enables you to choose the alignment of text (left, centered, right, or justified) and line spacing used in text
Special Effects	Controls how words are divided (or not divided) at print time; also controls hyphenation and overprint

The Utilities Menu

The Utilities menu holds the different commands you use to access the special features of WordStar. Here you find the spelling checker, thesaurus, calculator, and macro commands. To open the Utilities menu, press Alt-U or click the Utilities menu name. Figure 2.22 shows the Utilities menu.

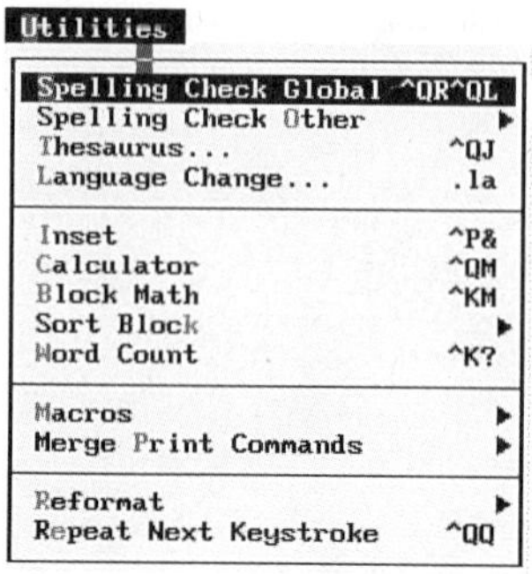

Fig. 2.22

The Utilities menu.

```
 Utilities
┌─────────────────────────────────┐
│Spelling Check Global  ^QR^QL     │
│Spelling Check Other            ▶ │
│Thesaurus...            ^QJ       │
│Language Change...      .la       │
├─────────────────────────────────┤
│Inset                   ^P&       │
│Calculator              ^QM       │
│Block Math              ^KM       │
│Sort Block                      ▶ │
│Word Count              ^K?       │
├─────────────────────────────────┤
│Macros                          ▶ │
│Merge Print Commands            ▶ │
├─────────────────────────────────┤
│Reformat                        ▶ │
│Repeat Next Keystroke   ^QQ       │
└─────────────────────────────────┘
```

Table 2.15 highlights the commands in the Utilities menu.

The Help Menu

You already know about the Help menu from earlier in this chapter (the Help menu on the opening screen and the Help menu on the edit screen are identical), but a couple of reminders never hurt anyone:

- At any point in the program, you can press F1 to get help relative to the operation you're performing.

- You can use the Help command in the Help menu to display a list of help topics.

- You can change the help level of the menus displayed by choosing Change Help Level from the Help menu.

The Style Bar

Now that you've finished wandering through the menus, you're ready to move on to the remaining screen elements. Below the menu bar, you see a rather suspicious-looking line of information: this line is known as the *style bar*. New with WordStar 7.0, the style bar provides immediate access to a number of settings concerning your text; you can make selections easily with the simple click of the mouse.

Table 2.15 The Utilities Menu (Edit Screen)

Command	Description
Spelling Check Global	Spell checks entire document
Spelling Check Other	Spell checks the specified word or portion of document
Thesaurus	Displays synonyms for words you enter
Language Change	Enables you to change the language dictionary being used for spell checking
Inset	Loads Inset, the graphics integration program
Calculator	Enables you to perform mathematical operations without leaving your document
Block Math	Calculates equations in a marked block and displays results at the top of the screen
Sort Block	Sorts marked text in alphanumeric order
Word Count	Provides the word count for the marked block or entire file
Macros	Gives you the option of playing, recording, editing, copy, deleting, renaming, or trouble-shooting macros
Merge Print Commands	Contains a submenu that controls all merge-printing operations
Reformat	Reformats document after changes have been made
Repeat Next Keystroke	Repeats the next keystroke you press until you stop the process by pressing another key

The style bar, as shown in figure 2.23, displays the following information:

- The chosen paragraph style
- The current text font
- The text style in use
- The alignment of text
- The line spacing of text

In the sections that follow, you learn about each of these special elements of the style bar.

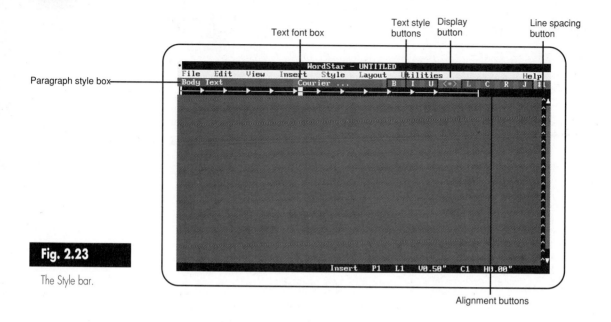

Fig. 2.23

The Style bar.

The Paragraph Style Box

As mentioned, paragraph styles are special formats you can assign to text. Suppose, for example, that you are creating a document that includes a bulleted list. You can use an existing paragraph style to format the text for you so that you don't need to go in and change margins, play with the spacing, and go through general trial and error before you find the right format for a bulleted list. WordStar 7.0 comes with several preset paragraph styles, and you can also design your own.

To see the different paragraph styles from which you can choose, simply click the paragraph style box. The Select Paragraph Style dialog box, shown in figure 2.24, appears. You can choose a style and press Enter, or press Esc to get back to the document.

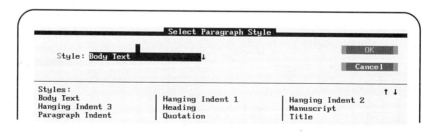

Fig. 2.24

The Select Paragraph Style dialog box.

What About Keyboard Users?

If you are using the keyboard, you can display the Select Paragraph
Styles dialog box by pressing Ctrl-OFS or by opening the Style menu
and choosing the Select Paragraph Styles command.

The Text Font Box

The text font box is to the right of the paragraph style box. In the text
font box, you choose the type of font you want to use in your document.
(The type and number of fonts you have available depend on the type of
printer you are using and the number—if any—of add-on fonts you have
purchased.)

If you are using a mouse, you can display your font choices by clicking
the text font box. If you are using the keyboard, you make your choices
by opening the Style menu (press Alt-S) and selecting the Font command. (You can bypass the menu selections by pressing Ctrl-P=. The
Font dialog box appears, as shown in figure 2.25. (**Note:** The Font dialog
box shown in figure 2.24 contains fonts that can be used with a
PostScript laser printer. Your fonts may be different from the ones
shown here.)

Finding Your Fonts

If you do not see the fonts for your printer in the Font dialog box
list, perhaps this document does not use your default printer. To
select the correct printer, choose the File menu by pressing Alt-F,
highlight Change Printer, and press Enter. You will see a list of installed printers. Highlight your default printer and press Enter. Now
look back at your list of fonts and see whether your fonts are
loaded.

```
                                    Font
        Font: Courier 10                              ██  OK  ██
                                                      ██ Cancel ██

        Fonts:          Printer: PSCRIPT                          ↑ ↓
        A Garamond ...  A Garamond SB...  Avant Garde ...  Bookman ...
        Courier ...     Helv Cond ...     Helv Narrow ...  Helvetica ...
        N Cntry Schl ... Palatino ...     Symbol ...       Times ...
        Zpf Chancery ... Zpf Dingbats ...
```

Fig. 2.25

The Font dialog box.

You can choose a new font and click OK (or press Enter), or you can press Esc to cancel the operation. (For now, you're just looking around; you'll get a chance to try out changing fonts and choosing styles in Chapter 3.)

The Text Styles Buttons

The next three options on the style bar are the text style buttons. You can choose B for boldface, I for italic, or U for underline. You can use these buttons in one of two ways:

- You can change the style of existing text by positioning the cursor at the place where you want to turn on the style and clicking the B, I, or U button. Then move the cursor to the point in the text you want to end that style and click the same button again. The text between the beginning and ending codes will be printed in the style you selected.

- You can enter text in the style you want by clicking the button and then typing the text. (All the text you enter after clicking the button appears in the style you chose.) You then click the button again to turn off the style so that text you type after that point is in regular style.

The Display Button

The display button is a small symbol between the style buttons and the alignment buttons. The display button controls the display of the command tags, which are displayed in your text and along the right side of the work area just inside the scroll bar. When you click the display button, the command tags appear in your text, and the flag column appears along the right edge of the screen, inside the scroll bar (see fig. 2.26). If you want to turn off the display of the flag column, click the button again.

The flag column shows you where you've pressed Enter or added special codes in your document. If you want to turn on the flag column by using the keyboard, open the View menu (by pressing Alt-V) and choose Screen Settings. When the Screen Settings dialog box appears, select Flag Column: Always On and press Enter.

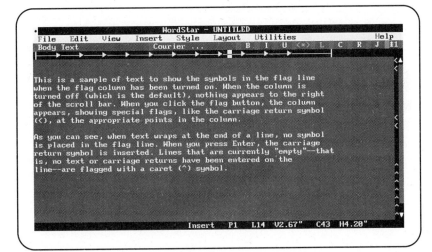

Document displaying
command tags and the
flag column.

The Alignment Buttons

The next four buttons control the alignment of text in your document.
You have four choices for the way your text is aligned:

Button	Alignment
L	Left, which aligns text along the left margin
C	Center, which centers text between margins
R	Right, which aligns text along the right margin and leaves the left edge ragged
J	Justified, which aligns text along both the right and left margins

You can choose an alignment and then enter the text, or you can place
your cursor before existing text and click the button. More about working with text alignment is explained in Chapter 3.

The Line Spacing Button

With the line spacing button, you can control a variety of options concerning the spacing and alignment of your document. When you click the
line spacing button, the Alignment and Spacing dialog box appears (see
fig. 2.27).

Fig. 2.27

The Alignment and
Spacing dialog box.

```
                         Alignment and Spacing
       Alignment:
          o   Flush Left      [X] Kerning              OK
          •   Centered        [X] Word Wrap
          o   Flush Right     [X] Hyphenation        Cancel
          o   Justified

       Line Spacing: [1]    Leading:  .17"    (Line Height)
```

As you can see, you can choose the alignment from this dialog box, as
well as control kerning (spacing between characters); word wrap; hyphenation; line spacing (single-spacing, double-spacing, and so on); and
leading (amount of space between lines). You can change the settings
and click OK; or click Cancel or press Esc to return to the document.

The Scroll Bar

The scroll bar, located along the right edge of your screen, enables you
to move around in the document easily. If you want to move to the end
of a long document, you can position the mouse in the lower portion of
the scroll bar and click the mouse button; you are taken to the end of
your document. Similarly, if you want to move to the beginning of the
document, place the mouse cursor at the top of the scroll bar and click.
You get the idea.

To scroll through the display in smaller increments, you can click the
arrows at either end of the scroll bar. This action moves you through
the display, one line at a time.

Mouse Tricks: Setting Margins

If you're using a mouse, you have a quick way to access a dialog
box that enables you to change the left and right margins and tab
setting. Simply move the mouse pointer up to the ruler line, just
below the style bar on the edit screen. Then click the mouse button. The dialog box appears, and you can make your changes.

The Status Line

The last line on the edit screen is the status line, found at the bottom
of the screen. The status line gives you important information about

your current operation. Consider the status line shown in the bottom of figure 2.28.

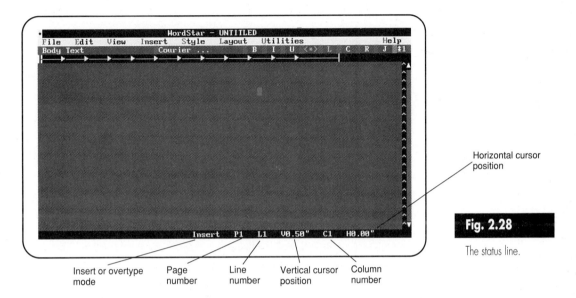

Horizontal cursor position

Fig. 2.28

The status line.

Insert or overtype mode

Page number

Line number

Vertical cursor position

Column number

As you can see in table 2.16, the status line tells you many different things.

Table 2.16 Status Line Items

Item	Description
Insert	Tells you that insert mode is in effect; when you begin typing, characters will be inserted into the text at the cursor position. The other setting that may appear here is Ins-off, which tells you that characters you type will overwrite existing characters.
P1	The cursor is positioned on page 1, or the page indicated by the number.
L1	The cursor is positioned on line 1, or the line indicated by the number.
V0.50"	The cursor is positioned vertically one-half inch from the top of the page, or the position indicated by the number.
C1	The cursor is positioned on character (or column) 1, or the character/column indicated by the number.
H0.00"	The cursor is positioned horizontally at the left edge of the page, or the position indicated by the number.

As you type, all these settings—except Insert—change to reflect the cursor position. You get a chance to see these changes in action in Chapter 3.

More Mouse Tricks: Using the Status Line

Mouse users have acccss to a few quick steps that keyboard users do not have:

Clicking the word *Insert* in the status line turns insert mode on or off.

Clicking the page number in the status line displays a dialog box enabling you to go to another page.

If you mark a section of text as a block, the beginning block marker <B> and the ending block marker <K> appear in the status line. If you click the <B>, your cursor automatically moves to the beginning of the block. If you click the <K>, your cursor automatically moves to the end of the block.

Chapter Summary

In this chapter, you've covered a great deal of ground. From a basic exploration of the opening menu, you've learned about all the menus on the opening and edit screens, found out about different commands and dialog boxes, and learned to use the elements on the edit screen. The next chapter gives you hands-on practice using all these basic elements in a tutorial that takes you through the process of opening a new document, entering, editing, enhancing formatting, spell checking, previewing, and printing text.

A WordStar Quick Start

I n the last chapter, you learned about all the basic tools—menus, commands, dialog boxes, and so on—that you use to create documents with WordStar. In this chapter, you get to put those tools to use. By the time you finish this chapter, you will have worked through the basic procedures for creating, editing, saving, and printing a document. (All the bells and whistles, such as macros and merge printing, come later.) Specifically, this chapter includes steps for performing the following tasks:

- Starting WordStar
- Opening a new document
- Entering text
- Doing simple keyboard editing
- Changing the font
- Changing the text style
- Changing alignment
- Changing the line spacing
- Applying a paragraph style
- Saving the document
- Previewing the document
- Printing the document

Because this chapter is a quick start, the steps for these tasks are provided in concise tutorial form so that you can follow along easily. References are provided so that you can turn to the appropriate chapters for more in-depth information about the different operations.

Starting WordStar

If you are just beginning your WordStar work session, you need to get WordStar up and running. Here's how:

1. Turn on your computer.

2. Change to the directory in which you've installed your WordStar files. (If you haven't installed the program yet, consult Appendix A for installation instructions.) To change to the WordStar directory, use the DOS Change Directory (CD) command followed by the name of the directory, such as

   CD WS

   WS is the default directory WordStar uses to store the files. If you changed the directory name when you installed WordStar, enter that directory name after the CD command. Press Enter.

3. Type *WS* and press Enter.

The copyright screen and then the opening screen appear. Figure 3.1 shows the opening screen.

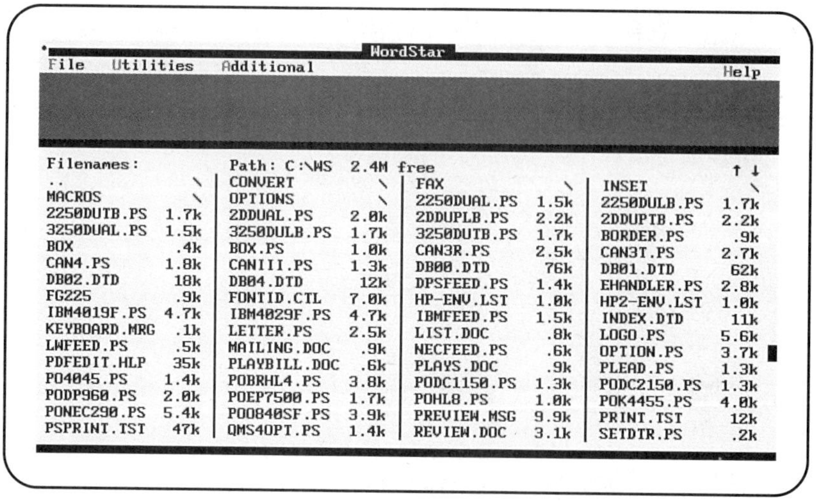

Fig. 3.1

The WordStar opening screen.

Opening a New Document

Any time you begin working on a new document, such as a report, a letter, or a newsletter, you start by opening a new file. WordStar offers several ways to open a new file. The simplest way is to press S.

With this keystroke, you are using the quick key for selecting New from the File menu. (You could open the File menu and choose the New command, if you prefer.) The edit screen appears, as shown in figure 3.2.

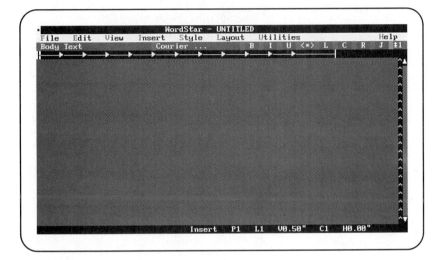

Fig. 3.2

The edit screen.

Entering Text

Now you can simply begin typing. If you are following along with the examples in this chapter, enter the following text, mistakes and all. (You'll correct the mistakes in a minute):

> Welcome to the Homeward Bound Publishing 1991 Annual Report. Wait—before you file this under the stack of papers in your in-basket—we want you to know we've adopted a new fomrat this year. No more dry stuff. Fewer statistics. More stories the best and worst of 91. (You may remember that the best and worst category was the popular most in last year's report.)

The first paragraph has three mistakes:

- The word *format* is misspelled as *fomrat* (sentence 2).

- The word *about* has been omitted between *stories* and *the* (sentence 5).

- The words *popular* and *most* have been transposed (sentence 6).

That's the end of the first paragraph. When the cursor is positioned after the closing parenthesis, press Enter twice. WordStar leaves a blank line and positions the cursor on the next line. Now type the second paragraph:

In this report, you'll find out about the following changes that 1991 brought: We've grown, peoplewise, 100 percent. We now distribute our own books in 12 cities along the West Coast. In 1991 alone, we published 23 books (seven more than in 1990).

Notice that as you type, WordStar automatically wraps the text to the next line. Unlike a typewriter, on which you have to press Enter (or the carriage return) at the end of each line, WordStar wraps text to the next line for you. You need to press Enter only at the end of a paragraph. Figure 3.3 shows the text you've entered in your first WordStar document.

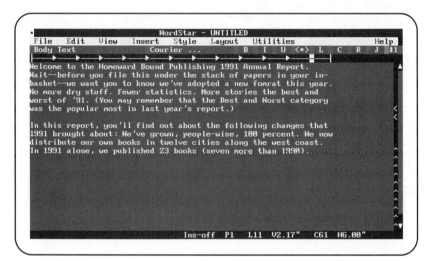

Fig. 3.3

The sample text.

Learning Simple Keyboard Editing

Now you need to fix the errors in the paragraph. In this section, you learn to move the cursor to the errors, use the Backspace key to correct misspellings, select text, and use a few simple editing commands to move misplaced text.

Moving the Cursor

You have already learned about the mouse cursor, the small arrow (or rectangular block, depending on the operation you are performing) that moves on-screen as you move the mouse. When you are working on a document in the edit screen, you use another cursor—the *text cursor*—to indicate the place on-screen where you want to enter or delete text. WordStar 7.0 provides several ways for you to move the text cursor:

- You can use the arrow keys on your keyboard.

- You can use WordStar's quick keys (The following are just a few; Appendix D contains a complete list.):

    Ctrl-D to move one character to the right

    Ctrl-S to move one character to the left

    Ctrl-E to move one line up

    Ctrl-X to move one line down

- You can position the mouse cursor where you want the cursor to be placed and click the mouse button.

Key Combinations

To press a key combination, such as Ctrl-E, press and hold the Ctrl key while you press the E. Release both keys simultaneously.

You can try all three methods. The cursor should still be positioned at the end of the second paragraph.

1. Press the up-arrow key three times. The cursor moves to the first line of the second paragraph. You're going all the way up to *fomrat* (in the first paragraph).

2. Press Ctrl-E once—oops! what happened?—the cursor jumped back to the first character position in the line when you got to the blank line between paragraphs.

3. Press Ctrl-E two more times. The cursor should be positioned on *worst*.

4. Now try the mouse. Move the mouse until you see the mouse cursor appear on the screen. (The mouse cursor is a small highlighted rectangle.)

5. Move the mouse until the mouse cursor is highlighting the *f* in *fomrat*.

6. Click the mouse button. The flashing cursor appears under the letter *f*.

Correcting Misspellings

Now you can edit the misspelled word easily. Here's how:

1. Press the right-arrow key twice. The cursor is positioned under the *m* in *fomrat* (in sentence 2).

2. Press the Delete key. The *m* disappears.

3. Press the right-arrow key once. The cursor is positioned on the *a*.

4. Press M. The *m* is inserted into the word so that it now appears correctly as *format*.

That's Not What Happened . . .

If, when you tried to insert the letter *m*, the character replaced the letter *a* (leaving you with the word *formt*), WordStar is in overtype mode. The default setting when you start WordStar is insert mode, meaning that any characters you type will be inserted into the word rather than overwriting existing characters. To change WordStar back into insert mode, press Ctrl-V.

Inserting a Word

The next editing task you take on involves inserting a word into existing text. You will insert the word *about* between *stories* and *the* (in sentence 5).

1. Make sure that WordStar is in insert mode by checking the status line. If WordStar is in insert mode, the word Insert appears at the beginning of the status line at the bottom of the screen. If Ins-off is displayed, press Ctrl-V to turn on insert mode.

2. Press the down-arrow key. The cursor moves to the letter *h* in the word *the*.

3. Press the left-arrow key. The cursor moves to the letter *t* in the word *the*.

4. Type *about* and press the space bar. WordStar automatically moves the words to the right of the new text to make room for the added word.

Selecting Text

The last editing change you make in this section involves highlighting a word and moving it to a new location in the paragraph. As you may recall, the words *popular* and *most* are transposed in the last sentence of the first paragraph. First, you need to select the word you want to move.

Whether you are selecting a character, a paragraph, or the entire document, any text you highlight (or mark) is known as a *text block*. You must select text as a block before you perform certain editing operations, such as copying, moving, or deleting text. You can select text with the mouse or the keyboard:

If you are using the mouse, follow these steps to highlight the word *popular*:

1. Move the mouse cursor to the beginning of the word *popular*.

2. Press and hold the mouse button.

3. Drag the mouse to the right until the entire word is highlighted.

4. Release the mouse button. The word is highlighted, as shown in figure 3.4.

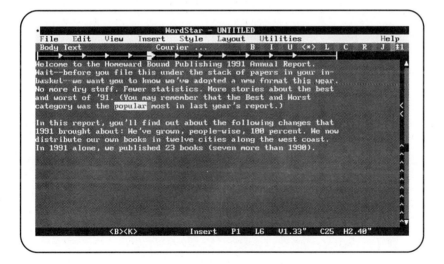

Fig. 3.4

The selected text.

If you are using the keyboard, follow these steps:

1. Move the cursor to the first letter of the word *popular*.

2. Open the Edit menu by pressing Alt-E.

3. Choose the Mark Block Beginning command (see fig. 3.5). WordStar returns you to the document. As you can see, a beginning block code <B> has been inserted into the text.

Fig. 3.5

Choosing the Mark Block Beginning command from the Edit menu.

4. Move the cursor to the space following the word *popular*.

5. Open the Edit menu.

6. Choose Mark Block End.

An ending block code <K> is inserted into the text, and the word is highlighted as a block.

Marking Blocks Quickly: Keyboard Method

You can mark blocks quickly from the keyboard by using the quick keys. Just position the cursor at the place you want to begin the block, and press Ctrl-KB. Then move the cursor to the end of the block and press Ctrl-KK. The block is then highlighted.

Moving Selected Text

Now you can solve the rest of your problem by moving the word you've selected. To do this, follow these steps:

1. Position the cursor where you want the word *popular* to go (on the *i* in *in*).

2. Open the Edit menu by clicking the menu name or by pressing Alt-E.

3. Choose the Move command. A small pop-up box appears beside the displayed Edit menu (see fig. 3.6).

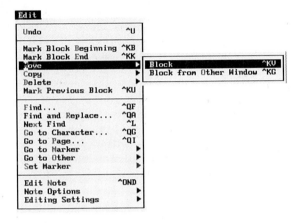

Fig. 3.6

The Move pop-up menu.

4. Choose Block.

WordStar automatically moves the marked block to the cursor position. Now your paragraph is correct, and you're ready to work with some different enhancement features of WordStar.

Reviewing the Style Bar

As you learned in Chapter 2, WordStar's edit screen contains all the settings you need as you edit and enhance the look of your document. The style bar, located just beneath the menu bar, displays the current settings and enables you to make changes for the following items:

- Paragraph style in effect at cursor position

- Font and size

- Style of text being entered

- Alignment of text

- Line spacing of text

If you need to review any of the style bar elements, refer to Chapter 2. The following sections give you practice working with text by changing settings in the style bar.

Changing the Font

As you can tell from the text font box in the style bar, the current font is Courier, a blocky, typewriterlike font that may not be suitable for your best-quality publications. You can easily change the font for the entire document or for a portion of the document. (***Note:*** The fonts available depend on the type of printer you installed with WordStar.)

What Is a Font?

If you're new to word processing, the term *font* may be new to you. A font is one particular type size and style within one typeface family. A *typeface* is a family of type, such as Courier, Times Roman, or Palatino. A font, then, would be Courier 10-point bold type or Times Roman 14-point italic type, and so on. For more information about working with fonts, see Chapter 8.

If you want to change the font for the entire document, first move the cursor to the first character at the beginning of the text. (You can do this quickly by pressing the Home key or, if your document is longer than one screen, Ctrl-Home.)

Then, if you are using the mouse, follow these steps:

1. Move the mouse cursor up to the text font box. (It currently says Courier).

2. Click the mouse button. The Font dialog box appears (see fig. 3.7). Your choices in this dialog box may vary, depending on the type of printer you have installed.

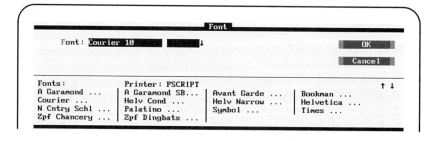

Fig. 3.7

The Font dialog box.

3. Move the mouse cursor to the font you want to use. (This example uses Palatino, a font available on PostScript printers.) Click the mouse button. The name of the font appears in the Font box.

4. If the Point Size box appears, type the size of the text you want to use. (Enter *12*).

5. Click OK.

Choosing Font Size

If you are using a PostScript printer and you choose a font with no ellipsis (. . .) after its name, the Point Size box appears, enabling you to specify the size of the font. Dot-matrix and other non-PostScript printers use fonts with a preset size, and you are not prompted to enter the size of the font. (The font's size is measured in *points*, with 72 points equalling 1 inch. The standard sizes for text are usually 10 or 12 points.)

When you return to the document, the new font you selected is shown in the text font box and a font code has been inserted at the cursor position (see fig. 3.8). Something else looks different—the text extends beyond the right edge of the screen, out of your line of vision. What's going on?

Font code —

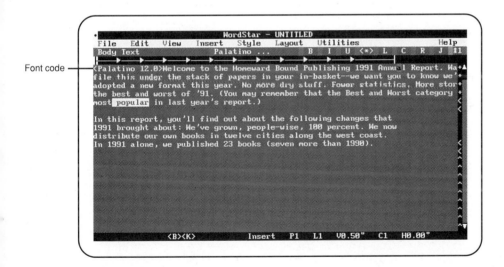

The Font code inserted into the text.

WordStar takes into consideration the fact that different fonts and sizes affect the width of text. Although in Courier the document fit nicely within the borders of the screen, changing the font to Palatino causes the text to extend beyond the right edge. Don't worry—in print, the document will appear correctly. On-screen, because Palatino is a proportionate font and Courier is a monospaced font, they look different. With *proportionate fonts*, different characters require different amounts of space, and you can fit more characters on a line. With *monospaced fonts*, each character is given the same amount of space, so they take up more room across the width of the page. (For more about working with fonts, see Chapter 8.)

WordStar is "thinking" about how many characters will fit across the width of the printed page. With a monospaced font, WordStar knows that it can fit 65 characters across the page (with the default margins). With a proportional font, WordStar can squeeze many more characters into that 65-character space because each character is given only as much room as it needs. The characters displayed on the screen, however, are not proportionate, so even though more characters can be printed on the page, they do not all fit within the width of the screen.

Finding Fonts Fast

You can bypass the menu selections by using the Ctrl-P= quick key combination to display the Font dialog box.

If you are using the keyboard, the method for changing the font is different. For this example, you move the cursor to the first character of the second paragraph.

1. Open the Style menu by pressing Alt-S.

2. Choose the Font command by highlighting it and pressing Enter (see fig. 3.9). The Font dialog box is displayed.

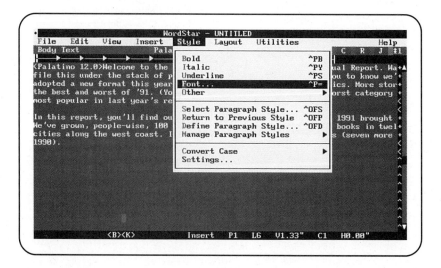

Fig. 3.9

Choosing the Font command.

3. Use the arrow keys to highlight the font you want to use. (For the example, choose New Century Schoolbook.)

4. Press Enter.

   If you are using a PostScript printer, the Point Size box appears. Type *12* and press Enter. (***Note:*** If you are using a dot-matrix or other non-PostScript printer, the Point Size box does not appear because the sizes for those printer types are fixed and cannot be changed.)

5. Press Enter. You are returned to the document, and the font code has been inserted.

Figure 3.10 shows the document after the keyboard method was used to change the font.

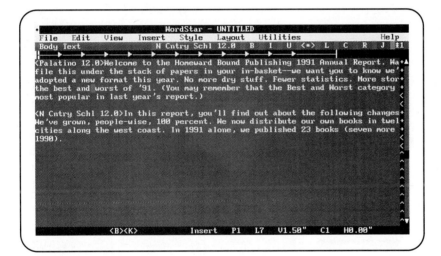

Fig. 3.10

Adding a different font to the document.

Understanding Embedded Codes

As you have seen, WordStar places certain codes in your text when you choose different options for your document. These codes may appear in angle brackets, or they may be displayed as dot commands (codes preceded by a period). When WordStar places one of these codes in your text, that code remains in effect until another code replaces it. When you change the font and the font code is added, for example, <Palatino, 12>, that font remains in effect unless you add another font code to change the font later in the document.

You'll see the effects of these changes when you preview the document later in this chapter.

Changing the Text Style

Suppose that you want to make the name of your company stand out. You can do this by using a different text style to highlight the text. WordStar gives you three different text styles—boldface (B), italic (I), and underline (U)—available right there on the style bar.

In this example, you change the text style of the words *Homeward Bound Publishing* in the first line of the sample document. To change the text style, follow these steps:

1. Move the cursor to the first letter of the phrase you want to change.

2. Click the B (bold) button to the right of the text font box, or if you are using the keyboard, press Ctrl-PB. A bold code, which appears as ^B, is placed at the cursor position. Your text also changes in intensity.

3. Now you need to add the ending bold code. Move the cursor to the end of the phrase.

4. Click B again or press Ctrl-PB. The ending bold code is added. Figure 3.11 shows the phrase after it has been changed to boldface style.

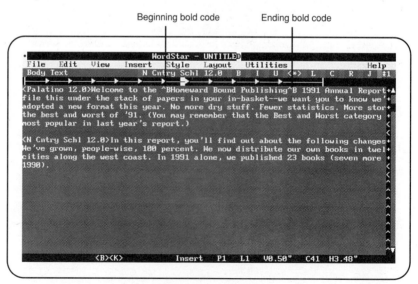

Beginning bold code   Ending bold code

Fig. 3.11

The boldfaced text.

Changing Alignment

Another aspect of the text you may want to change is the way it is aligned. WordStar gives you the option of aligning text in the following ways:

- *Left aligned*, the default setting, in which the text is aligned along the left margin but is ragged along the right

- *Centered*, in which the text is centered between the margins

- *Right aligned*, in which the text is aligned along the right margin and ragged along the left

- *Justified*, in which the text is aligned along both the left and right margins

---

More About Alignment . . .

You can find out more about aligning the text in your documents—from the standard left, center, right, and justified to more advanced column layouts and hanging indents—in Chapters 8 and 10.

To change the alignment of the text, follow these steps:

1. Position the cursor where you want the new alignment to take effect. (In this case, press Ctrl-Home to go to the beginning of the document again.)

2. Your next step depends on whether you're using the keyboard or the mouse.

   If you're using the mouse, click the button for the alignment you want. (For this example, click C for Center.)

   If you're using the keyboard, open the Layout menu and choose the Alignment and Spacing command. (Or if you prefer to skip a few keystrokes, press Ctrl-OS.) The Alignment and Spacing dialog box is shown in figure 3.12.

   Now, using the keyboard, type the highlighted letter of the alignment you want. (Press C to select Centered.) Then press Enter.

When you return to the document, you can see that WordStar has embedded an alignment code, .oj c, in your document. This code controls the alignment of all paragraphs following the code in your document—not just the one immediately following the code—until you enter another code to change the alignment again.

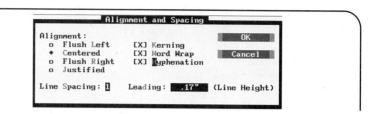

Fig. 3.12

The Alignment and
Spacing dialog box.

Reformatting Paragraphs

You won't see the effect of the inserted alignment, spacing, or font
codes until you reformat the paragraph. To reformat, press Ctrl-B.
WordStar reformats the paragraph according to the codes you have
inserted.

Changing the Line Spacing

You can also change the line spacing by using either the buttons on the
style bar or menu selections. Follow these steps:

1. First, position the cursor at the point where you want to change
   line spacing.

2. If you're using the mouse, click the 1 (spacing) button at the far
   right end of the style bar. If you're using the keyboard, press Ctrl-
   OS. Both operations display the Alignment and Spacing dialog box.

3. Type a new number for line spacing. (In this case, type *2*.)

4. Click OK or press Enter.

The document shows that a new code, .ls 2, has been inserted. To see
the effect of the change, press Ctrl-B (see fig. 3.13).

Applying a Paragraph Style

One of the major time-savers offered by WordStar is the addition of paragraph styles. *Paragraph styles* enable you to apply a preset format to
paragraphs so that you don't have to set alignment, font, spacing, style,
and indents for each paragraph in your document. WordStar comes with
nine preset paragraph styles. You can use these paragraph styles, or you
can create your own for styles you use often. (Chapter 8 introduces you

to all the WordStar paragraph styles and shows you how to create your own styles.)

Alignment code   Line spacing code

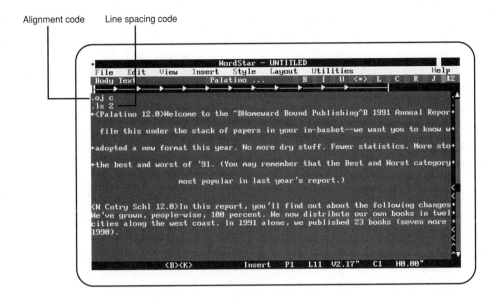

Document after changing the alignment and line spacing.

Try applying one of the preset paragraph styles to the second paragraph in the sample document. First, move the cursor to the beginning of the second paragraph.

If you're using the mouse, follow these steps:

1. Move the mouse cursor to the paragraph styles box at the left side of the style bar. (It currently says Body Text.)

2. Click the mouse button. The Select Paragraph Style dialog box appears (see fig. 3.14).

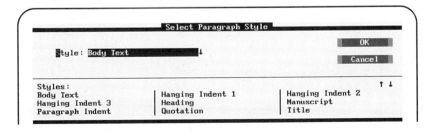

The Select Paragraph Style dialog box.

3. Click the style you want. For this example, choose Paragraph Indent.

4. Click the OK button.

When you return to the document, the style is inserted, and the paragraph is automatically reformatted.

If you are using the keyboard, follow these steps:

1. Position the cursor at the point where you want to apply the style.

2. Press Alt-S to display the Style menu.

3. Choose the Select Paragraph Style command. (You can press Ctrl-OFS to bypass the menu selections, if you prefer.)

4. The Select Paragraph Style dialog box appears. Press the arrow keys to highlight the style you want. (In this example, choose Paragraph Indent.)

5. Press Enter.

You are returned to the document, and the paragraph is reformatted to the new style. Figure 3.15 shows the second paragraph with the inserted code.

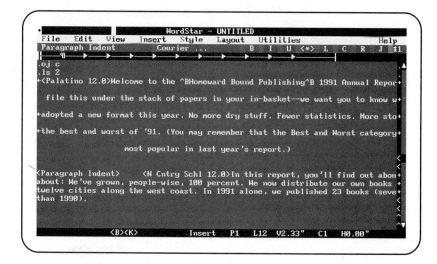

Fig. 3.15

Using a paragraph style in the document.

Saving the Document

OK, you've spent a great deal of time working on this document. What happens if a badly timed thunderstorm comes up and wipes out the power lines? What if a preoccupied co-worker trips over your computer's power cord? You lose all your work. For that reason, you need to be sure to save your file often—like every 10 or 15 minutes.

To save the file, follow these steps:

1. Open the File menu by pressing Alt-F or by clicking the menu name.

2. Choose the Save command (see fig. 3.16).

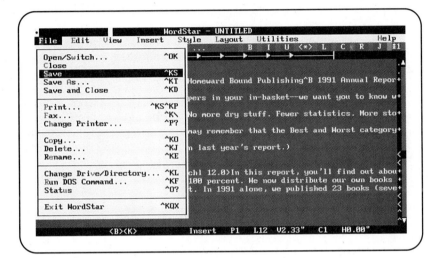

Fig. 3.16

Selecting the Save command.

3. The Save As dialog box appears (see fig. 3.17). Type a name for the file (in this case, *SAMPLE*) in the Filename text box.

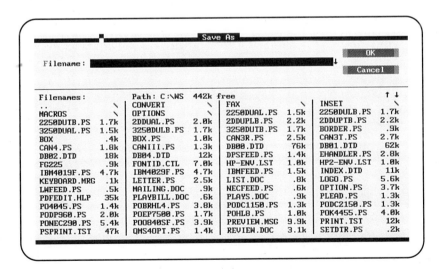

Fig. 3.17

The Save As dialog box.

4. Click OK or press Enter. WordStar saves the file and returns you to the document. The name of the file, SAMPLE, appears in the title bar of the edit screen.

Quick Saves

You can display the Save As dialog box quickly or perform a quick save on a file you've already saved by pressing Ctrl-KS.

WordStar also gives you the options of saving files in different formats or saving files under different names. Each time you save a file, WordStar makes a backup file automatically. (A backup file is given the extension BAK). For more about saving and retrieving WordStar documents, see Chapter 4.

Previewing the Document

Now that you've made all these changes to the original text, it would be nice to see what this document will look like in print. WordStar's preview feature gives you a chance to see your entire document on-screen, complete with the fonts, sizes, and styles you've chosen. (Chapter 9 explains in more detail how to use WordStar's preview feature.)

1. Open the View menu by clicking the menu name or pressing Alt-V.

2. Choose Preview. (You can bypass the menu selections by pressing Ctrl-OP, if you prefer.)

After a moment, WordStar displays the document in full-page view (see fig. 3.18). Across the top of the screen, you see a new menu system that includes commands you can use to view the document in preview mode. (More about preview is explained in Chapter 9.)

When you are ready to return to the document, press Esc.

Printing the Document

The final step in producing this sample document is printing. To print the document, follow these steps:

1. Open the File menu.

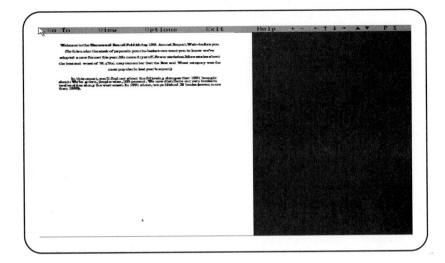

Fig. 3.18

The sample document
in preview mode.

2. Choose the Print command. The Print dialog box, shown in fig-
    ure 3.19, is displayed. As you can see, you have many options for
    the way you print.

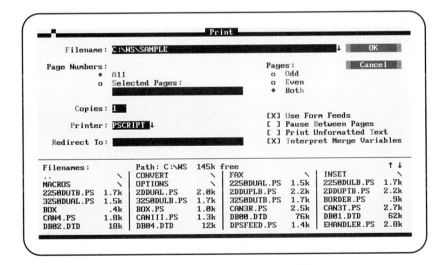

Fig. 3.19

The Print dialog box.

3. For your purposes, all the print options are all right the way they
    are. Click OK.

WordStar begins sending your document to the printer. A message,
Printing, appears in the top left corner of the title bar. Depending on

the type of printer you are using, your printer may begin working imme-diately, or it may take a minute or so to print your file. If your document does not print, make sure that your printer cable is connected securely and that your printer has a full supply of paper.

Chapter Summary

In this chapter, you have learned about the different procedures used to create WordStar documents. You've practiced techniques for starting WordStar; opening a new document; entering text; choosing text styles; selecting text alignment; performing simple keyboard editing techniques; and saving, previewing, and printing your document. In the next chapter, you learn to work with your WordStar files.

Working with WordStar Files

In the last few chapters, you've learned about the basics of WordStar 7.0 and tried your hand at several of the procedures involved in assembling a document. In this chapter, you learn to manage the files you create and work with during your WordStar work sessions.

Opening Files

This section explains how to open a new file with WordStar and shows you how to open files you've already created and saved.

Starting a New File

As you may recall, the process of starting a new file was introduced in the WordStar Quick Start (Chapter 3). In this chapter, you learn the various options available when you open a new file in WordStar 7.0.

When you first start the program, WordStar displays the opening screen (see fig. 4.1). From the opening screen, you access the File menu, which contains all the commands you need for working with the files you create. At the bottom of the opening screen, you see a list of files in the current directory. Your screen may show different files in this list.

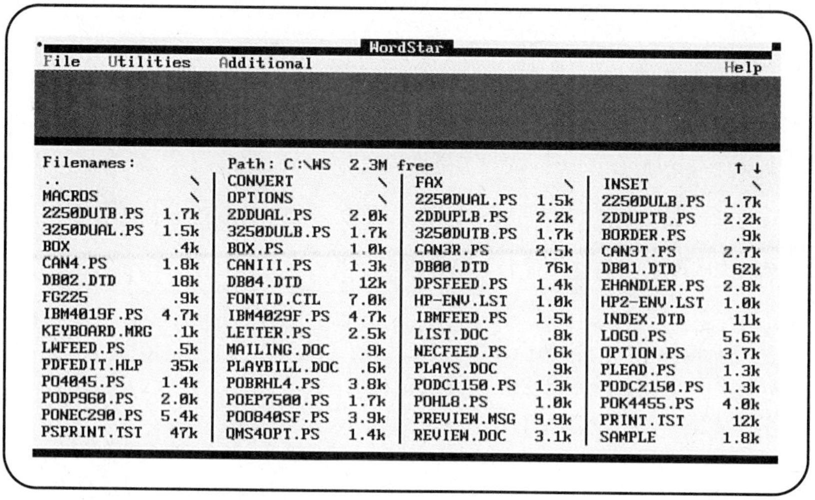

```
┌────────────────────────────────────────────────────────────────────────┐
│  •                                    WordStar                        ■   │
│  File   Utilities   Additional                                    Help    │
│ ▓▓▓▓▓▓▓▓▓▓▓▓▓▓▓▓▓▓▓▓▓▓▓▓▓▓▓▓▓▓▓▓▓▓▓▓▓▓▓▓▓▓▓▓▓▓▓▓▓▓▓▓▓▓▓▓▓▓▓▓▓▓▓▓▓▓▓▓▓▓▓▓▓  │
│                                                                           │
│  Filenames:        Path: C:\WS   2.3M free                         ↑ ↓    │
│  ..              \  CONVERT        \  FAX           \   INSET         \    │
│  MACROS          \  OPTIONS        \  2250DUAL.PS  1.5k  2250DULB.PS  1.7k │
│  2250DUTB.PS  1.7k  2DDUAL.PS   2.0k  2DDUPLB.PS   2.2k  2DDUPTB.PS   2.2k │
│  3250DUAL.PS  1.5k  3250DULB.PS 1.7k  3250DUTB.PS  1.7k  BORDER.PS     .9k │
│  BOX           .4k  BOX.PS      1.0k  CAN3R.PS     2.5k  CAN3T.PS     2.7k │
│  CAN4.PS      1.8k  CANIII.PS   1.3k  DB00.DTD      76k  DB01.DTD      62k │
│  DB02.DTD      18k  DB04.DTD     12k  DPSFEED.PS   1.4k  EHANDLER.PS  2.8k │
│  FG225         .9k  FONTID.CTL  7.0k  HP-ENV.LST   1.0k  HP2-ENV.LST  1.0k │
│  IBM4019F.PS  4.7k  IBM4029F.PS 4.7k  IBMFEED.PS   1.5k  INDEX.DTD     11k │
│  KEYBOARD.MRG  .1k  LETTER.PS   2.5k  LIST.DOC      .8k  LOGO.PS      5.6k │
│  LWFEED.PS     .5k  MAILING.DOC  .9k  NECFEED.PS    .6k  OPTION.PS    3.7k │
│  PDFEDIT.HLP   35k  PLAYBILL.DOC .6k  PLAYS.DOC     .9k  PLEAD.PS     1.3k │
│  PO4045.PS    1.4k  POBRHL4.PS  3.8k  PODC1150.PS  1.3k  PODC2150.PS  1.3k │
│  PODP960.PS   2.0k  POEP7500.PS 1.7k  POHL8.PS     1.0k  POK4455.PS   4.0k │
│  PONEC290.PS  5.4k  POO840SF.PS 3.9k  PREVIEW.MSG  9.9k  PRINT.TST     12k │
│  PSPRINT.TST   47k  QMS40PT.PS  1.4k  REVIEW.DOC   3.1k  SAMPLE       1.8k │
└────────────────────────────────────────────────────────────────────────┘
```

Fig. 4.1

WordStar 7.0's opening screen.

To display the commands you use to open a new file, press Alt-F, or move the mouse to the word *File* in the menu bar and click the mouse button. The File menu opens, as shown in figure 4.2.

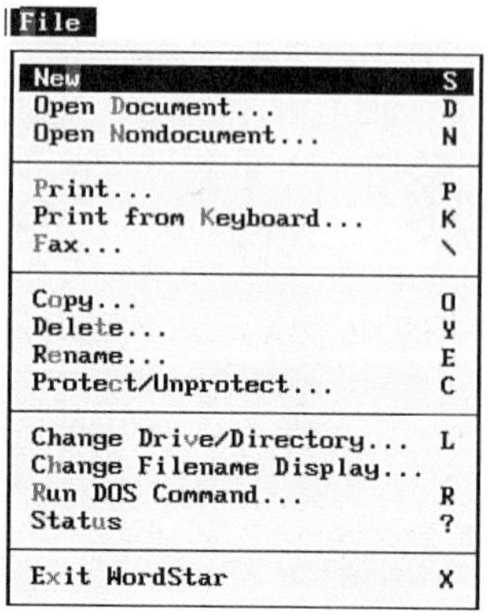

```
┌─────────────────────────────┐
│ ▌File                       │
├─────────────────────────────┤
│ ▌New                    S ▐ │
│ Open Document...         D   │
│ Open Nondocument...      N   │
│                              │
│ Print...                 P   │
│ Print from Keyboard...   K   │
│ Fax...                   \   │
│                              │
│ Copy...                  O   │
│ Delete...                Y   │
│ Rename...                E   │
│ Protect/Unprotect...     C   │
│                              │
│ Change Drive/Directory... L  │
│ Change Filename Display...   │
│ Run DOS Command...       R   │
│ Status                   ?   │
├─────────────────────────────┤
│ Exit WordStar            X   │
└─────────────────────────────┘
```

Fig. 4.2

The File menu.

You can start a new file by using any of the first three commands on the File menu: New, Open Document, or Open Nondocument. New, as you may expect, is used most often for opening new files. Open Document enables you to open existing documents; however, if you select this command and type the name of the file you want to create, WordStar displays the blank editing screen so that you can begin the new document. Open Nondocument opens an ASCII file—a file that stores text but no formatting codes. The following items further explain these commands.

- You select the New command by highlighting the command and pressing Enter, typing *S*, or clicking the New command.

- You can choose Open Document, type a name for the new file, and press Enter or click OK. Because this file is new (a file that WordStar has not previously saved), WordStar alerts you that it cannot find the file you specified. WordStar asks whether you want to create a new file (see fig. 4.3). Click OK or press Enter to begin the new file with the name you specified.

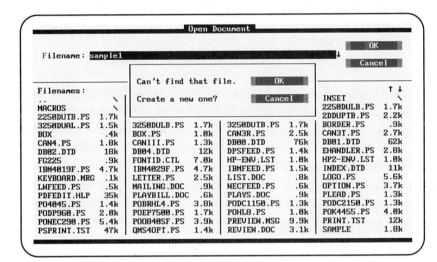

Fig. 4.3

Using the Open Document command to start a new file.

- You can choose Open Nondocument to begin a nondocument file. (A nondocument file is a file that includes only text in straight ASCII format. You might use a nondocument file, for example, when you plan to use your WordStar text with another program that cannot read WordStar's formatting codes.) When you type a name for the file and click OK or press Enter, WordStar tells you that it cannot find the file you specified and asks whether you want to create the file. Click OK or press Enter to create the file.

Retrieving an Existing File

After you've saved a file, you later may want to retrieve it from your hard disk or floppy disk. You can use any of the following three procedures from the File menu to open an existing file:

- Select the Open Document or Open Nondocument command in the File menu; type the name of the file you want, and click OK or press Enter.

- Press the down-arrow key to move the highlight to the Filenames list; then highlight the name of the file you want and press Enter.

- Double-click the file name in the Filenames list at the bottom of the opening screen.

At the bottom of the opening screen, WordStar displays the list of files in WordStar's start-up directory. (You learn more about directories later in this chapter.) You can use either the Filenames list or the commands in the File menu to open the file you want.

Follow these steps to open a file by using the File menu:

1. Press Alt-F or use the mouse to open the File menu.

2. Select the Open Document command by highlighting it and pressing Enter, by pressing D, or by positioning the mouse cursor on the command and clicking the mouse button. (If you are opening a nondocument file, choose the Open Nondocument command instead.)

   WordStar displays the Open Document dialog box, as shown in figure 4.4.

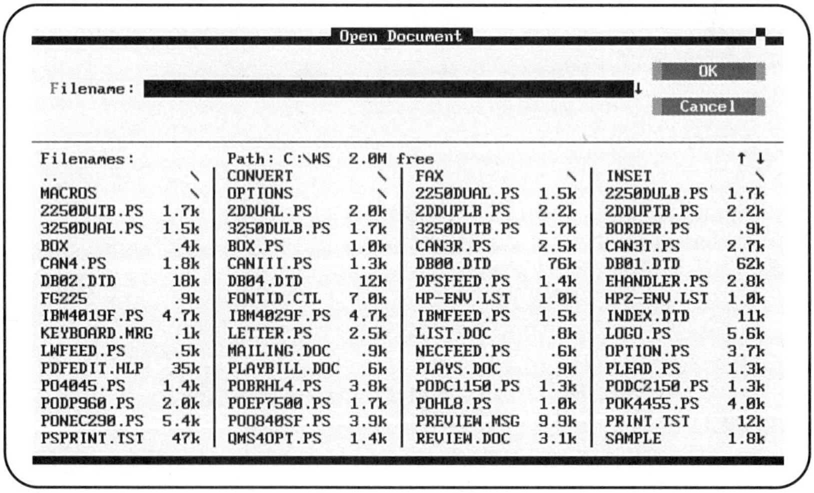

Fig. 4.4

The Open Document dialog box.

3. In the Filename text box, type the name of the file you want to open.

4. Click OK or press Enter.

WordStar then searches for the file you specified and displays it in the edit screen. If the file name you enter is not found, WordStar asks whether you want to create a file with that name. Click OK (or press Enter) to create the file, or click Cancel (or press Esc) to abandon the operation.

To open a file by using the Filenames list, follow these steps:

1. When the opening screen is displayed, press the down-arrow key. The cursor moves to the Filenames list.

2. Use the arrow keys to highlight the name of the file you want to retrieve, or if you're using the mouse, position the mouse cursor over the file name and click the mouse button (see fig. 4.5).

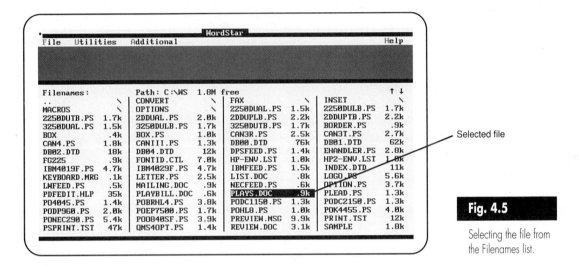

Selected file

3. Press Enter or click the mouse button again. You can also open the file you want by double-clicking the file name.

WordStar then opens the file you selected and displays it on the edit screen.

Understanding Directories

The preceding discussion is fine if you see the file you want in the Filenames list, but what if you can't remember the name of the file or you don't see it in the list? The second problem could be that the file you are looking for is not in the current directory. In this section, you learn about drives and directories and find out how to locate the files you need.

What Is a Directory?

Directories are most easily understood when explained from the bottom and working up. The most basic element is the file. A *file* is a collection of data you store on a disk; that collection of data may be a document, a mailing list, or something similar. As you continue to work with a program, you accumulate a number of files. These files are stored in directories. You can think of a *directory* as a file folder that stores similar types of information. The directory that stores your WordStar files, for example, may actually be a directory of files that are organized within another larger directory. The directories are stored on your disk drive.

Table 4.1 presents the drive, directory, and subdirectories of WordStar 7.0.

Table 4.1 WordStar Drives and Directories

Drive	Directory	Subdirectory	Comments
C:			The name for your hard drive. (In some cases, the hard drive is divided into more than one drive, so you could, for example, have drives C and D designated as hard drives.)
	\		The *root* directory, that is, the first directory on your hard disk in which all other subdirectories (individual program and data directories) are stored.
	WS		The main directory in which all WordStar files are stored. You write this directory designation, or *path*, like this: C:\WS. (During installation, you are given the option of naming the directory differently. If you modify the name of the directory that stores your WordStar files, the directory name in the path is different.

Drive	Directory	Subdirectory	Comments
		CONVERT	A subdirectory of WS, that stores Star Exchange conversion files. (Star Exchange, a utility included with WordStar, enables you to convert files easily.) This path is written as C:\WS\CONVERT.
		FAX	The subdirectory in which your fax files are placed after conversion. This path is written as C:\WS\FAX.
		INSET	A subdirectory of WS, that stores the Inset files. This path is written as C:\WS\INSET.
		MACROS	A subdirectory of WS, that stores the macros you create to automate your work with WordStar. This path is written as C:\WS\MACROS.
		OPTIONS	A subdirectory of WS, that stores different files for use in merge printing and in printing mailing labels. This path is written as C:\WS\OPTIONS.

WordStar automatically sets up these subdirectories for you when you install WordStar. You may want to add your own subdirectories to store your documents. For example, you can use the DOS command MD to create a WORK subdirectory. Follow these steps:

1. From the DOS prompt (C:\), type

   CD WS

   Press Enter.

2. Type *MD* followed by a space and type the name of the directory: *WORK*.

3. Press Enter.

DOS creates the subdirectory within the WS directory, and you have a place to store your files. (For more about working with DOS, consult *Using MS-DOS 5*, published by Que Corporation.)

Changing Directories and Drives in WordStar

When you want to change to a different drive or directory in WordStar (when the file you want is not shown in the Filenames list, for instance), you must first find out where you are in the program. The current directory is shown in the top line of the Filenames list (see fig. 4.6). The subdirectories of the current directory are displayed across the top of the list of file names.

Current directory

Subdirectories of current directory

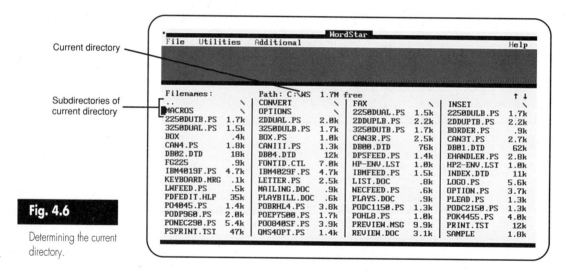

Fig. 4.6

Determining the current directory.

Changing Directories

Subdirectories of your current directory are shown in the first two lines of the Filenames list. The names of subdirectories are shown with a backslash (\) in the column immediately to the right of the subdirectory name:

    CONVERT   \

Files, on the other hand, appear with their file sizes on the right side:

    BOX.PS 1   .0k

To change to another directory, move the mouse cursor to the directory you want to select and double-click the mouse button. The files shown in the Filenames list change to show you the contents of that directory. If you are using the keyboard, you can change to another directory by pressing the down-arrow key, highlighting the directory you want, and pressing Enter. The directory you select is then displayed, and the top line of the Filenames list shows the new path to the directory you have chosen (see fig. 4.7).

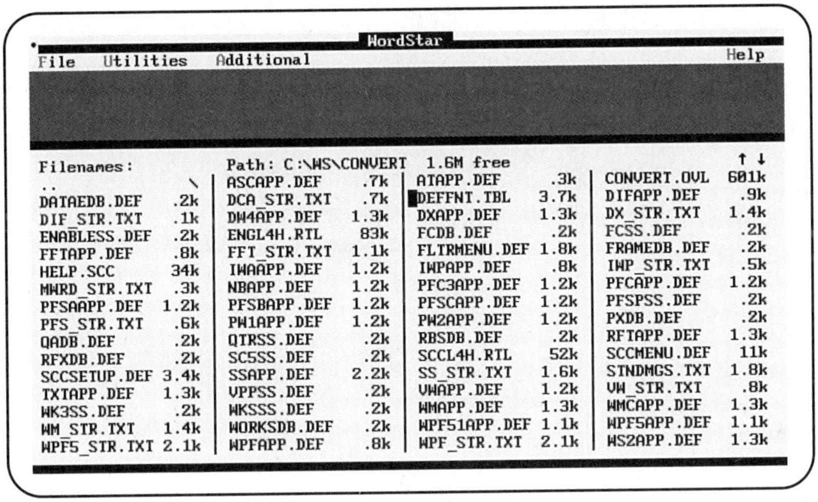

```
                              WordStar
 File    Utilities   Additional                              Help



 Filenames:         Path: C:\WS\CONVERT  1.6M free              ↑ ↓
                 \  ASCAPP.DEF    .7k  ATAPP.DEF    .3k  CONVERT.OVL 681k
 DATAEDB.DEF  .2k  DCA_STR.TXT   .7k ▌DEFFNT.TBL  3.7k  DIFAPP.DEF   .9k
 DIF_STR.TXT  .1k  DW4APP.DEF   1.3k  DXAPP.DEF   1.3k  DX_STR.TXT  1.4k
 ENABLESS.DEF .2k  ENGL4H.RTL    83k  FCDB.DEF     .2k  FCSS.DEF     .2k
 FFTAPP.DEF   .8k  FFT_STR.TXT  1.1k  FLTRMENU.DEF 1.8k FRAMEDB.DEF  .2k
 HELP.SCC     34k  IWAAPP.DEF   1.2k  IWPAPP.DEF   .8k  IWP_STR.TXT  .5k
 MWRD_STR.TXT .3k  NBAPP.DEF    1.2k  PFC3APP.DEF 1.2k  PFCAPP.DEF  1.2k
 PFSAAPP.DEF 1.2k  PFSBAPP.DEF  1.2k  PFSCAPP.DEF 1.2k  PFSPSS.DEF   .2k
 PFS_STR.TXT  .6k  PW1APP.DEF   1.2k  PW2APP.DEF  1.2k  PXDB.DEF     .2k
 QADB.DEF     .2k  QTRSS.DEF     .2k  RBSDB.DEF    .2k  RFTAPP.DEF  1.3k
 RFXDB.DEF    .2k  SC5SS.DEF     .2k  SCCL4H.RTL    52k SCCMENU.DEF  11k
 SCCSETUP.DEF 3.4k SSAPP.DEF    2.2k  SS_STR.TXT  1.6k  STNDMGS.TXT 1.8k
 TXTAPP.DEF  1.3k  VPPSS.DEF     .2k  VWAPP.DEF   1.2k  VW_STR.TXT   .8k
 WK3SS.DEF    .2k  WKSSS.DEF     .2k  WMAPP.DEF   1.3k  WMCAPP.DEF  1.3k
 WM_STR.TXT  1.4k  WORKSDB.DEF   .2k  WPF51APP.DEF 1.1k WPF5APP.DEF 1.1k
 WPF5_STR.TXT 2.1k WPFAPP.DEF    .8k  WPF_STR.TXT 2.1k  WS2APP.DEF  1.3k
```

Fig. 4.7

Changing to a different directory.

The .. symbol in the subdirectories portion of the Filenames list performs a special function. When you select one of the other subdirectories, you display a subdirectory one level "beneath" the current directory. For example, when C:\WS is the current directory and you double-click the OPTIONS subdirectory, the files in C:\WS\OPTIONS are shown. To move back up to the C:\WS directory, however, you double-click the .. symbol.

Changing Drives

In the last section, you learned a few quick steps for changing directories. WordStar also includes a built-in command you can use to change drives and directories.

Suppose that you have a file on a disk in drive A, and you want to view the contents of that disk. You can display the files by following these steps:

1. When the opening screen is displayed, press Ctrl-L. (If you prefer, you can open the File menu and choose Change Drive/Directory). The Change Drive\Directory dialog box appears, as shown in figure 4.8.

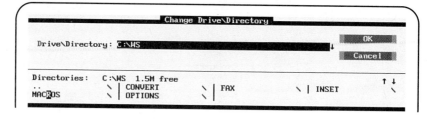

Fig. 4.8

The Change Drive\Directory dialog box.

2. In the Drive\Directory text box, type *A:* and press Enter.

WordStar then reads the information on the disk in drive A and displays in the Filenames list all the files and subdirectories on drive A.

It Didn't Work . . .

If you tried to log onto drive A and WordStar wouldn't let you, check to make sure that the disk is inserted properly and the drive door is closed. After you've checked those things, try logging on again.

Changing the File Name Display

You can change the way files are shown in the Filenames list at the bottom of the opening screen. You may want to make this change, for example, when you routinely work with a certain set of files and don't want to see all available files on the screen at once.

Suppose that, like the Filenames list in the examples in this chapter, your screen displays all files in the current directory no matter what the extension. You see PS files (PostScript printer files); HLP files (help files WordStar uses in processing); and everything else in the directory, including the document files you need. Rather than search the display for your files each time you open an existing document, you can change the file name display so that it shows only the files you work with. If you name all your documents with a DOC extension, for example, you can customize your Filenames list so that only DOC files are shown. To customize your Filenames list, follow these steps:

1. Open the File menu.

2. Choose the Change Filename Display command by pressing H or by clicking the command. The Change File Listings dialog box appears (see fig. 4.9).

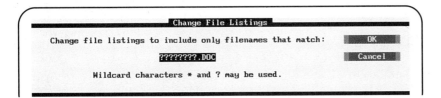

Fig. 4.9

Customizing the Filenames list.

As you can see, the text box in the center of the dialog box is filled with question marks. These question marks are called *wild cards*, and they stand for "any character," meaning that WordStar displays files that have any characters in place of the question marks. This entry explains why every file in the directory is currently displayed in the Filenames list.

3. Enter the characters that tell WordStar what kind of files you want displayed. For the example mentioned earlier, enter *DOC* after the period (as in fig. 4.9).

4. Click OK or press Enter.

When you return to the opening screen, only the files with characters that match those you specified are displayed on the screen (see fig. 4.10).

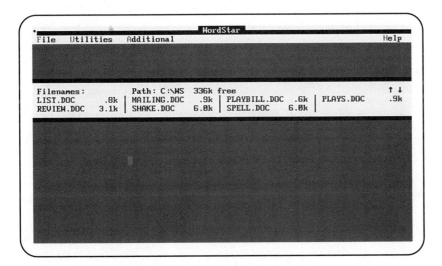

Fig. 4.10

The customized Filenames list—only files with DOC extensions are displayed.

You can change the display back by opening the File menu and choosing Change Filename Display. When the Change File Listings box appears, replace the DOC extension with the characters you want WordStar to search for. (If you want to display all files, replace the entry in the Change File Listings box with *.* and click OK or press Enter.)

Saving Files

Another important step in working with files involves saving files you've created. In the Chapter 3 quick start, you learned the basic steps for saving a document. This section shows you how to save a file under a different name (for times when you want to make a copy of a file but still keep the original intact).

Saving . . . The First Time

When you save a file for the first time, you choose a drive and directory for the file and enter a file name. Follow these steps to save a file for the first time:

1. Open the File menu.

2. Choose the Save command. The Save As dialog box is displayed (see fig. 4.11).

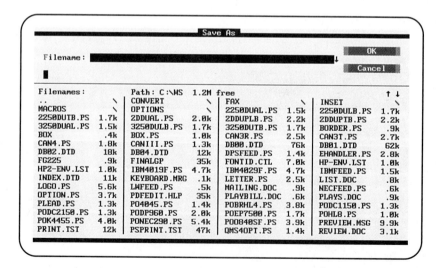

Fig. 4.11

The Save As dialog box.

3. In the Filename text box, type the name for the drive on which you want to save the file. (If you are saving the file in the current drive and directory, you don't need to enter a drive and directory designation.)

4. If you want to save the file in a directory other than the current one, type the directory path in the Filename text box, or double-click the directory in the Filenames portion of the screen. (If you're using the keyboard, press the down arrow and use the arrow keys to highlight the directory; then press Enter.)

5. Type a name for the file. You can type up to eight characters before the period and three characters after the period. You can enter any extension you like, but you may want to keep the extensions consistent so that you can find your WordStar files easily later. If you create a letter to Jim Smith, for example, you might name that file JSMITH.LTR.

6. Click OK or press Enter to save the file.

WordStar displays the message Saving, and after the file is saved, returns you to the edit screen.

Naming Conventions

As you get more experienced with creating and naming WordStar files, you'll want to come up with your own naming conventions. In the meantime, here are a few suggestions for ways to name your files so that you'll recognize them easily later:

Extension	File Type
RPT	Report files
MEM	Memo files
NWS	Newsletter files
FLY	Flier files
PR	Public relations files
BK	Book files

Saving Existing Files

Now you've saved the file once, but suppose that you open the file and make more changes. Now you need to save those changes—back in the same file. The process is simple. To save changes to an existing file, press Ctrl-KS.

This quick-key combination automatically saves the document for you without any further action.

If you want to save the publication under a different name, choose Save As from the File menu. The Save As dialog box is displayed again, and you can enter a new name and click OK or press Enter.

Saving a File to a Floppy Disk

At times, you may want to copy a file to a floppy disk. Suppose, for example, that you want to give a co-worker a copy of a publication you've been working on. You simply insert a blank, formatted disk into drive A. Then, with the publication you want to copy open on the screen, choose Save As. When the Save As dialog box is displayed, in the Filename text box (A:*filename*), type *A:* followed by a backslash and then the file name. Click OK or press Enter. The publication is then saved to the disk in drive A.

Working with WordStar Files

Now that you know how to open and save your WordStar files, you will want to understand the basic commands for working with the multitude of files you create. In the File menu, you find commands with which you perform the following operations:

- Copy files
- Delete files
- Rename files
- Protect and unprotect files

Copying Files

You can easily make a copy of a file by using the Copy command in the File menu. Whether the opening screen is displayed or you are working with a document in the edit screen, the command is available. To copy a document, follow these steps:

1. Open the File menu.

2. Choose the Copy command. The Copy dialog box appears, as shown in figure 4.12.

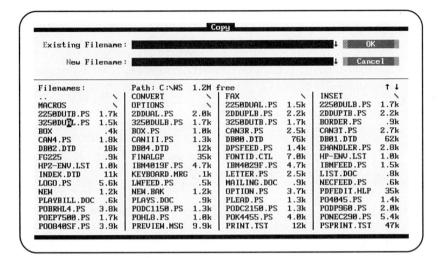

```
                                    Copy
   Existing Filename:  [                              ]↓     [   OK   ]
        New Filename:  [                              ]↓     [ Cancel ]

  Filenames:           Path: C:\WS  1.2M free                         ↑ ↓
  ..              \    CONVERT     \    FAX           \   INSET          \
  MACROS          \    OPTIONS     \    2250DUAL.PS  1.5k  2250DULB.PS  1.7k
  2250DUTB.PS   1.7k   2DDUAL.PS   2.0k 2DDUPLB.PS   2.2k  2DDUPTB.PS   2.2k
  3250DUDL.PS   1.5k   3250DULB.PS 1.7k 3250DUTB.PS  1.7k  BORDER.PS     .9k
  BOX            .4k   BOX.PS      1.0k CAN3R.PS     2.5k  CAN3T.PS     2.7k
  CAN4.PS       1.8k   CANIII.PS   1.3k DB00.DTD     76k   DB01.DTD     62k
  DB02.DTD      18k    DB04.DTD    12k  DPSFEED.PS   1.4k  EHANDLER.PS  2.8k
  FG225          .9k   FINALGP     35k  FONTID.CTL   7.0k  HP-ENV.LST   1.0k
  HP2-ENV.LST   1.0k   IBM4019F.PS 4.7k IBM4029F.PS  4.7k  IBMFEED.PS   1.5k
  INDEX.DTD     11k    KEYBOARD.MRG .1k LETTER.PS    2.5k  LIST.DOC      .8k
  LOGO.PS       5.6k   LWFEED.PS    .5k MAILING.DOC   .9k  NECFEED.PS    .6k
  NEW           1.2k   NEW.BAK     1.2k OPTION.PS    3.7k  PDFEDIT.HLP  35k
  PLAYBILL.DOC   .6k   PLAYS.DOC    .9k PLEAD.PS     1.3k  PO4045.PS    1.4k
  POBRHL4.PS    3.8k   PODC1150.PS 1.3k PODC2150.PS  1.3k  PODP960.PS   2.0k
  POEP7500.PS   1.7k   POHL8.PS    1.0k POK4455.PS   4.0k  PONEC290.PS  5.4k
  POO840SF.PS   3.9k   PREVIEW.MSG 9.9k PRINT.TST    12k   PSPRINT.TST  47k
```

Fig. 4.12

The Copy dialog box.

3. The cursor is positioned in the Existing Filename text box. Type the name of the file you want to copy. Press Tab.

4. WordStar enters the name and path in the New Filename text box. Type over or modify the path and name to reflect the location and name you want for the new file.

5. Click OK or press Enter.

WordStar makes a copy of the file and places the new file in the Filenames list at the bottom of the screen.

Figure 4.13 shows the Copy dialog box when the information has been completed. When you click OK or press Enter, WordStar copies the file named NEW and names the new file NEWCOPY.

Too Many Copies

If you are working in the edit screen, don't get the File menu's Copy command and the Edit menu's Copy command confused. The Copy command in the File menu is used to copy entire files, but the Copy command in the Edit menu is used to copy blocks of text. If you've chosen a command you don't want, press Esc to return to the document.

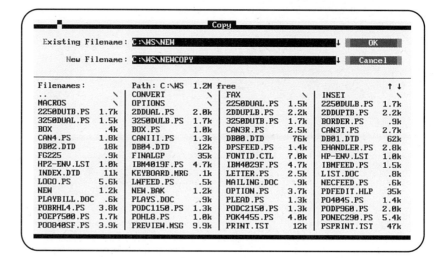

Fig. 4.13

Copying a file.

Deleting Files

Undoubtedly, there will be times when you want to weed out files you no longer need. You use the File menu's Delete command to remove these unnecessary files. Follow these steps to delete a file:

1. Open the File menu.

2. Choose the Delete command by pressing Y or clicking the command. The Delete dialog box appears, as shown in figure 4.14.

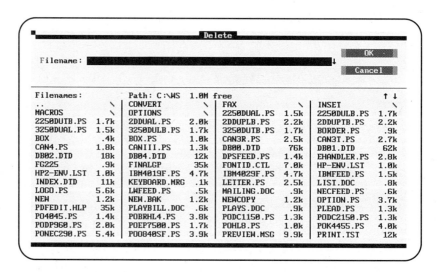

Fig. 4.14

The Delete dialog box.

3. In the Filename text box, type the names of the drive, directory, and file you want to delete.

4. Click OK or press Enter. WordStar displays a dialog box, alerting you that the file you selected is about to be deleted (see fig. 4.15).

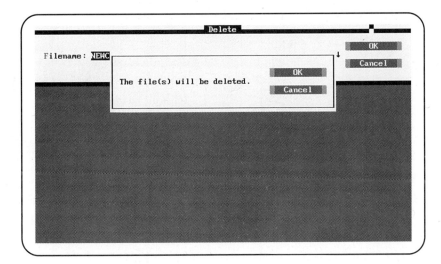

Fig. 4.15

The Delete warning dialog box.

5. Click OK or press Enter to delete the file; click Cancel or press Esc to cancel the deletion.

WordStar returns you to the screen you were working with (the opening screen or the edit screen), and the file is removed from the Filenames list on the opening screen.

Selecting Files

You can display the contents of a different directory by double-clicking the directory name in the Filenames list. Then, when you see the file you want, click the file name. WordStar automatically enters the name in the Filename box at the top of the screen.

Renaming Files

From time to time, you may want to rename a file. You can rename files from either the opening screen or the edit screen. Follow these steps to rename a file:

1. Open the File menu.

2. Choose the Rename command by pressing E or by clicking the command name. The Rename dialog box appears, as shown in figure 4.16.

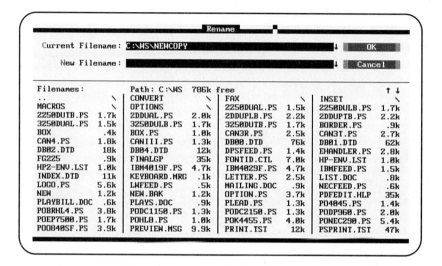

Fig. 4.16

The Rename dialog box.

3. The name of the most recently used file is displayed in the Current Filename box. If this file is not the file you want to rename, type the drive, directory, and name of the file you want to use.

4. Press Tab. The cursor moves to the New Filename box.

5. Type the new name for the file.

6. Click OK or press Enter.

WordStar then renames the file as you've specified. It appears, with its new name, in the Filenames list on the opening screen.

Protecting and Unprotecting Files

WordStar gives you the options of protecting and unprotecting files. *Protecting* a file keeps data from being written to a file—you can open and read through a protected file, but you cannot modify the file in any way.

The capability to protect and unprotect files is an important one when you are working with sensitive data. If you've spent hours working on a file that includes important information, for example, you may want to protect the file so that someone else using the system can't accidentally overwrite the information or delete the file. Protecting a file requires these steps:

1. Open the File menu.

2. Choose the Protect/Unprotect command. The Protect/Unprotect dialog box appears.

3. The name of the file you were working with most recently is displayed in the Filename box. If you want to protect a different file, type the name of the file you want to protect.

4. Click OK or press Enter. A dialog box appears telling you that the file is currently unprotected and asking whether you want to protect it (see fig. 4.17).

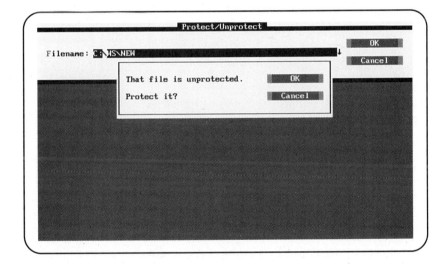

Fig. 4.17

The Protect/Unprotect dialog box.

5. Click OK or press Enter to protect the file.

The file is now protected. When you retrieve the file (by using the Open Document command in the File menu), the file is displayed in the edit screen. At the bottom of the screen, you see the message Protect (see fig. 4.18). If you try to edit the file, your computer beeps at you, telling you that you can look, but you can't touch.

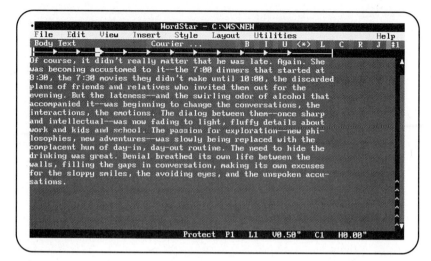

Fig. 4.18

The Protect file
message.

To unprotect the file, follow these steps:

1. Close the file.

2. Return to the opening screen.

3. Open the File menu.

4. Choose the Protect/Unprotect command.

5. Type the name of the file you want to unprotect. (If you haven't worked with any files since you viewed the protected file, that file name is entered in the Filename box for you.)

6. Click OK or press Enter. A message box appears, telling you that the file is currently protected.

7. Click OK or press Enter to unprotect the file.

When you open the unprotected file, the Protect message is gone, and you can edit the text as necessary.

Chapter Summary

In this chapter, you've learned all about working with files, directories, and drives in WordStar. You found out how to open and save files, and learned how to navigate your way through drives and directories. Additionally, you learned to use the File menu to perform basic file-maintenance tasks. The next chapter takes an in-depth look at the process of designing your WordStar documents.

Creating and Printing WordStar Documents

PART

II

OUTLINE

Designing the Document

In Part I of this book, you learned the basics of WordStar and ways to use the File menu commands to work with files you create. In Part II, you get down to work. This chapter presents the first step in creating and printing WordStar documents: designing the way you want the document to look.

The first step in creating your WordStar document involves planning the kind of publication you want to produce. As with anything else, you must set a goal from the outset in order to determine the general direction you want to go. Without a plan, if you start with a blank page and no general design, you may end up with a three-column report when you originally wanted a simple one-page fact sheet.

You may be wondering why this chapter is emphasizing design strategies when you're using a word processing program. How many different things can you do with words, anyway? The answer to that question is precisely the reason you should take a few minutes to think about the kind of document you want to produce. What do you *want* to do with words? Do you want to design a business card? A bulletin? A report? Will you use Inset to add graphics to your work?

When word processing programs first appeared in the market, they could do little besides print words on a page. Today, the features that the most popular word processors offer enable you to be creative by choosing exactly where you place the words, which fonts and type sizes you use, and whether you incorporate graphics into documents. By using text alignment, font, style, size, and placement features, you can create snazzy documents that rival those created in a true desktop publishing program.

This chapter explores the basic design elements you can use in your documents. Thinking about the document now saves you considerable time when you get down to work and actually start creating documents (the topic of Chapter 6). In this chapter, you consider some of the important factors in developing the following kinds of documents:

- Letters
- Long documents (such as reports or manuals)
- Newsletters
- Fliers
- Brochures
- Business cards and stationery
- Business forms
- Training handouts

Exploring Document Design Tips

Communicating on paper has its advantages and disadvantages. First, a well-designed, well-planned publication can communicate the creativity, strength, and professional dedication of your company. With a logo or strategic layout, you can communicate that your company is competitive, friendly, or serious. Your publication plays a crucial role in the impression you make on a prospective client, who may be learning about your company for the first time.

The down side of communicating on the one-dimensional page is that you can't correct a mistaken first impression. Your work represents *you*, whether the people reading your documents are prospective clients, employers, or stockholders.

The best publications mix a well-thought-out, eye-catching design with, of course, good writing that communicates the appropriate tone of the document. If you're creating a report for the accounting department of your company, for example, the tone and overall design of the document will be more serious than a document you might create for the local historical society or your child's preschool.

Think about publications you've seen recently. Undoubtedly, you immediately filed some in the waste-paper basket; for some reason, the publication did not hold your attention and you decided that reading it wasn't worth your time. Some items, however, caught your eye, inviting you to take a closer look. What was it about those publications that interested you? Chances are, it was the arrangement of the text, a catchy headline, or interesting artwork that made you want to read more closely.

In these days of information overload, materials must grab a reader's attention fast. Printed words and graphics on a page must speak for you in a way that holds the reader's interest right from the start. If you are sending out a packet of promotional literature, for example, you may not get a second chance to place your publications in front of that client. If your materials are poorly done, the next time the client sees something from your company, the reaction may be, "I've seen some things from them before. Throw that away—I'm not interested."

Of course, depending on the type of documents you create, the effectiveness of your work may not be a life-or-death business imperative. If you are creating a report that will be circulated only among the managers of your company, the design of the publication may not be as important as the design of a document going out to the public. Everyone, however, prefers to read a document with a creative, well-planned design instead of one poorly designed. Even if your audience is "only managers," therefore, take the time to plan your document design before you begin work.

In this section, you learn about design strategies you can use to plan your documents. Whether you are creating simple advertising fliers or sophisticated multipage reports that will be sent to investors, taking a few minutes to think about the basic goals of your document helps to ensure that your publication is effective.

Overall Design Tips

Before studying the specialized tips for specific project types presented later in this chapter, consider these general tips that apply to all types of documents.

Consider your audience. Who reads your publication? Make sure that the style of the text and the artwork you select are appropriate for your readers. If you are composing a serious newsletter for an organization of political activists, for example, avoid using light, cartoon-style graphics, which are too "cute" for your publication. A more serious, businesslike tone with charts to reinforce statistics in the text is more appropriate for such an audience.

Think about your objectives. What do you want to accomplish with this document? Are you telling clients about a new product that is going to be introduced? Are you creating invitations for the company Christmas party? Have you inherited the job of producing the company newsletter? Think about the reaction you want from your readers. Do you want to inform, inspire, or motivate? Do you need to be humorous or serious? Take time to think about the tone you want your publication to convey. You may want to talk with coworkers to see whether their views for the publication differ from yours.

Keep a folder of styles you like. Whether you produce simple correspondence, brochures, fliers, menus, or newsletters, keep samples of published materials you like. Clip out logos or general page designs that appeal to you. Typeset or not, copied or professionally printed, the idea is not how the publication was produced but whether you can use any of the appealing designs in your own work. (Remember, however, that company logos are generally protected, so use other people's logos only as inspiration for ones you create yourself.)

The next sections introduce you to individual design tips related to the types of publications you are producing. Tips are included for the following publications:

- Basic Correspondence
- Long Documents
- Newsletters
- Fliers and brochures
- Business cards and stationery
- Business forms
- Training handouts

Basic Correspondence

For many of your WordStar creations, you may be doing nothing more complex than simply typing text on a page and printing it. WordStar, however, includes a wealth of features you can use to produce everything from simple memos to complex multicolumn documents. This section includes tips you may want to consider as you create basic correspondence documents—letters, memos, and so forth. Although letters and memos are by far the easiest documents to create, don't underestimate the effect that a professional letter has over an unplanned, unformatted document.

As you begin creating your first document, think about these questions.

What is the tone of your letter? If you are writing to your Aunt Minnie, the basic organization and layout of your letter are probably not as important as the content of the letter. If you're writing to a client, a prospective employer, or someone else who may make decisions about you or your business based on the appearance of your letter, the tone and overall feeling of the letter are important. Do you want a dry, business-like tone or a friendly, chatty letter? The typeface you choose affects the tone; some typefaces, like Times Roman, convey a businesslike tone, whereas others, such as Avant Garde, give the letter a more relaxed, "artsy" tone. (You learn more about using typefaces and fonts in Chapter 8.)

What type of alignment best suits the correspondence? Different alignment types also convey different messages. The two most often used alignments are left alignment, in which the text is aligned along the left margin but ragged on the right, and justified, in which the text is aligned both on the left and right margins. Justified alignment provides the most businesslike tone; however, left alignment is used by many businesses. Figure 5.1 provides an example of a letter formatted with left-aligned text, and figure 5.2 shows the same letter with justified alignment. Right-aligned text, in which the text is aligned along the right margin but ragged on the left, is used only in specially designed documents that intend to call attention to a specific photo or chart. Traditional correspondence never uses right-aligned text. Figure 5.3 shows an example of a simple letter. The various elements of the letter—address, greeting, body text, and closing—are identified.

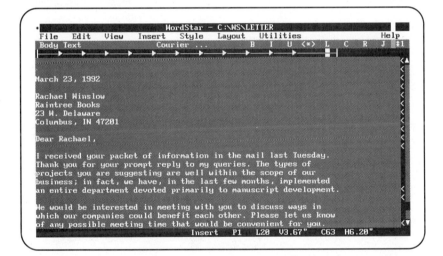

Fig. 5.1

A letter with left-justified text.

Do you plan to merge print the letter? If you plan to use MailList to help you merge a mailing list of names and addresses with a form letter, you must enter variables in the changeable parts of your letter. (Chapter 14 explains how to set up and use a mailing list with MailList and explains how to print form letters.)

Do you want to use the Calculator? Remember that you can use WordStar's built-in math features to help you calculate figures on your document. You can line up the numbers in table format and use the Calculator (available in the Utilities menu) to perform the calculations without your ever having to leave your document. (Chapter 10 introduces you to the Calculator.) Figure 5.4 shows an example of using the Calculator to add a result in a sample document.

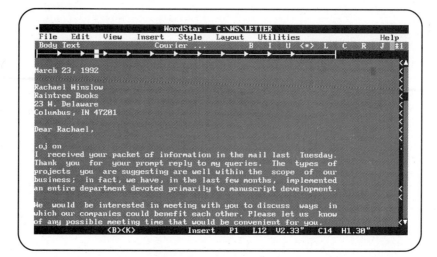

Fig. 5.2

The letter with justified text.

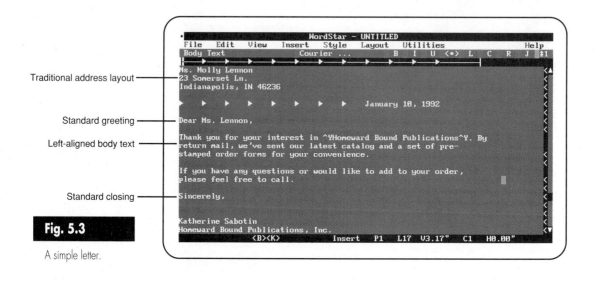

Traditional address layout

Standard greeting

Left-aligned body text

Standard closing

Fig. 5.3

A simple letter.

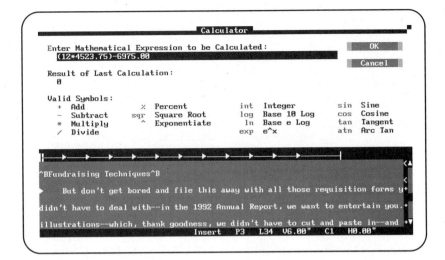

Fig. 5.4

Using the Calculator in
a document.

Do you plan to print the letter on traditional 8 1/2-by-11-inch paper?
Depending on the capabilities of your printer, you may be able to use
different paper sizes and orientation. The orientation of your document
refers to the way the text is printed on the page. With traditional *portrait*
orientation, the text is printed so that the lines are parallel to the shorter
edge of the paper in 8 1/2-by-11-inch format; with *landscape* orientation,
the text is printed so that the lines are parallel to the longer edge of the
paper in 11-by-8 1/2-inch format. (*Note:* Not all printers support landscape orientation, so depending on the capabilities of your printer, this
option may or may not be available to you.)

Do you want to print envelopes from WordStar? If you want to print
the envelopes for your letters from within WordStar, you can do so using
the MailList utility. Again, as with form letters, you must add variables at
the appropriate places if you plan to merge print a mailing list. If you
want to type one envelope at a time, you can use WordStar's Print from
Keyboard command (available in the File menu) to print the envelope as
you type. Chapter 14 explains how to use MailList to create mailing lists
of data you can incorporate into your WordStar documents.

Long Documents

Longer documents in WordStar become more of a challenge—not an
insurmountable one to be sure, but you do have a few more things to
think about. Examples of longer documents you can create with
WordStar include the following:

- Annual reports
- Manuals of office procedures
- Term papers
- Project proposals
- Book chapters
- Legal documents
- Instruction manuals for products

With longer documents, different design elements come into play. You want to make sure that readers don't get lost; so you need to provide page numbers and probably some kind of text in headers or footers. You can use headings to break up the text on the pages and perhaps graphics as well. The spacing of your document becomes more important. Do readers want to wade through 35 pages of single-spaced text, or will they be more comfortable with double-spaced paragraphs? Do you want to add an index so that readers can refer to specific topics easily? Will a table of contents help readers find the sections they need?

Keep the following points in mind as you start your document.

What typeface conveys the best tone? Your choice of typeface becomes more important with longer documents. If your readers must review a large amount of text, choose a typeface that is easy to read. Statistics have shown that readers are more comfortable reading a serif typeface for longer periods of time than they are reading sans serif typefaces. (*Serif* typefaces are typefaces, like Times Roman, that have small crossbars at the ends of the characters; *sans serif* typefaces, like the Avant Garde typeface, do not have crossbars.)

Think about the margin settings for the page. The left and right margins are also important because long lines of text are tiring to the eyes, especially when readers look over pages and pages of text. If your document is long, move the right margin in more than you would in shorter documents just to give the readers' eyes a rest.

What kind of spacing will you use for text? Remember that readers get discouraged when too much text is crammed into too small a space. In some documents, such as college term papers, double-spacing enables reviewers to write comments between the lines. (Of course, you may wish you didn't have to see the reviewer's comments . . . .) Figure 5.5 shows text of a term paper created with double-spaced text.

Does your document require an index? If you present a variety of topics in your document, an index provides the readers with a way to find topics of interest quickly. You can use WordStar's automatic index generator to create a simple or detailed index for your document. (Indexes are explained in Chapter 16.)

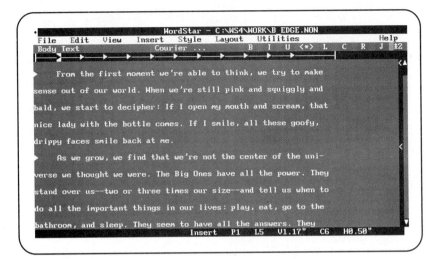

```
                    WordStar - C:\WS4\WORK\B_EDGE.NON
 File    Edit    View    Insert    Style    Layout    Utilities              Help
 Body Text                    Courier ...             B  I  U  <*>  L  C  R  J  ‡2

    ▶    From the first moment we're able to think, we try to make

sense out of our world. When we're still pink and squiggly and

bald, we start to decipher: If I open my mouth and scream, that

nice lady with the bottle comes. If I smile, all these goofy,

drippy faces smile back at me.

    ▶    As we grow, we find that we're not the center of the uni-

verse we thought we were. The Big Ones have all the power. They

stand over us--two or three times our size--and tell us when to

do all the important things in our lives: play, eat, go to the

bathroom, and sleep. They seem to have all the answers. They
                    Insert    P1    L5    V1.17"    C6    H0.50"
```

Fig. 5.5

A double-spaced document.

Do you want to use headers and footers? Headers and footers give readers a point of reference as they peruse the text. You may want to include your name or your company name, department, page number, date, or other information to help readers identify the document they are reading. Figure 5.6 shows a text page where the header shows the book title and the page number.

Does the document require a table of contents? A table of contents is a kind of "reader service" item that can make a difference in the way readers feel about your document. If they can easily find the topics they need to read about, they remember the document more favorably. Even in short documents, providing a table of contents helps readers know what to expect from the document and gives them the option of turning directly to the section they want.

Do you want to include graphics? Especially in text-intensive documents, graphics can provide a welcome break from page after page of words. Graphics can liven up your document and give the reader's eyes a well-deserved break. With WordStar, you can import graphics using the Inset program (available in the Utilities menu) to add special graphic touches to your document. Chapter 12 explains how to use Inset to add artwork to your documents.

Be consistent with your design. Use the same design items throughout the document. If you begin with headlines in Times Roman 14-point bold-faced text, for example, and then begin using headlines in Courier 12-point italic on page 6, readers will be confused. Keep the margin settings, text settings, and spacing the same from page to page. Tables and other special design elements can add variety; however, always remember to come back to your original design so that your readers can follow the organization of your document.

> 8   *Pumpkins and Other Miracles*
>
> *The world loomed above us;*
> *Stairways stretching to heaven,*
> *People as tall as skyscrapers,*
> *Frowns as big as doom.*
> *Our fingerprints,*
> *Our footsteps,*
> *Our muddy tennis shoes,*
> *All caused ripples of reaction,*
> *Like a pebble*
> *Dropped in clear blue water*
> *On a windless summer day.*
> *Our sins making our presence known,*
> *—even when we couldn't—*
> *And bringing on*
> *The flawed and fatal scales*
> *Of justice.*
>
> *And now we are giants*
> *And the rabbits in our care*
> *Won't eat their peas*
> *Or sit still at the table.*
> *They don't care about fingerprints,*
> *Or footsteps,*
> *Or muddy tennis shoes.*
> *And the scales of justice*
> *Have long since rusted and locked,*
> *Frozen for eternity in*
> *their irrelevance,*
> *Thank God,*
> *Thank God.*

Fig. 5.6

A sample document with a header.

Newsletters

Newsletters are a popular item. Corporations—big and small—are now using word processing and desktop publishing programs to keep their employees up-to-date on company happenings. Most of us receive newsletters from all kinds of organizations: insurance agencies, animal hospitals, people hospitals, schools, churches, community organizations, financial planners . . . and the list goes on.

Newsletters are an effective means of helping your clients get to know you. In a newsletter, you can include important industry information, news specific to your business, tips for clients, and artwork in the form of charts or pleasing graphics.

When you begin to plan your newsletter, consider the following.

What type of design is appropriate for your audience? If your publication is a serious medical document, for example, a light, airy typeface and humorous clip art do not fit the image you want to convey. If you are creating a flier advertising a high-school reunion, on the other hand, a typeface that is small and tight (indicating seriousness), may turn off readers. Along the same lines, the number of columns you include on a page can either support the impression you're trying to make or take away from it. In a more serious document, three columns on a page may be OK; in a light-hearted document, the audience may be overloaded by too much text on a page.

How long is the newsletter? If you are planning a multipage newsletter, think about the design of all the pages. Do you want to repeat some of the same elements, such as a logo or a business name, on every page? Do you want to use the same column format on every page, or do you want to vary the layout from page to page? Consider also how your newsletter is printed. A four-page newsletter consists of four pages, one after another. In this case, you may want to consider keeping the design similar from page to page. If your newsletter is printed on folded paper, so that pages 2 and 3 are facing pages, you should keep that in mind as you plan the layout (see fig. 5.7).

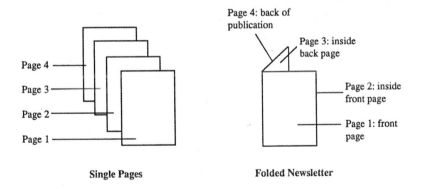

Single Pages   Folded Newsletter

Fig. 5.7

Planning a four-page newsletter.

How many articles will be involved? Block out the number of articles you plan to use. Think about the approximate lengths of the articles and plan where you want to place them in the newsletter. Sketching this layout on paper is especially helpful if you have several articles that continue on other pages of your publication. Planning the publication helps you fit everything together so that no text is left over and no gaping holes are left unfilled in your document.

What type of banner (the heading at the top of the publication that shows the publication's name) does your publication need? Typically, the banner includes the name of the publication with your company's name placed in smaller type. Are you designing the banner or does your company have a banner that is used on all publications of this type? Again, consider your audience: think about the kind of type (light and friendly or heavier and more serious) you want to use to communicate your tone. An appropriate, eye-catching banner can make a big impression on a first-time reader.

What kind of graphics do you want to use? As mentioned earlier, WordStar 7.0 uses the Inset graphics integration program to add graphics to your documents. What kind of art will you use? Is it currently available in electronic form? Would you like to be able to convert charts you create in a spreadsheet program into a format usable with WordStar? (WordStar automatically converts graphics files to PIX files, a standard graphics file format that is supported by most graphics programs.) If the art is not available in computer form, will you leave space in your publication so that the art can be manually pasted in at print time?

Table 5.1 lists some general guidelines you can use as you think about the overall tone of your newsletter.

Table 5.1 Newsletter Guidelines for Tone

Friendly	Serious
Light, humorous art	Charts or sophisticated art
Cartoon-style graphics	Smaller, serif typeface
A great deal of open space	More text on a page; two or three columns
Friendly, sans serif typeface	Bold, professional headlines
Light, open headlines	More structured layout of text and graphics
Innovative placement of graphics and text	Use of rules and boxes to guide reader's eye

Fliers and Brochures

Attention-getting fliers are easy to produce. In less than an hour, you can design, create, and print a flier that is ready to be photocopied or printed and distributed. Typically, a *flier* is a single-page document that uses few words to communicate information. You may send out fliers to announce a special sales promotion, for example, an upcoming party, or a new product. A *brochure* is a document that provides more in-depth information in a two- or three-fold layout. You may create a brochure, for example, to explain the services of your company, to describe a new product, or to provide pertinent information about an upcoming conference. When you are planning a promotional piece—whether it is a flier or fold-out brochure—consider these points.

What kind of business are you promoting? If the flier is advertising a service business, the text and graphics you choose for the flier or brochure should convey that idea. If you are promoting a product or advertising a sale at a local retail outlet, you may want to use Inset to bring in a picture that resembles the product or key products involved in your sale.

What is your most important message? A promotional piece is a "hit 'em fast" type of publication. Much of the communication power must rest on a few powerful words, and you need to choose your words carefully to convey the strongest message possible in just a few words. Particularly in promotional materials, being concise is important: don't use 10 words to say something you can say in 2. Figure 5.8 shows an example of a simple promotional piece.

How should your brochure be organized? Brochures typically convey more information than their skimpier cousins, fliers. In a brochure, you can take the extra words that you might try to squeeze in as few words as possible in other materials and use them to describe services, events, products, or benefits. Most brochures are single-page documents, but the individual page is folded to give the illusion of more than one page. You might use a two-fold or three-fold brochure for your document. Figure 5.8 shows an example of the inside of a three-fold brochure. When you are considering how you want to structure the layout of your brochure, think about the number of columns. (The brochure in fig. 5.9 was created using a three-column format.)

Use headlines to help readers find key points quickly. If possible, condense your text into paragraph-sized pieces that will fit nicely beneath boldfaced headlines. This practice helps readers find the aspect of your business (product, organization, and so on) that most appeals to them.

Consider the alignment of text as you create your brochure. In most documents that require the use of columns, choosing justified text (the alignment in which the text aligns along both the left and right margins) helps reinforce the vertical layout of the text. Of course, you can use a ragged-right margin if you choose, but justified text gives the brochure a "neater" look.

New!

Author *Keenan Bocke*

narrates

Beating the MidWinter Blues

(or 101 ways to stay sane in spite of snow)

Where: Al's Bookcellar
1529 W. Arlington Blvd.
Columbus, IN 47201

When: 1:00-2:00

Reservations required.

Fig. 5.8

A promotional flier.

Will you be mailing the brochure? If you plan to send out your brochure through the mail, be sure to leave a space for an address label and return address. Most simple brochures involve a single sheet of paper, printed on both the front and the back. The middle panel in the back of the page is usually left blank, reserved for address information and postage (see fig. 5.10).

What type of items will you use to grab readers' attention? Because business is people-oriented, a friendly-yet-serious image is best for many promotional pieces. You want the public to think that you run a personable business but that you take your work seriously. The text and graphics you choose should reflect the image you want to convey. A business that makes home-knitted baby booties, for example, could afford to be more relaxed in its businesslike portrayal; but generally, buyers want to know that they are paying for a professional product. The layout of text and the graphics you choose for your publication should reflect that professionalism, but where appropriate, add some fun.

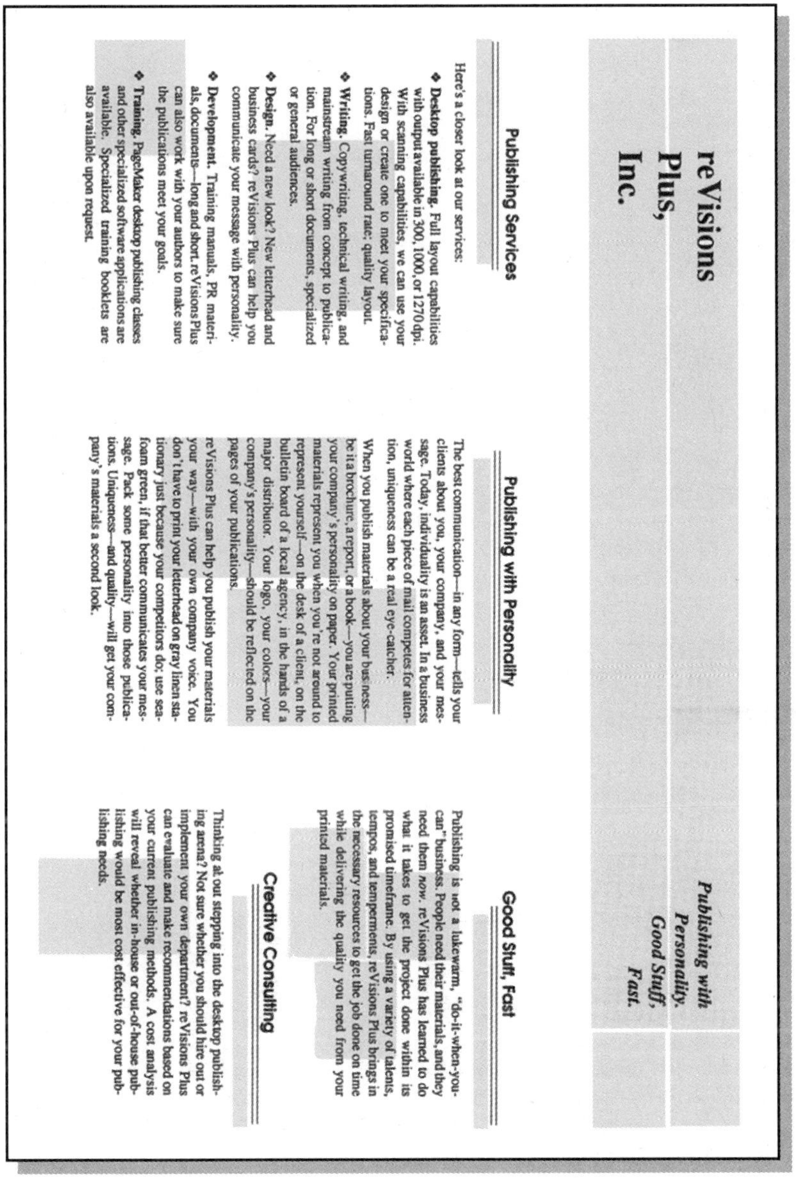

reVisions Plus, Inc.

Publishing with Personality.
Good Stuff,
Fast.

Publishing Services

Here's a closer look at our services:

◆ **Desktop publishing.** Full layout capabilities with output available in 300, 1000, or 1270 dpi. With scanning capabilities, we can use your design or create one to meet your specifications. Fast turnaround rate; quality layout.

◆ **Writing.** Copywriting, technical writing, and mainstream writing from concept to publication. For long or short documents, specialized or general audiences.

◆ **Design.** Need a new look? New letterhead and business cards? reVisions Plus can help you communicate your message with personality.

◆ **Development.** Training manuals, PR materials, documents—long and short. reVisions Plus can also work with your authors to make sure the publications meet your goals.

◆ **Training.** PageMaker desktop publishing classes and other specialized software applications are available. Specialized training booklets are also available upon request.

Publishing with Personality

The best communication—in any form—tells your clients about you, your company, and your message. Today, individuality is an asset. In a business world where each piece of mail competes for attention, uniqueness can be a real eye-catcher.

When you publish materials about your business—be it a brochure, a report, or a book—you are putting your company's personality on paper. Your printed materials represent you when you're not around to represent yourself—on the desk of a client, on the bulletin board of a local agency, in the hands of a major distributor. Your logo, your colors—your company's personality—should be reflected on the pages of your publications.

reVisions Plus can help you publish your materials your way—with your own company voice. You don't have to print your letterhead on gray linen stationary just because your competitors do; use sea-foam green, if that better communicates your message. Pack some personality into those publications. Uniqueness—and quality—will get your company's materials a second look.

Good Stuff, Fast

Publishing is not a lukewarm, "do-it-when-you-can" business. People need their materials, and they need them *now*. reVisions Plus has learned to do what it takes to get the project done within its promised timeframe. By using a variety of talents, tempos, and temperaments, reVisions Plus brings in the necessary resources to get the job done on time while delivering the quality you need from your printed materials.

Creative Consulting

Thinking about stepping into the desktop publishing arena? Not sure whether you should hire out or implement your own department? reVisions Plus can evaluate and make recommendations based on your current publishing methods. A cost analysis will reveal whether in-house or out-of-house publishing would be most cost effective for your publishing needs.

Fig. 5.9

A three-fold brochure.

Panel 1

Panel 6 reserved for
mailing information

Panel 5

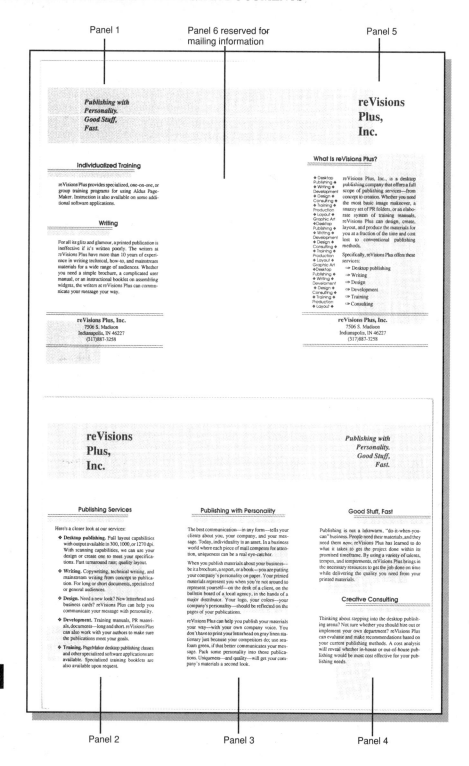

*Publishing with
Personality.
Good Stuff,
Fast.*

**reVisions
Plus,
Inc.**

Individualized Training

reVisions Plus provides specialized, one-on-one, or group training programs for using Aldus Page-Maker. Instruction is also available on some additional software applications.

Writing

For all its glitz and glamour, a printed publication is ineffective if it's written poorly. The writers at reVisions Plus have more than 10 years of experience in writing technical, how-to, and mainstream materials for a wide range of audiences. Whether you need a simple brochure, a complicated user manual, or an instructional booklet on assembling widgets, the writers at reVisions Plus can communicate your message your way.

reVisions Plus, Inc.
7506 S. Madison
Indianapolis, IN 46227
(317)887-3258

What Is reVisions Plus?

◆ Desktop Publishing ◆ Writing ◆ Development ◆ Design ◆ Consulting ◆ Training ◆ Production ◆ Layout ◆ Graphic Art ◆ Desktop Publishing ◆ Writing ◆ Development ◆ Design ◆ Consulting ◆ Training ◆ Production ◆ Layout ◆ Graphic Art ◆ Desktop Publishing ◆ Writing ◆ Development ◆ Design ◆ Consulting ◆ Training ◆ Production ◆ Layout ◆

reVisions Plus, Inc., is a desktop publishing company that offers a full scope of publishing services—from concept to creation. Whether you need the most basic image makeover, a snazzy set of PR folders, or an elaborate system of training manuals, reVisions Plus can design, create, layout, and produce the materials for you at a fraction of the time and cost lost to conventional publishing methods.

Specifically, reVisions Plus offers these services:

⇨ Desktop publishing
⇨ Writing
⇨ Design
⇨ Development
⇨ Training
⇨ Consulting

reVisions Plus, Inc.
7506 S. Madison
Indianapolis, IN 46227
(317)887-3258

**reVisions
Plus,
Inc.**

*Publishing with
Personality.
Good Stuff,
Fast.*

Publishing Services

Here's a closer look at our services:

◆ **Desktop publishing.** Full layout capabilities with output available in 300, 1000, or 1270 dpi. With scanning capabilities, we can use your design or create one to meet your specifications. Fast turnaround rate; quality layout.

◆ **Writing.** Copywriting, technical writing, and mainstream writing from concept to publication. For long or short documents, specialized or general audiences.

◆ **Design.** Need a new look? New letterhead and business cards? reVisions Plus can help you communicate your message with personality.

◆ **Development.** Training manuals, PR materials, documents—long and short. reVisions Plus can also work with your authors to make sure the publications meet your goals.

◆ **Training.** PageMaker desktop publishing classes and other specialized software applications are available. Specialized training booklets are also available upon request.

Publishing with Personality

The best communication—in any form—tells your clients about you, your company, and your message. Today, individuality is an asset. In a business world where each piece of mail competes for attention, uniqueness can be a real eye-catcher.

When you publish materials about your business—be it a brochure, a report, or a book—you are putting your company's personality on paper. Your printed materials represent you when you're not around to represent yourself—on the desk of a client, on the bulletin board of a local agency, in the hands of a major distributor. Your logo, your colors—your company's personality—should be reflected on the pages of your publications.

reVisions Plus can help you publish your materials your way—with your own company voice. You don't have to print your letterhead on gray linen stationery just because your competitors do; use seafoam green, if that better communicates your message. Pack some personality into those publications. Uniqueness—and quality—will get your company's materials a second look.

Good Stuff, Fast

Publishing is not a lukewarm, "do-it-when-you-can" business. People need their materials, and they need them *now*. reVisions Plus has learned to do what it takes to get the project done within its promised timeframe. By using a variety of talents, tempos, and temperments, reVisions Plus brings in the necessary resources to get the job done on time while delivering the quality you need from your printed materials.

Creative Consulting

Thinking about stepping into the desktop publishing arena? Not sure whether you should hire out or implement your own department? reVisions Plus can evaluate and make recommendations based on your current publishing methods. A cost analysis will reveal whether in-house or out-of-house publishing would be most cost effective for your publishing needs.

Fig. 5.10

The front and back of
a brochure.

Panel 2

Panel 3

Panel 4

Business Cards and Stationery

One of the most important aspects of the look and feel of your business cards and stationery is the company logo you use. In some cases, your company may already have designed a logo that you use in your publications. In other cases, you may get to design a logo of your own. Selecting a logo takes careful consideration: be sure to choose items that in some way are connected to your business. Simply selecting a picture for art's sake won't work when you're trying to build a reputation. Using a penguin in your logo when your company name is Ben's Biscuits doesn't make much sense to the reader, but if you're running the Petite Penguin restaurant, the logo works. Ideally, the logo reminds readers of your business.

Here are a few guidelines for selecting or designing a logo:

- Make sure that the logo is in some way connected to the service or product of your business.

- Choose a simple logo that readers can remember easily.

- Geometric shapes (such as rectangles, triangles, and so forth) and line-art drawings are popular in logos right now: if you use shapes or line art, be sure to keep the design simple.

- If you include the company name as part of the logo, make sure that the name is readable. Keep in mind that the logo may be reduced in size when printed on your materials.

- Be careful not to use anyone else's logo. Similar to other items like company name and slogan, logos are protected by trademark regulations.

- Remember that simple is best. Don't overwhelm your readers with complex graphics and too many characters. Make your logo simple so that readers can remember it easily.

When you plan business cards and stationery, consider the following points.

Make the design of your cards, stationery, and other printed items consistent. After you have decided on a logo, use that logo on all your printed materials. The consistency of seeing the same logo and basic text layout (where you place the company name and address, for example) helps readers identify your company.

Keep the design simple and memorable. Especially with business cards, don't give in to the temptation to fill the card with too much information. Remember that you have only a limited amount of space and that unused space on small publications is just as important as the printed words. Don't include your company name, address, phone, fax number, and company logo on a small 2-by-3-inch business card. Select the most important items and use those. Remember that cluttering a publication with too many words—whether the publication is a business card or a newsletter—causes readers to think that wading through the publication is more trouble than it's worth.

Remember the two basic functions of stationery: first, to correspond and, second, to get your company's name in front of people (otherwise you would use blank paper). You may be tempted to put quite a bit of information on your stationery, such as a logo, slogan, name, address, and telephone number. This information is important, but be sure to use a small type size to downplay the information and leave the greatest amount of space for the primary objective: correspondence.

Highlight the company name. On your stationery and business cards, place the company name and logo in a strategic place so that the reader's attention is drawn to the item. Remember that the use of blank space is important—it helps guide readers to the item you want them to focus on.

Business Forms

Another type of document that finds its way into the hands of the public is the forms you use in your transactions. Suppose that you manufacture a video game. When your customers order games, you ship the games with an invoice giving important information about the transaction.

Several guidelines should be kept in mind as you create business forms.

Use the same company logo on all forms. It helps customers build on their impression of you. Place the logo so that it is instantly recognizable as soon as the customer opens the envelope.

Think about the number of columns you need and divide the space appropriately. Although for some special layouts you may want to vary the widths of the columns you use, most simple two- or three-column document layouts use columns of the same width. When you're working with business forms, however, another question comes to mind: how much room will you need for the information entered in the columns? A Description column would take more space than a Quantity or Price column, for example. Whether you use one column or many, remember to divide the space so that the columns are appropriately proportioned.

Organize the form into understandable sections. Be careful not to squeeze the information onto the form in an disorganized fashion. Set off one area (preferably at the top of the form) that gives your company name, logo, address, and phone number; set off another area that includes the customer's name, address, and phone number. In another area, include the purchase information—stock number, description, quantity, price, and other important items. In another area, total all the costs involved in the transaction and show the customer clearly how those costs were figured. Also include an area that explains the terms by which your company expects payment. Organizing the form in this way helps customers understand the transaction taking place and shows that you care about the way your business interacts with clients. Figure 5.11 shows an example of a simple business form.

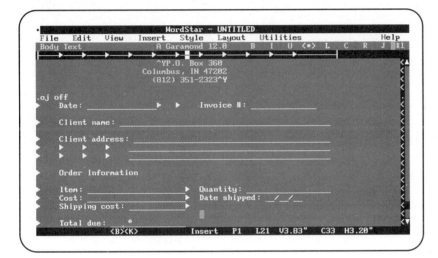

Fig. 5.11

A simple business form.

Use only a few typefaces. Be consistent within the body of your business forms. Use one typeface for the column headings in your invoice, for example, and another for the company information. Remember that using too many different typefaces can create a confusing look.

Use boxes to help keep things neat. Depending on the capabilities of your printer, you may be able to add special design boxes to notes or other information on your form. Boxes can help you group similar items to make the organization of your form easier for readers to follow. WordStar has several macros that help you add boxes to your documents (see Chapter 13).

Training Handouts

The goal of training handouts is to teach rather than to invite or inspire. Training handouts therefore require a different kind of design. The design of a training handout follows the same "quick look" idea that promotional literature uses; however, you use more words in training materials than you use in promotional pieces. The format of your training hand-outs also should guide readers through the handout in a certain manner. Figure 5.12 shows a sample training handout for a parenting course.

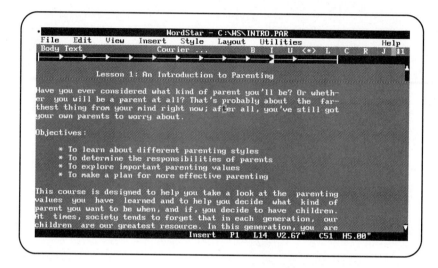

Fig. 5.12

A training handout.

When you are designing training handouts, consider these tips.

Make your objectives known. Place the objectives, or goals, of your course in an easily identified spot on the handout (as in fig. 5.12). If you are designing a course that includes several different lessons, include only the objectives for the current lesson on the individual training handout.

Keep the handout brief, with only enough information to refresh the reader's memory when the handout is read later. Remember that you don't need to restate the entire lesson in this backup material. Simply cover the key points in your discussion so that the reader can recall important facts.

You may want to include space for notes. Depending on the nature of your course and whether you are pressed for space on the handout, you may want to add a section where students can write notes from your presentation.

Make the major points easy to find. Use special styles to highlight the most important points on a page. You can use numbered steps, bold-faced type, or a picture, such as an icon, to draw the reader's eye to the most important items.

Use boxed material to reinforce concepts introduced in the text.
Boxed information can be effective in restating, or summarizing, a topic
introduced in text or in class. Keep boxed material brief. (You also may
want to use pull-quotes, which are small sections of text in a larger type
style set off by lines and set in the center of a text column, as shown in
fig. 5.13.)

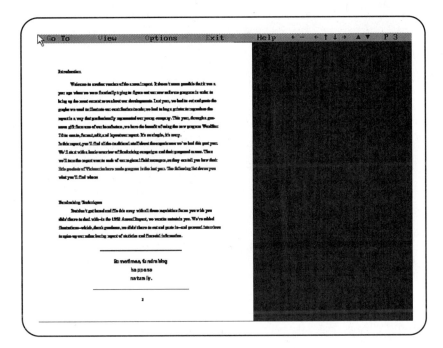

Fig. 5.13

A page with a pull-
quote.

Summary of Design Strategies

You have covered a considerable amount of ground in this section. If
you feel overwhelmed, don't worry—you learn a great deal about effective publications through trial and error. In the chapters that follow, you
learn more about individual designs. You also may want to refer to Chapter 17, "A WordStar Sampler," for more ideas that can be incorporated
into WordStar documents. As you prepare your documents, keep in
mind the following considerations:

- Your company's expectations

- The type of format that appeals to your readers

- The publication's purpose

- The publication's tone (friendly or serious)
- The type of graphics you want to import

When you have an idea of where you want to go with a document, you're ready to begin working with your first page. As you become more experienced with WordStar, you spend less time in the design stage. At least initially, however, the more time you spend deciding what type of publication you want, the less time you spend producing it.

Getting Ready

In the last section, you learned a number of factors to consider as you create your own publications. When faced with a blank page, some people, understandably, pale. The responsibility of creating an effective, well-designed document can be overwhelming for people just beginning to learn about word processing—and perhaps computers in general.

Perhaps the best advice at this point is to start small. Begin using WordStar by working on simple, uncomplicated projects; then work up to the documents that require the use of columns, headers, footers, indexes, and table of contents. If you don't have the luxury of starting with something simple, don't worry; nothing in WordStar is truly difficult. You do, however, have many different steps to remember. You will be reminded of these as you go along.

Chapter Summary

In this chapter, you have learned about one of the most important steps in document creation: planning. From a basic discussion of general design tips to more specialized examples of tips for letters, long documents, newsletters, fliers, business cards, and forms, this chapter has clued you in to some important design considerations that could reduce the time and effort you spend creating documents. The next chapter helps you begin creating documents in WordStar by entering and importing text.

Entering and Importing Text

I n the last few chapters, you learned the techniques of creating simple documents; you discovered all the menus and commands that you can use; and you learned how to manage the files you create. By now, though, you must be eager to start creating WordStar documents of your own. Well, get ready to roll up your shirtsleeves, because in this chapter you learn to enter text into WordStar documents. Specifically, you learn the following concepts and procedures:

- Entering text
- Understanding word wrap and paragraph breaks
- Using insert and typeover modes
- Moving the cursor
- Using simple keyboard editing techniques
- Applying paragraph styles
- Importing text
- Opening existing text files
- Understanding Star Exchange

Before you can do anything else, however, you must start WordStar, open a new document, and enter some text. These topics are explained in the following section.

Entering Text

If you haven't already started WordStar, change to the directory storing your WordStar files and start the program. When the opening screen appears, open a new document. You can open a new document in one of two ways:

- Open the File menu by pressing Alt-F, and select the New command.

- Press S.

After a moment, the new, blank document appears in the edit screen. The text cursor (the small flashing underscore) is positioned in the top left corner of the work area (see fig. 6.1).

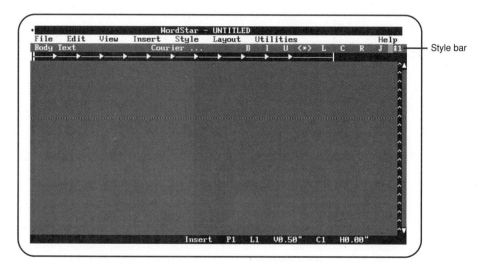

— Style bar

Fig. 6.1

The blank edit screen.

The style bar, located just below the menu bar, displays the default settings in effect as you type. New with Version 7.0, the style bar provides important information about the text: the paragraph style; the font used; the style (boldface, italic, or underline); alignment (left, centered, right, or justified); and the spacing. (Each style bar item is explained fully later in this chapter.)

Table 6.1 summarizes the initial (default) settings for the new document.

In subsequent chapters, you learn to change these settings to customize your documents. In this chapter, you use the settings as they are.

Table 6.1 Default Settings for the New Document

Item	Setting	Description
Paragraph style	Body Text	The initial paragraph style applied to text
Font	Courier	The font chosen for the entered text (Depending on the capabilities of your printer, your setting in the Font box may be different).
Style	No style selected	None of the styles— boldface, italic, or underline—is selected.
Flag column	On	The column to the left of the horizontal scroll bar displays the command tags and the block highlights.
Alignment	Left	The text you enter will be left-aligned (aligned along the left margin but ragged along the right).
Spacing	Single-spaced	The default spacing is for single-spaced text.

Now, get busy and enter some text. Start by entering the following paragraph, or if you prefer, create your own:

> What is a New Year's resolution? Some personal reform—like smoking, studying harder, or losing weight—you didn't accomplish in the past year, even though your conscience nagged you to the point of thinking about it on New Year's Eve? Is it something you know you have to face even though you'd rather avoid it (like making up with your mother, finishing that dissertation, or paying back income taxes)?

What happened as you typed? For one thing, you saw the characters you typed appear on-screen. As you continued typing and neared the end of the line, WordStar automatically wrapped the text to the next line for you, enabling you to keep typing without interruption. This feature is known as *word wrap*. WordStar continues to wrap lines for you until you press Enter to mark the end of the paragraph.

Press Enter twice. With the first keystroke, the cursor moves to the next line following the paragraph you just typed. With the second keystroke, the cursor moves down another line, leaving the preceding line blank to separate the paragraphs. Now continue entering text with the following paragraph or one of your own:

Why can't our New Year's resolutions be more pleasant? Do they always have to be something we don't really want to do? Doesn't that automatically stack the odds against us, so when we look back at the end of the year, we have yet another thing we haven't lived up to? Perhaps it would be a healthier and happier New Year if we made resolutions like these:

How are you doing? WordStar makes text entry and editing simple, so if you're making typos as you go along, don't worry. You learn how to correct those in a minute. For now, press Enter twice. The cursor moves first to the next line and then on to the next, leaving another blank line between paragraphs.

Now, you try something different. Press the Tab key. The cursor moves to the sixth character position; C6 appears in the status line at the bottom of the screen. Also, the tab symbol—a white triangle—appears at the beginning of the line (see fig. 6.2).

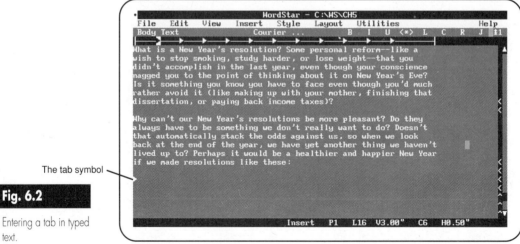

The tab symbol

Fig. 6.2

Entering a tab in typed text.

Now type the following line:

In 1992, I promise to eat at least 30 Milky Way candy bars.

Press Enter twice. That familiar blank line appears, and the cursor is positioned at the start of the next paragraph. Press Tab again. Once again, you see the tab symbol. Now type

In 1992, I promise to play more and work less.

Press Enter again. Your screen should now look something like the one in figure 6.3. As you can see, entering text in WordStar is not at all painful (and neither are these New Year's resolutions).

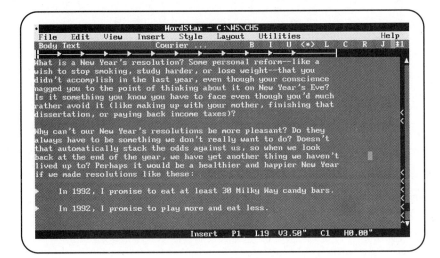

Fig. 6.3

The entered text.

Misteaks?

What if you made some typing mistakes back in the first paragraph? If the problem is relatively minor—like a misspelled word or a forgotten space—you can move the text cursor to the error and fix it easily by first pressing the Backspace key to delete characters and then retyping the word or words you want to correct. Your problem may be more serious, however, requiring you to move words around and reform paragraphs. Editing techniques like these are the topic of Chapter 7.

Moving Around in the Document

WordStar 7.0 provides several ways for you to view different parts of a document. You can

■ Use the mouse to point and click at the place where you want the text cursor to appear

- Use the mouse to click in the scroll bar located at the far right side of the document, enabling you to move through the document quickly

- Use the keyboard arrow keys to move through the document one line or one character at a time

- Use other keyboard keys—such as Page Up, Page Down, Home, and End—to move through the document quickly

- Use the Go To commands, available in the Edit menu, to move to a specified place in the document

In the following sections, you learn how to navigate in your document. The next sections explain how you can use the mouse to move through your file. Then you learn how to use the keyboard techniques for moving around in files.

Mouse Methods

The way in which you use the mouse to move through your document depends on the size of the document and the distance you want to move the cursor. If you want to move the cursor a short distance (say within the displayed text on-screen), simply point the mouse and click the mouse button to position the cursor. If you want to move the cursor to a point in the document you cannot see on-screen (you are viewing page 1, for example, and you want to display a paragraph on page 3), use the scroll bar method. Both methods are explained in the following sections.

Point and Click

The new mouse capabilities of WordStar 7.0 make it easy to move the cursor around the screen. To move the text cursor, follow these steps:

1. Move the mouse so that the mouse cursor is positioned where you want the text cursor to be placed.

2. Click the mouse button.

The text cursor moves to that point. You can move the cursor as many times as you like.

Scroll Bar Methods

Another mouse method is helpful when scrolling through a long document. The scroll bar, located at the right edge of the work area, provides a means of moving quickly through the document. Figure 6.4 shows the scroll bar located along the edge of the work area.

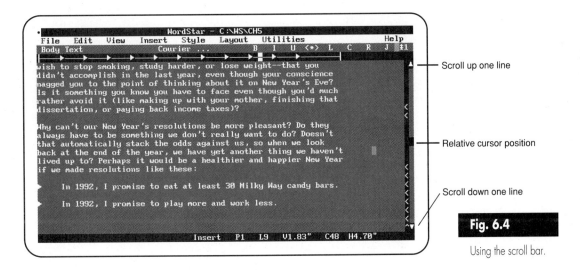

Fig. 6.4

Using the scroll bar.

The scroll bar contains an arrow at the top and at the bottom. You also see a small box somewhere in the scroll bar. This box shows you the position of the cursor relative to the beginning and end of the document.

To use the scroll bar, first position the mouse at the location in the scroll bar that corresponds to the place in the document you want to see. If you want to view the end of the document, for example, move the mouse cursor to the bottom of the scroll bar. To see text in the middle of the document, position the mouse cursor in the middle of the scroll bar. After positioning the mouse, click the mouse button. The portion of the document, relative to the point you clicked in the scroll bar, is displayed. To scroll the document one line at a time, click the up arrow or down arrow at either end of the scroll bar. The display moves up or down one line, respectively.

As you use the scroll bar, you may notice that the document itself—not the cursor—moves, displaying different parts of the document. When you click the down arrow at the bottom of the scroll bar, for example, the document scrolls up (similar to what happens when you press the carriage return on a typewriter).

Keyboard Techniques

If you're using the keyboard, you can use a variety of keys to navigate through the text in a document. Table 6.2 provides an overview of the various cursor-movement keys you can use.

Table 6.2 WordStar Cursor-Movement Keys	
Key	Description
Up arrow	Moves the cursor up one line
Down arrow	Moves the cursor down one line
Right arrow	Moves the cursor to the right one character or space
Left arrow	Moves the cursor to the left one character or space
Ctrl-right arrow	Moves the cursor one word to the right
Ctrl-left arrow	Moves the cursor one word to the left
Home	Moves the cursor to the top left corner of the screen
End	Moves the cursor to the bottom of the screen
Ctrl-Home	Moves cursor to beginning of document
Ctrl-End	Moves cursor to end of document
Page Up	Scrolls the document display up one page
Page Down	Scrolls the document display down one page

Now, play around a bit with the cursor movement. When the sample document is on-screen (the cursor should still be positioned at the end of the text), follow these steps:

1. Press the up-arrow key twice. The cursor moves up two lines.

2. Press the right-arrow key. The cursor moves to the right one character.

3. Press Ctrl-right arrow. The cursor moves to the beginning of the next word to the right.

4. Press Page Up. The cursor moves up one screen length (25 lines).

The Go To Commands

WordStar provides you with yet another method of moving through the document: using the Go To commands. In Version 6.0, WordStar's Go To commands occupied a menu all their own; now they are included with the commands on the Edit menu (see fig. 6.5).

```
┌─Edit─────────────────────────┐
│ Undo                    ^U    │
│                               │
│ Mark Block Beginning   ^KB    │
│ Mark Block End         ^KK    │
│ Move                      ►   │
│ Copy                      ►   │
│ Delete                    ►   │
│ Mark Previous Block    ^KU    │
│                               │
│ Find...                ^QF    │
│ Find and Replace...    ^QA    │
│ Next Find              ^L     │
│ Go to Character...     ^QG    │
│ Go to Page...          ^QI    │
│ Go to Marker              ►   │
│ Go to Other               ►   │
│ Set Marker                ►   │
│                               │
│ Edit Note             ^OND    │
│ Note Options              ►   │
│ Editing Settings          ►   │
└───────────────────────────────┘
```

Fig. 6.5

The Edit menu with the Go To commands.

As you can see, you have four different options for moving to a specific part of your document. You can move to a specific character by selecting Go to Character. If you want to change to a different page, you can use the Go to Page option. Go to Marker takes you to a place marker you've previously set. The last option, Go to Other, lets you move to command tags (such as format tags, paragraph style tags, bold codes, block beginning and ending codes, and so on) or enables you to scroll through the document pages. As you can see, two of these commands—Go to Character and Go to Page—have quick keys (Ctrl-QG and Ctrl-QI, respectively). The other two Go To commands display pop-up list boxes that provide you with additional options. Table 6.3 gives you an overview of the Go To commands.

Going to a Character

You can instruct WordStar to search for the next occurrence of a character and move the cursor to that position in your document. Suppose, for example, that you are putting together a company letter about a change in payroll policies. You now want to change something in the section that talks about current policies, but you can't remember where that information is in the document. You do know, however, that you used the word *existing* in that section. You can use the Go to Character command to find the *x* in *existing* and move the cursor to that point by following these steps:

Table 6.3 Go To Commands

Command	Quick Key	Description
Go to Character	Ctrl-QG	Moves the cursor to the next occurrence of the character you specify
Go to Page	Ctrl-QI	Moves the cursor to the beginning of the page you specify
Go to Marker		Moves the cursor to a marker you've created (numbered 0 to 9). Markers are explained later in this chapter.
Go to Other		Moves the cursor to other items in your document, including code tags, block markers, beginning or end of document, or previous position. Also enables you to scroll continuously through the document. (Chapter 7 covers more about block codes.)

1. Move the cursor to the beginning of the document.
2. Open the Edit menu by pressing Alt-E or by clicking the menu name.
3. Choose the Go to Character command. A small pop-up box appears (see fig. 6.6).
4. Type the character you want to search for (in this case, *x*).
5. Click OK or press Enter.

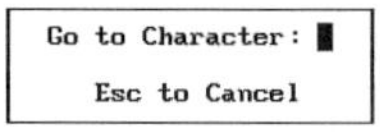

Fig. 6.6

Using the Go to Character command.

```
Go to Character: █
   Esc to Cancel
```

Quick Character Searches

You can go to a character quickly by pressing Ctrl-QG, typing the character, and pressing Enter.

WordStar then searches the document and moves the display (and the cursor) to the point where the character is found.

That's Not What I Had in Mind . . .

If WordStar finds a word with the character you specified but the word is not the word you are looking for, you can instruct WordStar to search for the same character again by pressing Ctrl-L.

Going to a Page

You can have WordStar move directly to another page by using the Go to Page command in the Edit menu. Follow these steps:

1. Open the Edit menu by pressing Alt-E or by clicking the menu name.

2. Choose the Go to Page command by pressing P or by clicking the command name. The Go to Page pop-up dialog box appears, as shown in figure 6.7.

3. Type the page number you want.

Fig. 6.7

The Go to Page pop-up dialog box.

4. Click OK or press Enter.

WordStar moves the display and the cursor to the first character position on the page you specified.

Changing Pages Quickly

You can move quickly to a specified page by using the quick-key combination. Press Ctrl-QI, type the page number, and press Enter. WordStar displays the chosen page. You also can use the mouse to select another page. Click the page number at the bottom of the edit screen (on the status line) and the Go to Page dialog box appears. You can then type the page number you want and press Enter.

Going to a Marker

As you may know, a marker is a small nonprinting flag you can place within text so that later you can return easily to that point. Suppose that you want to add a marker at a specific point in text. Move the cursor to that point and press Ctrl-K; then type a number for the marker (from 1 to 9). WordStar places the marker flag—<1>, if you typed *1*—at the cursor position. You can then return to the marker any time you work on the document by using the Go to Marker command and typing the marker's number. (The marker serves as a kind of electronic Post-it note, enabling you to move directly to the tag you marked.)

Setting Markers

You can place a marker in your text by positioning the cursor at the point where you want the marker, opening the Edit menu, selecting the Set Marker command, and choosing a number for the marker. WordStar then leaves a little flag in your text, indicating the marker placement. Don't worry; this marker will not print.

To move to a marker, follow these steps:

1. Open the Edit menu by pressing Alt-E or clicking the menu name.

2. Choose the Go to Marker command by pressing M or by clicking the command name. A small pop-up box of marker choices appears beside the displayed Edit menu (see fig. 6.8).

3. Select the marker you want by clicking it or by typing the marker number.

WordStar then moves the cursor to the marker you specified.

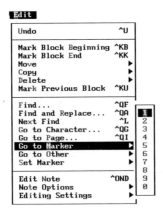

Fig. 6.8

Moving to a marker.

Going to Other Items

You can use the Go to Other command in the Edit menu to find all sorts of other items in your WordStar document. Not only can you move to a specific item, such as a font tag or block end, but you can also choose to scroll continuously up or down through the document. Figure 6.9 shows you the different options you have when you use the Go to Other command to move the cursor.

```
Edit
Undo                       ^U

Mark Block Beginning  ^KB
Mark Block End        ^KK
Move                    ▶
Copy                    ▶
Delete                  ▶
Mark Previous Block   ^KU

Find...                ^QF   Font Tag              ^Q=
Find and Replace...    ^QA   Style Tag             ^QK
Next Find              ^L    Note...               ^ONG
Go to Character...     ^QG   Previous Position     ^QP
Go to Page...          ^QI   Last Find/Replace     ^QV
Go to Marker            ▶    Beginning of Block    ^QB
Go to Other             ▶    End of Block          ^QK
Set Marker              ▶    Document Beginning    ^QR
                             Document End          ^QC
Edit Note              ^OND  Scroll Continuously Up    ^QW
Note Options            ▶    Scroll Continuously Down  ^QZ
Editing Settings        ▶
```

Fig. 6.9

The Go to Other
command choices.

Table 6.4 summarizes the different options for the Go to Other command.

Table 6.4 Options for the Go to Other Command

Option	Quick Key	Description
Font Tag	Ctrl-Q=	Finds the next font tag in the document
Style Tag	Ctrl-Q<	Moves to the next style tag in the document
Note	Ctrl-ONG	Displays a pop-up dialog box asking which type of note to find: Any Note, Footnote, Endnote, Annotation, Comment, Index Entry
Previous Position	Ctrl-QP	Moves the cursor to the preceding cursor position
Last Find/Replace	Ctrl-QV	Repeats the last find and replace operation (Find and replace is explained in Chapter 7.)
Beginning of Block	Ctrl-QB	Moves the cursor to the beginning of the selected block
End of Block	Ctrl-QK	Moves the cursor to the end of the selected block
Document Beginning	Ctrl-QR	Places the cursor at the beginning of the document
Document End	Ctrl-QC	Places the cursor at the end of the document
Scroll Continuously Up	Ctrl-QW	Scrolls, one screen at a time, up through the document
Scroll Continuously Down	Ctrl-QZ	Scrolls, one screen at a time, down through the document

To use the Go to Other command, follow these steps:

1. Open the Edit menu by pressing Alt-E or by clicking the menu name.

2. Choose the Go to Other command by pressing O or by clicking the command. The pop-up options box is displayed.

3. Choose the item you want WordStar to find. If you choose Note, another dialog box appears asking which type of note you want to

search for (see fig. 6.10). When you choose any of the other items, WordStar begins the search automatically and finds the item you specified. If you chose the Note option, make your selection from the Note options box, and WordStar begins the search.

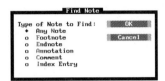

Fig. 6.10

The Note options box.

Going Back

If you move the cursor to another position and then wish you were back where you started, you can get there easily by pressing Ctrl-QP. WordStar takes you back to the preceding cursor position.

WordStar also gives you the option of scrolling continuously through the document. This feature comes in handy when you are scanning the document, perhaps looking for items that aren't formatted correctly or looking for a specific phrase or line. (If specific characters are involved, though, you can use the Go to Character command to move directly to those characters).

To scroll continuously through the document (up or down), you can use the Go to Other command and then select Scroll Continuously Up or Scroll Continuously Down. Alternatively, you can press Ctrl-QW to scroll up or Ctrl-QZ to scroll down. To end scrolling, you can press any key. Choose the command again to start scrolling again.

Understanding Insert and Typeover Modes

Now that you know how to navigate your way through a WordStar document, you must know what to do once you get to your desired location. You may want to add text, edit existing text, or change the font or style of text already there. In this section, you learn about the difference between insert and typeover modes—something important if you are planning to enter text in the middle of existing text. (Chapter 7 explains how to edit text in your document, and Chapter 8 shows you how to work with fonts and styles.)

As you know, WordStar gives you the option of inserting text into your document (*insert mode*) or typing over existing text (*typeover mode*). You control the mode by pressing Ctrl-V.

When you first open a document, WordStar is in insert mode. In this mode, the characters you type are inserted at the cursor position, and characters to the right of the cursor are moved to make room for the new text. Suppose, for example, that the cursor is positioned under the word *fox* in the following sentence:

The quick brown fox jumped over the lazy dog.

If WordStar is in insert mode, after you type the word *fuzzy* and press the space bar, the line looks like this:

The quick brown fuzzy fox jumped over the lazy dog.

Now, if you press Ctrl-V, WordStar changes into typeover mode. The status indicator at the bottom of the screen changes from Insert to Ins-off. With the cursor positioned under the word *fox*, if you type *kangaroo*, the line looks like this:

The quick brown fuzzy kangarooed over the lazy dog.

As you can see, typeover mode can be dangerous when you are entering information that should not overwrite existing text. To change typeover mode back to insert mode, press Ctrl-V again. Ins-off changes back to Insert on the status line at the bottom of the screen.

Understanding Paragraph Styles

One feature that falls under the heading of "enhancing" and that you should consider here is paragraph styles. *Paragraph styles* are preset formats that control basic settings for your paragraph. Generally, paragraph styles control the following elements:

- Font
- Text size
- Text alignment
- Text style (boldface, italic, underline, and so on)
- Text spacing
- Margins
- Indentation

You can, for example, select the Body Text paragraph style before you enter text so that the text appears in precisely the format and the text settings you want.

Chapter 8 explains how to use WordStar's preset paragraph styles and shows you how to create and use your own. Although in many cases you may want to apply paragraph styles to your paragraphs after you enter text, you do have the option of entering your text directly in the style you want so that you don't have to do any reformatting or changing later.

The first box in the style bar shows you the default paragraph style currently displayed (see fig. 6.11). You can display the different paragraph styles available by clicking the paragraph style box on the style bar or by opening the Style menu and choosing the Select Paragraph Style command. The dialog box shown in figure 6.12 is then displayed.

Default paragraph style

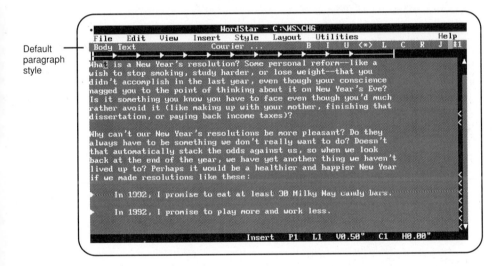

Fig. 6.11

The paragraph style box.

Current style

Available styles

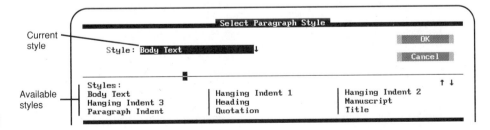

Fig. 6.12

The Select Paragraph Style dialog box.

The Style text box shows the current style, and other available styles are listed in the lower part of the dialog box. You can choose the style you want by highlighting it (use the arrow keys or the mouse) and clicking OK or pressing Enter. WordStar then returns you to your document and places a paragraph style code in the text just before the cursor position. When you begin to enter text, the text appears in the paragraph style you've chosen.

Working with Paragraph Styles

You can do much more than simply work with the paragraph styles shown in the dialog box; you can create your own styles. Do you use a special format in your two-column newsletter? Does your work involve many levels of indentation? You can create a paragraph style to take care of the formatting and text settings for you. Chapter 8 explains how to create, apply, and edit paragraph styles.

Importing Text Files

One of the greatest benefits of using a word processing program is that you can reuse the data you enter. Suppose that you create a 40-page annual report for your company. In a newsletter sent to clients, you want to include basic information about new products—something you've already written. With word processing, you don't need to rewrite or re-type anything: you can simply use in your new document the part of the file you've already created.

But what if you have just recently changed to WordStar and all your word processing files were created in another program? No problem. WordStar 7.0 includes a program called Star Exchange, which enables you to change files from most popular word processing programs into a format usable by WordStar. (You learn more about Star Exchange later in this chapter.)

With WordStar, you're not limited to importing only text files. You also can import some spreadsheet and database files, as well as standard graphics files. (More about this subject later in this chapter.)

The way in which you import information depends on the type of items you're trying to import. The following list explains the different procedures you use when you import text files:

■ If you want to import a text section into your existing WordStar document, you use the File command in the Insert menu to bring the section of text into your document.

■ If you are using WordStar from within Microsoft Windows, you can copy the text section you want to the Windows Clipboard and then paste the section into your WordStar document.

■ If you want to use a file you created in another program with WordStar, you use Star Exchange to convert the file to WordStar; then you can open the file and use it as you use any regular WordStar document.

Importing WordStar Text Files

This section begins with the easy stuff. Suppose that you want to import an existing file into your WordStar document. Follow these steps:

1. Open the document into which you want to import the file.

2. Position the cursor at the point where you want to insert the text.

3. Open the Insert menu by pressing Alt-I or by clicking the Insert menu name. The Insert menu is displayed (see fig. 6.13).

```
Insert
Page Break            .pa
Column Break          .cb

Today's Date Value    ^M@
Other Value            ▶
Variable               ▶
Extended Character... ^P@
Custom Printer Code    ▶

File...               ^KR
File at Print Time... .fi
Graphic...            ^P*
Note                   ▶

Index/TOC Entry        ▶
Par. Outline Number... ^OZ

Change Printer Codes...
```

Fig. 6.13

The Insert menu.

4. Choose the File command. The Insert File screen appears, as shown in figure 6.14.

5. Highlight the name of the file you want to import. (If you need to change to another directory, click the directory name you need before highlighting the file name.)

6. Click OK or press Enter.

WordStar immediately inserts the selected file at the cursor position.

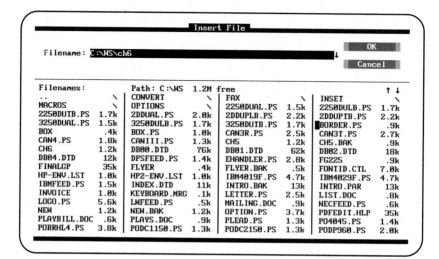

Fig. 6.14

The Insert File screen.

Importing a Portion of a File

If you don't want to bring an entire file into your current WordStar document, you can highlight the portion of the file you want and save it as an individual file before you open the file in which you want to place the selected section. Suppose, for example, that you want to use a portion of the annual report in your current document, but the report is 40 pages long. You don't want to import the entire file into your new document.

First, save and close the current document; then open the annual report file. Go to the portion of the file you want to use, and highlight the section by using the mouse or by using the Mark Block Beginning and Mark Block End commands in the Edit menu. Then press Ctrl-KW. This quick-key combination selects the Copy to Another File command (available in the Edit menu). Type a name for the file and press Enter. The highlighted section is saved as its own file, so that you can return to your original document and import the file as necessary. Chapter 7 explains more about this facet of the copy procedure.

Importing Other Types of Files

You also can import some spreadsheet and database files directly into your WordStar documents. If you're working with a large file and want to use only a portion of it in your WordStar document, be sure to copy the portion you want out to an individual file and import that file. (This step saves you a considerable amount of cutting time later.)

When you use the File command in the Insert menu to bring in a file other than a word processing file, WordStar automatically recognizes the file type and displays a screen of options about that file type. Suppose, for example, that when choosing File from the Insert menu, you select a spreadsheet file from the Filenames list, and click OK or press Enter. The Insert File screen shown in figure 6.15 is displayed.

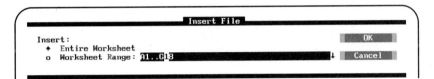

Fig. 6.15

Inserting a spreadsheet file.

You can choose to import the Entire Worksheet by clicking the button to the left of that option or by pressing E. If you want to import only a section of the worksheet, click the Worksheet Range option (or press R) and type the worksheet range you want to import. After you click OK or press Enter, WordStar imports the file and places it at the cursor position in your document.

Inserting a File

Files saved in ASCII (American Standard Code for Information Interchange) format can be opened and used in WordStar without any conversion. ASCII is a universal format that stores the data in a format recognizable by all computers. ASCII format stores only the basic information—no formatting or text style codes are included in the file.

But what happens if you import a file, and although WordStar doesn't give you an error message, a bunch of garbage appears on your screen? Simple—that file doesn't transfer directly into WordStar without conversion. In that case, you can use WordStar's file conversion utility, Star Exchange, to convert the file into a format usable in WordStar.

Understanding Star Exchange

Star Exchange is a file conversion program that enables you to use files created in more than 50 different programs. You start Star Exchange by selecting Star Exchange from the Additional menu on the opening screen. The quick keys to access Star Exchange are AS.

Star Exchange enables you to convert all sorts of files—word processing files, spreadsheet files, and database files—to a format usable in WordStar documents. Table 6.5 lists all the different programs and formats you can use.

Table 6.5 Programs Supported by Star Exchange

Program	Type
ASCII	Data format
dBASE	Database
DCA	Data format
Data Ease	Database
dBXL	Database
DEC WPS Plus	Word processor
DisplayWrite	Word processor
Enable	Database, spreadsheet, word processor
First Choice	Database, spreadsheet, word processor
FoxBase	Database
Framework	Database, spreadsheet
IBM Writing Assistant	Word processor
Lotus 1-2-3	Spreadsheet
Lotus Symphony	Spreadsheet
MASS-11	Word processor
Microsoft Excel	Spreadsheet
Microsoft Word[1]	Word processor
Microsoft RTF	Data format

Program	Type
Microsoft Works	Database, spreadsheet, word processor
Mosiac Twin	Spreadsheet
MultiMate	Word processor
Nota Bene	Word processor
Paradox	Database
PFS: Professional Plan	Spreadsheet
PFS: Write	Word processor
Professional Write	Word processor
Q&A	Database, word processor
Quattro	Spreadsheet
R:BASE	Database
Reflex	Database
Samna Word	Word processor
SmartWare II	Database, spreadsheet, word processor
VP Planner	Spreadsheet
Volkswriter	Word processor
Wang PC	Word processor
WordMARC Composer	Word processor
WordPerfect[1]	Word processor
WordStar	Word processor
WordStar 2000	Word processor
XYWrite	Word processor

[1] *Microsoft Word and WordPerfect can be converted from Macintosh format. Additionally, Star Exchange can convert MacWrite II files.*

After you select Star Exchange from the Additional menu, the Star Exchange opening screen appears (see fig. 6.16). You can then follow the on-screen prompts to convert the file of your choice into a format usable by WordStar. You can press F1 to get help on using the various Star Exchange procedures. When you're ready to exit Star Exchange, press 4 to return to WordStar.

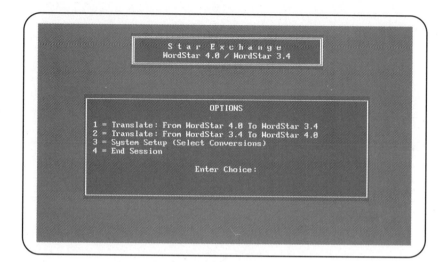

┌─────────────────────────────────────┐
│   S t a r   E x c h a n g e   │
│   WordStar 4.0 / WordStar 3.4   │
└─────────────────────────────────────┘

```
                       OPTIONS

    1 = Translate: From WordStar 4.0 To WordStar 3.4
    2 = Translate: From WordStar 3.4 To WordStar 4.0
    3 = System Setup (Select Conversions)
    4 = End Session

                   Enter Choice:
```

Fig. 6.16

The Star Exchange
opening screen.

Chapter Summary

In this chapter, you have learned how to enter text into your WordStar document. Additionally, you have found out how to import sections of text and entire files into your word processing documents. In the next chapter, you learn to edit the text you entered by working with text blocks, using the find and replace feature, and applying the spelling checker and thesaurus to your documents.

Editing Text

I n the last chapter, you learned to enter text into a WordStar document. If you followed along with the sample text in the chapter or created your own document, you now have text to work with on your screen. In this chapter, you learn how to use various editing features to fix any errors that find their way into your document and to use the spelling checker and thesaurus to help ensure the accuracy of your spelling and word choice. Specifically in this chapter, you learn how to perform the following tasks:

- Use the editing keys to correct typing and other errors
- Mark blocks of text
- Copy, move, and delete selected blocks of text
- Copy text to and from the Windows Clipboard
- Use the find and replace feature
- Use the spelling checker
- Use the thesaurus

Before you start editing, take a minute to save your file if you haven't already done so. As a general rule, you should save your working file each time you enter a new portion of text or edit existing text. Pressing Ctrl-KS every 15 minutes or so could save you a considerable amount of time in the long run by saving you from having to retype material lost due to a poorly timed power outage or someone's tripping over the power cord.

WordStar offers great flexibility in the way you can edit text in a document. If you want to correct typing or punctuation errors, you can use a few simple keystrokes to move to the problem and fix it. This process, for the sake of this discussion, is known as *keyboard editing*. If you want to revise your document on a larger scale, you can use WordStar's *block editing* procedures to move, copy, or delete blocks of text. You also have the additional editing tools of the spelling checker and thesaurus.

Keyboard editing enables you to perform such tasks as moving the cursor to the place in the document you want to make a correction and using editing keys to fix the error. Block editing, on the other hand, enables you to highlight text as a block and then copy, move, or delete the text block.

Keyboard Editing

Now, assuming that you have a sample document open on your screen, you can try some editing procedures. In this section, you learn some of the basic keys and procedures used in keyboard editing.

When working with keyboard editing techniques, you use a particular set of key combinations to move within the text and to edit it. Table 7.1 lists the editing keys available and describes the function of each key combination. The keys will save you enormous amounts of time. Suppose that you want to move the cursor from its present position to the beginning of the next word. You *could* press the right-arrow key to move the cursor—character by character—to the location you want. Or you can press Ctrl-F; WordStar automatically moves the cursor to the first character of the next word.

Take a few minutes to try out these editing keys. You can use the following exercise to try out the key combinations:

1. Press Home. The cursor moves to the top left corner of the work area.

2. Press Ctrl-X twice. The cursor moves down two lines.

3. Press Ctrl-F three times. The cursor is now positioned on the first character of the fourth word.

4. Press Ctrl-E. The cursor moves up one line.

5. Press Ctrl-Y. The current line is deleted, and the following line moves up to replace the deleted line.

6. Press Ctrl-U. The deleted line is returned to the document.

Table 7.1 Editing Keys

Key Combination	Description
Ctrl-D	Moves the cursor one character to the right
Ctrl-E	Moves the cursor up one line
Ctrl-S	Moves the cursor one character to the left
Ctrl-X	Moves the cursor down one line
Ctrl-F	Moves the cursor one word to the right
Ctrl-A	Moves the cursor one word to the left
Ctrl-G	Deletes character at the cursor position
Ctrl-H	Deletes character to the left of the cursor
Ctrl-T	Deletes word at the cursor position
Ctrl-Y	Deletes line at cursor position
Ctrl-U	Restores last deleted character, word, line, or block
Ctrl–Del	Deletes all characters to the left of the cursor on the current line
Ctrl-QY	Deletes all characters to the right of the cursor on the current line
Backspace	Deletes the character to the left of the cursor

At first, you may find It difficult to remember what each key combination does. Remember, though, that if you forget a key combination, you can always use either the mouse or the arrow keys to move the cursor. And with a little practice, these editing keystrokes become second nature.

Using the Mouse for Keyboard Editing

Although you can't use the mouse for actual editing—that is, you cannot delete or add characters using the mouse—you can use the mouse to replace the editing keys for moving the cursor. The mouse makes placing the cursor easy: you position the mouse pointer where you want the cursor and click the mouse button. All other keyboard editing procedures, such as those for deleting characters and lines, you have to do with the keyboard.

Working with Text Blocks

Not all the errors in your document can be corrected with the simple press of a keyboard editing key. Suppose that after reading through a report you've just finished, you notice that one of the sections is out of place: the document would be easier to understand if you moved one section to a place later in the document. How can you do that? With block editing, you can mark the entire section as a *block* of text and use WordStar's Move command to move the text to the new location in the document.

A block of text can be any amount of text you mark, from a single character to the entire document. Before you can move, copy, or delete text, you must mark it as a block. This section shows you how to mark text as a block and then perform various block operations.

Figure 7.1 shows you the Block & Save menu, which appears when you press Ctrl-K from the edit screen. As you can see, you can perform the following functions after you mark a block of text:

- Copy a block within your file
- Move a block
- Delete a block
- Copy a block to disk
- Calculate equations in the block
- Sort the lines of a block in ascending or descending order
- Count the number of words in the block
- Hide the block markers
- Mark the previously marked block
- Unmark the block
- Copy or move blocks between windows
- Change text to uppercase, lowercase, or sentence style capitalization
- Copy the block to and from the Windows Clipboard
- Add a text marker to the block

Block options   Block options with windows

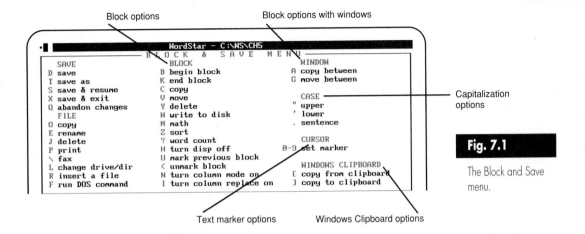

Capitalization options

Fig. 7.1

The Block and Save menu.

Text marker options   Windows Clipboard options

Block Rules

The following guidelines will help you work more efficiently with blocks:

- You can have only one block of text marked at one time.

- You must mark text as a block before you can copy or move it.

- You can save a text block as an individual file by pressing Ctrl-KW.

- You can recover a deleted block by pressing Ctrl-U.

- Do not highlight a block when you want to change the font, style, or spacing of text. (WordStar inserts codes to mark the beginning and end of those changes.)

- If you mark a block and are unsure what to do next, press Ctrl-K to display the Block and Save menu.

Marking Text Blocks

The first step in block editing involves, of course, marking the block. WordStar enables you to highlight only one block at a time. As soon as you begin to mark a subsequent block, WordStar unmarks the current one. You can mark a block in one of three ways:

- Highlight the block by using the mouse

■ Use key combinations to insert block markers (Ctrl-B to mark the beginning of the block and Ctrl-K to mark the end)

■ Use commands in the Edit menu

Marking a Block: Mouse Method

If you're using the mouse, you can highlight, or mark, the block easily by following these steps:

1. Position the mouse at the point where you want the block to begin.

2. Press and hold the mouse button.

3. Drag the mouse to the place where you want the block to end. The highlight extends to follow the mouse (see fig. 7.2).

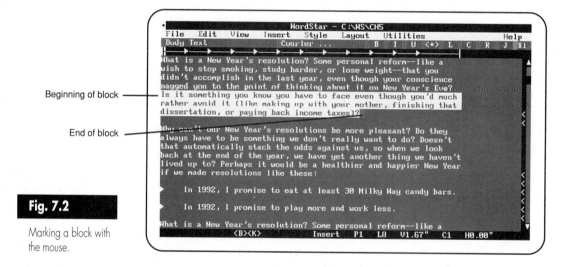

Beginning of block

End of block

Fig. 7.2

Marking a block with the mouse.

4. Release the mouse button.

That marks the block; now you can move, copy, or delete the block as necessary.

Marking a Block: Key Combinations

If you're more comfortable using the keyboard for text-based operations than you are using the mouse, you'll find that you have an easy alternative to using the mouse to mark blocks:

1. Move the text cursor to the place where you want to begin the block. (You can do this by using the arrow keys, the cursor-movement quick keys—such as Ctrl-F, Ctrl-E, and so on—or by using the mouse to position the cursor.)

2. Press Ctrl-KB. A beginning block marker—<B>—appears at the cursor position.

3. Move the cursor to the point where you want the ending block code to be inserted.

4. Press Ctrl-KK. The ending block marker—<K>—is placed in the text, and the text between the two markers is highlighted.

Marking a Block: Edit Menu

You can also use the Edit menu to insert the beginning and ending block codes into your text. Here's how:

1. Position the cursor at the place where you want the block to begin.

2. Press Alt-E to open the Edit menu.

3. Select the Mark Block Beginning command by clicking it or by pressing the down-arrow key once to highlight the command and then pressing Enter. The menu is closed, and the beginning block marker (<B>) is placed at the cursor position.

4. Move the cursor to the place in the text where you want the block to end.

5. Press Alt-E to open the Edit menu again.

6. Choose the Mark Block End command by clicking it or by highlighting it and pressing Enter. The menu is closed, and the end block marker (<K>) is inserted into the text. The text between the two markers is highlighted.

Unmarking Blocks

What if you've highlighted the wrong section of text? That pesky highlight won't go away without a little help from you. If you mark a subsequent block, WordStar automatically unmarks the previous block, because only one block can be marked at one time. However, if you want to unmark a block without marking another, you can simply press Ctrl-KH. (You can also press Ctrl-KH a second time to highlight the most recently marked block, if no block is currently highlighted.)

Copying Text

When you want to copy a block of text, you have several options for the way in which you copy the block and where you want the copied block to end up. The following options, explained in this chapter, are available for the copy procedure:

■ You can copy a block of text from one point in a document to another point in the same document.

■ You can copy a block of text to or from another file in a different window.

■ You can copy a block of text to or from the Windows Clipboard.

■ You can copy a block of text to another file.

Copying in the Same File

This section starts the easiest copy procedure. To copy a block of text within the same document, follow these steps:

1. Mark the block you want to copy.

2. Position the text cursor at the point where you want the copied block to be placed.

3. Open the Edit menu and choose the Copy command. A pop-up list of Copy options appears beside the open Edit menu (see fig. 7.3).

Fig. 7.3

Choosing a Copy option.

4. Choose Block.

WordStar leaves the marked block highlighted and places a copy of the block at the cursor position.

> **Quick Copy**
>
> You can copy a block quickly by marking the block, positioning the cursor, and pressing Ctrl-KC.

Copying to a Different Window

WordStar enables you to have more than one file open on-screen at once. When you open a second file (assuming that you already have one file open), WordStar opens a second window in the bottom half of the screen. Your second document appears in that window. (Chapter 9 explains how to open and work with windows in WordStar.)

If you're working with more than one window open on the screen, you can copy a block of text from one window to another. First, assume that your screen looks something like the one shown in figure 7.4 and that you want to copy the highlighted block in the top of the screen to the window in the bottom of the screen.

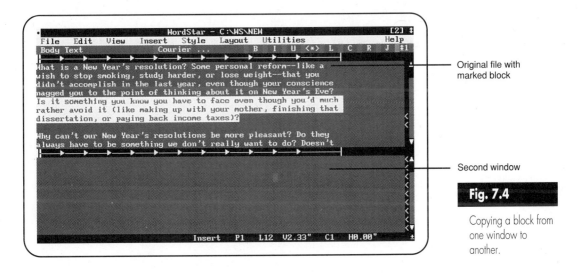

Original file with marked block

Second window

Fig. 7.4

Copying a block from one window to another.

To copy the block from the first window to the second window, follow these steps:

1. Mark the block you want to copy.

2. Position the cursor in the second window, where you want the copied text to be placed. (If you're using the mouse, you can position the cursor by clicking in the second window. If you're using the keyboard, open the File menu and press W to choose Switch.)

3. Open the Edit menu.

4. Choose the Copy command. The pop-up options list appears.

5. Choose Block from Other Window.

The block is then copied, and the copy is placed in the second window, as shown in figure 7.5.

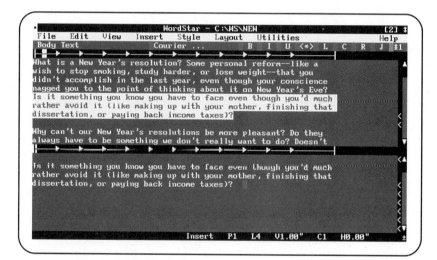

Fig. 7.5

The block copied to the second window.

Copying to Another Window—Fast

You can use the Ctrl-KA quick-key combination to copy a block from one window to another quickly.

Copying to the Windows Clipboard

If you run WordStar 7.0 from within Microsoft Windows (a graphical environment that enables you to open and run programs in different windows on the screen), you can use WordStar 7.0 to copy text to and from the Windows Clipboard. The Windows Clipboard is an unseen area of memory that stores text and pictures you copy and then enables you to paste them into other applications or other files.

Suppose, for example, that you are creating a report in WordStar, and you want to use a section of the WordStar text in a manual you're preparing using Aldus PageMaker (a desktop publishing program that runs under Windows). You can copy the section from your WordStar document and place it on the Windows Clipboard so that you can easily paste the text into the PageMaker document.

Not Working?

If you try the Windows copy procedure and it doesn't work the way it is supposed to, check the following:

■ Is Windows currently running in 386 mode?

■ Did you start WordStar from within Windows?

■ Does your computer have enough RAM to support both programs?

■ Have you installed WordStar to be recognized by Windows?

If the answer to any of these questions is no, consult your Windows documentation for information on how to set up the WordStar application program to run within your current version of Windows.

To copy the text to the Windows Clipboard, follow these steps:

1. Mark the text you want to copy.

2. Open the Edit menu.

3. Choose the Copy command.

4. When the pop-up options list appears, choose To Windows Clipboard.

WordStar then places the copy on the Windows Clipboard, ready to be used in other applications.

If you want to copy text *from* the Windows Clipboard, you perform basically the same procedures (choose Edit and then Copy), but when the pop-up options list appears, choose the From Windows Clipboard command instead. The text is then pasted into your document at the cursor position.

To and From Windows: A Shortcut

You can use the quick-key combinations to copy text to and from the Windows Clipboard. Mark the text block you want to copy and then press Ctrl-K] to copy the text *to* the Clipboard; press Ctrl-K[to copy *from* the Clipboard.

Copying to an Individual File

You also can copy a marked block of text to an individual file. You might want to copy to a separate file, for example, when you are saving a portion of a document to be incorporated into a different file. This procedure is known as saving the block to disk. To save the block to disk, follow these steps:

1. Mark the block you want to save.

2. Open the Edit menu.

3. Choose the Copy command.

4. When the pop-up options list appears, choose To Another File. The Copy to Another File dialog box appears, as shown in figure 7.6.

Filename text box ⟶

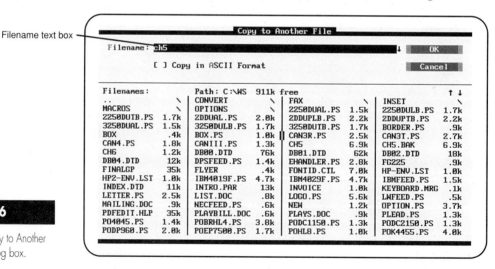

Fig. 7.6

The Copy to Another File dialog box.

5. In the Filename text box, type a file name for the file that will store the copied text.

6. If you want the text to be saved in ASCII format (a universal format that does not save formatting and style codes), click the Copy in ASCII Format check box or press A.

7. Click OK or press Enter.

WordStar saves the file under the file name you specified. You then can open and edit the file as you work with any other WordStar file.

Copying to Another File Quickly

You can copy a block to an individual file fast by marking the block, pressing Ctrl-KW, typing a name for the file, and pressing Enter. As soon as you press Ctrl-KW, the Copy to Another File dialog box appears.

Moving Text

Moving text doesn't provide you with quite as many options as the copy procedure provides. You may want to move a block of text, for example, when you reorganize a report and want to shift a block of text from one section to another. You don't want to use the copy procedure, however, because you don't need the text in two places in the same report. With the Move command, which is available in the Edit menu, you have two basic options:

■ To move the block within the same document

■ To move the block to another window

When moving text, remember to position the cursor *before* you choose the Move command. Otherwise, WordStar places the highlighted text wherever the cursor is located, which may be the point from which you are trying to move.

Moving Text Blocks

Moving text around in a document is not unusual: most people do a variety of moves and deletions before they are happy with the documents they've created. To move a block of text, follow these steps:

1. Mark the block you want to move.

2. Position the cursor at the point where you want the moved block to be placed.

3. Open the Edit menu.

4. Choose the Move command. A small pop-up list of options appears beside the menu (see fig. 7.7).

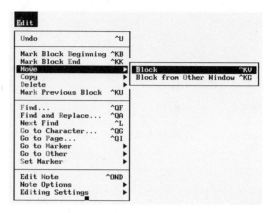

Fig. 7.7

Moving a block of text.

5. Choose Block.

WordStar then moves the marked block to the cursor position. If you're unhappy with the location of the moved block, you have to repeat the move procedure by opening the Edit menu and choosing Move and Block again. Undo (Ctrl-U) doesn't work in this instance.

Moving . . . Doubletime

You can bypass the menu selections and cut straight to the chase by moving your marked block with the Ctrl-KV key combination.

Moving between Windows

As you learned in the section about the copy procedure, WordStar enables you to open a second document by opening another window in the bottom half of the edit screen. In some instances, you may want to move text from the document in one window and place it in the document in the second window. Only a slight difference exists between this procedure and the more traditional move operation. First, you need to have both documents open on-screen. Then, follow these steps:

1. Mark the block you want to move.

2. Move the cursor to the document window in which you want the block to be placed. (If you're using the keyboard, open the File menu and choose Switch; if you're using the mouse, simply click in the second document window.)

3. Open the Edit menu.

4. Choose Move.

5. When the pop-up options list appears, choose Block from Other Window.

WordStar then moves the block from the first document window and places the block at the cursor position in the second document window.

Moving between Windows Quickly

The quick-key combination for moving text between document windows is Ctrl-KG. (Remember, however, to switch to the second document window and position the cursor *before* you press the key combination.)

Deleting Text

Deleting can be scary business. Any time you must remove words, lines, or sections, wiping the text from your computer screen has a sense of finality about it. Inevitably, however, you'll need to delete text, whether it's to streamline your document, shorten wordy sections, or remove text that is no longer current. Suppose that you have worked for hours on a project and now realize that you've exceeded your word limit. Something has to be cut somewhere. WordStar gives you several options for the way you delete text—and not all of them require that you mark the block first. With WordStar, you can delete the following units:

- A marked block of text

- A word

- A complete line

- The portion of the line to the left of the cursor

- The portion of the line to the right of the cursor

- All text up to a specified character

Although this section deals primarily with block deletions, (basic key-stroke deletions were presented earlier in this chapter), you learn all the step-by-step procedures for the following operations here:

- Deleting a text block

- Deleting unmarked text

Deleting a Text Block

The process for deleting a text block is simple—almost too simple. WordStar has a built-in safety net, however, so that if you accidentally press the delete quick key (Ctrl-KY), you can recover the almost-lost text by pressing Ctrl-U. Remember, however, that you can recover only the last item you deleted.

To delete a block of text, follow these steps:

1. Mark the block you want to delete.

2. Open the Edit menu.

3. Choose the Delete command. A pop-up list of options appears, as shown in figure 7.8.

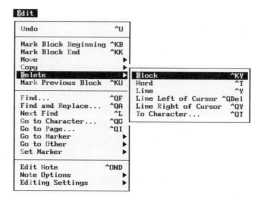

Fig. 7.8

The Delete pop-up list box.

4. Choose Block.

Wow—it's gone, just like that. Again, if you really meant to press Ctrl-KV or some other key combination and didn't actually want to delete any-thing, you may be in shock—but don't worry. You can recover the de-leted block by pressing Ctrl-U immediately after you accidentally delete the block.

> **What If You Really Mess Up a File?**
>
> Even in the worst case, all may not be lost. If you've previously
> saved your document—meaning, of course, that this file is not a
> new file—you can use the backup file WordStar creates automati-
> cally when you save a file. You need to rename the file by using the
> DOS RENAME command and change the BAK extension to some-
> thing else.

Deleting Unmarked Text

In the section on keyboard editing, you learned that you can delete some
sections of text—a word, a line, or parts of lines—without first highlighting the text you want to delete. You can press Ctrl-Y, for example, to
delete the entire line where the cursor is located without marking the
line first. In the Delete pop-up list, you'll find the menu selection you can
use rather than Ctrl-Y; however, the quick keys are much faster. You can
use Ctrl-T, for example, to delete a word rather than open the Edit menu,
choose Delete, and choose the Word option from the pop-up list. As you
can see, using Ctrl-T is much easier. Table 7.2 presents the Delete command options.

Table 7.2 Delete Command Options

Command Option	Quick Key	Description
Word	Ctrl-T	Deletes the word at the cursor position
Line	Ctrl-Y	Deletes the line at the cursor position
Line Left of Cursor	Ctrl-Q-Del	Deletes all text and spaces to the left of the cursor position in the current line
Line Right of Cursor	Ctrl-QY	Deletes all text and spaces to the right of the cursor position in the current line
To Character	Ctrl-QT	Deletes all characters between the cursor position and the character you specify

When you choose the To Character option of the Delete command, a small pop-up box appears asking you to enter the character to which you want to delete text (see fig. 7.9). Type the character in the text box; WordStar then deletes the text between the cursor position and the next occurrence of the letter you entered.

Fig. 7.9

Deleting text to a
specific character.

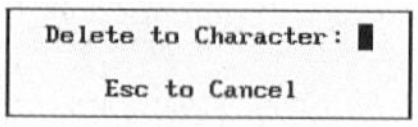

```
┌──────────────────────────┐
│ Delete to Character: █    │
│      Esc to Cancel        │
└──────────────────────────┘
```

Using Find and Replace

Find and replace is a fairly straightforward procedure: WordStar finds the text you specify and replaces it with something else that you specify. Suppose, for example, that you are preparing a report for an interdepartmental meeting. As you proofread the document, you notice that you misspelled your supervisor's name: *Hawthorne* instead of *Hawthorn*. You can use WordStar's find and replace feature to search for the misspelled name and replace it with the correctly spelled one.

With find and replace, you have the following options:

- To find—but not replace—the text you enter
- To find *and* replace the text you specify
- To search for whole words or individual characters and spaces
- To search the entire file (globally) or search for the next occurrence of the text you enter
- To search for both uppercase and lowercase matches
- To search forward or backward through the file
- To use wild-card characters in your searches

In the next sections, you learn about the two different commands in the Edit menu—Find and Find and Replace—that help you locate text in your document.

Finding Text

You start the find process by opening the Edit menu and choosing the Find command (see fig. 7.10). After you choose the command, the Find dialog box appears, as shown in figure 7.11.

As you can see, the Find dialog box presents several options. The cursor

Fig. 7.10

Choosing the Find
command.

Fig. 7.11

The Find dialog box.

is positioned in the Find text box, which is where you type the text
you're seeking. You can enter the text exactly as it appears in the document with the proper capitalization, or you can type just the characters
and have WordStar search for any characters—uppercase or lowercase—that match the characters in the Find box. Type the text you want
to find and press Tab. The cursor moves to the Options box.

In the Options box, you can type the letters that correspond to the
options you want to use. Table 7.3 lists the different options with the
letter you type in the Options box and provides a description of each
option. You don't have to type the letters in the Options box, however;
you can instead use the check boxes on the Find dialog box to choose
the options.

Table 7.3 Find Options

Option	Letter	Description
Next Occurrence	C	Finds only the next occurrence of the text you enter
Entire File/Global	G	Searches for every occurrence throughout the file
Whole Words	W	Finds the text you enter only when it appears as an entire word (for example, if you enter the word *at*, WordStar finds only the word *at*, not *that* or *attitude*).
Ignore Case	U	Ignores the case of the characters you enter and finds all occurrences of the letters (for example, if you enter *Whatever*, WordStar finds *whatever* or even *WhAtEvER*).
Backward	B	WordStar searches backward through the document from the cursor position
Use Wildcard ? Character	?	Finds any character in the place of ? (for example, if you enter *ba?*, WordStar finds *bad*, *bag*, or *bat*).

Whether you select an option by typing its highlighted letter in the Options line or clicking the option, WordStar gives you several choices for streamlining your text search. The two options beneath the Options line (in the Search section) enable you to decide whether you want to search the entire document for the text you entered (in the Find line) or search the document only to the next occurrence of the word. If you've misspelled the word *business* throughout the document, for example, you'll want to search for every occurrence so that you can make the correction. (Of course, you can also use the spelling checker.) On the other hand, if you have edited a document up to a particular point and typed your initials as a placemarker before closing the file, you need to search only for the next occurrence of the text in your Find operation.

These two search options are mutually exclusive, meaning that only one can be selected at a time. After you enter the text you want to find in the Find box, you can choose the Search option For Next Occurrence by clicking the button to the left of the option or by pressing C. Choose Entire File/Global by clicking its button or pressing G.

The Occurrence box enables you to enter the number of the occurrence you want to search for. Unlike the Search options, which enable you to search the entire file for all occurrences or simply search until the next occurrence is found, Occurrence enables you to specify exactly which occurrence you want to find. Simply type the number you want and press Tab. Suppose that you are looking for the third occurrence of the word *Smith*. In the Occurrence box, type *3*. When the search begins, WordStar skips the first two occurrences of the word *Smith* and positions the cursor on the third occurrence.

Selecting Find Options

You can choose the Find options in one of three ways:

- Type the character for the option in the Options box.

- Click the individual options you want.

- Press Tab to move from option to option and type the highlighted letter to choose the command.

On the right side of the Find dialog box, you see four additional Find options: Whole Words, Ignore Case (U), Backward, and Use ? Wildcard Character. These options control how WordStar looks for the search text. Whole Words matches exactly the text you enter in the Find box. If, for example, you enter the name *Sam* in the Find box but don't select Whole Words (so that the check box is left blank), WordStar finds not only *Sam* but also *sample* and *flotsam*. If you want WordStar to find only *Sam*, select Whole Words by clicking the check box or typing *W*.

When selected, Ignore Case enables you to search for all text with the characters you specified, no matter how they are capitalized. When Ignore Case is selected, WordStar finds *Sam, SaM, SAM, sAM, saM*, and so on. Select the option by clicking the Ignore Case check box or typing *U*.

As you may expect, selecting the Backward option begins the search from the current cursor position and searches backward to the beginning of the file. To select the option, click the check box or type *B*.

The final option on the Find dialog box is Use ? Wildcard Character. If you've used other programs or, more specifically, have had some DOS experience, wild cards aren't new to you. Put simply, a *wild-card character* is a character that WordStar reads as "any character." When you type *?am* in the Find box, for example, WordStar finds the following occurrences:

dam

ham

pam

ram

sam

When WordStar sees the ? character, the program looks for words that match the search text having *any character* in place of the ? but also having *am* as part of the word.

Finding—and Stopping—Fast

You can use the Ctrl-QF quick key to display the Find dialog box quickly. If you want to abandon the find operation during the search, press Ctrl-U. WordStar displays a message telling you that the search has been interrupted and asking you to click Continue or press Enter to return to the document.

Try using the Find procedure. Open the Edit menu and choose Find, if you haven't already done so. When the Find dialog box is displayed, follow these steps:

1. In the Find box, type *the*.

2. Press Tab. The cursor moves to the Options box.

3. You can type the letters of the options you want. Entering *UB*, for example, causes WordStar to search—backward through the document—for the characters you entered, regardless of their capitalization. If you prefer, you can choose these options by clicking their check boxes in the dialog box rather than entering the letters in the Options box. Press Tab. The cursor moves to the Search options.

4. Type the letter of the option you want or click the option. Press Tab. The cursor moves to the Occurrence box.

5. If necessary, type the number of the occurrence you want to find. Press Tab.

6. If you want to search for whole words only, type *W* or press the space bar. An X appears in the check box indicating that the option has been chosen. Press Tab. The cursor moves to Ignore Case.

7. If you want to search for the characters you've entered no matter what their capitalization, type *U* or press the space bar. Press Tab.

8. If you want to search backward through the file, type *B* or press the space bar.

9. If you want to use a wild-card character to make your search easier, type *?* or press the space bar. This character tells WordStar to read the question mark as a wild-card character and not as a regular question mark. (If you want to search for text the includes a question mark as a question mark—not as a wild-card character—make sure that this box is not selected.)

10. Click OK or press Enter to begin the search.

WordStar returns you to your document and places the cursor on the word or words you are trying to find.

Deselecting Options

What if you choose an option and then don't want to use it? You can deselect the options you've chosen by choosing them again: position the cursor in the option you want to turn off and press the space bar or type the option letter again. If you want to stop the find operation, you can press Esc to return to the document without searching.

Finding and Replacing Text

The find and replace procedure is similar to the find operation— except that you have another step to consider: in this case, you are replacing the found text with new text you enter. To start the find and replace operation, open the Edit menu and choose Find and Replace. The Find and Replace dialog box is displayed, as shown in figure 7.12.

You recognize many of the options in the Find and Replace dialog box: most are similar to those in the Find dialog box. In the Find text box, you type the text you're looking for (similar to the Find procedure). In the Replace text box, you enter the text you want WordStar to use in replacing the found text. If you want to search for the word *Sam* and replace it with *Samantha*, for example, type *Sam* in the Find text box and *Samantha* in the Replace text box.

The Find and Replace dialog box.

In the Options box, you again have the choice of typing the highlighted letters of the options you want or leaving the box blank and choosing the options manually. Several of the options should look familiar; with the three Search options you can search and replace only the next occurrence, the entire file, or the rest of the file from the cursor position on. The Replace Occurrences box enables you to replace only a specified number of occurrences (just type the number you want and press Tab).

In the Options on the right side of the Find and Replace dialog box, you see an entire column of choices. Some options—Whole Words, Ignore Case (U), Backward, and Use ? Wildcard Character—work the same as the ones you saw in the Find dialog box. The Align option, when selected, tells WordStar to realign your text after the replacement is made. The Don't Ask option searches and replaces all occurrences of the text in the Find box without asking you for confirmation. The Maintain Case option places the replacement text in the same capitalization as the Find text. To choose any of these options, click the check box to the left of the option or type the highlighted letter (A for Align, N for Don't Ask, or M for Maintain Case).

Table 7.4 summarizes the new options in the Find and Replace dialog box.

Table 7.4 Options Applying to Find and Replace Only

Option	Character	Description
Rest of File	R	Searches and replaces from the cursor position to the end of the file
Align	A	Realigns the text after the replacement
Don't Ask	N	Searches and replaces without confirmation from you
Maintain Case	M	Leaves all capitalization as is

To use find and replace, follow these steps:

1. Open the Edit menu and choose Find and Replace.

2. When the Find and Replace dialog box is displayed, type the text you want to find in the Find box. Press Tab.

3. In the Replace box, type the text you want WordStar to enter when it locates the text in the Find box. Press Tab.

4. In the Options box, type the characters for the options you want. (This step is optional; you can choose the options by clicking or by typing the letter of the option you want.) Press Tab.

5. In the Search options, click the option you want (For Next Occurrence, which replaces only the next occurrence of the text found; Entire File/Global, which replaces the text for the entire document; or Rest of File, which replaces the text from the cursor position to the end of the document). Press Tab.

6. In Replace Occurrences, type the number of times you want the Find text to be replaced. (This step also is optional: you can leave this option set to 0.) Press Tab.

7. Select the check boxes you want by clicking the box or by pressing Tab to move to the box and typing the highlighted character or pressing the space bar. Here's a review of the different options:

    Align reforms the paragraph after the replacement.

    Don't Ask searches and replaces without action from you.

    Whole Words finds exact word matches.

    Ignore Case finds the characters in uppercase or lowercase.

Maintain Case places the replaced text in same capitalization.

Use ? Wildcard Character enables you to use the question mark as a wild card.

8. When you're finished making your selections, press Enter or click OK.

WordStar then begins the find and replace operation. If you choose the Don't Ask option in the Find and Replace dialog box, WordStar speeds through your document and replaces all occurrences of the text you entered. If you do not choose the Don't Ask option, WordStar stops at each occurrence, and a prompt at the top of the screen asks you whether you want to replace the text. Type *Y* to replace the text or *N* to skip this occurrence and go on to the next one (see fig. 7.13).

The Replace prompt

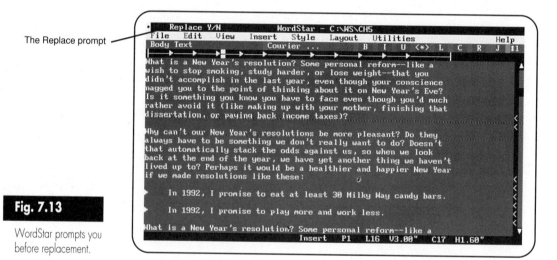

Fig. 7.13

WordStar prompts you before replacement.

When WordStar gets to the end of the document, you see a message telling you that the search is complete. Click the Continue button or press Enter to return to the document.

Stopping and Starting Searches

You can display the Find and Replace dialog box by pressing the quick key, Ctrl-QA. If, after you begin searching, you abandon the search by pressing Esc or Ctrl-U, you can restart the search by pressing Ctrl-L.

Using the Spelling Checker

The spelling checker is another kind of search operation that WordStar can perform. WordStar searches through your entire document looking for words that have the following errors:

- Misspellings
- Certain punctuation errors
- Unusual capitalization

The Spelling Checker is a program that evaluates each word in your document (or the words you specify) for accuracy by checking the words against an incredibly large dictionary, which was added to your hard disk automatically when you installed WordStar. WordStar searches through your text and alerts you whenever the program finds a word that does not match any word in WordStar's internal dictionary.

Although this dictionary is extremely large, it cannot include every word in the English language. As a result, if you are working on a document that uses words specific to your industry, WordStar interprets those words as misspellings, although they may be spelled correctly. (WordStar displays the words as misspelled words only because they are not in the internal dictionary.)

Knowing that each user would need to customize the dictionary to include often-used words, WordStar gives users the option of adding words to the dictionary. These additions, in effect, teach WordStar the new words, so you don't have to check them again and again as you spell check your documents. When you add words to the dictionary, you aren't actually changing WordStar's internal spelling dictionary; you are really creating your own dictionary. Each word you add to the dictionary is placed in the file PERSONAL.DCT, which is stored in the C:\WS directory. When you start the spelling checker, WordStar searches the document and checks the words against both the internal and the personal dictionaries.

You should know, however, that although WordStar can find the misspellings and typos in your document, it cannot uncover the following faux pas:

- Misused words (such as *form* for *from* or *their* for *there*)
- Incorrect grammar ("*There's problems in this sentence.*")
- Punctuation problems ("*I can't remember when to use commas, and semicolons.*")

Working with PERSONAL.DCT

After you've added a few words to your personal dictionary (you learn how in the next section), you may want to open the file and take a look at it. You open this file as you open any other file, but when the opening screen is displayed, press N to open a nondocument file. Then type *PERSONAL.DCT* and press Enter.

The PERSONAL.DCT looks like nothing more than a list of words, which is actually what it is. When WordStar encounters a word it doesn't recognize, the program looks in your PERSONAL.DCT file to see whether the word exists there. If the word is found, the spelling check continues. If the word is not found in the list, WordStar displays the Spell Check dialog box and waits for your response.

You can delete entries from PERSONAL.DCT or add your own, if you like. Remember to type each entry on its own line (press Enter at the end of the line). When you're finished adding or deleting entries, save the file as usual, by pressing Ctrl-KD.

In the Utilities menu are two commands that you can use to check the spelling of your document. The first command, Spelling Check Global, checks the entire document. The second command, Spelling Check Other, checks the rest of the document (from the cursor on), the spelling of an individual word, or spelling in notes that accompany your document.

Checking the Entire Document

To start the spelling checker, follow these steps:

1. Open the Utilities menu by pressing Alt-U or by clicking the menu name. The Utilities menu appears, as shown in figure 7.14.

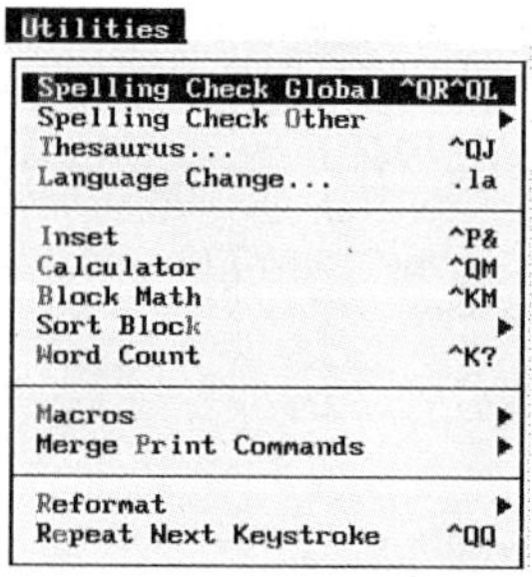

```
Utilities
Spelling Check Global  ^QR^QL
Spelling Check Other        ▶
Thesaurus...            ^QJ
Language Change...      .la

Inset                   ^P&
Calculator              ^QM
Block Math              ^KM
Sort Block                  ▶
Word Count              ^K?

Macros                      ▶
Merge Print Commands        ▶

Reformat                    ▶
Repeat Next Keystroke   ^QQ
```

Fig. 7.14

Choosing a spelling command.

2. Choose the Spelling Check Global command by pressing Enter. (This command is already highlighted.)

The spelling checker goes to work immediately. When the program finds a misspelled word, the Spelling Check dialog box appears (see fig. 7.15).

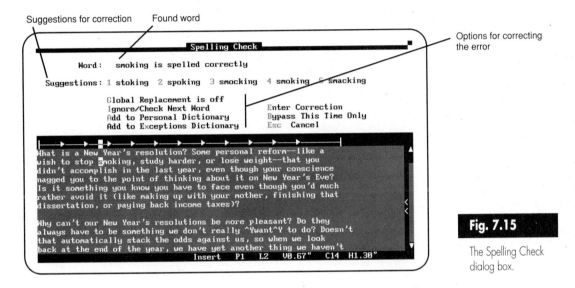

Suggestions for correction   Found word

Options for correcting the error

```
                    Spelling Check
       Word:   smoking is spelled correctly

  Suggestions: 1 stoking  2 spoking  3 smocking  4 smoking  5 Smacking

       Global Replacement is off
       Ignore/Check Next Word          Enter Correction
       Add to Personal Dictionary      Bypass This Time Only
       Add to Exceptions Dictionary    Esc  Cancel

What is a New Year's resolution? Some personal reform--like a
wish to stop Smoking, study harder, or lose weight--that you
didn't accomplish in the last year, even though your conscience
nagged you to the point of thinking about it on New Year's Eve?
Is it something you know you have to face even though you'd much
rather avoid it (like making up with your mother, finishing that
dissertation, or paying back income taxes)?

Why can't our New Year's resolutions be more pleasant? Do they
always have to be something we don't really ^Ywant^Y to do? Doesn't
that automatically stack the odds against us, so when we look
back at the end of the year, we have yet another thing we haven't
                Insert   P1   L2   V0.67"   C14  H1.30"
```

Fig. 7.15

The Spelling Check dialog box.

As you can see, you have several options for controlling the way WordStar corrects this word. Table 7.5 lists the options in the Spelling Check dialog box.

If the correct spelling of the word is shown in the Suggestions list, type the number of the correct word. WordStar automatically replaces the incorrect word with the correct one. If you want to skip the word, type *I;* if you want to add the word to your personal dictionary, type *A.* Additionally, you can press E to correct the spelling yourself. When you press E, the Spelling Correction dialog box appears (see fig. 7.16). You can type the correct spelling for the word and press Enter or click OK.

Table 7.5 Spelling Check Options

Option	Character	Description
Suggestions	Type the number of the suggestion you want	Provides correction suggestions
Global Replacement	G	Turns on global replacement: all occurrences of the misspelled word are corrected
Ignore/Check Next Word	I	Skips the word and goes to the next one
Add to Personal Dictionary	A	Adds the word to the personal dictionary. The word won't be found in a spelling check again
Enter Correction	E	Enables you to type the correct spelling of the word
Bypass This Time Only	B	Skips this occurrence of the word
Cancel	Esc	Cancels the spelling operation

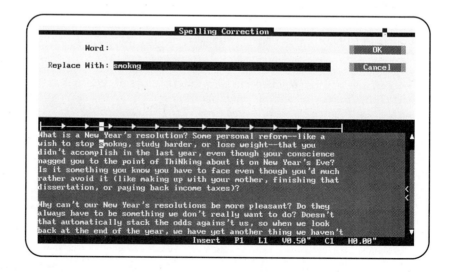

Fig. 7.16

The Spelling Correction dialog box.

As soon as you make the correction, WordStar continues the spelling check. When the search is complete, WordStar displays a screen telling you how many words were checked in your document and prompting you to click Continue (see fig. 7.17). You then are returned to the document.

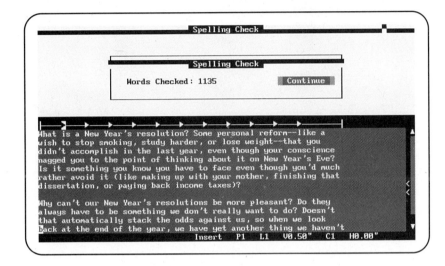

Fig. 7.17

The completed spelling check message.

Checking Partial Documents

If you want to check something other than the complete document, use the Spelling Check Other command in the Utilities menu. When you choose the command, a small pop-up options list appears (see fig. 7.18).

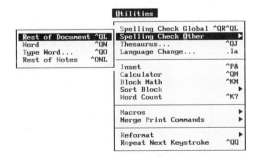

Fig. 7.18

The Spelling Check Other options.

You can then click the option you want or press the option's highlighted letter. Rather than use the menu selections to choose the options, however, you may want to save time by using the quick-key combinations.

For example, rather than open the Utilities menu, choose Spell Check Other, and choose Word, you can check the spelling of an individual word by placing the cursor on that word and pressing Ctrl-QN. Here are the quick-key combinations for the Spelling Check Other options:

If you want to do this	Press	Command
Check spelling from the cursor position forward	Ctrl-QL	Rest of Document
Check the spelling of the word at the cursor position	Ctrl-QN	Word
Check the spelling of a word you're about to enter	Ctrl-QO	Type Word
Check the spelling of notes in your document	Ctrl-ONL	Rest of Notes

If you choose Rest of Document (by pressing Ctrl-QL or by choosing the command from the Spelling Check Other options), WordStar begins the spelling check and displays the Spelling Check screen if a misspelled word is found. If you choose Word, WordStar checks the word at the cursor position. If you choose Type Word, WordStar displays a screen, asking you to type the word you want to check (see fig. 7.19). The final option, Rest of Notes, enables you to spell check any notes you've added to your document. (Chapter 10 explains how to add notes to your WordStar files.)

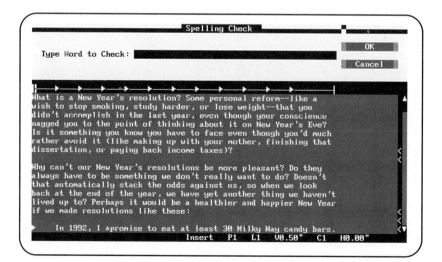

Fig. 7.19

Checking the spelling of a word you want to enter.

That's all there is to spell checking your document. Remember to save
your document after you correct the spelling, however; you don't want
to lose the work you and WordStar have done.

Using the Thesaurus

The last editing feature you learn about in this chapter helps you make
sure that you've used the right word in the right place in your document.
The thesaurus won't tell you when you've used *affect* for *effect* or confused *their* and *there*, but it helps you vary your word choice, enabling
you to make your documents more interesting and well-written.

The thesaurus is available to you in the Utilities menu. To start the thesaurus, position the cursor on the word you want to check and then
open the Utilities menu by pressing Alt-U or by clicking the menu name.
When you choose the Thesaurus command, the Thesaurus menu appears (see fig. 7.20).

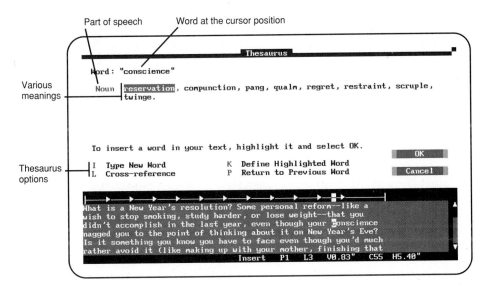

Fig. 7.20

The Thesaurus menu.

Finding Synonyms Quickly

You can access the thesaurus quickly by using the quick-key combination, Ctrl-QJ. This command displays the Thesaurus menu so
that you can examine your options and display definitions as
needed.

The word *stop* is being analyzed by the thesaurus in figure 7.21. As you can see, several alternatives for the word *stop* exist. WordStar lists the possible meanings and provides you with several different choices that could substitute for the word. Additionally, WordStar tells you what part of speech the word is (noun) and gives you options for continuing.

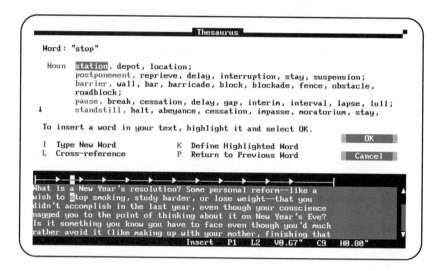

Fig. 7.21

The Thesaurus alternatives.

For some words, you may see only a few suggestions; for others, you see a screenful. For the word *stop*, you can see many alternative words. To see more words, you can click the down arrow in the left side of the dialog box. After clicking the down arrow several times, you see yet another category for *stop*: these are the verbs (see fig. 7.22). Notice, also, that now an up arrow appears at the top of the list; you can also scroll back up through the list to see earlier suggestions.

If you see a word you want to use, simply highlight it by using the arrow keys or by positioning the mouse cursor on the word and clicking the mouse button; then click OK or press Enter. WordStar substitutes the word you choose for the original word in the document.

At the bottom of the Thesaurus box, you see the following options:

- Type New Word
- Cross-reference
- Define Highlighted Word
- Return to Previous Word

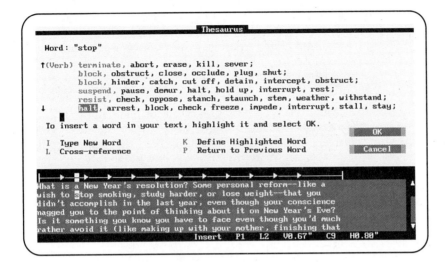

Fig. 7.22

More alternatives for the word *stop*.

You can choose Type New Word by pressing I or by clicking the option. When you choose this option, WordStar displays a dialog box in which you can enter a new word you want to look up in the thesaurus (see fig. 7.23). Type the word you want to see, and press Enter or click OK. WordStar instantly displays the thesaurus entry for the word you entered.

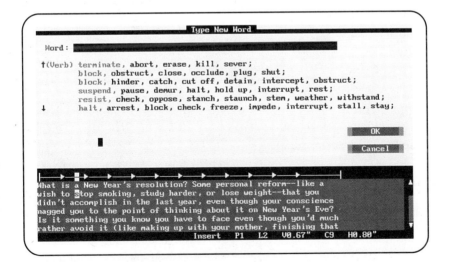

Fig. 7.23

Typing a new word for the thesaurus.

When you choose Cross-reference by pressing L or by clicking the option, WordStar displays a screen of synonyms for the word highlighted on the Thesaurus screen. If, for example, when you were scrolling through the synonym list for the word *stop*, you positioned the cursor on the word *depot*, when you press L, WordStar displays synonyms for the word *depot*.

Choose Define Highlighted Word (by pressing K or clicking the option) when you want to see the definition of the word currently highlighted on the Thesaurus screen. Figure 7.24 shows the screen that appears when you position the cursor on the word *constrain* and press K.

The defined word

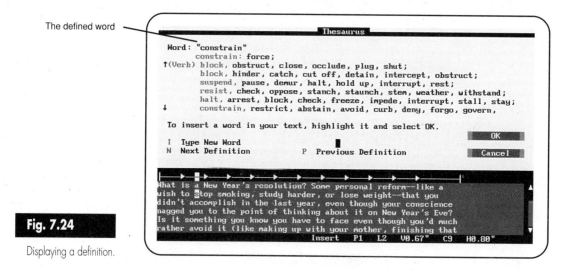

Fig. 7.24

Displaying a definition.

The options at the bottom of the screen change to show that you are now exploring word definitions. Instead of Cross-reference, you see Next Definition, which displays alternative definitions of the selected word. In place of Return to Previous Word, you see Previous Definition. To return to the Thesaurus options, click Cancel or press Esc.

You can choose the final option on the Thesaurus screen, Return to Previous Word, by pressing P or clicking the option. You can use this option, for example, when you have examined the synonyms for one word and then gone on to another. You can return to the first word by pressing P on the Thesaurus screen.

When you've made your selections, click OK or press Enter to return to the document. Remember, again, to save any changes you have made to your document by pressing Ctrl-KS.

Chapter Summary

In this chapter, you have covered a great deal of ground. From a discussion of simple editing keys to more involved procedures on various block operations—such as copying, moving, and deleting text blocks—this chapter has introduced the collection of editing techniques you use to create and revise your WordStar documents. In this chapter, you also learned about using the spelling checker and thesaurus to streamline the accuracy of your documents. The next chapter explains how you can enhance your text by working with fonts, text styles, alignment, and spacing.

Enhancing Text Styles

In the last chapter, you learned to edit the text in your WordStar document. This chapter concentrates on changing the way your document looks by showing you how to change fonts, styles, and formats. Specifically, in this chapter, you learn about the following:

- Understanding WordStar's paragraph styles

- Applying paragraph styles

- Creating new paragraph styles

- Understanding font basics

- Changing fonts in your documents

- Boldfacing text

- Italicizing text

- Underlining text

- Changing text alignment

- Adjusting line spacing

Before you get started, make sure that you have a document open on the screen. This chapter uses the sample article you started in Chapter 6, but you may want to use a document of your own. To open the document, press D when the opening screen is displayed. When the Open Document dialog box appears, type the name of the document you want to open, and click OK or press Enter. Your document is then displayed in the edit screen.

Applying Paragraph Styles

In Chapter 5, you learned a little about paragraph styles. As you know, a paragraph style is a group of settings that you can apply automatically to the paragraphs in your document. In this section, you learn how to use the paragraph styles that are included with WordStar 7.0. You also find out how to create your own paragraph styles; modify existing paragraph styles; and copy, rename, and delete paragraph styles.

Introducing Paragraph Styles

When your document is displayed in the edit screen, the current paragraph style is shown in the paragraph style box, in the far left side on the style bar (see fig. 8.1). Whether you have applied this style to your document or not, the currently selected style is displayed.

Current paragraph style ───

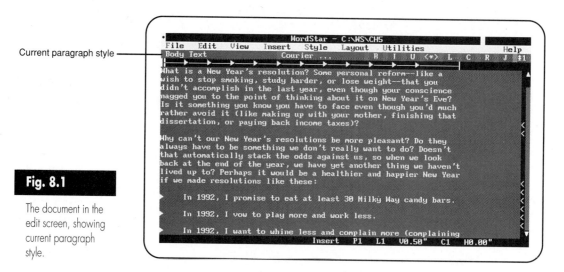

Fig. 8.1

The document in the edit screen, showing current paragraph style.

When you add a paragraph style to your document, WordStar inserts a paragraph style tag at the cursor position. If you select the default style, Body Text, the tag inserted at the cursor location is <Body Text>. This style is applied to your text from that point on—not just for the current paragraph—until WordStar encounters another paragraph style tag.

WordStar 7.0 comes with nine different paragraph styles you can use in your own documents:

- Body Text
- Hanging Indent 1
- Hanging Indent 2
- Hanging Indent 3
- Paragraph Indent
- Heading
- Quotation
- Manuscript
- Title

You can control a number of text settings by setting up a single paragraph style that specifies the text, font, tabs, margins, and alignment. You can also assign those settings manually.

You may want to use paragraph styles, for example, when you are creating a document that uses a variety of formats. Suppose that you are creating a business report which includes many block-style paragraphs, indented lists, numbered steps, pictures, two-column formats, and different heading styles. Rather than selecting the settings for one paragraph, then selecting settings for the headline, then the steps, and so on, you can create paragraph styles to apply to the different items in your document.

Figure 8.2 shows the items you can control by using an existing paragraph style or by creating one of your own. When you first display the Define Paragraph Style dialog box, WordStar displays the list of available paragraph styles at the bottom of the screen. As you move the cursor to the different options in the box, the list of options at the bottom changes to show your choices for the current option. When you move the cursor to the Font option, for example, the area at the bottom of the box displays the choices of fonts available for your printer.

As you can see, you can include in a paragraph style almost every setting you need—except the text, of course. The following list explains the various items you can set in a paragraph style:

- *Style name.* You can assign to a new style any name of up to 24 characters in any combination of capital letters, characters, and spaces.

Margin settings   Line spacing

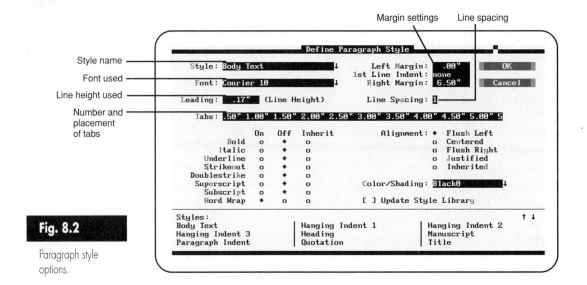

Style name ——

Font used ——

Line height used ——

Number and
placement
of tabs ——

Fig. 8.2

Paragraph style
options.

- *Font.* You can choose any font that is supported by your printer. You can tell which fonts are available to you by moving the cursor to the Font option in the Define Paragraph Style box and pressing Enter.

- *Leading.* You can control the amount of space used between lines in your paragraph.

- *Tabs.* You can set and move tabs. (The default paragraph style sets tabs at every half inch.)

- *Text styles.* You can choose from boldface, italic, underline, strikeout, doublestrike, superscript, or subscript.

- *Word wrap.* You can turn automatic word wrap on or off.

- *Margins.* You can set the left and right margins and specify a first-line indent for paragraphs.

- *Line spacing.* You can specify the number of blank lines inserted between lines (from 1 to 9).

- *Alignment.* You can choose left, centered, right, or justified alignment.

- *Color/Shading.* You can choose the color for the text in that particular style. (You can print in color only if you have a color printer, of course.) If you have a printer that supports shading, you can use this option to print in shades of gray.

As mentioned previously, WordStar 7.0 comes to you with nine preset paragraph styles, which you can use as they are or modify to suit your needs. If you work with indented lists of text (often used for bulleted items or numbered steps), for example, you should find the Hanging Indent styles helpful. Eachparagraph style provides a different margin variation for indented text. You may want to use the Body Text, Manuscript, and Paragraph Indent styles as they are for business documents; the Quotation style indents text a half-inch from the left and right margins of the page. The Title and Heading paragraph styles include settings for headlines and document titles. Table 8.1 gives you an overview of these styles.

Table 8.1 WordStar 7.0 Paragraph Styles

Paragraph Style	Item	Description
Body Text	Font	Courier 10
	Leading	.17
	Tabs	Every .5-inch
	Style	Normal
	Margins	Left: 0
		First line: none
		Right: 6.5
	Spacing	1
	Alignment	Left
	Color	Black
Hanging Indent 3	Font	Courier 10
	Leading	.17
	Tabs	Every .5-inch
	Style	Normal
	Margins	Left: 1.50
		First line: 1.00
		Right: 6.50
	Spacing	1
	Alignment	Left
	Color	Black
Paragraph Indent	Font	Courier 10
	Leading	.17
	Tabs	Every .5-inch
	Style	Normal
	Margins	Left: 0
		First line: .50
		Right: 6.5
	Spacing	1
	Alignment	Left
	Color	Black

continues

Table 8.1 Continued

Paragraph Style	Item	Description
Hanging Indent 1	Font	Courier 10
	Leading	.17
	Tabs	Every .5-inch
	Style	Normal
	Margins	Left: .50
		First line: none
		Right: 6.5
	Spacing	1
	Alignment	Left
	Color	Black
Heading	Font	Courier 10
	Leading	.17
	Tabs	Every .5-inch
	Style	Bold, underline
	Margins	Left: 0
		First line: none
		Right: 6.5
	Spacing	1
	Alignment	Left
	Color	Black
Quotation	Font	Courier 10
	Leading	.17
	Tabs	Every .5-inch
	Style	Normal
	Margins	Left: .50
		First line: none
		Right: 6.0
	Spacing	1
	Alignment	Justified
	Color	Black
Hanging Indent 2	Font	Courier 10
	Leading	.17
	Tabs	Every .5-inch
	Style	Normal
	Margins	Left: 1.00
		First line: .50
		Right: 6.5
	Spacing	1
	Alignment	Left
	Color	Black

Paragraph Style	Item	Description
Manuscript	Font	Courier 10
	Leading	.17
	Tabs	Every .5-inch
	Style	Normal
	Margins	Left: 0
		First line: .50
		Right: 6.5
	Spacing	2
	Alignment	Left
	Color	Black
Title	Font	Courier 10
	Leading	.17
	Tabs	Every .5-inch
	Style	Bold
	Margins	Left: 0
		First line: none
		Right: 6.5
	Spacing	1
	Alignment	Centered
	Color	Black

Applying Paragraph Styles

Now that you know what you've got to work with, how do you apply
the styles to the paragraphs in your document? When you select
a paragraph style, WordStar inserts a paragraph style tag (such as
<Body Text> for the Body Text paragraph style) at the cursor position.
Selecting a paragraph style is simple. First, if you've been exploring, return to the edit screen that shows the document you plan to work with.
Then, follow these steps to apply a paragraph style:

1. Move the cursor to the point in the document where you want the
   paragraph style to take effect.

2. Display the Select Paragraph Style box. You can display the box
   two ways, depending on whether you're using the keyboard or the
   mouse.

   If you're using the mouse, move the cursor to the paragraph style
   box in the style bar and click the mouse button. The Select Paragraph Style box appears (see fig. 8.3). The default paragraph
   styles—plus any styles you create—appear in the columns along
   the bottom edge of the dialog box.

If you're using the keyboard, press Alt-S to open the Style menu; then choose the Select Paragraph Style command. (If you prefer, you can bypass the menu selections by pressing Ctrl-OFS.) The Select Paragraph Style box appears.

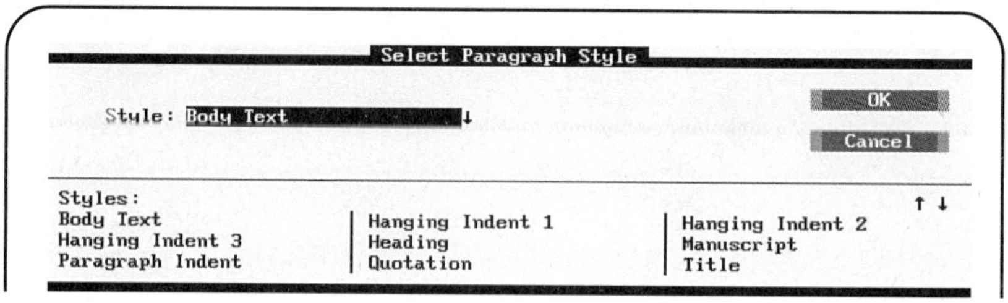

Fig. 8.3

The Select Paragraph Style box.

3. When the Select Paragraph Style box appears, you can choose the style several ways:

> You can type the name of the style you want in the Style box.

> You can use the mouse to click the style you want.

> You can press the down-arrow key to move the highlight to the style you want.

4. When you've selected the style (in this case, choose the Hanging Indent 1 style), click OK or press Enter.

WordStar then returns you to the document. As you can see, the paragraph style is already in place, and the text has been reformatted according to the specifications for that paragraph style. (Remember that the paragraph style remains in effect until WordStar encounters another paragraph style tag or the end of the file.) Figure 8.4 shows the document after the Hanging Indent 1 paragraph style has been applied to the second paragraph.

I Don't Like That Style . . .

If after you apply a paragraph style, you decide that you don't like it, simply position the cursor on the character immediately following the style tag and press the Backspace key. WordStar deletes the style and reformats the paragraph. If another paragraph style tag precedes the tag you delete, the text takes on that style. If no paragraph style tag precedes the deletion, text is given "no style."

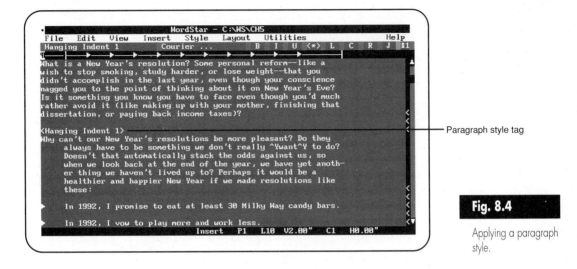

Paragraph style tag

Fig. 8.4

Applying a paragraph style.

Creating Your Own Paragraph Styles

Chances are, you want to create your own paragraph styles for use in your WordStar documents. Depending on the nature of your document, you may want to create styles that perform the following functions:

- Set the type style and alignment for headlines
- Center titles
- Add italic bylines
- Set the style and alignment for pull-quotes (short quotations taken from the body of your article, usually highlighted and centered in a text column)
- Control irregular spacing (such as using single-spaced excerpts in a double-spaced document)
- Create bulleted lists
- Make table generation easier

Any time you find yourself selecting the same settings over and over for paragraphs in your document, consider creating a paragraph style to help automate the process. You can create a paragraph style from scratch, or you can modify one of WordStar's existing paragraph styles.

To create a paragraph style, first position the cursor at the point where you want the new paragraph style to take effect. Then follow these steps:

1. Open the Style menu by pressing Alt-S or clicking the menu name.

2. Choose the Define Paragraph Style command by pressing D or by clicking the command name (see fig. 8.5). You can also use the Ctrl-OFD key combination to bypass the menu selections.

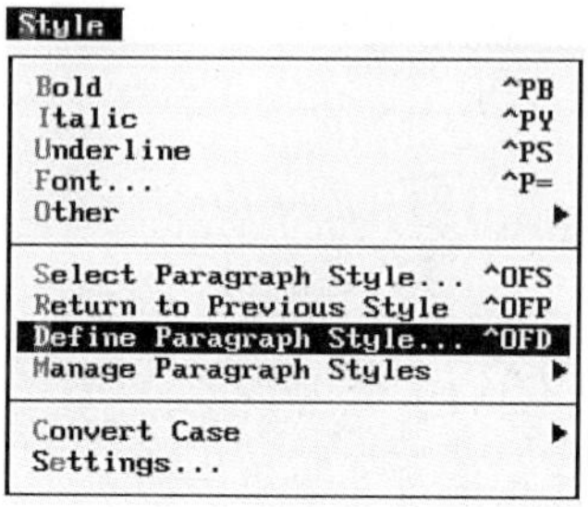

Fig. 8.5

Selecting the Define Paragraph Style command.

The Define Paragraph Style dialog box appears (see fig. 8.6). You use the options in this box to choose the settings for the paragraph style you create.

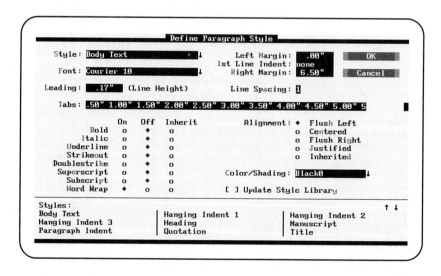

Fig. 8.6

The Define Paragraph Style dialog box.

3. Type a name for the style in the Style box. (In this case, type the name *Introduction*.)

4. Press Tab. The cursor moves to the Font box.

   As you can see, the font selections for your printer are shown at the bottom of the screen (see fig. 8.7).

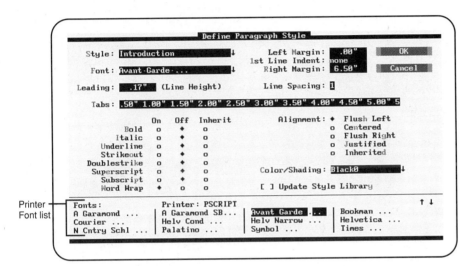

Printer
Font list

Fig. 8.7

Selecting a font.

5. Choose the font by clicking the font name or by typing the font name in the Font box. Press Tab.

Can't Find a Font?

If you do not see the fonts for your printer listed in the Define Paragraph Style dialog box, press Esc. Press Ctrl-P? to go to the Printer Selection menu. Highlight the name of your printer and press Return. Now go back to define paragraph styles (press Ctrl-OFD). You should see the font selection appropriate for your printer in the Font section.

Another line appears below the Font box, this one asking for the point size of the text you want to enter.

6. Type the size of the font (type *12* for this exercise) and press Tab.

   The cursor is positioned in the Leading box. (*Leading* is the term for the amount of space between lines.)

7. You can change this setting, if necessary, or leave the default value as it is. (Keep the default value for this example.) Press Tab. The cursor moves to the Tabs line.

8. You can change the tabs as necessary by deleting individual tab settings on the line and typing the ones you want. For this example, leave the tab settings alone. (You learn more about setting tabs later in this chapter.) Press Tab. The cursor moves to the Left Margin text box.

9. Type the setting you want for the left margin. (Leave this setting at 0 for the example.) Press Tab.

10. At 1st Line Indent, type the amount of space you want the first line of the paragraph indented from the left margin. (Again, for this example, leave the default setting.) Press Tab.

11. Type the measurement for the Right Margin. (Leave this option set to 6.50, if you're following the example.) Press Tab.

12. In the Line Spacing box, you can type the number of lines you want between text lines in the paragraph (for this example, *1* is sufficient). Press Tab. The cursor moves to the text style columns.

    For each text style, you have three choices: On, Off, or Inherit. On turns on the setting, Off turns off the setting, and Inherit applies the current document style to the style you're creating. When a text style option is selected, the dot turns to a diamond.

13. Choose the settings you want by pressing Tab or by typing the style's highlighted character to move to the style you want; then press the up- or down-arrow key to move the diamond among the choices. Figure 8.8 shows that the Italic text style has been chosen for the Introduction paragraph style.

Accidents Happen

If you accidentally press Tab and the diamond moves to the next selection, you can move backward through the selections by pressing Shift-Tab.

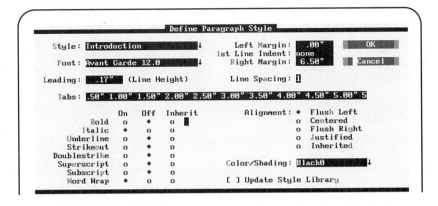

Fig. 8.8

Choosing a text style.

14. After you're finished entering style settings, press Tab. The cursor moves to the Alignment options.

15. Use the up-arrow and the down-arrow keys to move the diamond to the alignment you want (choose Centered). You can also type the highlighted letter of the option to select it. Press Tab.

16. When the cursor is in the Color/Shading box, you can select a color from the list displayed at the bottom of the screen. This choice affects your document only if you have a color printer; otherwise, WordStar ignores the setting. Press Tab.

17. If you want to update WordStar's style library, which makes all styles available to all documents, press the space bar. An X appears in the box, indicating that this new paragraph style will be available in all new documents you create.

18. When you've entered all your settings, click OK or press Enter.

WordStar returns you to your document. Now you need to select the paragraph style you just created and apply it to your text. Position the cursor where you want the paragraph style to be applied, and click the paragraph style box. (If you're using the keyboard, press Alt-SD.) After the Select Paragraph Style box appears, select the style you just created by double-clicking its name or by using the arrow keys to highlight the style name and pressing Enter. The new paragraph style is then applied to the current paragraph (see fig. 8.9).

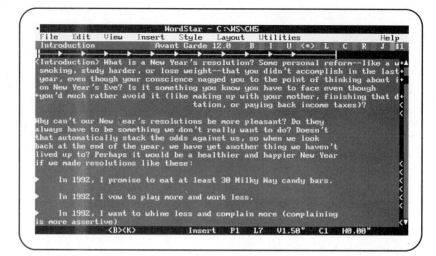

Fig. 8.9

The new style applied to the current paragraph.

Is This Right?

Depending on the options you selected in the Define Paragraph Styles dialog box, you may be surprised at what you see on-screen. Sure, you chose italic, but where is it? You also selected a different text size, but the text on the screen still looks the same. WordStar, although it enables you to see the text and the tags that control the format of the text on-screen, is not a true WYSIWYG (what-you-see-is-what-you-get) program. In order to see the different font changes, sizes, and styles, you need to use the Preview command from the View menu. Chapter 9 explains more about Preview.

Remember that when WordStar finds a paragraph style tag in your document, the program continues to use that style for the remainder of the document, until you enter a different paragraph style tag. For example, if you apply the Introduction paragraph style, created in the last section, and place the style code at the beginning of the document, the entire document is formatted in that style. If you want to change the paragraph style in the second paragraph, you must enter another paragraph style at that point, to turn off the Introduction paragraph style and begin the new paragraph style. Figure 8.10 shows that the document has been returned to the Body Text style after the first paragraph.

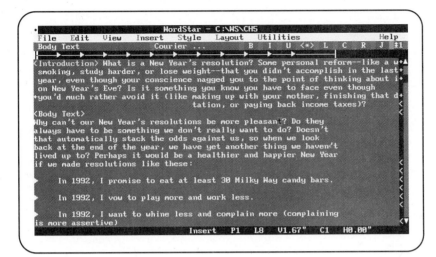

Fig 8.10

Adding a paragraph
style tag.

Now that you know the basics of creating and using paragraph styles, you need to know how to set font, style, and alignment options separately. The following sections explain those procedures.

Changing Fonts

Throughout this chapter, the term *font* is thrown around rather loosely. What is a font? Or a text style? Sans serif? Downloadable fonts? Before you learn how to change the font used in your WordStar document, you need some basic font information. The following list defines terms related to choosing the font, size, and style for your document.

- *Typeface (family)*. A family of type, including all point sizes and styles. For example, Times Roman and Avant Garde are typefaces.

- *Font*. One size and style in a particular typeface. For example, Helvetica 12-point Bold type is one font.

- *Type style*. The style applied to the font, such as boldface, italic, or underline.

- *Point size*. The size of the characters in points, a measurement used often in typography. (One point is equal to 1/72 of an inch.)

- *Sans serif*. A kind of type that does not have the small cross lines at the ends of the characters. The following line shows an example of a sans serif typeface:

    This is sans serif type.

■ *Serif.* A kind of type that does include the small cross lines at the ends of the characters. The following line shows what serifs look like:

This is serif type.

■ *Proportional type.* With proportional type, each character is given just the amount of space needed. For example, the letter *l* gets less space than the letter *w*. The characters are given space proportional to their widths. (The text of this book uses proportional type.)

■ *Nonproportional type.* With nonproportional type, each character is assigned the same amount of space. (This type also is known as monospaced type.) The letter *l* is given the same amount of space as the letter *w* (as in well).

■ *Downloadable fonts.* Downloadable fonts are fonts that are stored in your computer's memory—like any other kind of software—and then sent to your printer at print time.

■ *Internal fonts.* Internal fonts are fonts that your printer stores permanently in its memory. Some printers, such as dot-matrix printers, may have only 1 or 2 internal fonts; and others, like PostScript laser printers, may have 36 or more internal fonts.

■ *Cartridge fonts.*Some printers have plug-in cartridges that store information for individual fonts. When you want to print with a certain font, you plug in the cartridge, and the printer uses the extra memory and reads the font information before printing your file.

■ *Soft fonts.* Soft fonts are software fonts that your computer stores on disk. You use the PRCHANGE program to install the soft fonts with your version of WordStar; you must download the fonts at print time so that they are available to your printer.

Before you can make any changes to the font selected for your document, you need to see what's available. First, place the cursor at the point in your document where you want the new font to go into effect. Then, to display the fonts available with your version of WordStar and your printer, you have three options:

■ You can move the mouse to the font box and click the mouse button.

■ You can open the Style menu and choose the Font command.

■ You can press Ctrl-P= (equal).

When you perform any one of these actions, the Font dialog box appears, as shown in figure 8.11. The fonts you see displayed in the lower portion of the box may be different, depending on the type of printer you are using. The printer installed in this example is a PostScript laser printer, so if you are using a dot- matrix printer or a different type of laser printer, your fonts will be different.

Current font   Installed PRD (printer driver)

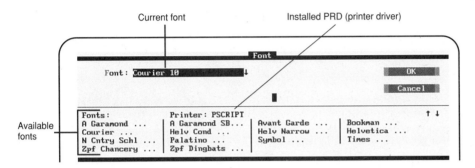

Available fonts

Fig. 8.11

The Font dialog box.

Can't Find Your Printer?

If the only font that you see listed here says Default, your document is not finding your printer. To tell your document where to find your printer, press Esc. Press Ctrl-P? to go to the Printer Selection menu. Highlight your printer name and press Enter. Now return to the font selection menu to see the fonts for your printer.

The Font dialog box shows you several things. First, you can see the currently selected font, displayed in the Font box. (In this case, the default font is Courier 10.) Below the dividing line, you see the list of fonts (which may be different depending on your printer) and the printer driver (in this case PSCRIPT) that you set up during installation.

You can select the new font by one of several ways:

- You can double-click the name of the font you want.

- You can press the arrow keys to highlight the font you want; then press Enter.

- You can type the name of the font in the Font text box and press Enter.

If you have chosen a scalable font (one with . . . after it), something curious happens. Another line appears below the Font text box, this one asking for the point size of the font you're selecting (see fig. 8.12).

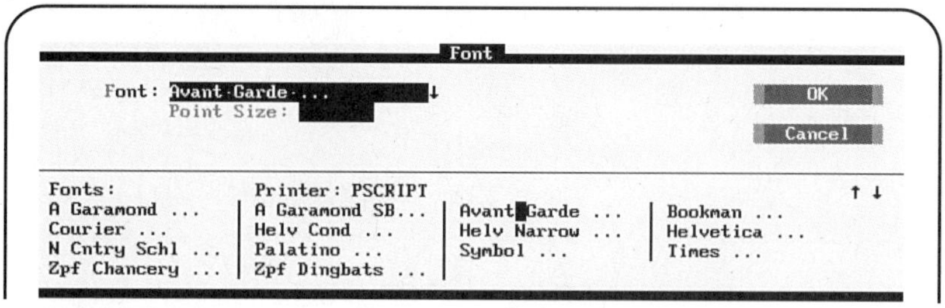

Fig. 8.12

Entering a point size.

Generally, if you're selecting a body text font, you want to use 10- or 12-point type. For headlines, you may want to use from 14- to 24-point type. For banners or titles, large type—from 36 to 72 points—is often used. If your printer supports scalable fonts, you can, of course, enter any point size you want for your individual document. Remember, however, that type which is either too small or too large makes reading difficult.

After you enter the point size, click OK or press Enter. You return to the document, and you see the font tag at the cursor position (see fig. 8.13). WordStar "sees" that font tag as the beginning point for the new font; everything after the tag is printed in that font, unless you change the font again later.

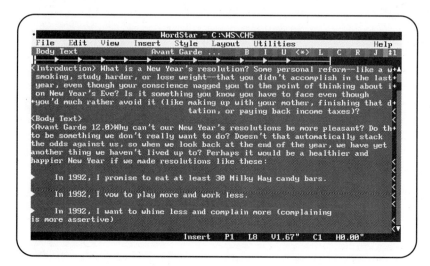

Fig. 8.13

A document containing a font tag.

That's all there is to changing the font for your document. If you change your mind and want to delete the font you've inserted, you simply position the cursor after the tag and press the Backspace key. WordStar removes the tag.

Cluttered Work Area?

Once you start adding paragraph style tags and font tags and such items to your document, it may begin looking a little cluttered. You have the option of turning off the display of all those tags. To turn off tags, press Ctrl-OD. When and if you want to turn the tags back on, simply press Ctrl-OD a second time. Or, if you prefer, you can use the mouse to turn the tag display on and off. Just move the mouse to the flag symbol (<*>) in the style bar at the top of the work area and click the mouse button. The tags disappear. To return the tags, click the symbol again.

Changing Text Style

As you have learned, the text style reflects the purpose of the words in your document. You can say something quietly with normal type. You can make an emphatic statement with boldfaced type. You can stress the importance of your point with italic type. In this section, you learn to use different type styles in your document.

No matter which method you use to change the text style in your document (and you find out how in this section), you need to enter one code to turn on the style and another code to turn off the style. For example, if you position the cursor at the beginning of the document and insert a boldface code at that point, WordStar puts the rest of your document in boldface, unless you place another boldface code somewhere in the document. That second boldface code turns off the boldface style and returns you to normal text.

You can add the style code in one of three ways:

- You can open the Style menu and choose the style.

- You can click the style button in the style bar (B for boldface, I for italic, or U for underline).

- You can press Ctrl-PY (for italic), Ctrl-PB (for boldface), or Ctrl-PS (for underline).

WordStar places the appropriate code into your document at the cursor position. If you click B (for boldface), for example, WordStar enters the code ^B into your text at the cursor position. Likewise, if you click I (or choose Italic from the Style menu), Word Star enters ^Y into you text. With U (or Ctrl-PS for underline), WordStar inserts ^S.

To turn off a style, use one of the following methods:

- Open the Style menu and choose the style that is currently in effect.
- Click the style button for the style in effect.
- Press Ctrl-PY (for italic), Ctrl-PB (for boldface), or Ctrl-PS (for underline).

The highlighting is then stopped with the end code.

To add a type style to your document, follow these steps:

1. Place the cursor at the point where you want to turn on the style.

2. Choose the style you want to begin.

   Figure 8.14 shows that an opening italic code has been entered just before the word *want*. As you can see, the rest of the text in the document appears in a different intensity, telling you that WordStar has placed the rest of the document in italic—at least until you enter the ending italic code.

Begin italic code

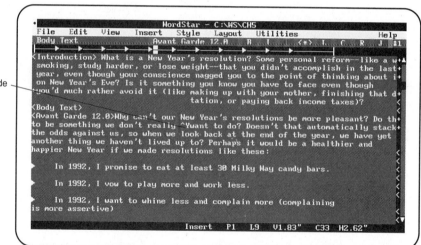

Fig. 8.14

Changing the text style.

3. Move the cursor to the point where you want to end the style.

4. Turn off the style by one of the methods described in the paragraph before these steps.

Figure 8.15 shows the document in which the beginning and ending italic codes have been entered.

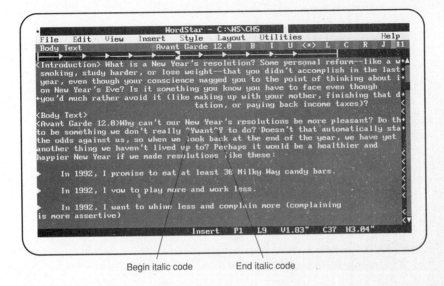

Begin italic code · · · End italic code

Fig. 8.15

The entered style codes.

That's Not What I Wanted . . .

If, after you enter the style tags, you decide that you really don't want to change the style of the text after all, you can delete a tag easily by positioning the cursor after the tag and pressing the Back-space key. Remember to delete both tags, however; if you delete only one, WordStar places the remainder of your document in that style.

Controlling Text Alignment

Earlier in this chapter, when you were exploring paragraph styles, you learned about your alignment options. WordStar enables you to align your text in the following ways:

- *Left aligned.* The text is lined up along the left margin but ragged on the right margin.

- *Right aligned.* The text is lined up along the right margin but ragged along the left.

- *Centered.* The text is centered between the right and left margins.

- *Justified.* The text is lined up along both the left and right margins.

Table 8.2 gives you a better idea of your alignment options.

Table 8.2 Alignment Options

Alignment	Style Button
Left	L

This paragraph is left-aligned text. Notice that the text aligns along the left margin but not along the right.

Center	C

This paragraph is centered text. The text is centered between the right and left margins.

Right	R

This paragraph is right-aligned text. Notice that the text aligns along the right edge but not along the left.

Justified	J

This is an example of justified text. Notice that WordStar inserts spaces between words to align the text along both the right and left margins.

WordStar looks at alignment settings as an on/off proposition: you need to enter a beginning alignment code and an ending alignment code if you want to turn off the alignment.

To change the alignment of a paragraph in your document, position the cursor at the point where you want to change the alignment. You then have several options:

- You can move the mouse cursor up to the style bar and click the alignment button you want (L for left, C for center, R for right, or J for justified).

- You can click the line spacing button (at the far right of the style bar) to display the alignment options in the Alignment and Spacing dialog box; you can then click the option or press the highlighted letter of the option you want (see fig. 8.16).

- You can open the Layout menu and choose the Alignment and Spacing command; then make your selection from the Alignment and Spacing dialog box.

- You can press Ctrl-OS to display the Alignment and Spacing dialog box; then select your choice.

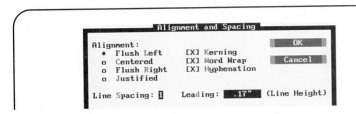

Fig 8.16

The Alignment and
Spacing dialog box.

After you choose the alignment you want, WordStar returns you to the
document and places a code in your text at the beginning of the paragraph containing the cursor. (Chapter 10 discusses the other options in
the Alignment and Spacing dialog box.) This code looks different from
the font and style tags—this code is preceded by a period and is placed
on the line before the paragraph you are currently working on, instead of
at the cursor position. This command is known as a *dot command*—a
command on a line beginning with a period—and tells WordStar to use
the alignment mode you've selected. Figure 8.17 shows another page of
the sample document, after right alignment has been selected.

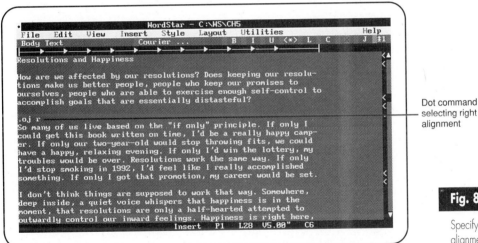

Dot command
selecting right
alignment

Fig. 8.17

Specifying a different
alignment.

As you can see, the command (or tag) has been added, but nothing else
happened. If you want to see the effect of the right alignment, position
the cursor at the beginning of the paragraph, and then press Ctrl-B to
reformat the paragraph. WordStar then reforms the paragraph in the
new right-aligned format (see fig. 8.18).

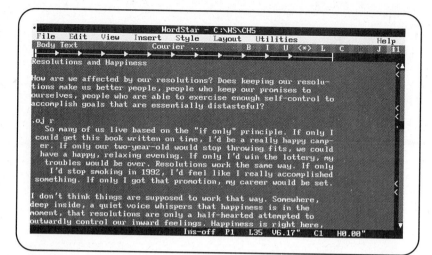

Fig. 8.18

The reformatted
paragraph.

Wrong Alignment?

If you don't like what you see and want to delete the alignment
code, simply position the cursor after the dot command and press
the Backspace key to delete the characters in the command. After
you delete the command, press Ctrl-B to reformat the paragraph.

WordStar also gives you the option of formatting a single line in your
document. You can center or right-align a single line in your document.

To center a single line, follow these steps:

1. Position the cursor on the line you want to center.

2. Press Alt-L to open the Layout menu or click the menu name. The
    Layout menu appears (see fig. 8.19).

3. Highlight the Center Line command or press C.

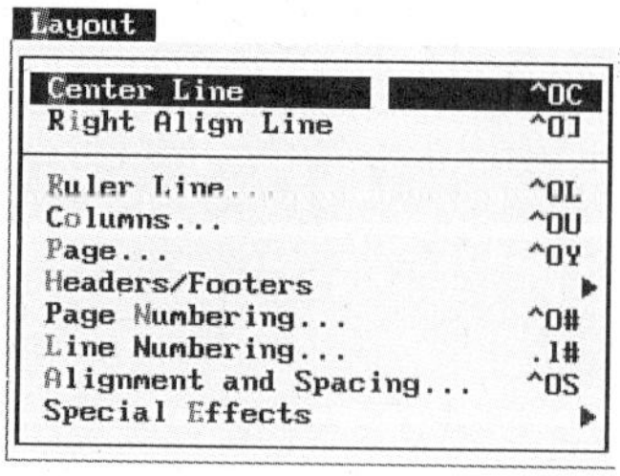

Fig. 8.19

The Layout menu.

WordStar then centers the line you have indicated (see fig. 8.20). If you want to right-align a selected line, you follow the same basic procedure but select Right Align Line instead of Center Line. The quick-key combinations for Center Line and Right Align Line are Ctrl-OC and Ctrl-O], respectively.

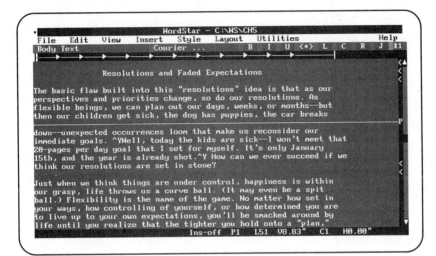

Fig. 8.20

The centered line.

Changing Line Spacing

One of the final items covered in this chapter involves the line spacing of your document. WordStar makes controlling the line spacing of your document a simple task: you simply select an option, make your choice, and WordStar does the rest.

To choose a new line spacing for your document, follow these steps:

1. Position the cursor at the point where you want the new line spacing to take effect.

2. Click the spacing button (at the far right of the style bar), or open the Layout menu and choose the Alignment and Spacing command. The Alignment and Spacing dialog box appears.

3. In the Line Spacing box, type the number of line spaces you want to use (see fig. 8.21). As you can see, the default is 1, indicating single-spaced text. If you want double-spaced text, type *2*. (You can enter values from 1 to 9.)

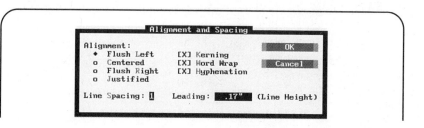

Fig. 8.21

Entering line spacing settings.

4. Click OK or press Enter.

WordStar returns you to your document. If you typed *2* for double-spaced text, WordStar places the dot command .ls 2 in your document. No other change is apparent. To see the effect of the command, press Ctrl-B. WordStar reforms the paragraph (see fig. 8.22). If you want to return to single-spaced text, you can delete the code at the beginning of the paragraph and press Ctrl-B to reformat the paragraph.

Line spacing dot command

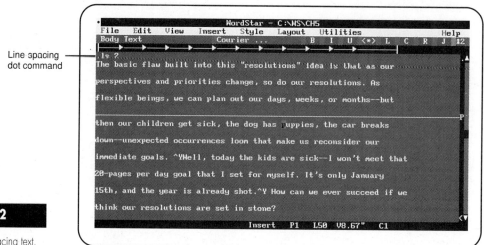

Fig. 8.22

Double-spacing text.

Notice that at the far end of the style bar, the spacing button changes from a 1 to a 2, showing you that double-spaced has been selected.

Chapter Summary

In this chapter, you have learned many different ways to change the look of the text in your document. You've experimented with paragraph styles; changed the font, size, and style of text; and modified text alignment and line spacing. As part of the examples in this chapter, you learned about different types of tags and codes inserted into your document. In the next chapter, you learn how those codes affect the way your document "really looks" in print by using different methods of viewing your document.

Viewing the Document

So far in this book, you've explored the techniques for entering, editing, and enhancing text. This chapter explains how to work with various WordStar options that enable you to change the way you view your document.

If you've been following along with the examples, the document on your screen is cluttered with font tags, style tags, and paragraph styles. In addition, you may have inserted one or two dot commands between paragraphs for alignment. Chances are that you want to see how your document *really* looks, that is, how it will look when printed. In this chapter, you learn how to view your document that way.

By now, you probably feel comfortable with WordStar's pull-down menus. You may want to experiment with the other menu levels, which can give you more on-screen space for working with your document. Other display topics covered in this chapter include changing the display of command tags, on-screen prompts, and block markers. Additionally, you learn about using windows in WordStar to display two different documents (or two different parts of the same document). Finally, you learn to preview the way your document will look in print.

Specifically, in this chapter, you learn about the following procedures:

■ Displaying dot commands

■ Hiding and displaying the flag column

■ Using soft space dots (nonprintable dots that show where you press the space bar) in your document

■ Displaying and hiding the scroll bar, style bar, ruler line, and status line

■ Displaying classic menus (menus available in earlier versions of WordStar)

■ Working with multiple windows

■ Resizing open windows

■ Previewing a document

■ Checking a document's memory usage

Changing the Display

As you may recall, the screen was getting crowded when you left the example in the last chapter. With all the paragraph styles and font tags, you may have had difficulty making sense out of the text. Figure 9.1 shows the sample document as you left it.

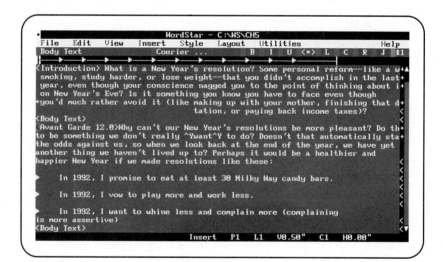

Fig. 9.1

The sample document.

You can change the display of the work area in the following ways:

■ Selecting a different help level, showing the classic WordStar menus

■ Suppressing the on-screen display of dot commands and tags

■ Turning off highlighting of the current text block

Using Different Help Levels

So far, you have used only help level 4, which displays the pull-down menus. Now, you are ready to try the WordStar classic menus—that is, the menus available in earlier versions of WordStar.

You can change the display of the menus at any time. To select a different menu system, follow these steps:

1. Open the Help menu.

2. Choose Change Help Level.

3. Type the number of the help level you want (see fig. 9.2).

4. Press Enter or click OK.

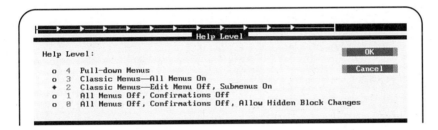

Fig. 9.2

Changing the help level.

Changing the Menu System Quickly

If you are using any of the help levels *except* level 4, you can move quickly among the different levels by pressing Ctrl-JJ to display the Help Level screen, typing the number of the help level you want, and clicking OK or pressing Enter.

Hey, wait a minute. In figure 9.3, you see that the classic menus don't save you any space at all on the edit screen. In fact, level 3 takes up more space than the level 4 pull-down menus require.

Now, try level 2—maybe that saves room on-screen. To select level 2, press Ctrl-JJ2, and then press Enter. Well, that's better, as figure 9.4 shows. Level 2 provides the same basic screen that the pull-down menus offer but with no pull-down menus. So how do you select a command? You must rely on your memory to tell you which keys combine with Ctrl to activate which classic menus. Or you can use the tear-out command card in the back of this book.

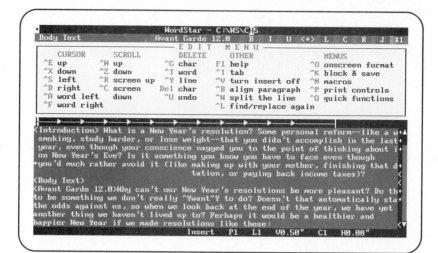

Fig. 9.3

The level 3 classic
menu.

Warning: When using help levels 3 and under, you can't access
the pull-down menus at all. Pressing Alt-F to access the pull-down
menus while in help level 3 does nothing. The menu keys that you
want to keep handy, therefore, are the keys to access the classic
commands—Ctrl-K, Ctrl-P, Ctrl-O, Ctrl-Q, and Ctrl-M—and not the
pull-down commands.

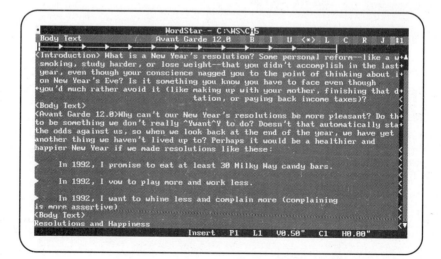

Fig. 9.4

The level 2 menu.

Changing Menu Information

In addition to changing the help level display, you can also control the amount of information displayed on each menu. By using the Settings command in the View menu, you can remove the quick-key combinations from the right side of the individual menus. Consider, for example, the menu in figure 9.5. As you can see, the command name is on the left, and the quick-key combination is on the right.

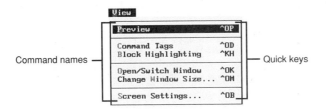

Command names ─ ... ─ Quick keys

Fig. 9.5

A typical menu display.

To remove the quick-key combinations from a menu, follow these steps:

1. Change back to help level 4 by pressing Ctrl-JJ4.

   You must be at level 4 in order to display the pull-down menus.

2. Press Alt-V to open the View menu, or click the menu name.

3. Select the Screen Settings command by pressing S. (You also can press Ctrl-OB to bypass the menu selections.) The Screen Settings dialog box appears, as shown in figure 9.6.

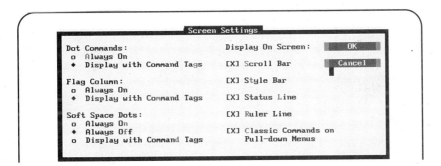

Fig. 9.6

The Screen Settings dialog box.

4. Press C to move the cursor to the Classic Commands on Pull-down Menus option. Pressing C moves the cursor to the Classic Commands option *and* toggles the selection to off (or on, as needed).

5. If an X is displayed in the check box, press the space bar to remove the X.

6. Press Enter or click OK.

When you return to the document and open a menu, WordStar no longer displays the key combinations (see fig. 9.7). You can return the display of the key combinations by again pressing Ctrl-OB and then pressing C.

Fig. 9.7

A menu displaying command names only.

Changing Other Screen Settings

In the last section, you were introduced to the Screen Settings dialog box, which contains several options for changing the look of your work area. Other features you can control on the Screen Settings dialog box include the following:

- Display of command tags

- Display of the flag column

- Dots used to indicate spaces

- Scroll bar display

- Style bar display

- Display of the status and ruler lines

To change any of these other screen settings, first open the Screen Settings menu either by opening the View menu and choosing the Screen Settings command or by pressing Ctrl-OB. When the Screen Settings dialog box appears, as shown in figure 9.8, make your selection.

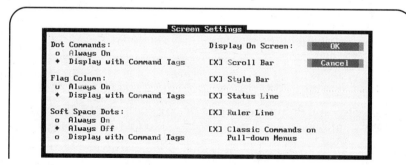

Fig. 9.8

The Screen Settings dialog box.

The Dot Commands options enable you to choose whether the dot commands are displayed at all times or displayed only with command tags. Dot commands in a document tell WordStar how you want the text to appear and to be printed. In some instances, you may want to suppress the display of other items, such as command tags so that you can better see the text in the document. If you select the Always On option, WordStar always displays the dot commands in your document. Even if you choose to suppress the display of other items, the dot commands remain on-screen. The default setting for this option, Display with Command Tags, causes the dot commands to be hidden when the other items are hidden. To change the option from its default, just press A. WordStar selects the Always On option.

The Flag Column options control whether the flag column is displayed. (The flag column appears at the right side of the work area just inside the scroll bar.) If you select Always On by pressing W, the flag column is displayed even when you suppress the display of other items. If you select the default option, Display with Command Tags, WordStar suppresses the flag column when you hide the command tags in your document.

The Soft Space Dots area includes three options: Always On, Always Off, and Display with Command Tags. You may never need to see the soft spaces in your document. (Usually this option is used when your printer or typesetting equipment is sensitive to the placement of spaces in your document, and you want to locate unnecessary spaces.) To turn on the display of soft spaces, press N to select Always On. You select the default, Always Off, by pressing F. If you want to display the soft spaces, but you want to hide them when you hide command tags, press D.

In the Display On Screen area, you can choose to display the scroll bar, style bar, status line, ruler line, and classic commands on pull-down menus. If you are new to WordStar, you may be most comfortable displaying these items for now. If you want to suppress the display of any of the items, simply type the highlighted letter of the option you want to change to place the cursor on that item, and press the space bar to remove the X from that check box.

After you enter your settings in the Screen Settings dialog box, click OK or press Enter. WordStar changes the display to match the settings you've entered and returns you to the document display.

Hiding and Displaying Tags

You have an easy option for displaying and hiding the command tags in your document. If you want to hide the command tags, follow these steps:

1. Open the View menu by pressing Alt-V or clicking the menu name.

2. Choose Command Tags by pressing C or by clicking the command.

The tags in your document are then hidden. Figure 9.9 shows the document without the command tags. Notice that all the settings controlled by the tags are still in effect, although the tags are hidden. As you can see, the screen looks much less cluttered without the tags displayed.

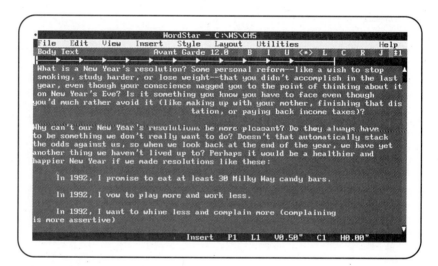

Fig. 9.9

Document with command tags hidden.

Hiding Tags Quickly

You can quickly hide and display the command tags in your document by using the Ctrl-OD quick-key combination. Press the combination once to turn off the command tag display; press the combination a second time to redisplay the tags. If you have a mouse, click the Display Tags button <*> to toggle display on and off.

Turning Off Block Highlighting

One WordStar feature that you may have noticed is that the block high-lights seem to last forever. The last block you marked—no matter how long ago—remains highlighted until you highlight another block or end your work session. How can you turn off that highlighting? Simple.

From any point in your document, press Alt-V to open the View menu and choose the Block Highlighting command. The last block you high-lighted is released from the highlight. Alternatively, if you don't have a block marked, selecting this command highlights the last block you had marked. The quick key for this procedure is Ctrl-KH.

Working with WordStar Windows

Another major benefit that makes WordStar such a flexible program in-volves using a second window to display another document. You can display the second document in a se_•ond window, or you can choose to display another part of the same document in the second window.

To open a second window, follow these steps:

1. Open the View menu by pressing Alt-V or clicking the menu name.

2. Choose the Open/Switch command (see fig. 9.10). You see the Open Document dialog box with the familiar Filenames list, as shown in figure 9.11.

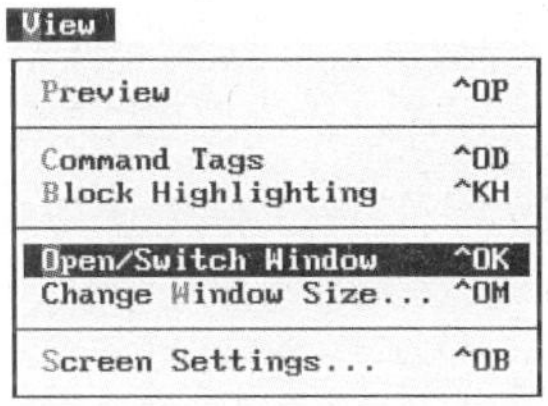

```
 View

 Preview              ^OP

 Command Tags         ^OD
 Block Highlighting   ^KH

 Open/Switch Window   ^OK
 Change Window Size...  ^OM

 Screen Settings...   ^OB
```

Fig. 9.10

Choosing the command to open a second window.

3. If you want to display the same file in both windows, press Enter. If you want to open a different file, type the file name in the Open Document dialog box and press Enter.

WordStar opens the document and displays it in the bottom half of the screen (see fig. 9.12). In the figure, the same document is open in both windows. Note that the cursor is positioned in the bottom window. You can move through the text as necessary by using the cursor-movement keys, the Go To commands in the Edit menu, or the scroll bar at the right edge of the screen.

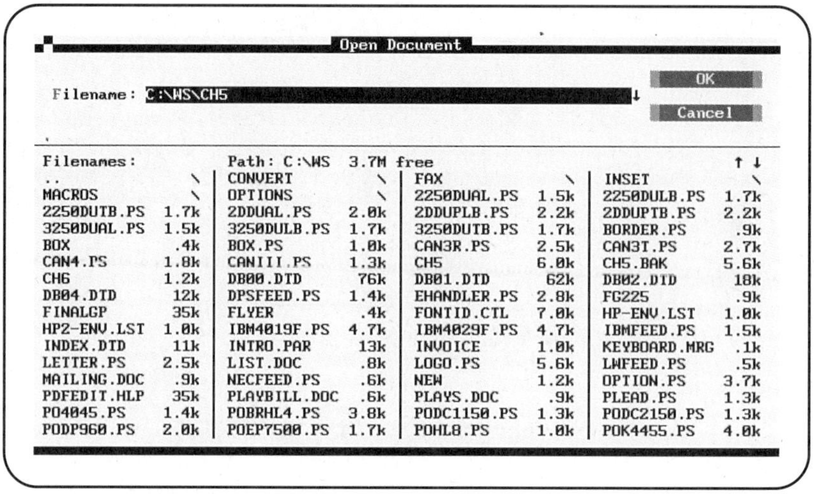

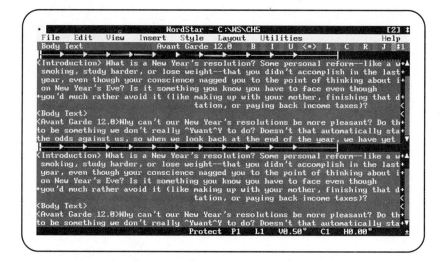

Fig. 9.11

The Open Document dialog box.

Fig. 9.12

A document opened in two windows.

If you are working with two copies of the same document, WordStar protects the document in the second window; that is, you cannot edit the text or make any other changes to the document in that window. If you are working with another document, you can edit both documents as usual.

If you are working with two documents, you can copy text from one window to another, as well as move, cut, or delete text. You can run the spelling checker and thesaurus in either window. Anything you can do in the first window, you can do in the second.

Switching Windows

If you plan to move from window to window, you must know how to move the cursor from one window to the other. You can move the cursor between windows by using the mouse or the keyboard:

- If you use the mouse, simply position the mouse cursor in the other window and click the mouse button. The cursor moves to that point.

- If you use the keyboard, press Alt-F to open the File menu and choose the Open/Switch command. The cursor moves to the other window.

Resizing Windows

You can also change the space assigned to the current window by using the Change Window Size command in the View menu. Follow these steps to resize a window:

1. Position the cursor in the window you want to change.

2. Open the View menu by pressing Alt-V or by clicking the menu name.

3. Choose the Change Window Size command by typing *W* or by clicking the command. The Change Window Size dialog box appears (see fig. 9.13).

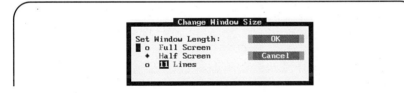

Fig. 9.13

The Change Window Size dialog box.

4. Choose the window length you want by typing the highlighted letter of the setting. Alternatively, you can type the number of lines you want for the current window by pressing L and then typing the number of lines you want.

5. Click OK or press Enter.

WordStar changes the size of the current window. You can change a window back to its original size at any time by repeating the procedure.

Closing a Window

When you want to close a window, first position the cursor in that window. Then, press Ctrl-KD. WordStar saves the file and returns you to the original window display. If you do not want to save the document, press Ctrl-KQ to abandon the document.

If you are using the mouse, position the mouse cursor on the close box in the upper left corner of the screen and double-click the mouse button. WordStar closes the window.

Previewing a Document

As you have learned in this chapter, WordStar displays a number of items. These on-screen display items enable you to review the paragraph styles, fonts, bold and italic highlighting, and other items you have selected. Sometimes, however, you may want to see how these features will make the document look when printed. For this reason, WordStar includes a preview feature, which displays the document with your selected fonts, styles, and formats.

Before you can preview the document, you must display it. First, open the document if you haven't already done so. Then, when the document is displayed in the edit screen, follow these steps:

1. Open the View menu by pressing Alt-V or clicking the menu name.

2. Select the Preview command by pressing Enter. (If you prefer, you can access preview mode by pressing Ctrl-OP.)

WordStar displays your document in preview mode. As you can see in figure 9.14, the preview screen is much different from the edit screen, which you have been using.

Understanding the Preview Screen

The document is displayed at full-page size on the left side of the screen. This part of your screen is the *document area*. You get a general idea of the layout of the text from this display, but you don't see anything up close. (You learn how to display different views of the document in this section.)

The *menu bar* at the top of the screen contains the menus you use in preview mode. Table 9.1 summarizes the capabilities of these menus.

Menu bar

Enlarges
page size

Reduces
page size

Moves highlight
through open menus

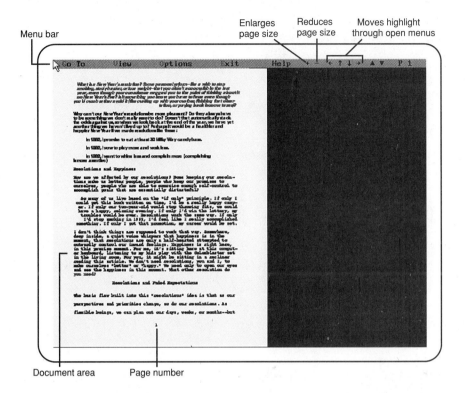

Document area

Page number

Fig. 9.14

Previewing the
document.

Table 9.1 Preview Mode Menus

Menu	Description
Go To	Contains commands for moving among the pages in the document
View	Enables you to display the entire page, facing pages, multiple pages, thumbnail display (displays many small pages in the preview area); magnify the display; or adjust window size
Options	Contains commands to scan text, fax text, or display a document grid (a series of horizontal and vertical lines that enables you to align text and graphics)
Exit	Returns you to the WordStar edit screen
Help	Displays help on the feature with which you are working

To the right of the menu names on the menu bar of the preview screen are a collection of symbols: a plus and a minus sign, directional arrows, two solid triangles (one pointing up and the other pointing down), and the symbol P 1. To use these symbols, position the mouse pointer on the symbol you want and click the mouse button.

When you are working in preview mode, you use the symbols for the functions summarized in Table 9.2.

Table 9.2 Preview Mode Keys and Functions

Symbol	Description
+	Enlarges page display
−	Reduces page display
Left arrow	Opens the menu to the left and closes the current menu
Up arrow	Moves highlight up one command in an open menu
Down arrow	Moves highlight down one command in an open menu
Right arrow	Opens the menu to the right and closes the current menu
Up triangle	Moves the display to the preceding screen of text; the same function as pressing Page Up on the keyboard
Down triangle	Moves the display to the next screen of text; the same function as pressing Page Down on the keyboard
P 1	Indicates the page currently displayed; in this case Page 1

Using Preview

Now you get a chance to try some of the preview techniques you learned about in the last section. In this section, you practice changing the way the document is displayed, moving among pages, displaying thumbnail pages that show the entire document on one screen, and adding grid lines.

The View menu contains the commands you use to change the way your document appears on the screen. Table 9.3 summarizes the various commands in the View menu.

Table 9.3 Commands in the View Menu

Command	Press	Description
Entire Page	E	Displays the entire page (This is the default setting.)
Facing Pages	F	Displays facing pages in the document
Multiple Pages	M	Places multiple pages on the screen
Thumbnail Display	T	Displays small thumbnail representations of the document pages
2x Zoom	2	Enlarges the document to two times full-page size
4x Zoom	4	Enlarges the document to four times full-page size
Adjust Window	A	Enables you to select the portion of the page you want to view

Getting a Closer Look

When you're working in preview mode, you can tell from the full-page display how the text and graphics are going to appear on the page. Preview mode gives you the "big picture" of your pages. You cannot, however, see the details of the text; you need to magnify—or *zoom*—the view so that you can see individual characters. To look more closely at your document, follow these steps:

1. Open the View menu by pressing V or clicking the menu name. The View menu opens (see fig. 9.15).

2. Select the 2x Zoom command by typing *2* or by clicking the command.

   The preview screen changes to display the document enlarged to two times its original size. As you can see in figure 9.16, the document can be seen clearly. Remember: you cannot edit the information on this screen; you can only view it, and make note of any changes you want to make when you return to the edit screen.

You also can use the mouse method to change the display. Move the mouse pointer to the minus (–) sign in the menu bar, and click the mouse button. Or you can press the plus (+) key and minus (–) key on the numeric keypad to zoom in and out, respectively. The document returns to full-page view.

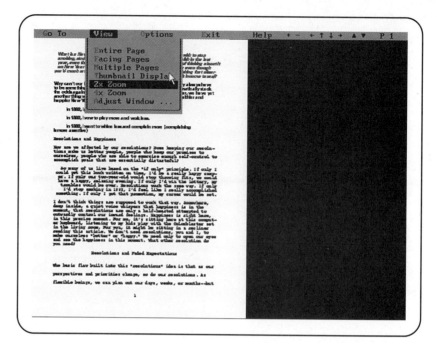

Fig. 9.15

The View menu in preview mode.

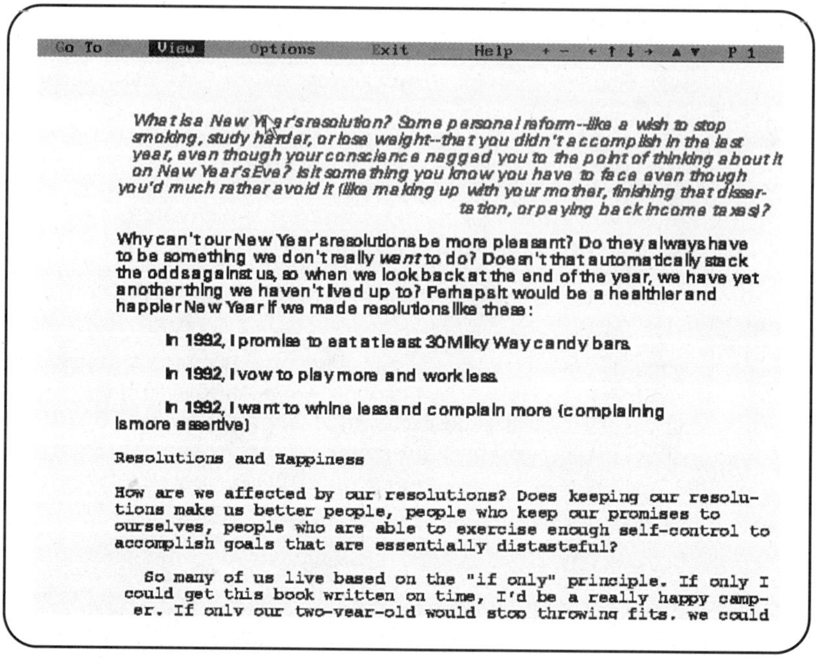

Fig. 9.16

Result of choosing the 2x Zoom command.

Moving among Pages

To look at another page on the preview screen, you first must display the contents of the Go To menu. To display the Go To menu, press G or click the menu name. The Go To menu has five options, which are described in table 9.4.

Table 9.4 Commands in the Go To Menu		
Command	**Press**	**Description**
Specified Page	S	Displays a pop-up dialog box; type the number of the page you want to see.
First Page	F	Takes you to the first page of the document
Last Page	L	Takes you to the last page of the document
Next Page	N	Displays the next page
Previous Page	P	Displays the preceding page

To move to a specific different page, press S to select the Specified Page command. A small dialog box appears in the center of the screen (see fig. 9.17). Type the number of the page you want to see and press Enter. WordStar displays the page you specified.

Displaying Thumbnails

The preview feature enables you to display your document in different ways. You can display, for example, a single page, or you can display many smaller pages (thumbnails) at one time. (Displaying a single page is the default.) In this section, you learn to use the different display options.

To change the display to thumbnail display, follow these steps:

1. Press V to open the View menu.
2. Press T to select Thumbnail Display, or click the option with the mouse.

Small iconlike pages appear on your screen. If your document consists of only a few pages, like the one shown in figure 9.18, a considerable amount of blank space appears on your screen. You can return to normal view by pressing V to open the View menu and pressing E. If you're using a mouse, click the + button to enlarge the display.

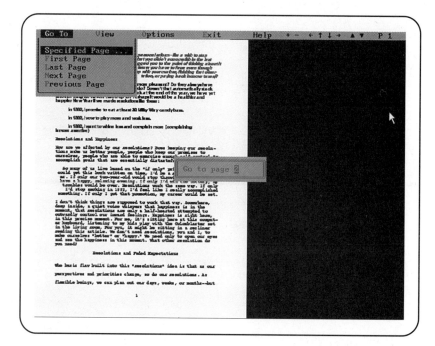

Fig. 9.17

Specifying a page to
preview.

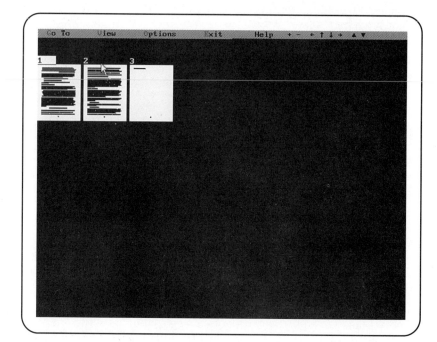

Fig. 9.18

The document
displayed in thumbnail
view.

Using the Options Menu To Add a Grid

The Options menu provides commands for scanning through pages, creating fax files, and displaying a grid for your document. Table 9.5 summarizes the commands on the Options menu.

Table 9.5 Commands in the Options Menu

Command	Press	Description
Automatic Scan	A	Scrolls through the entire document
Scan Range	S	Displays a dialog box so that you can enter the range of pages you want to see
FAX Files for entire Document	F	Creates a fax file from entire document
FAX Files for Range	R	Creates a fax file for pages you specify
Grid Display On/Off	G	Turns a grid on and off

This example explains how to add a grid to the previewed document. A *grid* adds nonprinting horizontal and vertical lines to the document, providing you with a means to align text and graphics. You may want to use a grid whenever you use columns of text or import graphics. You can use the grid to make sure that you have the items aligned properly.

To turn on the grid, follow these steps:

1. Press O to open the Options menu.

2. Press G to select Grid Display On/Off, or click the command name.

WordStar adds the grid to the display (see fig. 9.19). You now can check the items in your document for proper alignment and return to the edit screen to make corrections. To hide the grid, press O to open the Options menu and then press G again. The grid is removed.

Exiting Preview

When you finish previewing the desired page or pages in your document, you will want to exit the preview display screen. To exit preview, use the commands in the Exit menu. Open the Exit menu by pressing E or by clicking the menu name. The Exit menu contains only two commands:

Original Page and Current Page. If you want to return to the edit view of the page displayed when you started preview, select Original Page. If you want to return to the page you're currently viewing in preview, select Current Page. You then return to the edit screen.

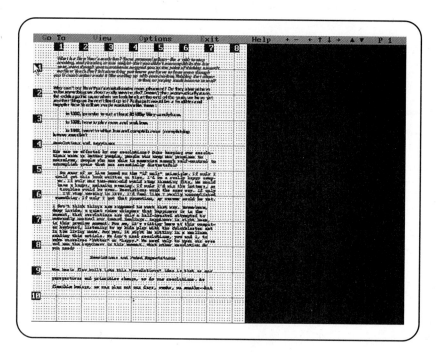

Fig. 9.19

Screen display with a grid.

Checking Document Status

The Status command on the File menu is another feature you may find useful as you create WordStar documents. The status feature enables you to tell at any time how much memory your document is using.

To check the status of your document, follow these steps:

1. From the edit screen, open the File menu by pressing Alt-F or by clicking the menu name.

2. Select the Status command by typing U or by clicking the command name.

   WordStar displays the Status screen (see figure 9.20).

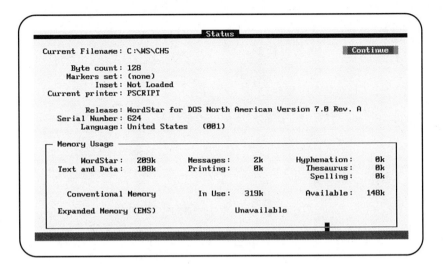

Fig. 9.20

The Status screen.

The Status screen displays a great deal of information about your file, including the current file name, file size (in bytes), the number of markers used, the current printer installed, the version and serial number of WordStar, and an overview of memory usage. After you've finished checking the Status screen, click Continue or press Enter to return to the document.

Chapter Summary

In this chapter, you have learned about the options available for displaying a document. WordStar 7.0 enables you to display a variety of different help menus and to control on-screen display options, such as command tags and highlighting. Additionally, you learned to work with WordStar windows and to preview the page before printing it. Finally, this chapter presents how to check the status of your document to determine the amount of memory a document is using and the amount of memory still available. The next chapter shows you how to use margins, tabs, columns, kerning, and other special features to complete your document's layout.

Finishing Page Layout

A re you ready for the finale? In the preceding chapters, you've
learned to perform a variety of tasks. You've entered text, edited
paragraphs, enhanced text within a document, used the Preview command to view your creation before printing, and discovered WordStar
windows. You basically have your document in place.

You now are ready to fine-tune your document—the final step before
printing. In this chapter, you learn to tie up some loose ends before
printing. You learn to work with the page layout, which determines the
appearance of your printed document. Specifically, this chapter presents the following procedures:

- Checking the margin settings
- Controlling page orientation
- Setting tabs
- Adjusting line spacing
- Working with columns
- Adding headers and footers
- Adding page numbers
- Creating tables
- Using the calculator

To perform these procedures, you make extensive use of the commands
on the Layout menu (see fig. 10.1). In Chapter 8, you learned about the
two alignment commands—Center Line and Right Align Line—on the
Layout menu. You learn about the remainder of the commands in this
chapter. Table 10.1 gives you a brief description of each command.

```
Layout
┌─────────────────────────────────────┐
│ Center Line                    ^OC   │
│ Right Align Line               ^O]   │
│                                      │
│ Ruler Line...                  ^OL   │
│ Columns...                     ^OU   │
│ Page...                        ^OY   │
│ Headers/Footers                 ▶    │
│ Page Numbering...              ^O#   │
│ Line Numbering...              .1#   │
│ Alignment and Spacing...       ^OS   │
│ Special Effects                 ▶    │
└─────────────────────────────────────┘
```

Fig. 10.1

The Layout menu.

Table 10.1 Layout Menu Options

Command	Hot Key	Explanation
Center Line	Ctrl-OC	Centers current line of text
Right Align Line	Ctrl-O]	Aligns the current line of text at the right margin
Ruler Line	Ctrl-OL	Changes settings for left, right, paragraph margins and tabs
Columns	Ctrl-OU	Sets up newspaper-style columns
Page	Ctrl-OY	Changes settings for margins, orientation, page length, paper bin, and suppression of blank lines at the top of the page
Headers/Footers		Inserts a header or footer into the document
Page Numbering	Ctrl-O#	Sets whether page numbers are printed at the bottom of the page and determines their position on the line and the number to be used
Line Numbering		Starts line numbering and sets line-numbering options
Alignment and Spacing	Ctrl-OS	Sets alignment, kerning, word wrap, hyphenation, line spacing, and line height
Special Effects		Overprints lines or characters, inserts optional hyphens, centers text vertically on the page, and keeps text together on lines or pages

Now, open a sample document if you haven't already done so. In the next section, you learn to check the page setup options (such as margin and tab settings, alignment, and line spacing) and modify them, if necessary.

Checking Page Setup

To display the Page Layout dialog box, first open the Layout menu by pressing Alt-L or by clicking the menu name. When the Layout menu is displayed, select the Page option. The Page Layout dialog box appears (see fig. 10.2).

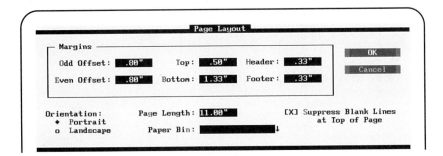

Understanding Margins

In the Margins box, you see a few items not previously discussed in this book. The Odd Offset and Even Offset measurements control the way the text is placed on the page. Are you creating a document to be placed in a three-ring binder or one that will be bound along the inside edge? By entering *1.00* or *1.20* in the Odd Offset and Even Offset boxes, you can leave enough space in the inner margins of your pages to bind the document without cutting into the text. Figure 10.3 illustrates how the Odd and Even Offset measurements affect the page.

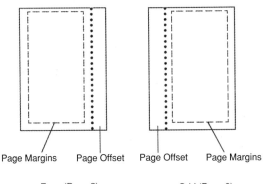

Page Margins   Page Offset   Page Offset   Page Margins

Even (Page 2)   Odd (Page 3)

Note that the Odd Offset sets the inner margin for odd-numbered pages and that the Even Offset controls the inner margin for even-numbered pages. You can enter settings for the Odd Offset and Even Offset options and then preview the document by pressing Ctrl-OP when the edit screen is displayed.

Offset and Page Margins

Any individual margins you set—either in paragraph styles or in dot commands you insert within the text—are added to the original Offset amount you enter in the Page Layout box. If the Odd Offset is set to 1.00 and you change the margin in the document to .50, for example, the total amount of white space from the edge of the page to the beginning of the text will be 1.5 inches.

The Top and Bottom margin settings hold no surprises: you enter in these text boxes the amount of blank space you want to leave at the top and bottom of the page. Remember, however, to leave enough space to print any headers and footers included on the page. Leave at least the default settings (.5 for top and 1.33 for bottom) unless you must have extra space.

The Header and Footer margin options enable you to set the amount of space you want between the last printed line of the header and the first printed line of text, or the last printed line of text and the first printed line of the footer. The amount of space you enter for the header line must be smaller than the amount of space you enter for the top margin. Likewise, the footer line number must be smaller than the bottom line amount. Headers and footers are detailed later in this chapter.

Measurement Options

Although you've been dealing primarily with inches, you can use other units of measure with WordStar. WordStar reads the following measurements:

Measurement	Procedure to move the margin	Enter
Columns	7 columns	7r
Lines	7 lines	7l
Centimeters	7 centimeters	7c
Points	30 points	30p
Inches	2 inches	2"

Selecting Orientation

Orientation was virtually unheard of before the advent of laser printers. Now, most high-end—and some low-end—printers are equipped with the means to print not only in the traditional portrait orientation (that is, vertically on an 8 1/2-by-11-inch sheet of paper) but also in landscape orientation (lengthwise on an 11-by-8 1/2-inch sheet). Figure 10.4 shows the difference between portrait and landscape orientation.

8 1/2-by-11 inches   11-by-8 1/2 inches

Portrait Orientation   Landscape Orientation

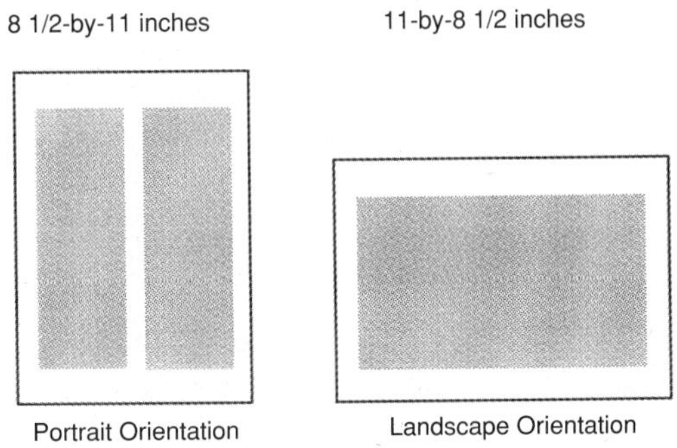

Fig. 10.4

Portrait and landscape orientation.

For most standard documents, use portrait orientation. It is the accepted way of printing correspondence, memos, letters, manuscripts, and other documents. When creating a booklet, a brochure, or some other multi-column document, you have the option of printing the page in landscape orientation. Another use for landscape orientation is producing transparencies or charts for presentations.

Planning Orientation

If you know that you want to print the document you are creating in landscape orientation, select the Landscape Orientation option in the Page Layout dialog box *before* you begin creating your document. Although selecting this option after you've entered and enhanced text creates no problems, you will have a better idea of the margins and general layout of the text if you select the orientation when you create the document.

Selecting Paper Size and Source

When you open the Page Layout dialog box, the setting in the Page Length box shows the default value WordStar expects for your paper size. By looking at the Page Layout dialog box, you can see that WordStar expects you to use paper that is 11 inches long. If you are working with legal-sized paper or paper of an irregular length, you can change the setting by clicking the Page Length box and typing the correct page length. If you have selected landscape orientation, the length of your standard page is now 8 1/2 inches, so be sure to change the page length before you print.

The Paper Bin setting in the Page Layout dialog box tells WordStar the source of the paper. If your printer has only one bin from which paper is taken, you won't need to change the Paper Bin setting. If you have a choice of paper bins, press Tab to move the cursor to the Paper Bin option. A list of available bins is displayed along the bottom of the Page Layout box (see fig. 10.5). Press the down-arrow key to highlight the name of the bin you want, or move the mouse cursor to that bin name and click. WordStar enters your selection in the Paper Bin box.

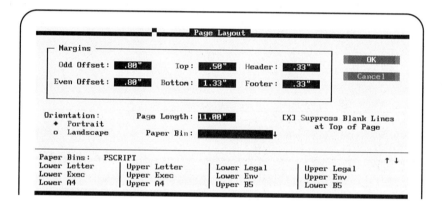

Fig. 10.5

Choosing a paper bin.

Suppressing Blank Lines

Occasionally as you print, you find that in your document a blank line or two winds up at the top of the page. Perhaps you reformatted the text or you forgot to check the page breaks by using preview. You can have WordStar automatically skip blank lines when they appear at the top of a document page, keeping the top margin of your document consistent and avoiding wasted space. As the default setting, the Suppress Blank Lines at Top of Page option is not checked, indicating that WordStar does not automatically skip blank lines. If you *do not* want the blank lines kept at the top of the page, press Alt-S to place an X in the check box.

When you've finished entering all the settings in the Page Layout box, click OK or press Enter to return to your document.

Working with Page Margins and Tab Stops

In the last section, you learned about controlling some basic settings for the overall layout of the page. In this section, you learn about the specific text settings—left and right margins, first-line indent, and tab stops—that help you fine-tune the way text is placed in your document.

To access these options, open the Layout menu and choose the Ruler Line command. The Ruler Line dialog box appears (see fig. 10.6).

```
                        ┌──────── Ruler Line ────────┐
   Left Margin:  .00"    1st Line Indent:            OK
  Right Margin: 6.50"                              Cancel
    Tab Stops: .50" 1.00" 1.50" 2.00" 2.50" 3.00" 3.50" 4.00" 4.5
```

The Ruler Line dialog box contains the Left Margin, Right Margin, 1st Line Indent, and Tab Stops options. Table 10.2 explains the purpose of each of these features.

Table 10.2 The Ruler Line Options

Option	Description
Left Margin	Marks the position where the left edge of the text will be printed, measured from the left edge of the page. (If Odd or Even Offset settings were entered in the Page Layout dialog box, the Left Margin entry is added to the Offset value.)
Right Margin	Marks the position where the right edge of text will be printed, measured from the left edge of the page. (If Odd or Even Offset settings were entered in the Page Layout dialog box, the Right Margin entry is added to the Offset value.)
1st Line Indent	Controls indentation of the first line of a paragraph
Tab Stops	Sets tabs in the document (the default is every half inch) so that you can easily align tabular material, such as tables, lists, and bulleted items

Entering Margins and First-Line Indents

You can enter the Left Margin setting for your text simply by typing the desired value in the Left Margin text box. Remember that you can use inches (the default), points (p), columns (r), lines (l), or centimeters (c). WordStar moves the text the specified amount of space from the left edge of the page.

Margins and Offset

Remember that the Odd and Even Offset values (the amount of space left blank on the inside margin of odd- and even-numbered pages, respectively) are added to the Left Margin setting. Although the amount of the Offset does not appear in the Left Margin box, remember to take this amount into account when you are entering a value for the left margin.

After entering a setting for the left margin, press Tab to move to the 1st Line Indent setting. This box is blank, indicating that the paragraphs in your document are not automatically indented. If you want to indent the first line of each paragraph, type a value in the box. (Usually, .25 is sufficient for a paragraph indent.)

Next, press Tab to move to the Right Margin setting. WordStar has automatically entered the value 6.50, telling you that the right margin is set 6 1/2 inches from the *left* edge of the page. You can change this margin as necessary to increase or decrease the length of the printed line.

Working with Tab Stops

The final setting in the Ruler Line dialog box contains the tab stops for the document. WordStar automatically sets tab stops every half inch. This setting means that each time you press the Tab key, the cursor moves to the next tab stop, one-half inch away.

If you've ever worked with a typewriter, you already know that tabs come in handy when you want to align text within the body of a document. You may, for example, want to use tabs to make alignment easier when you are entering the opening address of a letter, creating a table, addressing envelopes, or indenting a line of text.

You may want to enter new tabs in the Tab Stops line, and you may want to delete existing tabs so that the cursor doesn't stop unnecessarily.

Suppose, for example, that you are preparing to type an envelope, and you want to remove all tab stops except the one at 3.5 inches. You can delete the entire line of tabs by pressing Ctrl-Y; then type *3.5"* in the Tab Stops text box. If you want to add a decimal tab, which aligns numbers along a decimal point, enter the pound, or number symbol (#), before the tab measurement (for example, *#3.5"*). Figure 10.7 shows the Tab Stops line with all default tabs removed and one new stop entered.

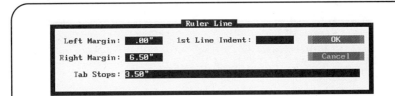

Fig. 10.7

Entering a tab stop.

If you want to modify a tab stop in the original tab line, you don't have to delete the entire line of tabs. You can use the arrow keys to move the cursor to the tab you want to change, delete the necessary numbers, and type the numbers you want.

Tab Reminders

To do this	Press this
Delete all tabs	Ctrl-Y
Enter a tab	Type the measurement (such as *.5"*)
Create a decimal tab	Type # before the measurement (such as *#.5"*)

Viewing Margin Changes

When you're finished changing tabs and entering settings on the Ruler Line dialog box, press Enter or click OK to return to your document. At the top of the document, you see that WordStar has made note of the changes you made in the Ruler Line dialog box. The dot commands for the settings you selected (.lm for left margin, .rm for right margin, .pm for first-line indent, and .tb for tabs) have been inserted at the top of your document (see fig. 10.8).

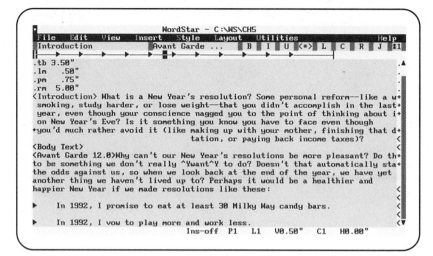

WordStar — C:\WS\CH5

| File | Edit | View | Insert | Style | Layout | Utilities | Help |

Introduction .... Avant Garde ...   B   I   U <*> L   C   R   J ‡1

```
.tb 3.50"
.lm  .50"
.pm  .75"
.rm 5.00"
<Introduction> What is a New Year's resolution? Some personal reform--like a u+
  smoking, study harder, or lose weight--that you didn't accomplish in the last+
  year, even though your conscience nagged you to the point of thinking about i+
  on New Year's Eve? Is it something you know you have to face even though
+you'd much rather avoid it (like making up with your mother, finishing that d+
                        tation, or paying back income taxes)?         <
<Body Text>                                                           <
<Avant Garde 12.0>Why can't our New Year's resolutions be more pleasant? Do th+
to be something we don't really ^Ywant^Y to do? Doesn't that automatically sta+
the odds against us, so when we look back at the end of the year, we have yet
another thing we haven't lived up to? Perhaps it would be a healthier and
happier New Year if we made resolutions like these:                   <
                                                                      <
 ▶   In 1992, I promise to eat at least 30 Milky Way candy bars.      <
                                                                      <
 ▶   In 1992, I vow to play more and work less.                       <▼
                    Ins-off  P1   L1    V0.50"   C1   H0.00"
```

Fig. 10.8

Viewing the effects of margin changes with paragraph style in effect.

Wait a minute; something's wrong here. You can see the dot commands at the top of the document, but nothing has happened to the text. The ruler line isn't even different. What went wrong?

By looking at figure 10.8, you can see a paragraph style tag at the beginning of each paragraph. This tag tells you that a paragraph style has been applied to that paragraph. A paragraph style contains its own margins and other settings, and these paragraph style settings override the values you entered in the Ruler Line dialog box. To show the effects of the new margin, first-line indent, and tab stop settings, the paragraph style assigned to the first paragraph (Introduction) has been deleted in figure 10.9. As you can see, the paragraph is reformatted to match the settings you entered in the Ruler Line dialog box.

Creating and Calculating Tables

Now that you know how to enter and use tab stops, you may want to consider adding tabular material to your text. Whether your information consists only of textual data or also includes numbers, you can have WordStar align and even calculate tables. Suppose, for example, that you set tabs at .5, 1.5, and 3.0 on the edit screen, and you want to include a table for the following data:

Apples	Oranges	Bananas
14	12	36
23	24	21
10	13	40

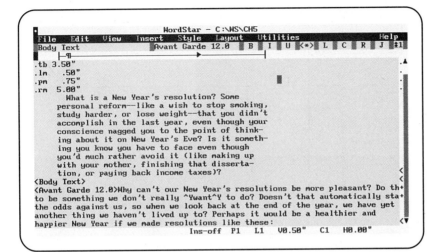

Fig. 10.9

The margin and indent settings with paragraph style removed.

In addition, you want the table to include the number of all baskets of fruit sold, which requires a total of all numbers in the table. To create the table, first open the Ruler Line dialog box and enter the tab stops at the appropriate points. Then enter and align your data.

You then can instruct WordStar to calculate the total for you by using the Block Math command, available in the Utilities menu. First, highlight the numbers as a text block; then open the Utilities menu by pressing Alt-U and select the Block Math command. WordStar instantly calculates the equation and tells you that the result is 193.

Adjusting Spacing

In earlier chapters, you learned to set the alignment of your text by clicking L, C, R, or J in the style bar. You also learned that if you are using the keyboard, you can choose the alignment by selecting the Alignment and Spacing command from the Layout menu. Additionally, you can choose the line spacing either from the style bar (clicking the line spacing button at the far right end of the bar) or by typing the number you want in the Alignment and Spacing box.

A few more options in the Alignment and Spacing box have to do with the placement of your text. These settings include kerning, word wrap, hyphenation, line spacing, and line height. To access these additional options, first open the Layout menu by pressing Alt-L or by clicking the menu name. Then choose the Alignment and Spacing option by pressing A or clicking the command name. The Alignment and Spacing dialog box is displayed (see fig. 10.10).

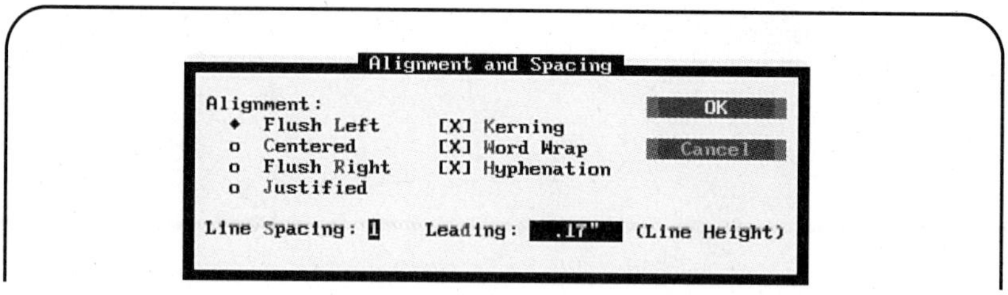

Fig. 10.10

The Alignment and Spacing dialog box.

```
                          Alignment and Spacing
       Alignment:
          •  Flush Left      [X] Kerning          OK
          o  Centered        [X] Word Wrap
          o  Flush Right     [X] Hyphenation     Cancel
          o  Justified

       Line Spacing: 1    Leading:  .17"  (Line Height)
```

The familiar Alignment options are on the left side of the dialog box, and the Line Spacing box, which you've seen before, is positioned on the bottom left side of the box (see Chapter 8 for more information about alignment options). The other options—Kerning, Word Wrap, Hyphenation, and Leading—are the focus of this section.

Understanding Kerning

What is kerning? It sounds like something you do to a vegetable, but it's a common word in typography. *Kerning* is the process of fitting letters together to make the type easier to read. Not all printers have the capability to kern letters—only printers that have proportional fonts. (In proportional fonts, individual characters are assigned different widths; for example, the letter *w* is given more space than the letter *t*.) Thus, you can use the kerning feature of WordStar 7.0 only if you have a laser printer that supports proportional, scalable fonts. (*Scalable* means that the font can be resized to different scales.)

Kerning generally is used in headings or titles, or at any time when large fonts are being used. Kerning letters in large fonts makes them easier to read.

When you first open the Alignment and Spacing box, the Kerning feature is already turned on. To turn off the feature, you must remove the X from the check box to the left of the option. To remove the X, tab to the Kerning option and press the space bar. The X is removed.

Understanding Word Wrap

Word Wrap is an automatic "given" with WordStar 7.0. As soon as you begin typing, you can see the effect of word wrap; your characters begin to move off the right side of the screen, and then, as you type, like magic, they jump to the next line and continue without any further intervention from you. So if you are used to working with the typewriter, resist the urge to press Return at the end of each line. WordStar takes care of ending the lines for you.

All this happens because in the Alignment and Spacing dialog box, the word wrap feature is enabled. Suppose that you want to turn off word wrap. (Perhaps in one particular part of a document, for example, you want to let a line extend beyond the margin.) To turn off word wrap, press Tab to move to the Word Wrap option and press the space bar. The X is removed, and word wrap is turned off. You can easily activate word wrap by selecting the command again and pressing the space bar to redisplay the X.

Setting Hyphenation

When word wrap is in effect, you don't always know where WordStar is going to break lines. For this reason, having a feature that automatically hyphenates broken words for you is a great benefit. WordStar knows the correct place to hyphenate most words and automatically breaks the words for you.

When the Alignment and Spacing dialog box is first displayed, Hyphenation is turned on. If you want to disable the feature, press H to move to the Hyphenation option. The X is removed.

Understanding Leading

Leading is another typographical term used to indicate the amount of space between lines in your printed document. Leading is measured from the bottom of one line of text to the bottom of the next; for example, consider the following text:

This is line one.

This is line two.

When determining the leading for the text, enter the amount of space you want to allow from the bottom of the characters in line 1 to the bottom of the characters in line 2. Generally, the average leading for standard text produces 6 lines per inch; the setting is shown in the Leading box as .17.

If you want more (or less) leading between lines, press D to move to the Leading box and type the new value. Remember that, as an option, you can set line spacing to 2 to get more space between lines.

So what's the difference between line spacing and line height? When you use line spacing, you specify whether you want the text to be single-spaced or double-spaced, and the blank lines between printed lines are physically inserted into the document. This feature enables you to see the single- or double-spacing on-screen and makes the document file larger, thereby taking up more disk space. Line height, on the other hand, can be set in hundredths of an inch. No physical blank lines are inserted into the text, and changes in line height do not appear on-screen.

Working with Columns

When working with columns, you're getting into the more difficult stuff. Actually, nothing in WordStar is truly difficult, but working with columns in most word processing programs can be a bit of a stretch for novices. Fortunately, WordStar 7.0 makes it simple to create multicolumn layouts right from the edit screen.

You start by positioning the cursor at the point in the document where you want to begin breaking the page into columns. (You don't need to put the whole document in columnar form; you can begin columns in the middle of a page, on the second page of your document, or anywhere the change is necessary.)

Next, open the Column Layout dialog box. Display the box by opening the Layout menu and selecting Column Layout. The dialog box shows the options available: specifying the number of columns, the space between columns, and the right-page margin (see fig. 10.11). WordStar automatically adjusts the column for even-width columns based on the settings you enter in this dialog box.

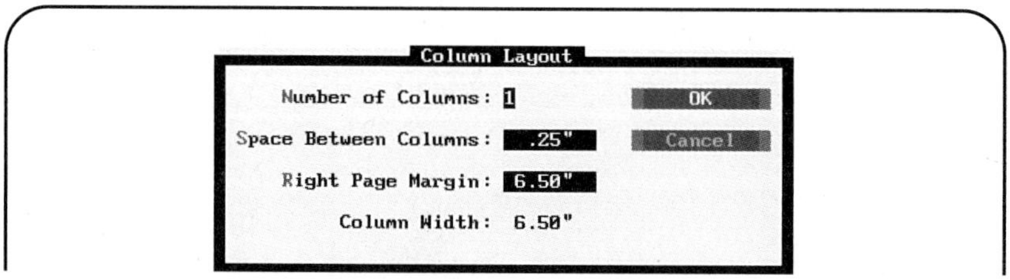

Fig. 10.11

The Column Layout dialog box.

By looking at the Number of Columns entry in the dialog box, you can see that one column is chosen. The Space Between Columns—commonly called *gutter width*—controls the amount of room you want, in inches, between the right edge of the first column and the left edge of the second column. The Column Width setting changes when you change the Number of Columns setting. The Right Page Margin setting governs the right margin of the page.

To set up multiple columns in your document, follow these steps:

1. When the cursor is positioned in the Number of Columns box, type the number of columns you want (in this case, enter *2*).

   After you enter the number, the cursor moves automatically to the Space Between Columns box. Notice that when you type a new number for the columns, the Column Width setting is automatically changed to show you the width of the columns you've specified (see fig. 10.12).

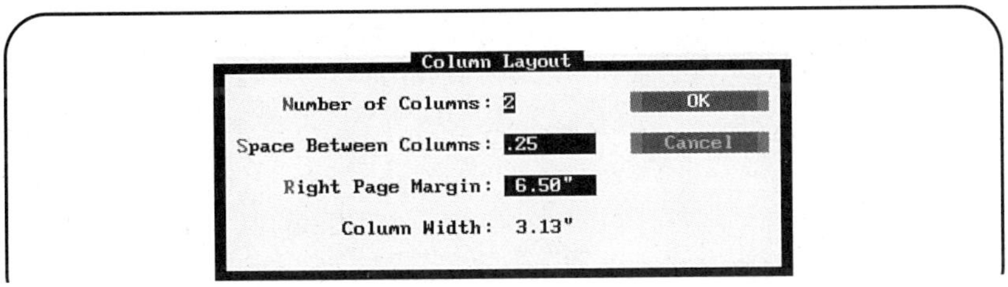

```
┌─────────────────────────────────────────┐
│            Column Layout                 │
│   Number of Columns: 2      ┌────OK────┐ │
│   Space Between Columns: .25 ┌─Cancel─┐ │
│   Right Page Margin: 6.50"               │
│      Column Width:  3.13"                │
└─────────────────────────────────────────┘
```

Fig. 10.12

WordStar calculates the column width.

2. Type the amount of space you want to reserve between columns (usually .5 or .25 is sufficient).

3. If you want to change the right margin of the page, press Tab to move to the Right Page Margin setting and type the new margin.

4. Click OK or press Enter.

When you return to the document, you can see that WordStar has done several things. Most noticeable is the fact that along the left side of the text, you see a line of dashes (see fig. 10.13). This is WordStar's visual clue that you have placed that text in columnar mode. Additionally, note that two dot commands have been inserted preceding the cursor position:

- .rm 3.00 says that the right margin of this column has been set to 3 inches.

- .co 2, .50 tells you that two columns have been selected, with a half-inch space between columns.

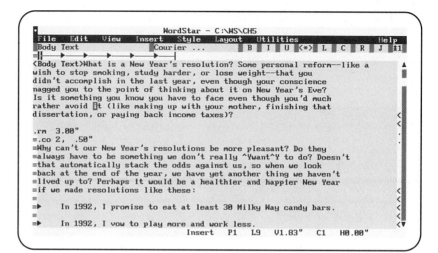

Fig. 10.13

The document after the column layout has been selected.

Another change you notice is that the ruler line at the top of the screen is shortened to the 3-inch width of the column. The text of the paragraph, however, still extends to the original margin. If you press Ctrl-B, the paragraph reforms. Figure 10.14 shows you how the text looks in columnar mode. If you want to reform the entire document, press Ctrl-QU. WordStar moves from the cursor position through the rest of the document, reformatting the entire document.

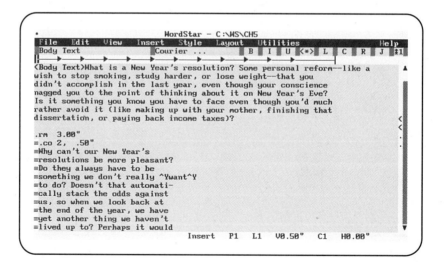

Fig. 10.14

The text in columnar mode.

As you notice in the figure, you see only one column on-screen, although you specified two. To see how your document looks in print, press Ctrl-OP to activate preview mode. The two columns are put in place beside each other when you preview the document (see fig. 10.15). Return to your document by pressing Esc.

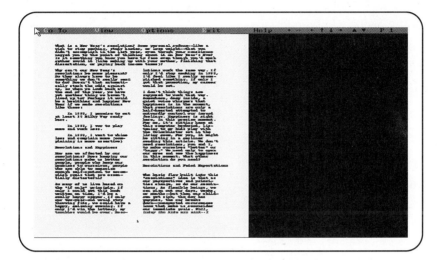

Fig. 10.15

Previewing the two-column document.

Once you've reformatted your document into columns, you may decide that you liked it better in single-column format. You can easily change the document back to one column by moving the cursor to the dot commands preceding the column break and pressing Ctrl-Y to delete the command lines. The document then automatically reformats to single-column mode.

Inserting Column Breaks

WordStar does a good job of distributing your text on the page, but you may not want to leave the alignment of columns totally to the program. You can insert your own column breaks at the points of your choosing. You position the cursor at the place you want the column to break, open the Insert menu, and choose the Column Break command. WordStar inserts the code .cb at the cursor position. When you preview the document, you see the results of the column break you entered.

Adding Headers and Footers

A *header* is placed at the top of every document page; a *footer* is placed at the bottom. Because you can easily forget where you are when you are reading through a large volume of text, headers and footers give you something to refer to. Headers and footers can be used to give the reader special information, such as

- The company name
- The title of the report
- Your department's number
- The date the document was written or revised
- The author's name
- The page number

You use the Headers/Footers command in the Layout menu to add a header or a footer to your document. First, open the Layout menu and choose the Headers/Footers command by pressing H. A small pop-up option list appears, waiting for your choice of header or footer (see fig. 10.16).

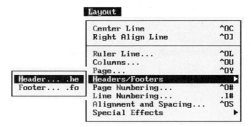

When you make your selection (in this case, choose Header), another dialog box appears (see fig. 10.17). The dialog box in the figure is the Header dialog box. If you choose Footer, the Footer dialog box is displayed. (The Footer box is identical to the Header box except the word *Footer* is substituted for *Header*.)

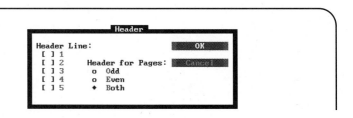

The cursor is positioned in the check box preceding the *1* in the Header Line options. If you want to enter text for line 1 of the header, press the space bar to reserve line 1 of this header for text. An X appears. Continue to select the other lines on which you want to enter text by pressing the down-arrow key to move to the check box for each line number and pressing the space bar to select the item.

When you're finished selecting the header lines you want to use, press Tab to move to the Header for Pages option. (You can simply press the highlighted letter of the option you want, if you prefer.) Select Odd if you want the header to be printed on odd pages only, Even for even pages only, or Both for both odd and even document pages.

Click OK or press Enter to return to the document. As you can see, WordStar moves the cursor to the first line, after the dot command .h1 (for header line 1). Type the text you want to appear in the header line. You can use any paragraph style, font, text style, or alignment you would use in the normal body of the document. Additionally, if you want to include a header or footer page number, you can type *Page* # in the header or footer; WordStar substitutes the actual page number for the # symbol when you print the document. (**Note:** This command is different from the Layout menu's Page Numbering command, which adds a page number at the bottom of the document.)

If you select more than one header line, you see lines that start with .h2 (header line 2), .h3, and so forth. You can press Ctrl-X or use the arrow keys to move the cursor to the second line of the header (.h2). You can type text in this line, or you can leave it blank.

When you add footers, the process is the same. When the Footers dialog box is displayed, select the lines on which you want to enter footer information and choose the pages (Odd, Even, or Both) on which the footer should appear. After you press Enter, type the footer text in the place provided just beneath the header lines. Figure 10.18 shows a previewed page with a header and footer.

Deleting Headers and Footers

You can easily remove headers and footers by simply positioning the cursor in the header or footer line and pressing Ctrl-Y. WordStar deletes the entire line.

Header ——

Footer ——

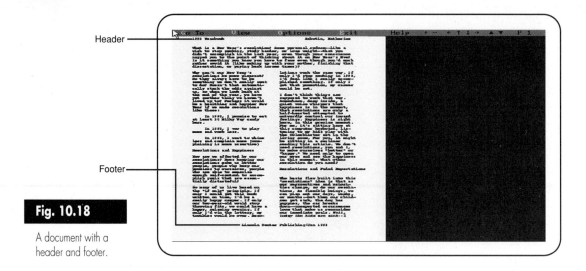

Fig. 10.18

A document with a
header and footer.

Adding Page Numbers

Another WordStar feature that comes in handy when you are working
with long documents is the capability of adding page numbers. In the
last section, you learned that you can add page numbers to the header
or footer in your document by simply typing *Page* # in the header or
footer line. WordStar offers you an alternative method with the Layout
menu's Page Numbering command, which places the current page number centered at the bottom of the document page. The Page Numbering
command also enables you to control the printing of page numbers, the
starting page number, and the page number position.

When you use the Page Numbering command, WordStar always places
the page number in the same place: centered at the bottom of the page.
If you've used footers in your document, however, your page numbers
won't show up. Thus, you can use the Page Numbering command to add
page numbers only if you have not used footers.

If you haven't used footers, you can add page numbers with the Page
Numbering command by following these steps:

1. Open the Layout menu.

2. Choose the Page Numbering command by pressing N. The Page
   Numbering dialog box appears (see fig. 10.19).

3. If the Print Page Numbers setting is not checked, press the space
   bar. An X appears. Press Tab. The cursor moves to the Set Page
   Number text box.

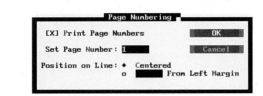

Fig. 10.19

The Page Numbering
dialog box.

4. Type the page number you want to appear on the current page of your document (such as 1). Press Tab.

5. In the Position on Line area, choose whether you want the page number centered or positioned a certain amount of space from the left margin. If you want to center the page number, press C; if you want to enter a measurement for the From Left Margin box, press M and type the measurement of your choice (such as *2.5"*).

6. Click OK or press Enter.

You are returned to the document, but no page number is apparent. In order to see the page number, you must preview the page by pressing Ctrl-OP. Figure 10.20 shows a two-column page with a centered page number.

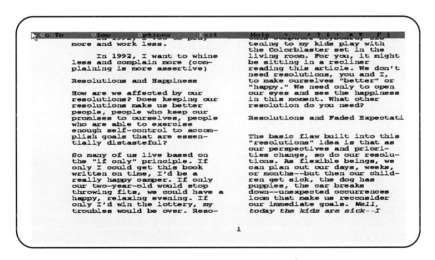

Fig. 10.20

A page with a
centered page
number.

Adding Line Numbers

Depending on the type of document you're creating, it may be helpful to add line numbers to your documents. You can print line numbers in the left margin of your document as you print line numbers in a legal paper. Line numbers don't appear on-screen but do appear in page preview and on the printed page.

To add line numbers, first open the Layout menu and select Line Numbering by pressing L or by clicking the command name. The Line Numbering dialog box appears (see fig. 10.21).

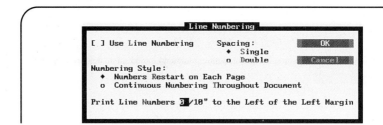

Fig. 10.21

The Line Numbering dialog box.

The cursor is positioned in the Use Line Numbering box. Press the space bar so that an X appears in the box, indicating that it has been selected. Press Tab to choose the spacing you want and then use the arrow keys to choose single- or double-spacing; then select the Numbering Style. You can modify Print Line Numbers to indicate where you want the numbers to be placed outside the left margin, or you can leave the default as is. When you finish entering settings, click OK or press Enter.

The only difference you see in the document is the addition of another dot command, .1# p1. This command indicates that you have chosen to use line numbers—but the line numbers don't appear on the edit screen. To see the line numbers in the document, press Ctrl-OP to preview the page (see fig. 10.22).

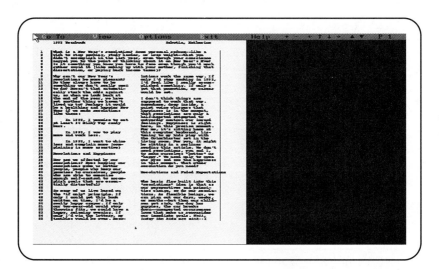

Fig. 10.22

Displaying line numbers.

Adding Paragraph Outline Numbers

Similar to adding line numbers to your document, you can also add paragraph outline numbers to your document. This feature can be especially beneficial as you design an outline and write your document to fit a particular outline. To add outline numbers to your paragraphs, use the Insert menu's Par. Outline Number command. When you choose this command, you are given the option of choosing one of WordStar's outline styles or creating your own. For more about using paragraph outline numbers, see Chapter 17, "A WordStar Sampler."

Adding Footnotes and Endnotes

In addition to adding headers and footers in your document, you can enter footnotes, endnotes, annotations, and nonprinting comments. As you may know, a *footnote* is a numbered notation placed at the bottom of the page on which it is referenced. Footnotes cite the sources of quotations, statistics, and other data used within the document. Footnotes also provide a way to include related information that does not fit with the flow of the text.

Similar to a footnote, an *endnote* is placed at the end of the document and is numbered sequentially and referenced in the text. *Annotations* are similar to footnotes except that they use a symbol as an in-text reference rather then having a numbered sequence. *Nonprinting comments* are like electronic notes you can store with your document.

You choose the kind of note you want from a menu accessed through the Notes command on the Insert menu. If you choose Comment, Footnote, or Endnote, a note window is opened at the bottom of the screen. If you choose Annotation, a small pop-up window appears, prompting you to type the character to mark the note (such as * or ##). Type the character you want to use to mark the annotation; then press F10 to display the note window. Figure 10.23 shows the note window displayed when Footnote is selected; figure 10.24 shows the Annotation Mark dialog box.

To add a note (comment, footnote, endnote, or annotation) to your document, follow these steps:

1. Position the cursor at the place in the text where you want to add the footnote.

2. Open the Insert menu by pressing Alt-I or by clicking the menu name.

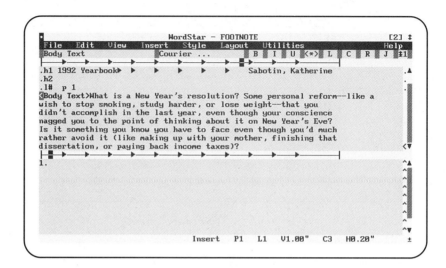

Fig. 10.23

The footnote window.

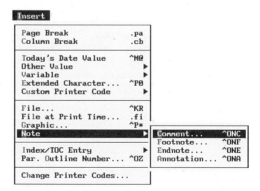

Fig. 10.24

The Annotation Mark
dialog box.

3. Choose the Note command by pressing N or clicking the command
   name. A pop-up menu appears, showing you the options for working with notes (see fig. 10.25).

```
 Insert
┌──────────────────────────────┐
│ Page Break              .pa   │
│ Column Break            .cb   │
├──────────────────────────────┤
│ Today's Date Value      ^M@   │
│ Other Value               ▶   │
│ Variable                  ▶   │
│ Extended Character...   ^P@   │
│ Custom Printer Code       ▶   │
├──────────────────────────────┤
│ File...                 ^KR   │
│ File at Print Time...   .fi   │
│ Graphic...              ^P*   │
│ Note                      ▶  ┌──────────────────────┐
├──────────────────────────────┤ Comment...      ^ONC │
│ Index/TOC Entry           ▶  │ Footnote...     ^ONF │
│ Par. Outline Number... ^OZ   │ Endnote...      ^ONE │
├──────────────────────────────┤ Annotation...   ^ONA │
│ Change Printer Codes...      └──────────────────────┘
└──────────────────────────────┘
```

Fig. 10.25

The Note pop-up
menu.

4. Select the type of note you want to create.

5. Type the note text in the window at the bottom of the screen (refer to fig. 10.23).

6. When you're finished entering text, open the File menu and choose the Save and Close command.

WordStar closes the window and places a note marker in your text (see fig. 10.26). The footnote number does not appear until you preview the document. You can remove the note, if you wish, by deleting the note marker in the text.

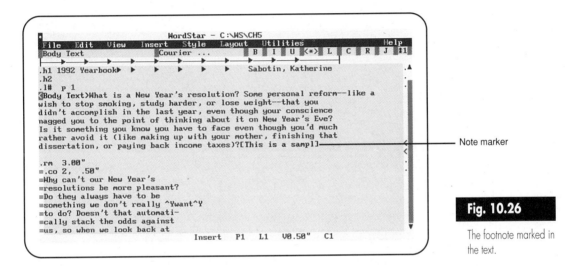

Note marker

Fig. 10.26

The footnote marked in the text.

If you want to see how WordStar places the note on your document, press Ctrl-OP to preview the text. WordStar places the note's number or symbol (if you've chosen Annotation) at the appropriate place in the text and puts the note at the bottom of the page or at the end of the document, whichever you've specified (see fig. 10.27).

Adding Comments

If you choose to use the Insert menu's Note command to add a note to your text, the note appears on-screen in boldfaced type and enclosed in brackets (similar to the footnote, endnote, and annotation notes). However, a comment you insert into your text does not print at print time and is not assigned a number.

Footnote number —

Footnote —

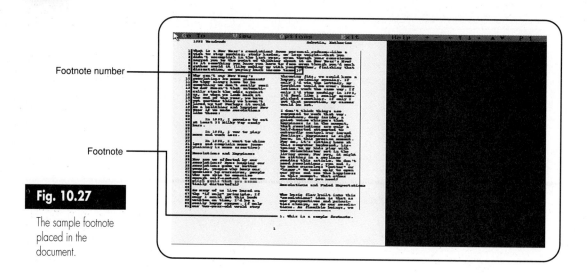

Fig. 10.27

The sample footnote placed in the document.

Are You Finished? A Layout Checklist

Now that you've spent considerable time adding the finishing touches to your document, take a few minutes to review your changes. If you think you need to review some areas, please refer to the appropriate chapters for assistance. You may want to preview the document (by pressing Ctrl-OP) as you review these items:

- Are you happy with the font selected for the body of your document?
- Are the headlines well-spaced and easy to read?
- Is the spacing of your document effective?
- Are the column breaks even?
- Is the alignment the best for your publication?
- If you've used columns, is the gutter large enough between columns?
- Are headers and footers aligned properly?
- Have you used tabs to align tabular material?
- Are you satisfied with the margin settings?
- Have you inserted page numbers?

■ Have you used the kerning feature to make the most of your proportional fonts?

Chapter Summary

In this chapter, you have learned many different procedures to help ensure that you placed the text just the way you want it. From a basic discussion of page setup, margins, tabs, and indents, this chapter has progressed to instructions for creating columns, adding headers and footers, and adding various notes to your documents. In the next chapter, you learn to prepare your file for printing, to add and manage fonts, and how to print your document.

Printing Your Documents

N ow that you've been through the whole set of basic WordStar functions, you're probably eager to see your work in print. In this chapter, you first go through a printer primer to find out more about the various types of printers you can use with WordStar. Then, you learn to prepare your document for printing, to select the printer you want to use, to print the document, and to troubleshoot printing problems.

Reviewing Printer Installation

This chapter—in fact, this entire book—is based on the assumption that you've already installed WordStar on your computer system. During installation, you used the WSSETUP utility to copy the program files to your hard disk, set up the various WordStar directories, and choose a monitor and printer.

WordStar enables you to install more than one printer so that at print time, you can choose the printer you want to use. If you want to install additional printers or make changes to the basic printer setup (you may want to add or delete fonts, for example, or choose a different printer port), use the WINSTALL program. (See Appendixes A and F for more information about WINSTALL.)

When you first installed the program, you chose the type of printer you were using and typed the name of a printer description file (PDF) in which WordStar stores important information about the type of printer you chose. You can perform many procedures in this chapter without changing the basic installation if you are using the same printer you installed during the initial setup. If you want to install another printer or add fonts to your current setup, you may want to turn now to Appendix A for more information.

Understanding Printers: A Primer

The kind of output you produce with WordStar depends largely on the type of printer you use. Can your printer scale a variety of fonts, or do the characters consist of dots arranged in a particular way on the page? In this chapter, you get an overview of the different printer types, including dot-matrix and laser printers, and find out which printers are supported by WordStar 7.0.

For some people, having a printer is an "optional necessity." If you use your computer primarily for organizing database information or tracking financial data, you *might* be able to get by without a printer. Chances are if you're using WordStar, however, not only do you want to enter text, you also want to print it.

As many different printers and printer capabilities are on the market as output needs exist. Perhaps you need a low-end printer, with which you can get the information on paper just for your own use. On the other hand, you may want a high-end printer, which enables you to produce high-quality printouts complete with graphics and a variety of fonts. You can find printers at both ends of the scale and a wide range of printers in between.

One type of low-end quality printer is the *dot-matrix printer*, which offers at an affordable cost the basic "put it on paper" approach to printouts. Each character created by a dot-matrix printer is actually a matrix of dots printed on a page. If you look closely, you often can see the dots that make up a character. As the technology evolved, the quality of dot-matrix printers improved, and you can find dot-matrix printers that offer good quality. Dot-matrix printers are limited in the number of fonts they can print, however, and the special capabilities of the printer—such as the capability to print graphics, print in landscape orientation, or use scalable fonts—may not exist at all.

Inkjet printers offer a higher quality printing resolution than a dot-matrix printer offers but not quite as high quality as most laser printers give you. An inkjet printer works by spraying a thin jet of ink onto the paper to form characters and graphics. Some inkjet printers have the capability to use *cartridge fonts*, fonts stored on a cartridge that is plugged into the printer, and *soft fonts*, fonts that are stored on your computer and then downloaded to your printer. Inkjet printers offer users an afford-able alternative to laser printers.

Laser printers represent the high-end of the printer spectrum. Two differ-ent types of laser printers are available: PCL and PostScript laser print-ers. A PCL printer typically uses its own internal fonts, font cartridges, or soft fonts to send the font descriptions to the printer. Each individual font size, style, and typeface used in the document must be stored in the printer's memory so that the font can print. A PostScript laser printer uses a different technology—the PostScript page description language— to print the various fonts in your document. PostScript printers also give you the option of producing high-resolution graphics. Of course, this extra boost in print quality and flexibility adds a significant chunk to the printer's price tag.

In the following sections, you learn more about types of printers. First, however, you should learn a few printing terms:

- *Color printer.* A printer that can print in four colors. (WordStar 7.0 supports color printing.) Color printers include some high-quality dot-matrix, inkjet, and laser printers.

- *Dot-matrix printer.* A low-end printer that forms letters by creating characters from a cluster of dots.

- *Downloadable fonts.* Fonts that are stored in your computer's memory and sent to the printer at print time. Downloadable fonts, or *soft fonts*, are available for dot-matrix, inkjet, and laser printers.

- *dpi.* The acronym for *dots per inch*, a measurement used to indicate the quality of text or graphics output produced in print.

- *Letter quality.* A term used loosely to describe the quality you can achieve from typewritten text. Often, dot-matrix printers are de-scribed as producing letter-quality or near-letter-quality output.

- *PostScript printer.* A type of laser printer that uses a special page description language (called PostScript) to receive and print files. PostScript gives you a wide range of fonts, which you can scale to any size possible within the amount of RAM available in your printer, and enables you to print high-resolution graphics.

- *Print head.* The printer mechanism in a dot-matrix printer, that forms characters by pressing pins against the printer ribbon and onto the page.

- *Print mode.* A type of print quality provided by a printer. Most dot-matrix printers can print in more than one quality, or mode. Draft mode, for example, gives you a quick printout, but the quality is fairly poor. Near-letter-quality (NLQ) mode produces text with more clearly formed characters but takes longer to print.

Compressed mode prints twice as many characters within the same amount of space used for draft or NLQ mode. (Not all printers support all modes.)

- *Printer cable.* The cable that connects your computer to the printer.

- *Printer driver.* The file that your computer uses to store printer-related information, including information about internal fonts and printing capabilities.

- *Printer memory.* The amount of memory in your printer; stores external fonts and, in laser printers, stores fonts that are downloaded during a work session.

- *Printer port.* The plug-like receptacle on the back of your computer into which you attach the printer cable.

- *Printer ribbon.* The inked ribbon—like a typewriter ribbon—used in dot-matrix printers.

- *PCL printer.* A laser printer capable of printing high-quality text (300 dpi) and using internal fonts, font cartridges, or soft fonts to create characters.

- *Resolution.* The number of dots per inch in a printout; used to measure the clarity and quality of the text and graphics. The greater the number of dots, the higher the resolution and the better the quality. Laser printers (usually 300 dpi) arc known as high-resolution printers; dot-matrix printers (usually around 72 dpi) are known as low-resolution printers.

- *Sheet feeder.* An add-on mechanism available for printers, that holds paper until needed and then sends separate sheets of paper to the printer. Also known as *cut-sheet feeder.*

- *Toner cartridge.* The plug-in cartridge for laser printers that stores a powder-like substance, known as *toner,* which places the text and graphics on the page.

- *Tractor feed.* On a dot-matrix printer, a device built into the printer itself or an add-on mechanism that fits on the top of the printer above the paper feed slot. The tractor feed has "teeth" on which you place the punch holes of continuous paper so that the pages move smoothly through the printer without getting caught in the printer or shifting out of alignment.

- *Wide-carriage printer.* A dot-matrix printer that can print on double-width paper.

Dot-Matrix Printers

Dot-matrix printers boast the widest variety of models and manufacturers. If you use a dot-matrix printer, you already know that your machine prints characters on the page by pressing the print head against the ribbon, which imprints the characters on the page. The basic technology is similar to that of the typewriter: you press the key, the hammer presses against the ribbon, and the letter prints on the page.

If you look closely at the print head (or take it apart, which is not recommended), you should see that the head is actually a collection (or *matrix*) of small pins, or wires. Some dot-matrix print heads have 9 pins in the print head; others have 24 pins.

At print time, depending on the character sent to the printer, the printer pushes a certain pattern of these pins against the ribbon, and the character appears on the page. A dot-matrix printer with 24 pins in the print head provides much better resolution than one with 9 pins in the print head. With scrutiny, you can see the individual dots that comprise each character.

Dot-matrix printers are popular for several reasons—the most persuasive of which, perhaps, is cost. You can buy a dot-matrix printer for as little as $100, although generally the lower the cost, the lower the print quality. In recent years—since the introduction of the powerful laser printer—companies have been producing a variety of fonts you can use with your dot-matrix printer to give your documents more personality. Dot-matrix users, unless they need to produce the highest quality output possible, are generally happy with the speed, flexibility, and readability of their printed text.

Laser Printers

At first glance, laser printers look suspiciously like office photocopiers. How do laser printers work? What benefits do they offer that can justify a cost ranging between $800 and $8,000?

The quality of your printouts is the most dramatic advantage that a laser printer can offer and dot-matrix printers cannot. Although a dot-matrix printer may print at near-letter quality, you can still see the series of dots that make up each character. With some lower-end laser printers, you can make out a dot pattern, but you must look *very* closely. The characters are printed at 300 dpi resolution. With higher-end laser printers, such as PostScript printers, you can't see dots because the printer uses a different technology to form the letters. Curves are smoothly formed; graphics and text appear crisp and clear.

How Do Laser Printers Work?

Laser printers use a technology similar to that of an office copier to put information on paper. When you send a file to the printer, the electronic data is sent through the printer cable to your printer's memory. The data is digitized onto a charged drum inside the printer. As the paper moves through the printer, the electrically charged toner sticks to the page in the designated pattern of characters and graphics. The result is printed output.

Two different types of laser printers are popular for today's output. PCL laser printers, like the Hewlett-Packard LaserJet, use laser technology to place characters and graphics on the page. PostScript printers, like the QMS PS810+, make use of a unique page description language to receive and send signals to and from the computer.

With PCL lasers, you have only a few internal fonts, which are stored permanently in the printer's memory. Each font must have specific computer instructions that tell the printer how to create every size and style of each available typeface. If you want to use additional fonts other than the ones built into your PCL printer, you must buy font cartridges, which plug into some models and store additional font descriptions, or soft fonts, which are stored in your computer's memory and sent to the printer at print time. As a result, your investment in your PCL laser printer may rise as you build up a library of fonts for your documents and upgrade your printer's memory to support them.

PostScript laser printers, on the other hand, don't need individual descriptions of each font, size, and style you use. The PostScript language includes a basic font description for many different fonts, and the printer's technology enables the printer to create different sizes and styles by using mathematical formulas to change the size and orientation of the characters as needed. This important benefit is known as *scalable fonts*.

With scalable fonts, you save memory, money, and trouble. You also give your document a significant boost in quality. Because PostScript characters are not formed from a series of dots, but instead created by internal formulas, the text and graphics appear sharp and clean with no jagged edges or loss of proportion.

Preparing To Print

Although the print routine itself is straightforward, you can save yourself a considerable amount of time and trouble by making sure that all the options are set up properly before you print. This section presents a printer checklist so that you can make sure that everything is connected properly. You also learn to make a few decisions about the text in your document so that you don't have any surprises when you print.

Checking the Hardware

To minimize any trouble, consider the following questions before you begin printing:

- Is the printer cable connected securely to the correct printer port on the back of your computer?

- Is paper in the printer?

- Is the printer on-line?

- If you are using a tractor feed, is it connected securely to your printer? Is the paper aligned properly?

- Have you installed the printer and font(s) you want to use?

Now that you've checked to see that everything is in working order, you're almost ready to print. Open the document you want to print by pressing D from the opening menu and selecting your file. In the next section, you learn how to place the text on the page just the way you want it.

Controlling Text Placement

Seeing your document in print is always nice. No matter how long you've worked on the text, printing the document brings a feeling of accomplishment. Too often, however, the first printout is not what you expect: paragraphs are divided in the wrong places, words are left hanging at the ends of paragraphs, or columns seem to have reformatted themselves.

WordStar provides the Special Effects command on the Layout menu to help avoid these surprises. When you open the Layout menu (by pressing Alt-L) and choose the Special Effects command (by pressing E), a list of Special Effects options appears (see fig. 11.1).

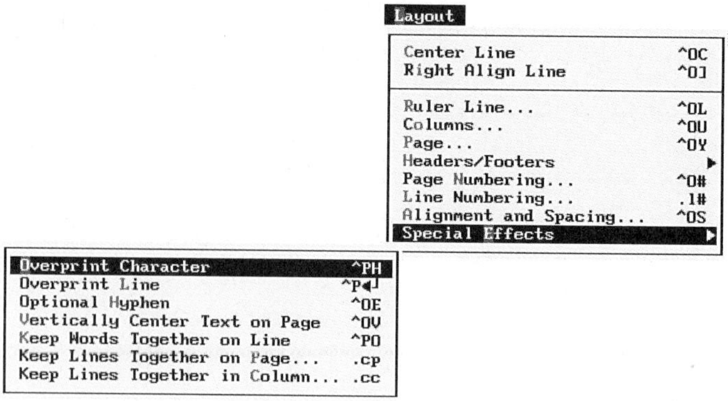

```
Layout
  Center Line                    ^OC
  Right Align Line               ^OJ

  Ruler Line...                  ^OL
  Columns...                     ^OU
  Page...                        ^OY
  Headers/Footers                  ▶
  Page Numbering...              ^O#
  Line Numbering...              .1#
  Alignment and Spacing...       ^OS
  Special Effects                  ▶
```

```
Overprint Character            ^PH
Overprint Line                 ^P↵
Optional Hyphen                ^OE
Vertically Center Text on Page ^OV
Keep Words Together on Line    ^PO
Keep Lines Together on Page... .cp
Keep Lines Together in Column... .cc
```

Fig. 11.1

The Special Effects options.

The first two commands in the Special Effects submenu, Overprint Character and Overprint Line, enable you to print over existing characters or lines in your document. Using Overprint Character or Overprint Line enables you to print two characters on top of one another to create one character. You may use these options when you want to add a special accent to a character your printer does not include as a single item.

To use Overprint Character, position the cursor immediately after the character you want to overprint. Press Ctrl-PH to choose the Overprint Character command; then type the character you want to add. The symbol ^H appears to mark the place between the overprint characters.

If you want to overprint an entire line, use the Overprint Line command by positioning the cursor at the end of the line you want to overprint. When you press Ctrl-P and press Enter or select the command from the submenu, WordStar displays a hyphen at the end of the line. Then, type the line that you want printed over the first line.

The next command in the Special Effects submenu is the Optional Hyphen command. You use this command when you want to indicate where to divide a word if it occurs at the end of a line. Position the cursor at the point in the word you want the hyphen to appear and press Ctrl-OE. If at print time the word falls at the end of a line, WordStar hyphenates the word as you specified. If the word is not at the end of a line, the hyphen does not print. You also can use Optional Hyphen to tell WordStar *not* to hyphenate a word by positioning the cursor at the beginning of the word and pressing Ctrl-OE.

You can use the fourth command, Vertically Center Text on Page, when creating a title page or a page for a presentation. When you press Ctrl-OV or choose the command from the submenu, WordStar centers the text vertically by measuring the half-way point from the cursor position and the end of the page. To center the entire document vertically, you need to place the cursor on line 1, column 1 of the editing screen and press Ctrl-OV.

The next three commands control where words, lines, and columns print. In some cases, whether one or two lines of a paragraph or list are printed together on the same page may not make much difference. In other cases, printing the lines on the same page may be vitally important. These commands give you the option of keeping words and lines from being moved to the next page at print time.

When you want words positioned on the same line, rather than add a space with the space bar, enter the key combination for the Keep Words Together on Line option (Ctrl-PO) between words. Suppose that you are typing a line that extends beyond the right margin of your document. You know that at some point WordStar is going to wrap some words to the next line, but keeping certain words together on a line is important. Perhaps you do not want to have a person's first name on one line and last name on the next line. You can "glue" the words together by pressing Ctrl-PO rather than the space bar between words. That way, when these words wrap to the next line, they do so as a unit.

In figure 11.2, the space bar was used to separate the words in the top example. If you use Ctrl-PO to keep the words together, small rectangles rather than spaces separate the words, as in the bottom example. You can remove the rectangles and view the words as usual by pressing Ctrl-OD. Still, when you go to print, the words remain together on the line.

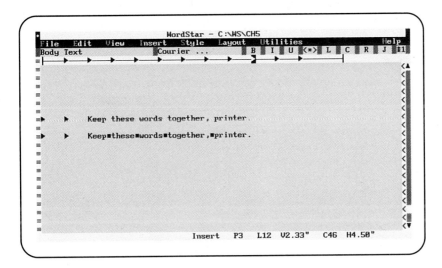

Fig. 11.2

Keeping words together on a line.

The next command on the Special Effects menu, Keep Lines Together on Page, controls the way paragraphs are divided at print time. If you want to preserve a certain paragraph or make sure that particular lines stay together, you can use this command to keep them as a unit.

To use the Keep Lines Together on Page command, first position the cursor at the starting point of the lines you want to keep together. When you select this command, the Keep Lines Together on Page dialog box appears, asking how many lines you want to affect (see fig. 11.3). Type the number of lines and click OK or press Enter. WordStar inserts the dot command .cp and the number of lines you entered immediately before the paragraph. If WordStar tries to keep the lines together on the page but the paragraph is too long to fit on the page, the entire group of lines is moved to the next page.

Fig. 11.3

The Keep Lines Together on Page dialog box.

Like the preceding command, the Keep Lines Together in Column command enables you to group lines in a column. Perhaps you want to keep a title and subtitle of a newsletter article in the same column. Keep Lines Together in Column enables you to "glue" these lines together so that they always appear in the same column. After you position the cursor above the text that you want kept together and then choose the command, the Keep Lines Together in Column dialog box appears (see fig. 11.4). Type the number of lines you want to keep together and then click OK or press Enter. This time, WordStar adds the dot command .cc before the text with the number of lines you specified.

Fig. 11.4

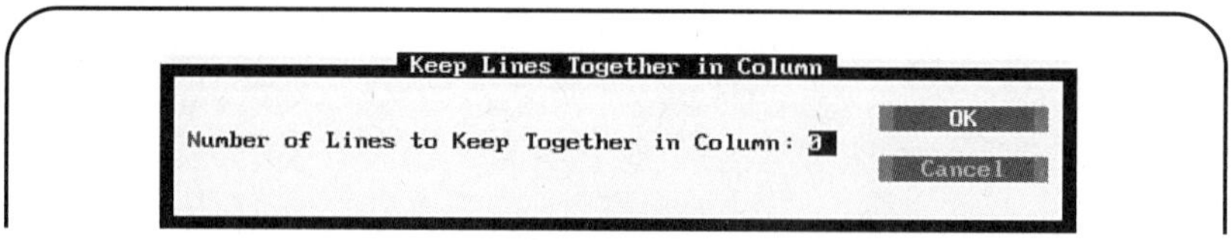

The Keep Lines Together in Column dialog box.

After you make these changes to your document, perform a quick save by pressing Ctrl-KS.

Selecting or Changing Your Printer

As mentioned earlier in this chapter, you can install more than one printer with WordStar. If you have access to more than one printer, you may, for example, want to print your rough draft on a dot-matrix printer and produce the final version on a laser printer. You can easily change the printer you are using from within WordStar before you print.

You can change the printer from the edit screen while working on the document or from the Print dialog box at print time. In the following example, the change is made from the edit screen.

To change the selected printer, follow these steps:

1. Open the File menu by pressing Alt-F and then choosing Change Printer by pressing H (see fig. 11.5). The quick key to change the printer from the editing screen is Ctrl-P?.

Fig. 11.5

Choosing the Change Printer command.

The Change Printer dialog box appears (see fig. 11.6).

Fig. 11.6

The Change Printer dialog box.

2. Select the printer you want to use by clicking its name or by pressing the arrow keys to highlight the one you want.

3. Click OK or press Enter to choose the printer.

Remember that the printer cable must be connected and the printer must be on-line and ready to print.

Printing with WordStar

You will not always need to go through all the checks and steps explained in the preceding sections. You will find, however, that the preparation that you do frequently will soon become second nature. You are ready now to learn about the actual procedure of printing a document. In the following sections, you also learn about printing in the background, pausing during printing, and canceling a print job before it has finished.

Sending a File to the Printer

When you're ready to print your document, follow these steps:

1. With the opening screen displayed, press F to open the File menu.

2. Choose the Print command by pressing P or by clicking the command name. The Print dialog box appears (see fig. 11.7), with the cursor positioned in the Filename text box.

   If you are in the document that you want to print, press Ctrl-KP to bring up the Print dialog box.

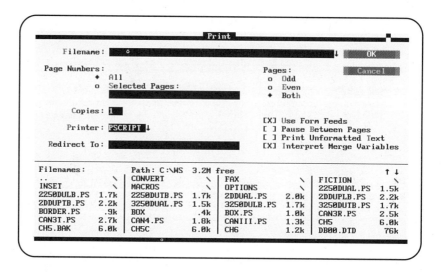

Fig. 11.7

The Print dialog box.

3. Select the file you want to print by highlighting its name in the Filenames list (below the Print dialog box) or by typing the file name in the Filename text box. Press Tab.

4. If you want to print the entire document, leave the Page Numbers setting set to All. If you want to print only a few pages, press S to choose Selected Pages and type the page or pages you want to print. If you want to print pages 3, 4, 7, and 8, for example, enter *3-4, 7-8*. Press Tab.

   The cursor moves to the Copies text box.

5. Type the number of copies you want to print (from 1 to 999 copies). Press Tab.

   The cursor moves to the Printer text box, and a list of available printers appears below the Print dialog box.

6. If you want to choose another printer, choose the printer driver from the list, or type the name of the printer driver. Press Tab.

7. In the Redirect To text box, you can have WordStar send the file to a different port or to a file on disk. If your printer is connected to your computer in a port other than LPT1, you need to type that port name here. Other common port names are LPT2, LPT3, COM1, and COM2.

   If you want to print your file to disk—meaning that the printed file actually is sent to a second file rather than to the printer—type a file name in the Redirect To text box. You can then review the letter on-screen before putting it on paper.

   For now, press Tab to move to the Pages option.

8. From the Pages options, choose whether you want to print odd, even, or odd and even pages by typing the highlighted letter of the option. Then press Tab.

   The Use Form Feeds option (selected by default) sends a code to your printer that advances the paper through the printer after a page has been printed. For most uses, you should leave the option selected.

9. Press Tab to move to the next option.

   The Pause Between Pages option enables you to have the printer stop and wait for further action from you before printing subsequent pages. After the printer pauses, you see a message on-screen that says `Press C to continue`. You may use this option when you are hand-feeding paper into the printer as you print.

10. Press Tab to move to the next option.

    The Print Unformatted Text option enables you to print the straight text in your document without any formatting.

11. Press Tab to continue.

    The Interpret Merge Variables option reads any merge variables in your document at print time and places data you've organized for a merge print operation. (For more information on merge printing, see Chapter 14, "Creating Form Letters and Labels.")

12. After you make all your selections, click OK or press Enter.

WordStar begins sending the file to the printer. At the top left corner of the screen, the message Printing appears (see fig. 11.8).

```
  ■  Printing                    WordStar
  File    Utilities    Additional                                        Help



Filenames:                  Path: C:\WS  3.2M free                              ↑ ↓
 ..                  \     CONVERT          \     FAX            \     FICTION          \
 INSET              \     MACROS           \     OPTIONS        \     2250DUAL.PS  1.5k
 2250DULB.PS  1.7k   2250DUTB.PS  1.7k   2DDUAL.PS    2.0k   2DDUPLB.PS   2.2k
 2DDUPTB.PS   2.2k   3250DUAL.PS  1.5k   3250DULB.PS  1.7k   3250DUTB.PS  1.7k
 BORDER.PS    .9k   BOX          .4k   BOX.PS       1.0k   CAN3R.PS     2.5k
 CAN3T.PS     2.7k   CAN4.PS      1.8k   CANIII.PS    1.3k   CH5          6.0k
 CH5.BAK      6.0k   CH5C         6.0k   CH6          1.2k   DB00.DTD      76k
 DB01.DTD      62k   DB02.DTD      18k   DB04.DTD      12k   DPSFEED.PS   1.4k
 EHANDLER.PS  2.8k   FG225        .9k   FINALGP       35k   FLYER         .4k
 FONTID.CTL   7.0k   HP-ENV.LST   1.0k   HP2-ENV.LST  1.0k   IBM4019F.PS  4.7k
 IBM4029F.PS  4.7k   IBMFEED.PS   1.5k   INDEX.DTD     11k   INTRO.PAR     13k
 INVOICE      1.0k   JIM          1.2k   JIM.BAK       .6k   KEYBOARD.MRG  .1k
 LETTER.PS    2.5k   LIST.DOC      .8k   LOGO.PS      5.6k   LWFEED.PS     .5k
 MAILING.DOC   .9k   NECFEED.PS    .6k   NEW          1.2k   UUPSCH5      6.1k
 OPTION.PS    3.7k   PDFEDIT.HLP   35k   PHILOSOP      24k   PHILOSOP.BAK  23k
 PLAYBILL.DOC  .6k   PLAYS.DOC     .9k   PLEAD.PS     1.3k   PO4045.PS    1.4k
```

Fig. 11.8

The Printing message displayed.

Printing in the Background

WordStar gives you the option of printing one file while working on another. This process is known as *background printing* because the file is printing in the "background" while you work. To have WordStar print in the background while you work on another file, follow the usual steps for printing outlined in the preceding section.

After WordStar sends the document to the printer and returns you to the edit screen, you can work as usual on any document. When the file is finished printing, the message Printing is removed from the top left corner of the screen.

You may notice a slight difference in speed as you work on your document—that is, the cursor may move a little more slowly, and a slight delay may occur when you choose certain options. You also can't preview your current document until the background document has finished printing.

Pausing Printing

Sometimes you may want to stop the printer from printing in mid-document. Perhaps you've noticed that the printer is almost out of paper or the paper is out of alignment. To pause the printer during printing, follow these steps:

1. Press Ctrl-KP. The Printing dialog box appears (see fig. 11.9).

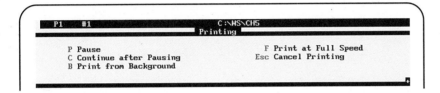

Fig. 11.9

The Printing dialog box.

2. Press P to select Pause. WordStar alerts you that printing has been paused and gives you the option of pressing C to Continue or P to pause again at the end of the next page.

When you want to resume printing, press C for Continue or F, which causes the printer to print at full speed. WordStar then returns you to the edit screen and your current document and continues printing the file as usual.

Table 11.1 summarizes the commands in the Printing dialog box.

Table 11.1 Printing Dialog Box Commands

Command	Press	Description
Pause	P	Pauses the file until you press C (Continue), F (Print at Full Speed), B (Print from Background), or Esc (Cancel Printing)
Continue after Pausing	C	Continues printing the file
Print from Background	B	Continues printing the file while you work on another file
Print at Full Speed	F	Continues printing the file at fastest speed possible
Cancel Printing	Esc	Stops sending the file to the printer and returns you to your document or the opening screen

Canceling Printing

WordStar also makes abandoning the print job easy for you. Suppose that you realize that you're printing the wrong version of the file. Follow these steps to stop printing:

1. Press Ctrl-KP. The Printing dialog box appears.

2. Press Esc.

Depending on how much of your file WordStar has already sent to the printer, the printer prints whatever data is in its memory before stopping. You are returned to the edit screen (if you are printing in the background) or to the opening screen.

Printing from the Keyboard

WordStar includes a print command that enables you to print as you type. This print command turns your computer system into a typewriter, enabling you to print directly on the printer the characters you type on the computer keyboard.

The Print from Keyboard command is useful when you need to have complete control over the placement of characters on your printout—for example, when you want to address an envelope quickly, add a special salutation to a document, fill out a form, or add a title at a specific point on the page.

To print from the keyboard, follow these steps:

1. At the opening screen, open the File menu by pressing F.

2. Choose Print from Keyboard by pressing K or clicking the command (see fig. 11.10).

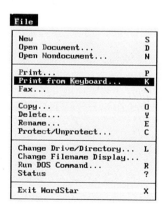

Fig. 11.10

Selecting the Print from Keyboard command.

3. The Print from Keyboard dialog box appears (see fig. 11.11). In this dialog box, you choose a template file to type the text you want to print. (**Note:** The template file contains dot commands that control basic margin, page numbering, and merge print information.) You can choose a different template file or use the default one displayed in the Template Filename text box. You also can set the printer to which you will be sending output in the Printer box.

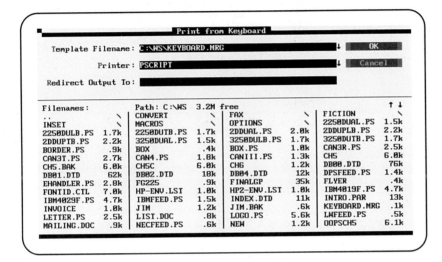

Fig. 11.11

The Print from Keyboard dialog box.

4. For now, press Enter or click OK. A Print from Keyboard screen appears, telling you to enter the text you want to print and then press Esc after you finish (see fig. 11.12).

    The cursor is positioned after the on-screen message Line to print?

5. Type the line of text you want to print—for example, type *Sample 1*.

6. Press Enter. Another Line to print? prompt appears.

7. Type *Sample 2*.

8. Press Esc.

WordStar immediately sends the text to the printer. Depending on the printer you are using and the margin settings in the template file, the printed text may or may not be positioned where you want it. If you want to change the margins or create your own nondocument template file, open the file (or create a new one by pressing N at the opening screen), and enter or modify the margin settings. If you're creating a new file, be sure to save the file with the extension MRG, which tells WordStar that the file is a template file.

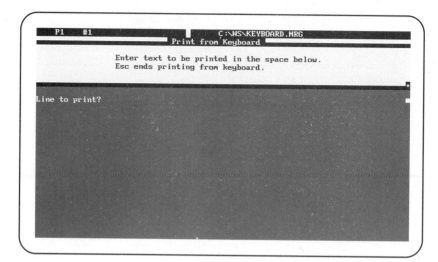

Fig. 11.12

The second Print from Keyboard screen.

Up to this point, you've learned various options for performing a simple print job with WordStar. Inevitably, as your experience with WordStar increases, you may want to try different types of printing procedures. The following list tells you where you can find more information about different types of printing:

For more about	See Chapter
Merge printing	14
Printing graphics	12
Adding fonts	Appendix A
Installing printers	Appendix A
Preparing fax files	15
Printing a macro list	13

In the next section, you learn to avoid (or get out of) trouble spots frequently encountered when printing.

Troubleshooting

The following are some common questions and answers concerning printing.

I'm getting only half a page of output when I print my documents.

Check to make sure that you're not overloading your printer's memory. If you are working with a document that uses many fonts and includes special items, such as Inset graphics, your printer's memory may not be large enough to support all the items in your document. You can create and print a test document (by copying the original and removing the Inset graphics) to see whether memory is the problem.

My printer is substituting the Courier font for the font I've selected.

For some reason, WordStar is not finding the font you specified when you were working with the document in the edit screen. Open the document and check the fonts and paragraph styles you've applied to the document. Then, open the Fonts dialog box (by pressing Ctrl-P=) and make sure that the fonts you've chosen are available on your current printer. If you are using downloadable fonts, remember that you must download the fonts to the printer before you print; otherwise, WordStar does not know where to find the font information at print time.

My dot-matrix printer starts to print and then prints mysterious characters rather than my file.

Because your printer is initially printing the file correctly, the problem must be occurring as the printer gets overloaded with the flow of data WordStar is sending out. You can solve this problem by using the WINSTALL program (discussed in Appendix A) to change the print speed.

The headers are cut off at the top of the page.

Depending on the printer you are using, your printer may or may not need the line feed command inserted at the beginning of each document. The margins also required by your particular printer type may vary from the default margins. Try to solve the header problem by entering a larger top margin setting.

After I click OK to begin printing, WordStar beeps and displays `Print Wait` *at the top of the screen.*

In this case, WordStar has tried to send the file to the printer but has encountered some sort of problem. Your printer may be out of paper, or the printer cable may not be connected securely. Press Ctrl-KP to display the Printing dialog box, which may display a message telling you what the error may be; then check all connections and make sure that your printer has paper and is ready. Press C to Continue printing.

The margins in my document are not printing the way I specified.

Some printers—especially laser printers—have built-in margins; that is, the printer does not print beyond a certain point on the page. The margins you specify are added to this nonprinting point on your pages;

depending on the margins you have set (and any added page offset margins), the margins may be larger than you want. You can fix this problem by entering a smaller margin value or by changing the offset (available by selecting the Page command from the Layout menu) for your document.

My printer won't print.

Make sure that the printer cable is connected securely to the back of the computer and to the printer itself. Also make sure that paper is in the printer and the printer is on-line. If the document still doesn't print, make sure that you've selected the right printer port. (You can see which printer port you selected by using the PRCHANGE utility, described in Appendix A.)

The message `Printer may not be ready` *keeps appearing.*

Again, WordStar is having trouble sending your file. Check all the physical connections, and make sure that WordStar is sending the data to the correct port. You also may need to use PRCHANGE to make sure that you've installed the correct printer.

Chapter Summary

In this chapter, you have learned how to print a document. From an introduction to different printer types to specific instructions for printing documents, this chapter presents how to print, pause, resume, and cancel printing. You have also learned how to print a file in the background while you work on other files. In the next chapter, you learn how to add a touch of art to your WordStar documents by using the Inset graphics integration program.

WordStar's Special Features

PART

III

OUTLINE

Adding Graphics

I n today's world of personal publishing, no competitive word processor is complete without some method of integrating graphics and text. Inset, a popular graphics integration program provided with WordStar, gives you the option to add charts, spreadsheets, and special artwork to your documents. With Inset, you can take a picture of literally anything on-screen and then incorporate the picture into your documents just by inserting a line into your text.

WordStar also comes with a number of clip-art images ready to be imported into your document. *Clip art* is a term used to describe a library of graphic images, symbols, and other drawings. You can select, or clip, any of these images for use in your document. To view one of these clip-art files, start Inset, choose View, and type the name of the clip-art file you want to see. The clip-art file names are SYMBOLS.PIX, LOGOS1.PIX, LOGOS2.PIX, LEISURE.PIX, EGALOGOS.PIX, DINGBATS.PIX, and BORDERS.PIX.

In this chapter, you learn to use Inset and WordStar for the following tasks:

- Performing initial setup tasks
- Loading Inset for the current work session
- Activating Inset
- Working with Inset menus
- Capturing a screen shot
- Exiting Inset
- Adding Inset files to WordStar documents
- Previewing the document in WordStar to see Inset files

In the next section, you get a closer look at the Inset program.

Understanding Inset

Inset is a program that takes a picture (known as a *screen shot*) of everything on-screen at a given instant. You can use Inset with most popular programs. Suppose that you are working in Lotus 1-2-3 and want to take a picture of a chart that now is on-screen. With a few simple keystrokes, you can take a picture of the chart and save the picture in a file. Then you can import the picture into your WordStar file, clip out any unwanted sections of the picture, and print the picture in your WordStar document.

Inset provides many options that relate to the way you save the file. You don't have to use these options: you can invoke Inset, take the picture, and save it with a few keystrokes. If you choose, however, you can use the commands in Inset's menus to perform the following operations:

- View other pictures you've captured with Inset
- Crop the picture to capture a particular section of the picture
- Rotate the image
- Change the shading
- Add a border
- Draw pictures or add text to a picture
- Copy, move, or delete an image you've drawn
- View the many clip-art images that come with WordStar

Getting Inset Help

Inset also includes its own help utility so that you can get help with different Inset operations after you start the program. To start help in Inset, select Help from the Inset main menu.

Particularly if you are creating documents that relate to software, having Inset loaded and ready at a moment's notice to capture a screen shot is a great benefit. With Inset, you have the following, and more, capabilities:

- You can incorporate into your document a chart that you can't create in WordStar.
- You can show a recent promotion's sales results, which are recorded in a spreadsheet; you don't have to re-create the table in WordStar.

- You can draw a simple diagram for use in your document; Inset has tools you can use to draw your own pictures.

- You can write a manual explaining how to use a new software program; you can use Inset to capture screen shots to illustrate the text.

- If you have created a company logo in a file that is not compatible with WordStar, you can take a picture of the logo and, using it as an Inset file, incorporate the graphic into your document.

- You can import a photograph you've scanned into a graphics file.

In the next section, you learn to set up Inset for use with your system.

Setting Up Inset

When you first installed WordStar, you probably installed the Inset files on your hard disk. If you don't remember whether you initially installed the program, you can check to see whether WordStar has created an INSET subdirectory. The subdirectory, if it exists, is shown in the Filenames portion of the opening screen (see fig. 12.1). If you didn't install the Inset files, the INSET subdirectory does not appear in your directory.

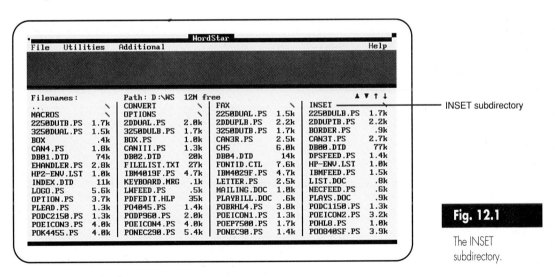

INSET subdirectory

Fig. 12.1

The INSET subdirectory.

To install the Inset files, follow these steps:

1. Exit WordStar by pressing X at the opening menu.

2. At the DOS prompt, type *WINSTALL* (upper- or lowercase letters) and press Enter. The WINSTALL main menu appears.

3. Choose the Add or Remove a Feature option.

4. When the Add or Remove a Feature menu appears, press the down-arrow key to move the cursor to the Inset feature and press +. A plus sign appears next to the Inset feature. If you see a filled box next to the Inset feature, you have already installed Inset (see fig. 12.2). You can press Esc to exit from WINSTALL.

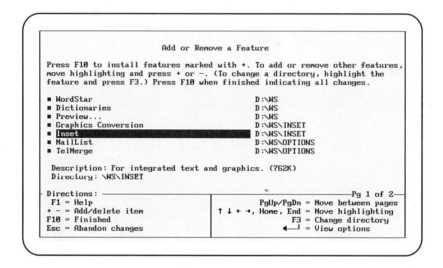

Fig. 12.2

Inset has already been installed.

5. Press F10. WordStar prompts you to insert the correct WordStar installation disk so that the installation program can copy the files to your hard disk. After the installation is finished, your Inset files have all been copied.

You set up Inset the first time you load the program. Setup enables you to configure Inset for your system by choosing your monitor and printer types. You can try it now. If you're in WordStar, press X from the opening screen to get to the DOS prompt. You always need to exit from WordStar to change, set up, or load Inset. After Inset is loaded, you can access it from any other program. To set up Inset the first time you load it, follow these steps:

1. Change to the INSET subdirectory by typing *CD INSET* and pressing Enter.

2. Type *INSET* and press Enter. A message appears stating that Inset has not been set up (see fig. 12.3).

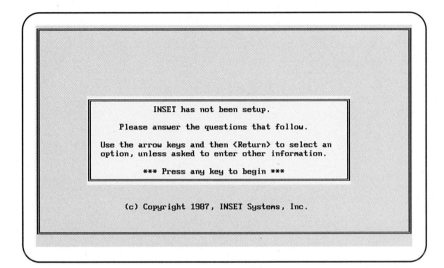

```
           INSET has not been setup.

     Please answer the questions that follow.

 Use the arrow keys and then <Return> to select an
 option, unless asked to enter other information.

         *** Press any key to begin ***


       (c) Copyright 1987, INSET Systems, Inc.
```

Fig. 12.3

The Inset setup screen.

3. Press Enter. The Inset Screen Driver Installation screen appears, showing you the various choices for the screen driver you use. One driver type is highlighted, and a line at the bottom of the screen tells you that Inset's own tests indicate that you need to use the highlighted driver.

4. If you want to use the highlighted driver, press Enter. If you want to choose a different driver, use the arrow keys to move the highlight to the one you want and press Enter. The Printer Driver Installation screen appears (see fig. 12.4).

5. If you want to use the highlighted driver, press Enter. You can choose a different driver by using the arrow keys to move the highlight to the driver you want and then pressing Enter. Inset displays the Color Printer? screen.

6. If you are using a color printer, press the down-arrow key to highlight the Color option and press Enter. If you are using a standard black-and-white printer, leave the highlight on B&W and press Enter.

Inset then displays the Hardware Configuration Setup screen, showing default values for various settings in the program (see fig. 12.5). Table 12.1 explains the various options on the Hardware Configuration Setup screen.

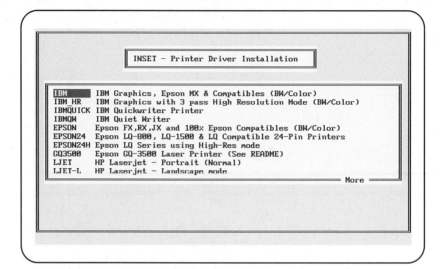

Fig. 12.4

The Printer Driver Installation screen.

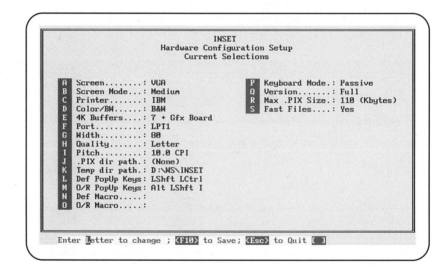

Fig. 12.5

The Hardware Configuration Setup screen.

Table 12.1 Inset Hardware Configuration Setup Options

Key	Option	Choices	Description
A	Screen	Supported monitors	Displays the list of monitors that Inset supports (the Screen Driver Installation screen)

Key	Option	Choices	Description
B	Screen Mode	Medium CGA_High EGA_High VGA_B&W VGA_High Current	Enables you to choose the resolution (picture quality) of the screen shots you capture; choose the mode that matches the display mode of your monitor.
C	Printer	Supported printers	Displays the list of printers that Inset supports (the Printer Driver Installation screen)
D	Color/BW	B&W Color	Enables you to choose whether your printer prints in black and white or color
E	4K Buffers	7–15	Enables you to choose the number of 4K memory buffers Inset uses for capturing screens (each buffer uses 4,000 bytes of RAM)
F	Port	LPT1 LPT2 LPT3	Enables you to choose the port from which you print Inset files. If you plan to print from within WordStar, you can use the default setting or can change the setting to reflect the port you use.
G	Width	80 132	Choose 80 column if you are producing portrait (8 1/2-by-11) pictures; choose 132 if you are creating landscape (11-by-8 1/2) pictures.
H	Quality	Draft Letter	Controls the quality you use for printing Inset files: Draft produces normal resolution, Letter produces high-resolution graphics.
I	Pitch	10.0 User entry	Enables you to enter the pitch of the characters you type in Inset
J	.PIX dir path	None Current Other	Enables you to choose the path Inset uses to save the files you create. You can use the default path, choose None to have the files placed in the INSET subdirectory, or enter your own path by choosing Other.

continues

Table 12.1 Continued

Key	Option	Choices	Description
K	Temp dir path	User entry	Enables you to enter a path to the directory in which Inset saves your files
L	Def PopUp Keys	User entry	Enables you to choose the keys you want to use to invoke Inset
M	O/R PopUp Keys	User entry	Enables you to choose the keys used in override mode (used to invoke Inset when the default PopUp keys don't work)
N	Def Macro	User entry	Enables you to enter a macro that automates the keystrokes for starting Inset
O	O/R Macro	User entry	Enables you to enter a macro that automates the keystrokes for the override method of starting Inset
P	Keyboard Mode	Passive Semi-Active Active	Enables you to choose the modes that fit the program you are using: use semi-active or active if you're using Inset in "stubborn" programs (where the normal PopUp keys don't work); use passive for programs in which Inset comes up easily
Q	Version	Full Small	Enables you to choose whether to install the full version of Inset with all editing features or to install only the screen capture utility
R	Max .PIX Size	110 (default) User entry	Enables you to set the maximum file size for your Inset files. The smallest minimum size is 15K; the largest maximum size is 447K.
S	Fast Files	No Yes	Enables you to create a FST file when you print Inset documents

How do you know which options to change? For most purposes, you can use the default settings for your hardware items—such as the screen driver, printer driver, and screen mode. You may want to change the PIX Dir Path or Temp Dir Path settings so that Inset places the files you create in the directory you want. If you use Inset often, you also may want to create macros that enable you to invoke Inset easily.

The other two options that are important as you start an Inset work session are Keyboard Mode (Passive, Semi-Active, or Active) and Version. If you are working in a program and find that the keys that activate the program, or PopUp keys (Left Shift-Left Ctrl), don't work, you may be working with what Inset calls a "stubborn" program. In this case, you may want to change the keyboard mode from passive to active or semi-active.

The Version setting affects how much of the Inset program is loaded into memory. If you are using Inset to capture only screen shots, you may not need all the editing features. In this case, you can install the Small version of the program to save on RAM required by your computer. If you're using the full features of Inset, leave the Version option's default set to Full.

After you make all your selections on the Hardware Configuration screen, press F10 to save the settings. Inset displays a screen providing you with an overview of all the settings you've chosen and returns you to the DOS prompt (see fig. 12.6).

```
 ┌──────────────────────────────────────────┐
 │ InSet: Graphics and Text Integrator       │
 └──────────────────────────────────────────┘
(c) Copyright Inset Systems Inc. 1989
Release 2.2 D
Full System Installed.  Use /S for Small system, /C for Capture only.
Mouse Found : Left Button = RETURN : Right Button = ESCAPE
Screen driver installed...: VGA.EXE
Printer driver installed..: IBM.PRD
Default Pop-Up key(s).....: Left_Shift Left_Ctrl
Override Pop-Up key(s)....: Alt Left_Shift I

[D:\WS\INSET]
```

Fig. 12.6

The settings chosen in Inset setup.

This final screen shows you several important items about the selections you've made during setup:

■ The version of the program installed (and the keystrokes required to load a smaller version of the program)

■ The function of your mouse buttons

■ The screen driver selected

- The printer driver selected

- The default and override PopUp keys you can use to invoke Inset

Now that you've gone through the setup routine, you don't have to set any of these options during your work with Inset. You can modify these settings at any time, however, by exiting WordStar, going to the INSET subdirectory, and typing *SETUP* at the prompt.

Loading Inset for the Current Work Session

To use Inset, you must have 512K of available RAM; otherwise, Inset cannot load, and the program displays an insufficient memory error message. If you try to load Inset and get an insufficient memory message, check to see whether you have any other memory-resident programs (such as SideKick) now in RAM. You may need to release the other programs that are eating up RAM space before you can load Inset. (The way to release such programs depends on the program you are using. Consult that program's documentation for instructions or reboot your computer.)

The way you load Inset depends on the version of Inset you want to use. In the last section, you set the Version option on the Hardware Configuration screen, but you still have the option of loading a partial version of Inset for the current work session. First, move to the INSET subdirectory by typing *CD\WS\INSET* at the DOS prompt and pressing Enter. Then, type one of the following command names:

Command	Version Loaded
INSET	The full program
INSET/S	The smaller version of the program
INSET/C	The capture utility only

After you type the command, press Enter. Inset then is loaded into RAM. The screen showing the options you've selected appears (refer to fig. 12.6). You're now ready to move into the program you want to use and begin taking pictures to import into your WordStar document.

Using Inset

Inset is a simple program to understand and use. Here's how Inset works. First, you display the graphic image you want to import into your document on-screen. This image could be a table in Lotus, a graphic from Harvard Graphics, or basically any screen from any program. Then, in a process similar to taking a snapshot and preserving it on film, you capture the on-screen image and store it in a file. That file can then be imported into your WordStar document.

To capture an image, first, start the program of which you want to take a picture. Then press the following key combination:

Left Shift-Left Ctrl

The Inset menu appears at the bottom of the screen (see fig. 12.7). If the menu line does not appear, try pressing the override PopUp keys, Alt-Left Shift-I. If the line still does not appear, you may need to return to the INSET subdirectory, type *SETUP* at the DOS prompt, press Enter, and change the Keyboard Mode setting to Active.

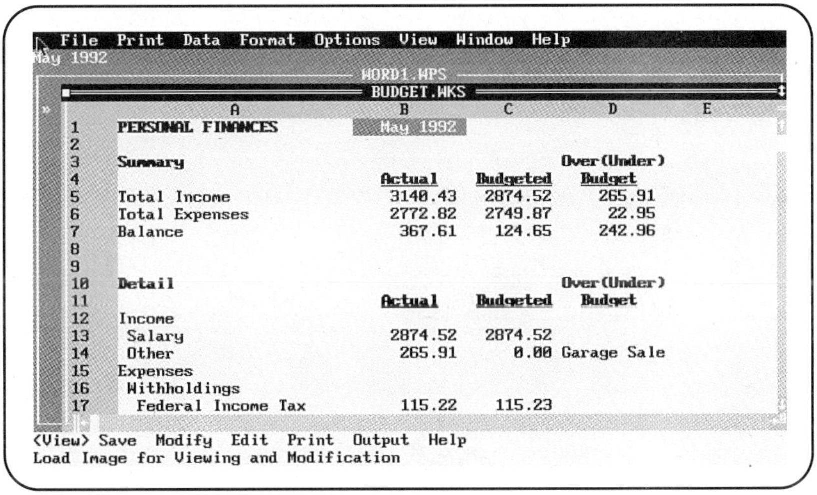

Fig. 12.7

The Inset menu along the bottom of the screen.

Quick Screen Capture

In the sections that follow, you learn all the different options you can use to tap into Inset's flexibility and power. Don't get the wrong idea, however; Inset is extremely easy—and quick—to use. The steps you can use to capture a simple screen shot follow. As you can see, the whole process takes only a few seconds:

1. Press Left Shift-Left Ctrl to display the menu.

2. Press the left-arrow key to select Save and then press Enter, or click Save.

3. The Save line appears. Type a name for the file (but don't enter an extension).

4. Press Enter. The file is saved. When the picture is taken, you hear an audible click, and the main menu returns to the screen.

In the next section, you learn about the various options in the Inset menus.

Understanding the Inset Menus

The Inset main menu line consists of seven different menus: View, Save, Modify, Edit, Print, Output, and Help. You choose a menu by highlighting it and pressing Enter. Table 12.2 explains the function of each menu.

Table 12.2 Inset Menus

Menu	Description
View	Enables you to enter the name of a file you want to view. Type the name of the file and press Enter. Inset then displays the file in the viewing area; you can make changes if necessary.
Save	Displays a line on which you can enter the name for the file you want to save. Type the name for the file, but not the extension; Inset adds the PIX extension to the file name.
Modify	Enables you to modify the picture as a whole. The commands in this menu are Clip, Rotate, Expand, Ink (which controls the way the item is printed), Pass (which controls whether the printer makes single or double pass when printing), Border, Status, and NoMenu (which removes the menu).

Menu	Description
Edit	Enables you to add and edit individual items in the picture. The menu includes drawing and editing commands: Line, Rect (Rectangle), Circle, Dots, Magnify (which enlarges a section of the picture), Text, Block, Fill, Erase, and Options (which enables you to choose colors, set line width, and set the screen mode).
Print	Enables you to print the picture and control various printing options, such as margins, form feed, moving the paper up or down, or moving the paper to the top of form
Output	Enables you to choose the offset margin for the picture, set the pitch of characters, select the quality of the printout, and choose whether to create a fast (FST) file. An FST file is created the first time you print so that subsequent printings will be 3 to 16 times faster.
Help	Provides an overview of help for using Inset

Choosing Menus and Commands in Inset

Finding your way around Inset is simple. Whether you you're using the keyboard or the mouse, you can easily choose a menu or command by following either of these procedures:

■ If you are using the keyboard, use the arrow keys to move the angle brackets to the menu or command you want to choose; then press Enter. Alternatively, you can type the first character of the menu or command you want to select.

■ If you are using the mouse, move the mouse in the direction you want to move the angle brackets. When the angle brackets enclose the menu or command you want, click the left mouse button.

After you choose a command, you can return to the Inset menu by pressing Esc or clicking the right mouse button. The following example uses the keyboard and the mouse:

1. Display the Inset menu if it's not already on-screen (press Left Shift-Left Ctrl).

2. Press the right-arrow key twice to move the angle brackets to the Modify menu.

3. Press Enter. The Modify commands appear across the bottom of the screen.

4. Move the mouse so that the brackets are positioned around Expand.

5. Click the left mouse button. Another line of options appears, displaying the available choices for the Expand command.

6. Click the *right* mouse button. The Modify submenu appears.

7. Press Esc. You are returned to the Inset main menu.

In the next section, you learn about saving screen shots.

Capturing a Screen Shot

As mentioned earlier in this chapter, capturing screen shots with Inset is simple. After you load Inset at the DOS prompt and open the program from which you want to capture a graphic, it's a matter of a few simple steps:

1. Move to the point in the program where you want to take a picture.

2. Start Inset by pressing Left Ctrl-Left Shift. The Inset menu appears.

3. Press the right-arrow key or use the mouse to move the angle brackets to the Save command (see fig. 12.8).

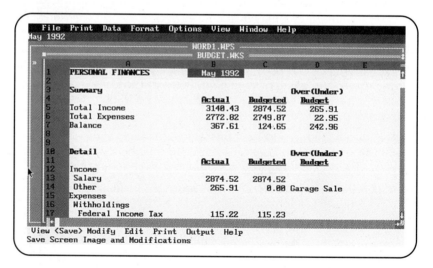

Fig. 12.8

Saving a screen shot.

4. Press Enter or click the left mouse button. Across the bottom of the screen Inset displays a line on which you can enter a name for the file you want to save (see fig. 12.9).

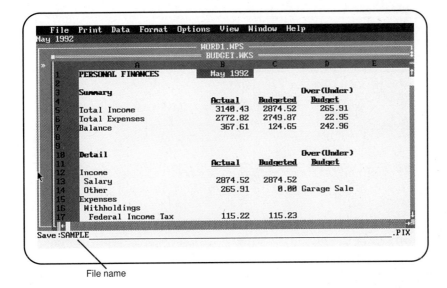

File name

Fig. 12.9

Entering a file name.

5. Type a name for the file, but don't enter an extension. Inset adds the PIX extension.

6. Press Enter.

The menu disappears for a moment while Inset saves the picture. You hear a click—like the snap of a camera shutter—and then Inset reappears at the bottom of the screen. If you want to take another picture, repeat the process. If you want to remove the Inset menu, press Esc or click the right mouse button.

Editing a Screen Shot

You can use the Modify and Edit menus within Inset to change the image you've captured on-screen. The Modify menu contains commands for dealing with the image as a whole: clipping, rotating, expanding, changing the colors or darkness of the image, or adding or removing a border. The Edit menu, on the other hand, contains commands for changing the picture on-screen: adding lines, rectangles, circles, free-hand lines, text; changing colors of items; erasing items; and other options.

Because this book is about WordStar, it doesn't cover all the different features Inset has to offer. You may want to spend some time, however, experimenting with the different options. Remember that the more time you spend getting your pictures just the way you want them in Inset, the less time you spend in WordStar making the picture fit the goals of your document. Some aspects you may want to consider before you leave Inset and return to your document include the following:

- **What size do you want the picture to be?** You can change the size of the picture by using the Modify menu's Expand command.

- **Do you need to change the shading of the picture so that it looks clear in your WordStar document?** You can change the colors or shading by using the Modify menu's Ink command.

- **Would your picture benefit if you add boxes, lines, or notes to help explain information to your readers?** You can use the drawing commands in the Edit menu to add these features to your picture.

- **Do you need the entire figure or part of the figure?** If you want to use only a portion of the picture, use the Modify menu's Clip command.

- **Do you want to add a border to the screen shot?** You can add a border to the picture by using the Modify menu's Border command.

Exiting Inset

After you've taken all the pictures you want, you can remove Inset from the viewing area by pressing Esc. The Inset menu disappears, but Inset is still active. You can redisplay the menu by pressing Left Shift-Left Ctrl again.

Removing Inset from Memory

After you finish using Inset, you can remove Inset from memory by following these steps:

1. Change to the INSET subdirectory by typing *CD\WS\INSET* and pressing Enter.

2. Type *RI* (for Remove Inset).

3. Press Enter.

Inset then is removed from your computer's RAM. You can reload Inset at any time simply by typing *INSET* in this subdirectory.

Using Inset in WordStar Documents

This entire chapter has been leading up to this point: now that you've created Inset files, how do you incorporate them into your WordStar document?

First, start WordStar by changing to the WS directory: type *CD\WS*; then type *WS* at the prompt and press Enter. The WordStar opening screen appears. Open the document you want to use, and position the cursor at the point in the document where you want the picture inserted. Then follow these steps:

1. Open the Insert menu.

2. Choose the Graphic command (see fig. 12.10). The Insert Graphic dialog box appears (see fig. 12.11).

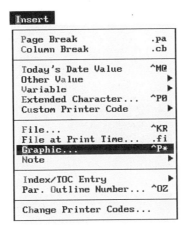

Fig. 12.10

Choosing the Graphic command.

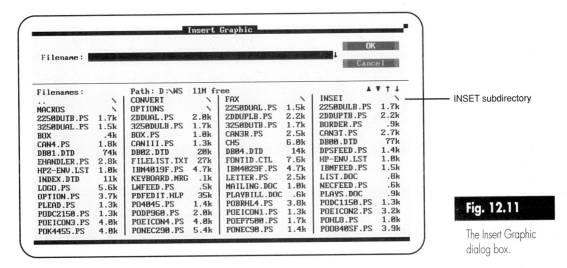

INSET subdirectory

Fig. 12.11

The Insert Graphic dialog box.

3. In the Filename text box, type the name of the Inset file, or click the INSET subdirectory and choose the file from the Filenames list.

4. Click OK or press Enter. WordStar then returns you to the document.

As you can see in figure 12.12, the program has added a line at the cursor position. This line tells WordStar where to find the graphics file and lists the name of the file.

Graphics insert line ——————

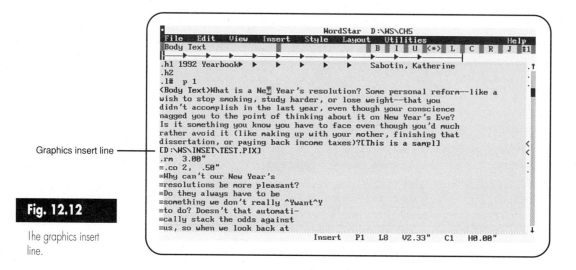

On the edit screen, you see only the insert tag. To see how the document will look when printed, press Ctrl-OP to start preview mode.

As you can see in figure 12.13, you have a problem with this sample document when you insert the picture: the text overwrites the graphic. To solve this problem, add a few spaces before and after the insert graphics line. You can use the standard keys to readjust your text to make the appropriate amount of room for the picture (use Enter or Tab, and change the margins, if necessary). Figure 12.14 shows the picture in preview mode after the spacing problem is corrected.

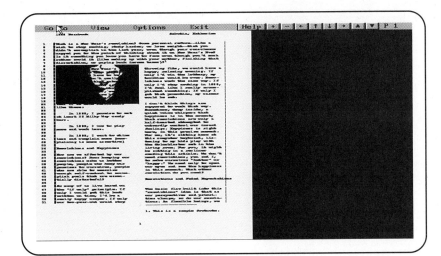

Fig. 12.13

The previewed
document with a
picture added.

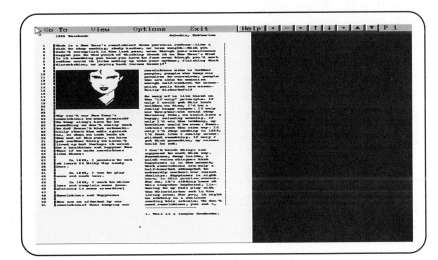

Fig. 12.14

The corrected
document.

Editing Graphics Tags

You don't have to use the Graphics command to insert the graphics tags. You can press Ctrl-P* to display the Insert Graphic dialog box.

If you realize that you've used the wrong file name or have placed the tag in the wrong place after you insert the tag, you can edit the information in the tag or move the tag to another location in your document, as you edit or move any other text. To move the tag, highlight it as a block, move the cursor to the point in your document where you want the tag to appear, and then press Ctrl-KV. To delete the tag, use the Backspace key to remove the characters or position the cursor on the line with the tag and press Ctrl-Y.

Printing Graphics Files

After you adjust the spacing of your text to enable the graphic to display properly, you're ready to print.

When you're printing your document with Inset files embedded in the text, remember that the quality of your picture is only as good as the quality of your printer. If you use a low-end, dot-matrix printer, you can see the individual dots, and the curves in your picture may look jagged. With a laser or PostScript printer, your output is of higher quality. (For more information about printing and printer types, see Chapter 11.)

Remember, however, that graphics images add substantially to the amount of memory needed to store your document. If you start to print the document and nothing is produced, you may want to check the size of your file (by using the Status command in the File menu) to see whether your printer's memory supports a file of that size.

Chapter Summary

In this chapter, you've learned about one of WordStar's companion programs, Inset, which enables you to bring pictures into your WordStar documents. Whether you want to add charts, spreadsheets, data forms, or artwork to your text, Inset makes taking a picture of the information on-screen and incorporating that information into a document easy. In the next chapter, you learn to automate your WordStar operations by using WordStar 7.0's powerful macro features.

Creating and Using WordStar Macros

With the introduction of WordStar 7.0 came a fully developed macro feature. WordStar versions before 7.0 provided Shorthand macros, which used the Esc key and additional key combinations heavily in an effort to make your computing life easier. Although the Shorthand macros worked, they could, at times, be cumbersome to create and use.

WordStar 7.0 has changed all that, however. Now you have sleek new macro capabilities. The Macros command, located on the Utilities menu, houses a full range of macro recording, editing, and managing options.

In this chapter, you learn what all the macro fuss is about and find out how to create and use your own macros. Specifically, this chapter introduces you to the following topics:

- Understanding macros
- Using WordStar's built-in macros
- Creating your own macros
- Playing back your macros
- Editing your macros
- Copying a macro
- Renaming a macro
- Deleting a macro
- Printing macro information

None of these topics, however, will make much sense to you if you don't understand the concept behind macros. That concept is the basis of the next section.

Understanding Macros

Macros sound more mysterious than they are. In reality, a macro is just a series of keystrokes you can carry out with one key combination, called a *hot key*. The quick keys you use to bypass menu selections are actually macros. Consider, for example, the keystrokes you must press to select the Vertically Center Text on Page command (available in a submenu of the Layout menu):

1. Position the cursor at the appropriate point in the document.

2. Press Alt-L to open the Layout menu.

3. Press E to select the Special Effects command.

4. Choose the Vertically Center Text on Page command.

If you knew that you can position the cursor and press one key combination—Ctrl-OV—to do the same thing, would you still prefer the menu selections? Initially, as you are getting comfortable using WordStar, you may prefer to see the commands you're selecting. But as your experience with WordStar grows, you'll look for ways to cut down on unnecessary keystrokes and speed up the creation of your documents.

A *macro* is a series of keystrokes, stored in a named file on disk and available from any WordStar document. Macros come in handy for a variety of uses: automatically adding headers to your document, inserting text you use repeatedly, formatting paragraphs a certain way, adding bullet information, and so on. You can make the macros as simple or as complex as you like—you're limited only by your imagination.

Working with Macros

You can work with macros from two different points in WordStar. If you now are working on a file in the edit screen, you can get to the macro options by opening the Utilities menu in the edit screen and choosing the Macros command. If you're not working on a file and the opening screen is displayed, you can press U to open the Utilities menu and choose Macros from there. When you create and execute the macros, where you are in the program when you begin working with them makes no difference.

After you create a macro, WordStar saves the macro in a macro file and gives it a WSM extension. When you press the hot key for a macro you've created, WordStar looks in the file and carries out the keystrokes it finds there.

In the next section, you learn about the different macros included with WordStar 7.0.

Understanding WordStar 7.0 Macros

As you may expect, WordStar 7.0 comes equipped with a full library of macros that you can use as they are or modify to suit your needs. Basically, you can divide the macros included with WordStar 7.0 into the following categories:

- *Block macros.* Block macros provide hot-key options for marking the beginning and ending of a block, copying, deleting, hiding highlighting, and moving blocks of text. Rather than use the traditional menu selection method of marking blocks (or use the mouse to point and click), you can position the cursor and press a simple key combination to perform a block operation.

- *Text style macros.* At times, selecting options from menus or clicking a style button seems a little silly each time you want to use a different text style in your document. With text style macros, you can cut your involvement down to one key combination when you're changing the style of text.

- *Formatting macros.* Several formatting options enable you to enter formatting instructions into your document without opening the necessary menus or typing long dot commands. You can change margins, reformat the document, center text, or insert a page break by using a simple macro.

- *Drawing macros.* Not found on the menus of WordStar 7.0, these macros provide several different options for adding lines and drawing boxes in your documents. Using the ASCII characters for individual lines and corners, these macros enable you to build boxes, add rules, and make designs in your text.

- *Editing macros.* The editing macros give you quick ways to delete lines and words, move to a specific point in your document, find and replace text, undo deletions, and run the spelling checker.

■ *Display macros.* The display macros enable you to turn on or off various items that relate to the display of the document. You may want to add a ruler line with a simple press of the F8 key, for example. You can also suppress and redisplay command tags and activate preview mode by using the macros provided.

As you can see, WordStar includes a library of macros you can use. You can try them out as they are or modify them, as necessary, to fit the kinds of operations you're trying to perform. (Macro-editing techniques are explained later in this chapter.) Table 13.1 lists the macros by name and gives the corresponding hot keys and a brief description of each macro.

Table 13.1 Macros Supplied with WordStar 7.0

Category	Name	Hot Key	Description
Block macros			
	BK_BEGIN	Shift-F9	Marks the beginning of a text block
	BK_COPY	Shift-F8	Copies the current block
	BK_DEL	Shift-F5	Deletes the current block
	BK_END	Shift-F10	Marks the end of the current block
	BK_HIDE	Shift-F6	Hides or displays block highlighting
	BK_MOVE	Shift-F7	Moves current block
Text style macros			
	BOLD	F4	Places a bold code at the cursor
	STYLE	Alt-0	Displays the choices of paragraph styles
	UNDERLIN	F3	Places an underline code at the cursor
Formatting macros			
	MARGIN_L	Ctrl-F5	Enables you to set the left margin
	MARGIN_P	Ctrl-F7	Sets the paragraph margin to .5 for the first-line indent
	MARGIN_R	Ctrl-F6	Enters the dot command for the right margin setting (You enter the measurement.)

Category	Name	Hot Key	Description
	PG_BREAK	Ctrl-F8	Inserts a page break at the cursor
	CENTER	Shift-F2	Centers the current line
	REFORMAT	F7	Reformats the current paragraph
Drawing macros			
	DRW_B_L	Alt-F5	Draws bottom left corner of a box
	DRW_B_R	Alt-F6	Draws bottom right corner of a box
	DRW_HORZ	Alt-F2	Draws a horizontal line
	DRW_H_DN	Alt-F7	Draws a horizontal split character, facing down (T)
	DRW_H_UP	Alt-F8	Draws a horizontal split character, facing up
	DRW_T_L	Alt-F3	Draws top left corner
	DRW_T_R	Alt-F4	Draws top right corner
	DRW_VERT	Alt-F1	Draws a vertical line
	DRW_V_L	Alt-F10	Draws a vertical split, facing left
	DRW_V_R	Alt-F9	Draws a vertical split, facing right
Editing macros			
	DEL_LINE	F5	Deletes the current line
	DEL_WORD	F6	Deletes the word at the cursor
	FIND	Ctrl-F1	Displays the Find dialog box
	FIND_NXT	Ctrl-F3	Finds next occurrence of entered text
	FIND_RPL	Ctrl-F2	Starts a find-and-replace operation
	GOTO_LNL	Ctrl-F9	Moves cursor to the beginning of the line (left)
	GOTO_LNR	Ctrl-F10	Moves cursor to the end of the line (right)
	GOTO_PG	Ctrl-F4	Displays the Go to Page dialog box
	SAVE	F9	Saves the file
	SPL_ALL	Shift-F3	Starts the spelling checker

continues

Table 13.1 Continued

Category	Name	Hot Key	Description
	SPL_WORD	Shift-F4	Checks the spelling of the word at the cursor
	UNDO	F2	Cancels last deletion
Display macros			
	DISPLAY	Shift-F1	Suppresses and redisplays command tags and block highlighting
	RULER	F8	Adds a ruler line at the cursor position in text
	PREVIEW	Alt-1	Activates preview mode

Choosing and Playing a Macro

Now that you know something about the different kinds of macros included with WordStar 7.0, you need to learn how to use them. In this section, you find out how to choose and play a WordStar macro.

First, load a sample document you can use in a few macro experiments. Then follow these steps:

1. Press Alt-U to open the Utilities menu (or click the menu name).

2. Select the Macros command, as shown in figure 13.1, by pressing M or by clicking the menu name. A small pop-up options list appears, as shown in figure 13.2.

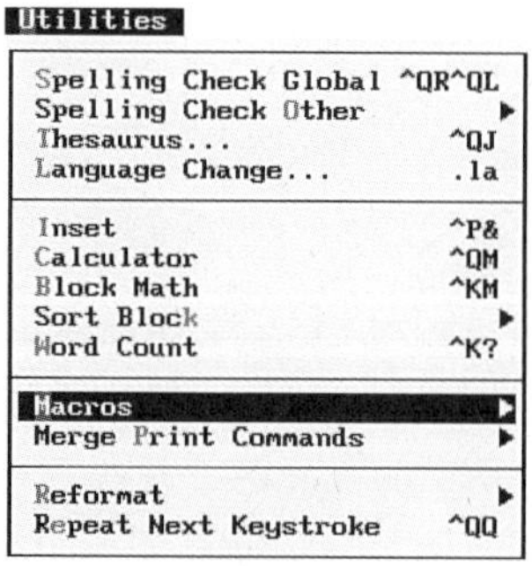

```
Utilities
Spelling Check Global    ^QR^QL
Spelling Check Other         ▶
Thesaurus...             ^QJ
Language Change...       .la

Inset                    ^P&
Calculator               ^QM
Block Math               ^KM
Sort Block                   ▶
Word Count               ^K?

Macros                       ▶
Merge Print Commands         ▶

Reformat                     ▶
Repeat Next Keystroke    ^QQ
```

Fig. 13.1

Choosing the Macros command.

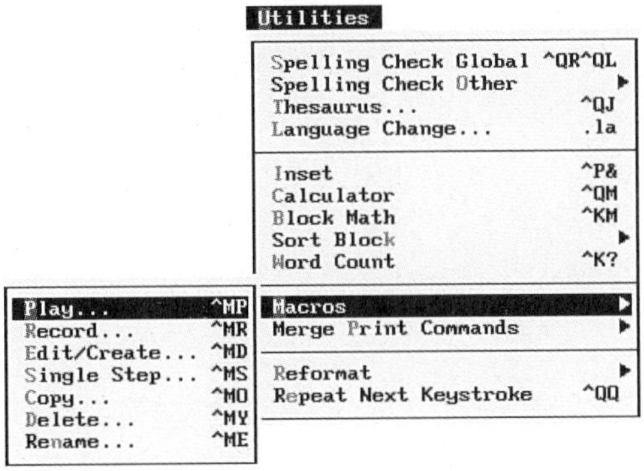

Fig. 13.2

The Macros submenu.

On that options list are all your macro options, wrapped up in one nice, neat little box. Table 13.2 introduces each command in more detail. The commands also are further discussed later in this chapter.

Macro Alternatives

Remember that you don't have to be in the edit screen to display the macro options. You can also access WordStar's macro capabilities from the Utilities menu on the opening screen.

Table 13.2 The Macros Submenu Commands

Command	Quick Key	Description
Play	Ctrl-MP	Displays Play Macro dialog box, enables you to choose a macro to play back
Record	Ctrl-MR	Records your keystrokes for inclusion in a macro
Edit/Create	Ctrl-MD	Enables you to edit a recorded macro or write your own macro
Single Step	Ctrl-MS	Plays a macro step-by-step so that you can check for errors
Copy	Ctrl-MO	Copies a selected macro to a different file
Delete	Ctrl-MY	Deletes a selected macro
Rename	Ctrl-ME	Renames a selected macro and assigns a new hot key

Now that you know where to find the necessary options for running and creating macros, try one of the built-in macros. You use the Play Macro dialog box, accessed through the Play option of the Macros submenu, to start the macro (see fig. 13.3). The Play Macro dialog box enables you to select the macro you want to use by typing the macro name in the appropriate box or by using the arrow keys to highlight the macro in the displayed list, and then pressing Enter. If you're using the mouse, you can position the mouse cursor on the name of the macro you want and double-click.

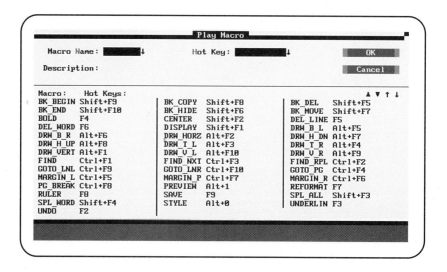

Fig. 13.3

The Play Macro dialog box.

To play a macro, first press Esc to back out of all menus. Then follow these steps:

1. Position the cursor at an appropriate point in your document.

2. Open the Utilities menu.

3. Choose the Macros command.

4. Select Play by pressing P or clicking the command name. The Play Macro dialog box appears (refer to fig. 13.3).

5. Use the arrow keys or the mouse to select the macro you want. You can look through the macros and display their descriptions by pressing the arrow keys and reading the Description line.

   Figure 13.4 shows the Play Macro dialog box after the SPL_ALL macro has been selected. (The SPL_ALL macro begins a global spelling check in the current document.)

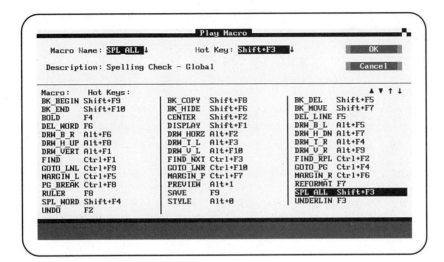

Fig. 13.4

Selecting a macro to
be played.

6. Press Enter or click OK. WordStar begins checking the spelling in
   your document and displays the Spelling Check dialog box. You
   then can proceed with the spelling check as usual, or press Esc to
   cancel the activity.

You may want to experiment with the various macros included with
WordStar 7.0. Undoubtedly, as your experience with WordStar grows,
you may think of ways to enhance the macros already there and come
up with macro ideas of your own. The next section shows you how to
create your own macros using WordStar.

Playing with Quick Keys

You don't have to use the menu selections when you want to play a
macro; you can bypass the menus by pressing Ctrl-MP. Or you can
press the two-letter hot-key combination, and the macro executes.

Creating a Macro

WordStar gives you two different options for the way you create your
macros. You can record the macros—that is, you can have WordStar
record the keystrokes you press as you perform an operation you use
often. WordStar then assigns those keystrokes to the hot key you

specify. The next time you press the hot key, the commands are carried out instantly. The other option for creating a macro is a little more complex—in this case, you use WordStar's macro language to write your own macros. This section explains both techniques.

Recording and Playing a Macro

Start with something simple. Suppose that you are responsible for creating documents for the marketing department of your company. On every document, you routinely enter a header that includes the company name, the department, and your name. Rather than enter the same header information time after time, you can create a macro and have WordStar do the work for you. To create the macro, you follow the steps you follow to enter and format the information. The one restriction is that you must use the keyboard methods; you cannot use the mouse when you are recording a macro. Give your macro a name that lets you recognize what the macro does; follow the usual DOS naming conventions for macro names.

First, start with a sample document. (You may want to begin a new document for this example.) Then, follow these steps:

1. Open the Utilities menu and choose the Macros command.

2. Choose the Record command by pressing R or by clicking the command. The Record Macro dialog box appears (see fig. 13.5).

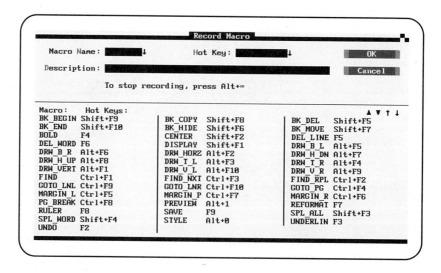

Fig. 13.5

The Record Macro dialog box.

Quick-Key Recording

You can use a quick-key combination to start the recording process
and display the Record Macro dialog box. Position the cursor at the
point in the document you want to begin recording, and press Ctrl-
MR. Then enter the name and hot key for the macro you're about to
create.

---

3. In the Macro Name box, type a name for the macro (in this example, *HEADER1*) and press Tab. The cursor moves to the Hot Key
   text box, and the display at the bottom of the screen changes to
   show your options of available hot keys (see fig. 13.6).

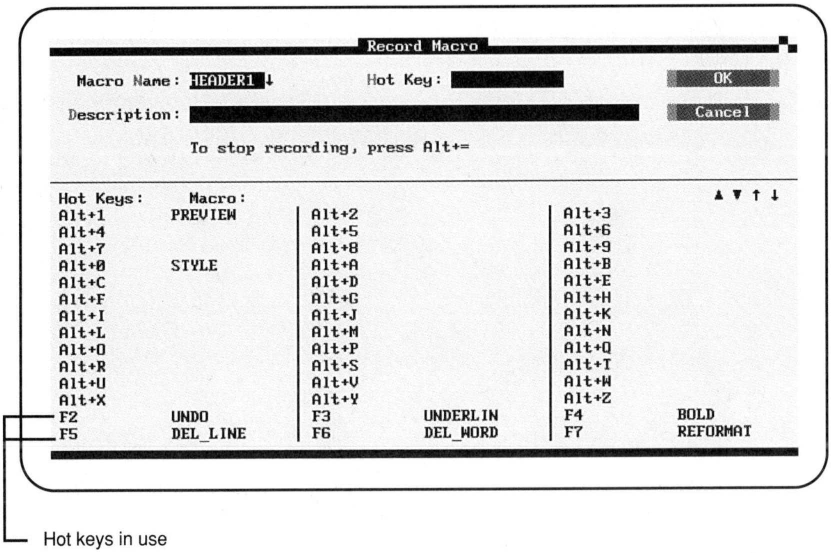

```
                          Record Macro
    Macro Name: HEADER1 ↓        Hot Key:                    OK

    Description:                                            Cancel

              To stop recording, press Alt+=

                                                           ▲ ▼ ↑ ↓
    Hot Keys:     Macro:
    Alt+1     PREVIEW      Alt+2                Alt+3
    Alt+4                  Alt+5                Alt+6
    Alt+7                  Alt+8                Alt+9
    Alt+0     STYLE        Alt+A                Alt+B
    Alt+C                  Alt+D                Alt+E
    Alt+F                  Alt+G                Alt+H
    Alt+I                  Alt+J                Alt+K
    Alt+L                  Alt+M                Alt+N
    Alt+O                  Alt+P                Alt+Q
    Alt+R                  Alt+S                Alt+T
    Alt+U                  Alt+V                Alt+W
    Alt+X                  Alt+Y                Alt+Z
    F2        UNDO         F3      UNDERLIN     F4      BOLD
    F5        DEL_LINE     F6      DEL_WORD     F7      REFORMAT
```

Hot keys in use

Fig. 13.6

Selecting a hot key.

4. Type or click a hot key for the macro. Remember that if you enter a
   hot key that is already in use, WordStar overwrites the existing
   macro that now uses that hot key.

   For this example, choose an unused hot key, Alt-2. Press Enter. The
   bottom display disappears, and the cursor is positioned in the Description text box.

5. Type a description for the macro. (This step is optional, but having
   such a description comes in handy after you create a number of
   macros.) For this purpose, enter *Header line 1*.

6. Press Enter or click OK to begin recording.

   WordStar returns you to the edit screen. At the top of the screen, you see the message `To end Recording press Alt+=`. From this point, WordStar records any keystrokes you make.

7. Type *.h1 Visionary, Inc.*

8. Press Tab three times to move the cursor across the document.

9. Type *Marketing Department, K. Smith.*

10. Press Enter.

11. Press Alt-= to end recording.

WordStar has recorded your macro. You now can play back the entire sequence by pressing a simple key combination, Alt-2. The header types itself across the screen (see fig. 13.7).

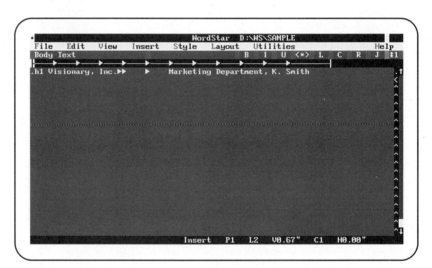

Fig. 13.7

The header generated by the macro.

See how easy macros are? In the next section, you learn to create a macro by using the macro language.

Writing and Saving a Macro

You probably understand by now the main difference between the two ways to create macros. With one method (recording), WordStar actually writes the macro as you press the keystrokes. With the other method (writing), you write the macro yourself by entering commands and keystrokes in a file. You then save the file and play the macro as usual.

One word of caution, however: this method of writing macros is not for the faint-hearted. If programming lines confuse you and program code causes you to break out in a rash, this method of creating macros may not be for you. Except for very complex macros, you should be able to create all the macros you need with the recording method.

Displaying the Macro Edit Screen Quickly

You can display the macro code of your macro quickly by using the quick-key combination Ctrl-MD. This keystroke displays the Edit/Create Macro screen so that you can choose the macro you want to see.

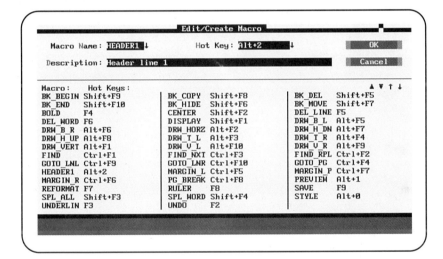

Fig. 13.8

The Edit/Create Macro dialog box.

To get an idea of what macro language looks like, look at the macro you just created:

1. Open the Utilities menu and choose Macros.

2. Select Edit/Create from the Macros submenu. The Edit/Create Macro dialog box appears (see fig. 13.8).

3. WordStar displays the most recently used macro (HEADER1, which you just created) in the Macro Name text box. Press Enter to select this macro.

WordStar then displays the macro code in the macro edit screen (see fig. 13.9). As you can see, the text looks unlike anything else you've seen in WordStar 7.0. Those lines of code are actually the macro you created in record mode.

Tab keystrokes

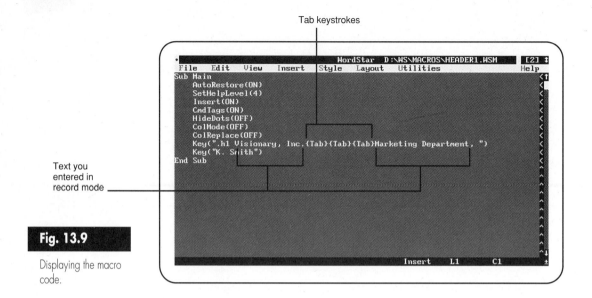

Text you
entered in
record mode

Fig. 13.9

Displaying the macro
code.

You can recognize many of the commands from other procedures you've
performed in WordStar: for example, INSERT(ON) means that WordStar
is in insert rather than typeover mode, and CmdTags(ON) means that
the command tags and highlighting now are set to be displayed. At the
bottom of the code, you see the lines of text you entered during the
example. At the beginning of this line is the Key() function, which tells
WordStar to enter the text enclosed in the parentheses exactly as it
appears.

Editing a Macro

To understand this writing-style method of creating and modifying macros, try adding a line of text to the displayed macro. The following steps
show how:

1. Move the cursor to the end of the line that says Key("K. Smith").

2. Press Enter. The cursor moves to the next line.

3. Press the space bar four times to align the cursor with the indented
    text.

4. Type the following line:

    Key(".h2 May 1992{ENTER}")

Your file now should look like the one in figure 13.10.

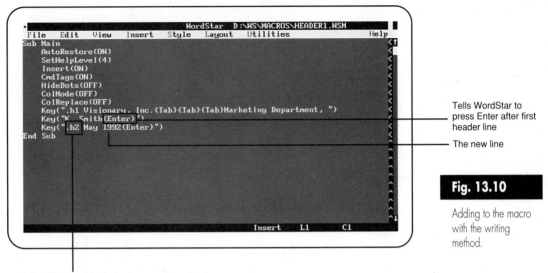

Tells WordStar to press Enter after first header line

The new line

Tells WordStar this line is the second header line

Fig. 13.10

Adding to the macro with the writing method.

Saving the Edited Macro File

Now you have modified the macro by writing a line of your own. Before you can try the macro, you need to save it to its macro file. Follow these steps:

1. Press Alt-F to open the File menu.

2. Choose the Save and Close command by clicking the command or pressing L.

WordStar returns you to the document in the edit screen. The macro is saved and "back there," ready to be used with the hot key assigned to it.

Playing the Modified Macro

Now you can try out the macro you've just changed by pressing the macro's hot key, Alt-2. The macro works as planned. (*Note:* If you're adding this header in an empty file, your header may not display until you enter some additional body text.)

Understanding the Macro Language

As mentioned earlier, WordStar's macro language is powerful and complex. In this section, you've learned to view the contents of the macro file to see how WordStar reads the macro language commands. If you want to learn more about programming your own macros—whether you want to create macros from scratch or modify existing macros—consult the WordStar reference manual that came with your software.

Testing a Macro

At some point, you may create a macro that just doesn't work the way you thought it should. You can use the Macros submenu's Single Step command to move slowly through the macro so that you can see where the problem lies.

To use single-step mode to test your macro, follow these steps:

1. Open the Utilities menu, and choose the Macros command.

2. After the Macros submenu is displayed, choose the Single Step command. (You can bypass the menu selections by pressing Ctrl-MS.) The Single Step dialog box appears, as shown in figure 13.11. As you can see, this dialog box is almost identical to the Create/ Edit Macro dialog box discussed previously.

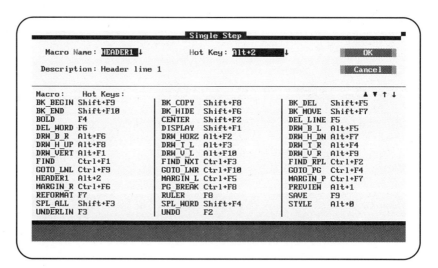

Fig. 13.11

The Single Step dialog box.

3. Select the macro you want to test by clicking its name or by typing the name of the macro in the Macro Name box.

4. Click OK or press Enter.

WordStar then returns you to the edit screen, where you can single-step through the document. Press the space bar to have WordStar move through the macro, step-by-step. That is, you go through the macro one command at a time and watch what happens at each command so that you can locate any errors. When you locate an error, you can press Esc to stop single-step mode. You then may want to record the macro again or use the Edit/Create command in the Macros submenu to correct the error in the code.

Copying a Macro

In some cases, you may want to copy a macro that has been particularly useful. Perhaps you've created part of a macro that you can use in other macros. When you want to make a copy of the macro, follow these steps:

1. Open the Utilities menu.

2. Choose Macros.

3. Select the Copy command by pressing C or by clicking the command name. The Copy Macro dialog box appears (see fig. 13.12). In this dialog box, you see the familiar places for the Macro Name, Hot Key, and Description. Here, another line—Name of Copy—has been added so that you can type the new name for the copied macro.

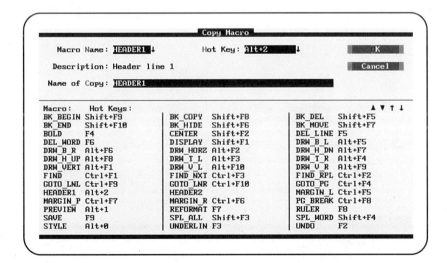

Fig. 13.12

The Copy Macro dialog box.

4. Select the macro you want to copy by typing the macro name or by highlighting the macro in the Macro list and pressing Tab or clicking the mouse button. The cursor moves to the Hot Key text box.

5. Press Tab again. The cursor moves to the Name of Copy text box. Type the name for the copied macro—for this example, type *HEADER2*.

6. Press Enter or click OK.

WordStar displays a dialog box telling you that the macro has been copied and that you can assign a hot key by using Macro Rename (see fig. 13.13).

Fig. 13.13

The copy has been performed.

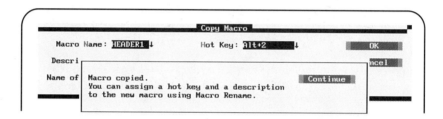

You now may want to open the macro in nondocument mode and edit it as necessary, deleting and adding lines where appropriate.

Copying Quickly

You can display the Copy Macro dialog box without selecting the necessary commands if you press the quick-key combination Ctrl-MO. You then can enter the name of the macro you want to copy and the name you want to assign to the copied macro.

Renaming a Macro

The next logical step is to use the Rename command to assign a hot key (rename) and a description to the macro you just copied. (Of course, you can rename any macro by using the Rename command.)

To start the renaming process, follow these steps:

1. Open the Utilities menu.

2. Choose Macros.

3. Choose the Rename command. The Rename Macro dialog box appears (see fig. 13.14). As you can see, WordStar still displays the most recently used macro, HEADER1. You need to change the macro to HEADER2 and assign a new hot key for the macro.

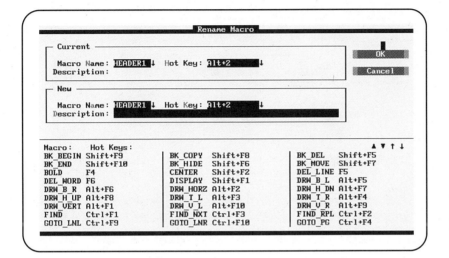

Fig. 13.14

Using the Rename Macro dialog box.

Quick-Key Renaming

You can display the Rename Macro dialog box quickly by pressing Ctrl-ME.

4. Because you're changing the hot key of the macro you just copied, type *HEADER2* in the Macro Name text box at the top of the screen. Press Tab. The dialog box changes by removing the Hot Key entry.

5. Press Tab again, leaving the first Hot Key box blank. (Currently, no hot key is assigned to HEADER2.) The cursor now is positioned in the New section, at the HEADER2 entry.

6. Press Tab twice, to leave HEADER2 as the selected macro and to move the cursor to the Hot Key text box.

7. Type a new hot key for the macro (something currently unused). For the example, type *Alt-3*. Press Tab.

8. The cursor moves to the Description text box. You can type an optional description of up to 48 characters.

Your screen should look something like the one shown in figure 13.15.

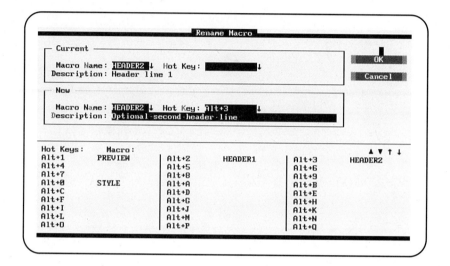

Fig. 13.15

Assigning a hot key and entering a new description.

9. Click OK or press Enter.

WordStar saves your changes and returns you to the edit screen or the opening screen, from whichever point you invoked the Macros command.

Deleting a Macro

From time to time, your macros may become outdated. Suppose that you have created a few macros to help with a special document you were creating. Now you are finished with the document and no longer need the macros. You can delete the unnecessary macros by following these steps:

1. Open the Utilities menu.

2. Choose the Macros command.

3. Choose the Delete command by pressing D or clicking the command name. The Delete Macro dialog box appears (see fig. 13.16).

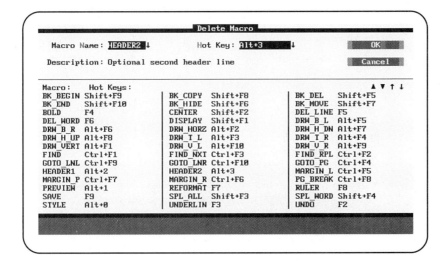

Fig. 13.16

The Delete Macro
dialog box.

4. In the Macro Name text box, enter the name of the macro you want to delete.

5. Click OK or press Enter. WordStar warns you that the file is about to be deleted.

6. Click OK or press Enter to delete the macro; click Cancel or press Esc to abandon the deletion.

After you press Enter, WordStar deletes the macro. You then return to the opening screen or the edit screen, from whichever point you selected the Macros command.

Deleting Macros Quickly

You can display the Delete Macro dialog box quickly by pressing Ctrl-MY. You then can specify which of the displayed macros you want to delete.

Printing a Macro File

In some cases, you may want to keep a printout of the code in your macro file. WordStar provides you with a means of printing the contents of a macro file. To print the macro file, follow these steps:

1. Open the Utilities menu.

2. Choose Macros.

3. Select Edit/Create a Macro. The macro code is displayed.

4. Press Alt-F to open the File menu.

5. Choose the Print command. The Print dialog box appears with the name of the current macro file in the Filename text box (see fig. 13.17).

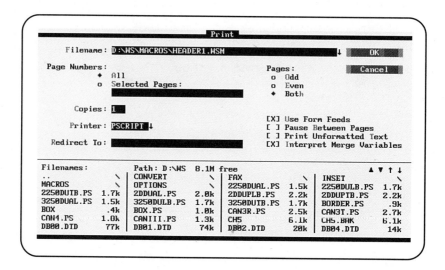

6. Choose any necessary print options, just as you choose options for printing a document; then click OK or press Enter to print the file.

After you press Enter, WordStar returns you to the macro edit screen and displays the message Printing at the top while the file is being sent to the printer. When you're ready to close the file, press Ctrl-KD to save and close the macro file.

Creating Sample Macros

This section gives you some ideas for additional macros you may want to create for your own documents. Specifically, you find instructions for creating the following macros:

- Adding a header
- Adding a footer
- Maintaining a work log
- Specifying columns
- Entering repetitive text
- Highlighting a sentence
- Adding a table heading

This section includes only the bare instructions. You can add to or modify the macros as needed to suit your document. Remember that after you create the macro, you can play it back easily by pressing the hot key you assigned to the macro.

Adding a Header

Follow these steps to create a macro that adds a header in your document:

1. Open a document.
2. Press Ctrl-MR (Record).
3. Enter a name (*HEADER1*) and a hot key (*Alt-2*).
4. Type a description, if desired.
5. Click OK or press Enter to begin recording.
6. Type the header dot command *.h1* followed by your header text.
7. Press Alt-= to stop recording.
8. Play back the macro by pressing Alt-2.

Adding a Footer

The procedure for a macro that adds a footer is as simple as adding a header. Follow these steps:

1. Open a document.
2. Press Ctrl-MR (Record).
3. Enter a name (*FOOTER1*) and a hot key (*Alt-3*).

4. Type a description, if desired.

5. Click OK or press Enter.

6. Type the footer dot command *.f1* followed by your footer text.

7. Press Alt-=.

You can play back the macro by pressing Alt-3.

Maintaining a Work Log

A work log comes in handy when you find that you split your day working on several different projects. This macro enables you to open a work log file, which you've already created, and move the cursor to the end of that file:

1. From the opening screen, press MR (Record).

2. Enter the macro name (*LOG*) and a hot key (*Alt-4*).

3. Type a description, if desired.

4. Click OK or press Enter. WordStar returns you to the opening screen.

5. Press D.

6. Type the name of your work log file and press Enter.

7. Press Ctrl-QC to move to the end of the file.

8. Press Ctrl-M@ and then press the space bar twice to add the date.

9. Press Ctrl-M! and then press Tab to add the time.

10. Press Alt-= to stop recording.

You can press Alt-4 to play back the macro any time the opening screen is displayed.

Specifying Columns

If you use columns often in your work, a macro that enables you to bypass entering the settings in the Columns dialog box may be helpful. To create a macro to set columns for you, follow these steps:

1. Open the document.

2. Position the cursor where you want to add columns.

3. Press Ctrl-MR.

4. Type a name for the macro (*COLUMNS*) and press Tab.

5. Enter a hot key for the macro (*Alt-7*) and press Tab.

6. Type a description, such as *Enters column settings*.

7. Click OK or press Enter. WordStar begins recording.

8. Press Alt-L to open the Layout menu.

9. Press O to choose Columns.

10. Type *3* (or the number of your choosing) for the number of columns.

11. Press Enter or click OK.

12. Press Alt-=.

WordStar adds the column dot commands according to your specifications. You can use this macro at any time by pressing Alt-7.

Entering Repetitive Text

Often, in business correspondence, you find yourself saying the same things over and over. You can cut down on the time you spend entering repetitive text by using this macro:

1. Open a sample document.

2. Press Ctrl-MR.

3. Type a name (*TEXT_ADD*) and a hot key (*Alt-3*).

4. Type a description, if you prefer.

5. Click OK or press Enter. WordStar begins recording.

6. Type the text you want assigned to the macro. You may include the following text, for example:

   Thank you for your time and consideration in this matter. If you have any questions, please feel free to call our office at (812) 555-5770.

   Sincerely,

   Robyn Reynolds
   President
   Visionaries, Inc.

7. After you finish typing the text, press Alt-=.

Any time you press the Alt-3 hot key, WordStar inserts into your document the text from the macro.

Highlighting a Sentence

When you're performing editing tasks, specifically copying and moving text, having a macro to do the highlighting for you can be an advantage. This macro highlights the current sentence for you:

1. Open the document you want to use.

2. Press Ctrl-MR.

3. Type a name (*SENTENCE*) and a hot key (*Alt-5*).

4. Type a description, if you like.

5. Click OK or press Enter. WordStar begins recording.

6. Press Ctrl-KB to mark the beginning of a block.

7. Press Ctrl-QF to start the Find procedure.

8. In the Find text box, type a period (.), which tells WordStar that you want to search for a period (marking the end of the sentence).

9. Press Enter or click OK to begin the search. The cursor moves to the period at the end of the sentence.

10. Press Ctrl-D to move the cursor to the space following the period.

11. Press Ctrl-KK to mark the end of the block.

12. Press Alt-= to stop recording.

You can activate this macro and highlight the current sentence at any time by pressing Alt-5.

Entering a Table Heading

Depending on how frequently you use tables in your documents, having a macro to apply a paragraph style and center the heading for you can cut some of the busywork out of your routine. The following steps create a macro that adds table headings:

1. Open the document you want to use.

2. Press Ctrl-MR.

3. Type a name (*TABLE*) and a hot key (*Alt-6*).

4. Type a description, if you like.

5. Click OK or press Enter.

6. Press Alt-S to open the Style menu.

7. Press S.

8. Use the arrow keys to highlight the Title paragraph style.

9. Press Enter.

10. Type *Table* and the table number; then press Enter.

11. Type the name for the table and press Enter.

12. Press Alt-= to stop recording.

From that point on, you can add a table heading to your document by pressing Alt-6.

Chapter Summary

In this chapter, you've learned much about macros. From a basic discussion that explains the macro concept to more specialized sections on using the various macro features, this chapter has provided you with enough macro information that you should be ready to create your own. Remember that you can automate in a macro any procedure you perform repeatedly, saving you a considerable amount of time and numerous keystrokes. This chapter concludes with a set of macros you can use in your own documents or modify to suit your needs. The next chapter explains how to create mailing lists and labels with WordStar 7.0.

Creating Form Letters and Labels

One of the biggest benefits of word processing software is the "reusable data" concept. Rather than type your documents over and over on a typewriter, you can type your text once and use it repeatedly. But what if each version of the letter you create varies slightly? Suppose that you want to send a form letter to 100 different customers. In each letter, the customer's name and address is different. You can solve this problem in two ways:

- You can make 100 copies of the same letter and type the correct name and address information.

- You can create a form letter and a data file (which contains the name and address information) and have WordStar merge the two files when you print.

As you can imagine, the first option doesn't save you much time and effort. The second option—the topic of this chapter—enables you to keep a running data file of important information, which you can print in a letter by pressing a few simple keystrokes.

WordStar 7.0's merge-printing capabilities enable you to create a form letter and have WordStar merge information from a data file into the individual letters you print. This version of WordStar also includes the MailList utility, which provides you with an easy way to enter and organize your data, which you then can print in your documents.

In this chapter, you learn how to perform the following tasks:

- Create a standard form letter
- Choose a data file
- Define and enter variables on the form letter
- Use a WordStar nondocument file to enter data to be inserted into the form letter at print time
- Use the MailList utility to choose a data form and create a data file
- Print form letters
- Use MailList to create mailing labels
- Print mailing labels
- Print a data list

Understanding Variables

A form letter is slightly different from a regular letter in that all the information you type is not printed exactly as it is entered into your document. The form letter includes items called *variables*, which mark the places where, at print time, WordStar substitutes data from the data file. You show WordStar which items are variables by enclosing the variable name in ampersands (&). If you want to use a customer's first name in the greeting of the letter, for example, you type

Dear &Firstname&,

WordStar prints the word *Dear*, inserts the space, and prints the comma after the variable, as you have entered them. When the program encounters the &Firstname& variable, WordStar searches the data file you've chosen to merge with the file (you learn how to choose the data file later in this chapter), finds the data that goes with the variable name you've entered, and merges the data at print time. In the printed document, the line appears as follows:

Dear Brenda,

First, consider the kind of information you want to use as variable information. In a typical form letter, you might use the following variables:

Item	Variable	Example
First name	&Firstname&	Brenda
Last name	&Lastname&	Reynolds
Title	&Title&	President
Company name	&Company&	Baskets, Inc.
Address	&Address&	1420 W. Elm
City	&City&	Columbus
State	&State&	IN
ZIP code	&ZIP&	47201

The preceding list includes variables you typically would use in the opening of a business letter. You can use any variable name you like; you don't have to use the ones shown here. Depending on the kind of letter you're preparing, you also may want to include variables such as &Phone&, &AccountNo.&, and &ShipDate&.

You can also place variables in the body of your document. You may want to use a variable, such as &Product&, for example, so that you can substitute the name of the product the customer is interested in. In the following sentences, &Product& is replaced with the name of the product you list in the data file:

> We appreciate your interest in our new line of &Product&. We've received your request form and will be sending you our complete &Product& catalog in today's mail.

The &Product& for one client may be children's books, and another client may be interested in educational tapes. By including this variable in your document, you save yourself the trouble of specifying manually the item in which the client is interested.

Follow these guidelines for adding variables in your documents:

- **Don't include spaces in the variable name.** Use &Firstname& instead of &First name&, for example.

- **If you're using the first and last names of the client, put the names in different variables**—for example, &Firstname& and &Lastname&. If you use only one variable, such as &Clientname&, you cannot break the names up in your document.

- **Remember that the variable is replaced with the data exactly as the variable is entered**—from the first & to the last &. If you add extra spaces before or after the ampersands, WordStar leaves those spaces in your document at print time.

■ *You can use a variable to insert the date.* The &&& variable inserts the DOS date your computer uses in your document at the specified location.

■ *You can have WordStar perform calculations based on the variables you enter.* If you have one variable named &Sales1& for the sales results for the first quarter, and a second variable named &Sales2& for second-quarter sales results, for example, you can have WordStar add the sales for the first two quarters by using the Set Variable to Math Result command. (See "Performing Math Functions with Variables" for more information on the Set Variable command.)

Understanding Merge Print Commands

You find all the commands you need for setting up variables on the Utilities menu. Start by opening a new document. When the blank edit screen appears, open the Utilities menu by pressing Alt-U or by clicking the menu name. Then press P to choose the Merge Print Commands or click the command name. The Merge Print commands appear, as shown in figure 14.1.

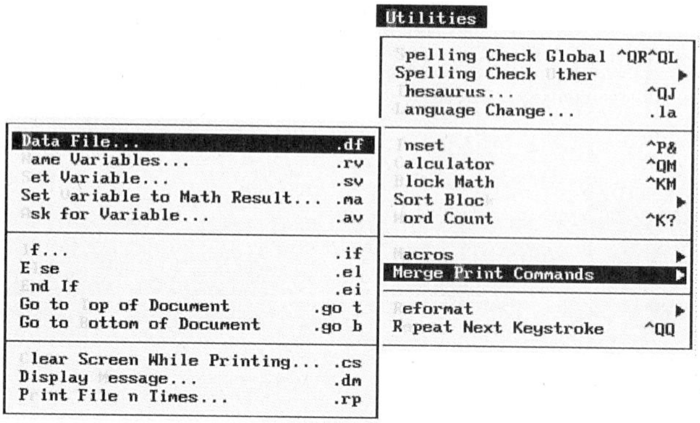

Fig. 14.1

The Merge Print commands.

You get some practice using these commands throughout this chapter. Table 14.1 summarizes the commands and their functions.

Table 14.1 Merge Print Commands

Command	Description
Data File	Enables you to specify the data file you want to use
Name Variables	Enables you to enter variable names into a document
Set Variable	Assigns a variable name to a specific value
Set Variable to Math Result	Enables you to include calculations in variables
Ask for Variable	Pauses printing at specific place and waits for user to enter variable information
If	Enables you to enter conditional information
Else	Prints conditional information when the If condition is not found to be true
End If	Marks the end of the If command and returns you to normal printing
Go to Top of Document	Goes to the beginning of the document before printing
Go to Bottom of Document	Goes to the bottom of the document before printing
Clear Screen While Printing	Enables you to clear the screen while the documents are being printed
Display Message	Displays printing messages on-screen
Print File *n* Times	Enables you to print multiple copies of a document

Creating the Form Letter

The first step is to begin the form letter. To set up a document to be merged with a data file, follow these general steps:

1. Tell WordStar which data file you plan to use.

2. Define the variables to be used in the merge print operation.

3. Enter the variables and the text.

4. Enter a page break at the end of the document.

5. Save the document.

Choosing a Data File

Somewhere you need to link your document to a data file so that WordStar knows where to find the data you want entered into the document at print time. You can easily link the document by using one of the Merge Print commands.

No Data File?

If you haven't decided what data file you want to use (or haven't created the data file yet), don't worry. You can set up your form letter by defining the variables and entering the text now. Before you merge print, however, you need to move the cursor up to the beginning of the document and enter the name of the data file you want to use. You can do this by choosing the Data File merge print command or by typing *.df* followed by the file name you want to use.

Entering the name of the data file you want to use is recommended before you enter variables and text. Follow these steps:

1. Open the Utilities menu by pressing Alt-U or clicking the menu name.

2. Choose Merge Print Commands by pressing P or clicking the command name.

3. Choose Data File from the displayed list. The Merge Print Data File dialog box appears, as shown in figure 14.2.

4. Select from the Filenames list box the file you want to use as a data file, or type the file name in the Filename text box. If the file is in a different directory, type the path (such as C:\LOTUS\SAMPDATA).

5. Click OK or press Enter. WordStar returns you to your document and places the dot command .df at the top of the file (see fig. 14.3).

After you are familiar with this command, you can type the `.df` command followed by the full path and file name on the first line of your document.

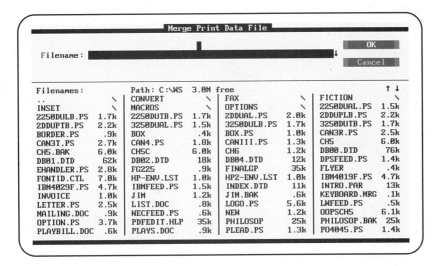

Fig. 14.2

The Merge Print Data File dialog box.

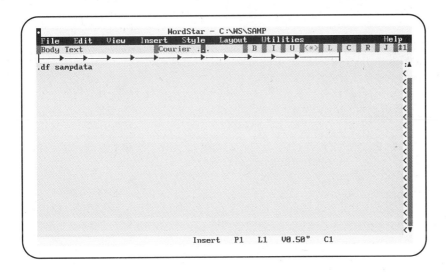

Fig. 14.3

Specifying the data file to be used at print time.

Now WordStar knows which file to turn to when looking for your merge-print data. Your next step is to define the variables for your publication.

Defining Variables

When you plan the variables you want to use, consider the following items:

- Name and address information
- City and state
- Phone and facsimile numbers
- Account numbers
- Date
- Order numbers
- Shipment dates
- Account representative

After you compile a list of variables, you can define the variables so that WordStar knows what words to recognize as variable information when the program merges the data file with the form letter. To define the variables, follow these steps:

1. Open the Utilities menu.

2. Choose Merge Print Commands.

3. After the submenu appears, choose Name Variables. The Name Variables for Merge Printing dialog box appears.

4. Type the names for your variables, following these guidelines:

   - Enter all the variables in the space provided (the line scrolls to the left if you use all available space).

   - After each variable, type a comma and press the space bar before typing another variable name.

   Figure 14.4 shows an example of variables entered in the Name Variables for Merge Printing dialog box.

5. After you enter all variables, click OK or press Enter.

WordStar returns you to the document and adds a new dot command, .rv, and the entire list of variables. Figure 14.5 shows the document thus far.

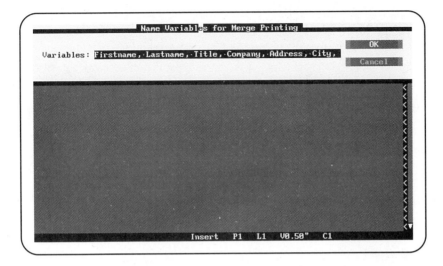

Fig. 14.4

Defining variables for merge printing.

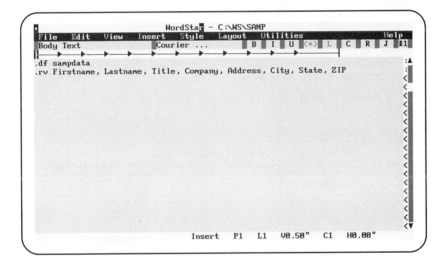

Fig. 14.5

The defined variables in the document.

Entering Variables

Now you're ready to begin entering the variables into the document. If you're creating a standard business letter, most variables you use may be in the first few lines.

When you enter a variable, you type the variable name (exactly as you specified it in the Name Variables for Merge Printing dialog box), enclosing the variable in two ampersands (&). The variable *Firstname*, for example, is written as

&Firstname&

First, type the opening address, using the variables for your form. Remember to place any spaces, commas, periods, or other textual information in the appropriate places. You can use this format or one that better suits your needs:

&Firstname& &Lastname&
&Title&
&Company&
&Address&
&City&, &State& &ZIP&

Dear &Firstname&,

Now you can type the body text for the letter. Before you add the text, you may want to add a date variable so that WordStar inserts the current date into your document. (Most computers have an internal time clock that keeps current record of the date and time. If your computer does not keep track of the date and time automatically, you can set the date and time when you first load DOS.)

Figure 14.6 shows the document created so far. As you can see, a date variable has been added before the name and address information.

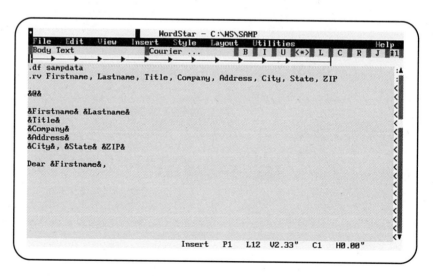

Fig. 14.6

The document with variables added.

Notice also that no margin or paragraph style settings have been entered at the beginning of this document. For your own document, enter format and type specifications as you would for any normal document. For this example, however, the extra codes were omitted to keep the letter as simple as possible.

Variable Options

You can work wonders with the variables in your merge-print documents. You may want to consider the following suggestions as your experience with merge printing grows:

- By using the Set Variables command, you can assign a specific value to a variable without using a different data file. Suppose that your company offers three different kinds of products: children's books, educational tapes, and educational software. You are creating a mass mailing to go out to clients. You can assign three different variables (such as V1, V2, and V3) to the product types. Then, when you want to specify one of the product types in the document, you can enter the variable that corresponds to that product type and have WordStar do the rest.

- You can use the Set Variable to Math Result to calculate equations in your variables and produce the result, without any further action from you.

Setting Variables to a Specific Value

When you assign a specific value to a variable, WordStar doesn't pull the data from the data file you merge with the document: the program saves the value assigned to the variable with the document file. Suppose that you are creating a letter to clients in which you describe three new product lines your company is introducing: children's books, educational tapes, and educational software.

Assuming that your company offers many more products than the ones being described in this document, you can assign these three items to specific variables. To set the variable items to a specific value, follow these steps:

1. Position the cursor after all other merge-print dot commands at the top of the file.

2. Press Alt-U to open the Utilities menu.

3. Choose Merge Print Commands.

4. From the submenu, choose Set Variables. The Set Variables for Merge Printing dialog box appears.

5. In the top Variable text box, type the first variable (such as V1). Remember to choose a variable name different from variable names already in the document.

6. Press Tab. In the top text box in the Data column, type the data you want to assign to the variable.

7. Press Tab to move to the second variable line. Continue entering variables and data as necessary.

   Figure 14.7 shows the Set Variables for Merge Printing dialog box after you enter three variables and their data.

```
┌─────────────────────────────────────────────────────────────┐
│                    Set Variables for Merge Printing          │
│  Variable:              Data:                                 │
│  ──────────────────────────────────────────────────    OK    │
│  v1              children's·books                      Cancel │
│  v2              educational·tapes                            │
│  v3              educational·software                         │
│                                                               │
│                                .                              │
│                                                               │
│  Dear &Firstname&,                                         ‹  │
│                                                            ‹  │
│  Thank you for your recent contribution to Visionaries, Inc. We│
│  are in the process of publishing a newsletter that explains how│
│  your contributions will be put to work this quarter. We're really│
│  excited about the different programs we have implemented in  │
│  Yugoslavia and Armenia and are anxious to hear the response of│
│  our supporters.                                           ‹  │
│                                                            ‹▼ │
│                         Insert   P1  L18  V3.33"  C1  H0.00"  │
└─────────────────────────────────────────────────────────────┘
```

Fig. 14.7

Setting variables to a specific value.

8. Click OK or press Enter.

When WordStar returns you to the document, you can see that the program has added a new dot command, `.sv`, for each variable you specified. After you add text to your document and specify these set variables (by entering &v1&, for example), WordStar replaces the variable with the values you entered. Figure 14.8 shows you a sample document in which the set variables have been used. When you print the document, WordStar inserts the values instead of the set variables.

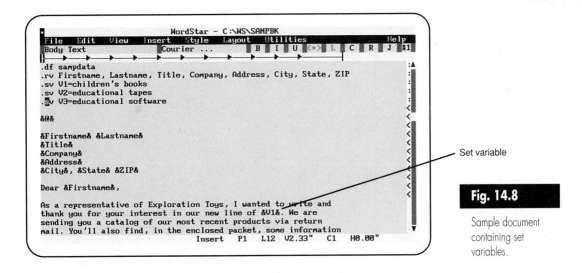

Set variable

Fig. 14.8

Sample document
containing set
variables.

Performing Math Functions with Variables

When you're working with mathematical data, great importance rests on
the accuracy of the figures in your document. You can reduce your margin of error by having WordStar calculate numeric values for you.

As you know, you can set variables to substitute numerical or textual
information. You also can have WordStar actually perform the calculations (adding, subtracting, dividing, and multiplying information), even
when those calculations occur within other variables.

The example letter shown in figure 14.9 includes several numeric
variables:

- &acctno&, for the account number

- &pymt&, for the client's monthly payment

- &duedate&, for the date on which the bill is past due

- &chrge&, for the calculated variable that displays the late fee

To use the math feature to calculate information in your variables, follow
these steps:

1. Position the cursor after the other dot commands at the top of the
   document.

2. Press Alt-U to open the Utilities menu.

3. Choose Merge Print Commands.

4. From the submenu, choose Set Variable to Math Result. The Set
   Variable to Math Result dialog box appears.

Late fee charge variable

Account number variable

Payment variable

Due date variable

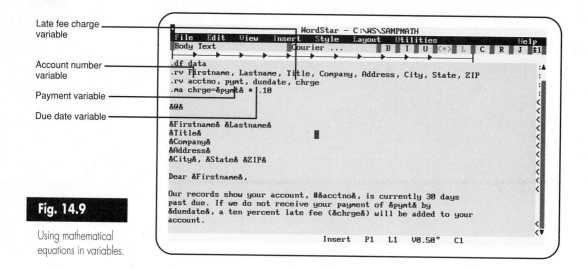

Fig. 14.9

Using mathematical equations in variables.

5. In the Variable Name text box, type the variable name you want to display the result of the calculation (in this case, *chrge*). Don't enter the ampersands (&) around the variable when you type the variable name in this line. Press Tab.

6. Enter the calculation you want WordStar to perform in the Mathematical Expression to be Calculated text box. If you use another variable to calculate the result, enclose that variable in ampersands. For this example, enter

&pymt& * .10

Figure 14.10 shows the information entered in the Set Variable to Math Result dialog box.

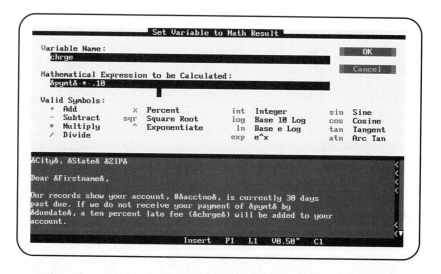

Fig. 14.10

Entering information for math variables.

7. Click OK or press Enter.

When you return to your document, WordStar has added the following dot command to your document:

```
.ma chrge=&pymt& * .10
```

When WordStar merge prints the document with its corresponding data file, the program calculates and prints the result in the correct place.

Entering Text

Now you can type the text as usual for your document. Use any paragraph styles, margin settings, or other options you think are necessary for the layout of your document.

Take a few minutes and compose a sample document. If you prefer, you can use the following example (remember that you entered the variables and the greeting in an earlier section):

Thank you for your recent subscription to *Home and Office*. We feel strongly that you will find the articles, tips, and time management features included in our publication—every month—will help you make a success of your individual home/office endeavor.

For most of us, the adjustment from corporate life to home/office life is both freeing and taxing. Now, with &Company&, you have the flexibility to set your own hours, but you also have the added responsibility of making everything work. We've enclosed, for your consideration, a postage-paid postcard that you can return to us if you are interested in networking with other home/office entrepreneurs in the &State& area.

Sincerely,

Figure 14.11 shows the document in its current state.

After you create the document, you need to save it as usual. Open the File menu and choose the Save command. When the Save dialog box appears, enter a file name and click OK or press Enter.

Taking Notes

Before you leave your document and begin working on the data file, you may want to make a list of the variables used in the document. Write the variables down, in the order they are used in the publication. This list should come in handy when you begin entering data in the data file.

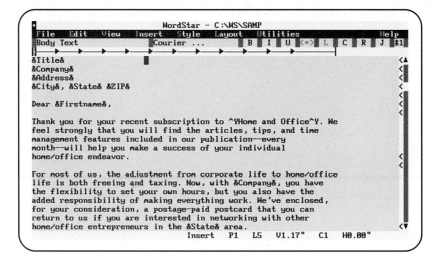

Fig. 14.11

The current document.

Creating the Data File

Now you're ready to create the data file. You have two options for the way you establish a data file. You can use nondocument mode to open a file and type the data, following a careful format; or you can build a database of information by using MailList, a utility created specifically for use in a merge operation. In this section, you learn to use WordStar to enter the data for your merge print operation.

If you are working with only a small amount of data, you should use WordStar rather than MailList because you may find entering a small amount of data easier in nondocument mode. The following section tells you how to use WordStar to create your data file. In the next section, you learn to use MailList to create a data file.

Using WordStar Nondocument Mode

As you may recall, WordStar gives you a choice when you open a file: you can create a document or a nondocument. Nondocument mode uses no formatting commands; the words don't wrap to the next line automatically; and no dot commands are inserted. When you create a file in nondocument mode, you essentially are creating an ASCII file. A document file, on the other hand, includes all the formatting commands, codes, and special tags used to lay out and print your text with the specifications you want.

When you use WordStar to create a data file, you open a nondocument file. You can do so by opening the File menu from the opening screen and choosing Open Nondocument (or press N). The nondocument edit screen appears (see fig. 14.12).

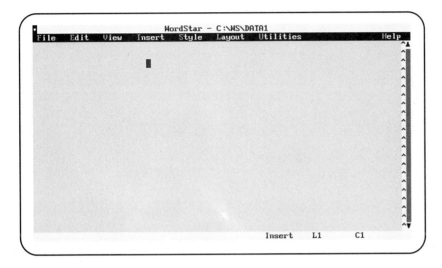

```
                        WordStar - C:\WS\DATA1
 File    Edit    View    Insert    Style    Layout    Utilities                        Help
```

```
                              Insert    L1         C1
```

Fig. 14.12

The nondocument edit screen.

You now can type the data for the file, in the order of the variables you entered in the document. Use the following guidelines for entering data:

■ Use a comma to separate each variable entry from the next, but don't put a space between the comma and the first letter of the next word.

■ If you enter a comma in the middle of an entry (such as *1420 Elm, Suite 240*), you must enclose the entire entry in quotation marks: *"1420 Elm, Suite 240"*.

■ Press Enter at the end of each data set (the data used for one form letter).

■ Enter the capitalization of the characters as you want them to appear in the text.

Save the data file as you save any other file, by opening the File menu, choosing the Save command, typing a file name, and pressing Enter.

Remember That File Name

The first thing you did when setting up the data form involved specifying the data file to be used in the merge-print operation. If you didn't use the Data File command (in the Merge Print Commands submenu) to specify the data file you wanted to use, do so now before you print. Otherwise, the data is not merged with the document.

Using MailList To Create a Data File

Before you can use MailList to create the data file, you need to start the MailList utility. Start MailList by following these steps from the WordStar opening screen:

1. Open the Additional menu by pressing A (see fig. 14.13).

Fig. 14.13

Starting the MailList utility.

```
Additional

MailList       AM
TelMerge       AT
Star Exchange  AS
```

2. Choose the MailList command.

After you choose the MailList command, the MailList menu appears, as shown in figure 14.14. As you can see, the MailList screen is much different from the menus and screens you've been working with in WordStar. MailList is basically a kind of database program that enables you to enter, edit, organize, sort, and view information you save in a data file.

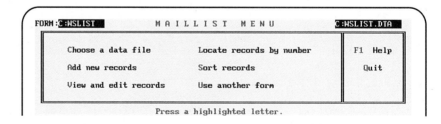

```
FORM: C:WSLIST            M A I L L I S T   M E N U            C:WSLIST.DTA

     Choose a data file          Locate records by number      F1  Help

     Add new records             Sort records                      Quit

     View and edit records       Use another form

                        Press a highlighted letter.
```

Fig. 14.14

The MailList menu.

Before you start, look at a few definitions:

- *Data form.* With MailList, you enter information into a data form similar to any standard business form. Depending on the form you choose (MailList comes with two forms: INVNTORY.DEF and WSLIST.DEF), the form provides spaces for you to enter the record number, names, title, company, address, city, state, ZIP code, and phone information.

- *Record.* A record is a complete data set. You enter many different data items about one customer (name, address, city, state, and so on), for example. The entire grouping of information about that one person is considered a record.

- *Field.* A field is an individual data item. Company is one field, for example; Title is another.

The overall process for creating and using a data file in MailList includes these steps:

1. Choose the form you want to use. (You can choose WSLIST.DEF or INVNTORY.DEF.)

2. Choose the data file you want to work with.

3. Add records.

4. View, edit, search for, or sort records as necessary.

MailList Help

MailList comes with its own help utility, which is always available when you press F1. The MailList help system is context-sensitive, meaning that the help topic displayed is related to the operation you are trying to perform when you press F1.

The following sections show you how to create a data file and work with records in MailList.

Choosing a Data File

MailList comes with two different data forms you can use to enter, store, and sort data: WSLIST.DEF and INVENTORY.DEF. WSLIST.DEF is a traditional data-entry form, including for each record generic entries such as Name, Address, City, State, and so on (see fig. 14.15). INVNTORY.DEF, on the other hand, includes fields to store information you may enter if you are keeping track of an inventory, such as Item, Description, Quantity, and Price.

```
FORM:C:WSLIST          A D D   N E W   R E C O R D S          C:WSLIST.DTA

  ^Copy from previous record      ^Write/save record in file      F1  Help

                                                                   Escape

                          Type data and press ←─┘.

    Record Number: 00003                            Date: 00/00/00
           Mr./Ms.: _____                     mm/dd/yy
 First, Init., Last: _____ ___ _____  Jr./M.D.: _____
             Title: _____

           Company: _____
    Address Line 1: _____
    Address Line 2: _____
   City, State, Zip: _____ ___ _____
           Country: _____
           Phone-1: _____
           Phone-2: _____
 User Fields—          Remarks—
 1: _____     _____
 2: _____     _____
 3: _____     _____
```

Fig. 14.15

The WSLIST.DEF data form.

For this example, you use the default WSLIST.DEF data form. If you want to change to the INVNTORY.DEF data form, press U to choose Use Another Form on the MailList menu. MailList asks you to choose the data form. Because INVNTORY.DEF already is highlighted, press Enter to choose the highlighted form.

WordStar then prompts, Data file or directory to use?. This prompt is asking for the name of the file in which you want to store your data. You can press Enter to choose the highlighted file or type the name of the file you want to use and press Enter. WordStar then returns you to the MailList menu and displays the name of the chosen data form in the upper left corner of the screen. In the upper right corner of the screen, the name of the data file you're using appears. Figure 14.16 shows that the WSLIST.DEF data form and the NEWDATA.DTA data file have been chosen.

Name of the data form   Name of the data file

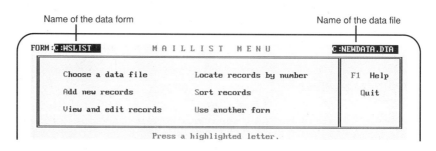

```
FORM:C:WSLIST          M A I L L I S T   M E N U          C:NEWDATA.DTA

    Choose a data file         Locate records by number      F1  Help

    Add new records            Sort records                  Quit

    View and edit records      Use another form

                      Press a highlighted letter.
```

Fig. 14.16

The MailList menu after the WSLIST data form and the NEWDATA.DTA data file are chosen.

What's the Difference between Files and Forms?

Although the two terms may seem synonymous at first, files and forms are different. MailList comes with two data forms on which you can enter data for many different data files. For example, you can use the WSLIST.DEF data form to create three different files: one that stores client information (CLIENT.DTA); one that stores personnel information (EMPLOYEE.DTA); and one that stores stockholder information (PARTNER.DTA). The form you use is always the same (WSLIST.DEF), but you use that form to create the different files.

Starting a New Data File

In the last section, you chose the form you wanted to use and chose the data file in which you plan to add data. But what if you want to begin a new data file? After you choose the form you want to use, you can start a new data file by following these steps:

1. Press C to select Choose a Data File.

2. At the Data file or directory to use? prompt, type the name of the new file and press Enter. (MailList enters the DTA extension for you.)

MailList then makes the new file the current file and returns you to the MailList menu.

Entering Data

Up to now, you have started MailList and chosen the form and the data file to be used. Now you're ready to enter the data. Follow these steps:

1. Press A to choose Add New Records. The data form you chose appears with the cursor in the Record Number field (see fig. 14.17).

2. Type the record number and press Enter. The cursor moves to the Date field.

3. Enter a date, if necessary, and press Enter. The cursor moves to the Mr./Ms. field.

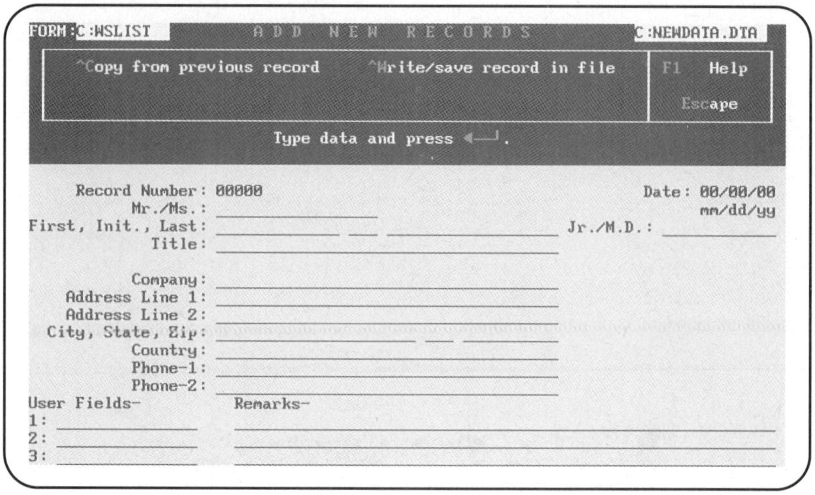

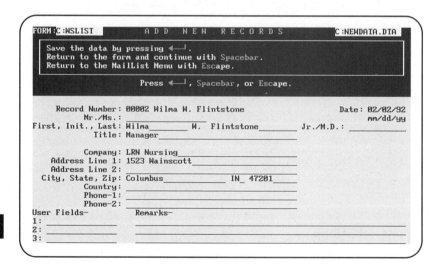

Fig. 14.17

Adding a new record
to a data file.

4. Continue to type the data you want in the various fields. If you want to skip a field, press Enter when the cursor is positioned in that field, and MailList moves to the next field.

5. After you finish entering data, press Ctrl-W. MailList tells you that you can save the data by pressing Enter, return to the form by pressing the space bar, or return to the main menu by pressing Esc (see fig. 14.18).

Fig. 14.18

Saving the record.

Copying Data

For some records, the data you enter may be repetitious. Suppose that you are entering information for clients in California. The entries you type into the City, State, and Zip fields may be identical in that group of records. If you want to copy the information from one record to the next, position the cursor in the field you want to copy the information to and press Ctrl-C. MailList brings the data from that field on the last record and fills in the current field.

Viewing and Editing Records

MailList gives you the option of looking through and editing the records you've entered. You use the View and Edit Records command in the MailList menu.

Press V to choose View and Edit Records. The View and Edit Records menu appears at the top of the screen (see fig. 14.19).

The View and Edit Records menu includes four commands that you can use to find and modify the records in the data file. The commands are summarized in table 14.2.

```
FORM C:WSLIST      V I E W   A N D   E D I T   R E C O R D S      C:NEWDATA.DTA

   ^Previous/^Next record        ^Write/save modified record    F1   Help

   ^Erase record                 ^Create/change record filter    Escape
                     Type any changes and press <──┘ .


      Record Number: 00001 Janice I. Walker           Date: 02/02/92
             Mr./Ms.: _____                               mm/dd/yy
   First, Init., Last: Janice_____  I.  Walker_____ Jr./M.D.: _____
              Title: Manager_____
           Company: LRN Nursing_____
      Address Line 1: 1523 Wainscott_____
      Address Line 2: _____
    City, State, Zip: Columbus_____  IN_ 47201_____
           Country: _____
           Phone-1: (812)378-5555_____
           Phone-2: _____
   User Fields─          Remarks─
   1: _____          _____
   2: _____          _____
   3: _____          _____
```

Fig. 14.19

The View and Edit Records menu.

Table 14.2 The View and Edit Records Commands

Command	Description
Previous/Next Record	Displays preceding or next record in the data file
Erase Record	Erases the data in the current record and renumbers subsequent records
Write/Save Modified Record	Saves the modified record to disk
Create/Change Record Filter	Enables you to search for specific records in the data file (for example, you may want to search for files that have IN in the State field)

Choose the command you want to use by pressing Ctrl and the high-lighted letter of the command. When you choose Create/Change Record Filter, MailList displays the Record Filter screen and displays asterisks in all the fields (see fig. 14.20).

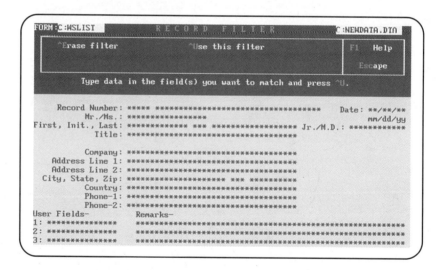

Fig. 14.20

The Record Filter screen.

This screen looks more complicated than it is. Move the cursor to the field in which you want to locate the information. (For example, if you want to find the records in which the Date field displays 02, press Enter to move the cursor to the Date field.) Then type the information you want to search for. When you press Ctrl-U, MailList searches for and displays the records that have the specified information in that field.

Locating Records

MailList gives you the option of moving to a specific record in the data list by entering the number of the record you want. Follow these steps:

1. From the MailList menu, press L to choose Locate Records by Number.

2. The Locate Records by Number screen appears. The cursor appears in the Record Number field, and you are prompted to type the number of the record you want to view.

3. Type the number of the record you want.

MailList moves to the record you specified. You then have the choice of using the other options on the Locate Record by Number screen. You can view the preceding or next record, erase the current record, or write the current record to the data file.

Sorting Records

Depending on the kind of data you are working with and the number of records you have entered in your data file, you may find organizing your data in a certain way helpful. Your company, for example, may be divided into several regions: one region includes California, one includes Washington, one includes Nevada, and one includes Oregon. If you are dealing with a large volume of records, you may want to sort the records so that the records from each state are grouped together. That way, when you search through the records—or when you merge print the data in WordStar—the records that go to the same regions are organized together.

You can start the sort procedure by choosing Sort Records from the MailList menu. The Sort Records screen, shown in figure 14.21, is displayed.

Field on which to sort

Data file in use

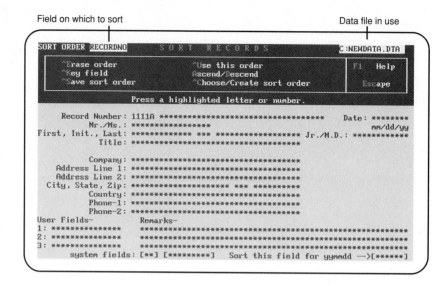

Fig. 14.21

The Sort Records
screen.

In the top left corner of the Sort Records screen, you see the message SORT ORDER, followed by the word RECORDNO. This message tells you that MailList now is prepared to sort on the Record Number field. The Record Number field shows 1111A, which means that the field has been chosen as the first sort field (the field that is sorted first), in ascending (A) order.

You can choose more than one field to be sorted during the sort procedure. You may want to sort all records by state (such as WA), and then sort the City field in alphabetical order (A), for example. MailList fills the field of the first sort with 1s and fills the second field with 2s. To specify sort orders, follow this procedure:

1. To specify the first sort, move the cursor to the field you want to use for the first sort.

2. Press Ctrl-K.

   The asterisks in the field are replaced with 1s. After the 1s, you see the letter *A*, which indicates that MailList has chosen ascending order by default. If you want to change the order to descending order (so that MailList sorts the records from Z to A), press D while the cursor is positioned in the field.

3. To specify the second sort, move the cursor to the field you want to use as the second sort.

4. Press Ctrl-K.

   The asterisks are replaced with 2s. Again, choose the sort you want. Press A for Ascending or D for Descending.

5. Press Ctrl-U to save the sort order and sort the records.

MailList displays a message, alerting you that the sort process is going on. After a few seconds (the length of time depends on the number of records in your file), a message appears telling you that the sort has been completed. You then can press Esc to return to the MailList menu.

Custom Sort Orders

As your experience with MailList grows, you may find that you use the same sort specifications over and over again. For this reason, MailList includes a feature that enables you to custom design sort orders and save them out to a file. You can choose the sort order you want, and MailList adds the specifications to the sort screen. You then can use Choose/Create Sort Order to choose the sort order you've created.

Exiting MailList

After you enter, edit, and sort your files, you're ready to leave MailList and return to your WordStar document. When the MailList menu is displayed, press Q to exit from MailList.

Merge Printing

Whether you are merge printing by using a data file you typed in nondocument mode in WordStar or by using a file you created with MailList, you need to make sure that you've done the following things before you print:

- Entered the name of the data file at the top of the document (using the .df dot command to specify the file name)

- Defined the variables used in the document (using the .rv dot command)

- Added a page break at the end of the document

If you created the variables yourself, undoubtedly you've typed the variables in the document and in the .rv lines at the top of the document. If you've used MailList's predesigned form, however, how do you know what variables to enter in the document? Table 14.3 lists the different fields and their corresponding variables. Remember that you must include every variable name in your .rv line, whether or not you filled in that variable field in the data file. For instance, if you skip the Country or Remarks field while filling in the data file, you still need to add those variable names to the .rv line. If you have used WSLIST.DEF as your form, you can quickly insert all the .rv lines into your document by placing your cursor on line 1 of your document and pressing Ctrl-KR. Type the file name *c:\ws\options\maillist.dot* in the blank provided and press Enter. After inserting the file, you can remove the line that reads (Type text and variable names here).

Table 14.3 Variables in WSLIST.DEF and INVNTORY.DEF

Data File	Field	Variable
WSLIST.DEF	Record Number	&number&
	Mr./Ms.	&Mr-Ms&
	First	&first&
	Initial	&mI&
	Last	&last&
	Jr./M.D.	&Jr-MD&
	Title	&title&
	Company	&company&
	Address Line 1	&addr1&
	Address Line 2	&addr2&
	City	&city&
	State	&state&
	Zip	&zip&
	Country	&country&
	Phone-1	&phone1&
	Phone-2	&phone2&
	Date	&date&
	User Field 1	&user1&

Data File	Field	Variable
	User Field 2	&user2&
	User Field 3	&user3&
	Remark 1	&remark1&
	Remark 2	&remark2&
	Remark 3	&remark3&
	yymmdd	&ymd&
INVNTORY.DEF	Record Number	&number&
	Date	&date&
	Item	&item&
	Code	&code&
	Status	&status&
	Description Line 1	&desc1&
	Description Line 2	&desc2&
	Description Line 3	&desc3&
	Account 1	&acct1&
	Quantity 1	&qty1&
	Price 1	&price1&
	Account 2	&acct2&
	Quantity 2	&qty2&
	Price 2	&price2&
	Account 3	&acct3&
	Quantity 3	&qty3&
	Price 3	&price3&
	User Field 1	&user1&
	User Field 2	&user2&
	User Field 3	&user3&
	Remark 1	&remark1&
	Remark 2	&remark2&
	Remark 3	&remark3&
	yymmdd	&ymd&

Now, if you've checked everything and are ready to print, you can save your file and choose the Print command from the File menu. After the Print dialog box appears, make your print selections. Specifically, make sure that the Interpret Merge Variables check box is selected (see fig. 14.22) to tell WordStar to merge data from the data file with the document being printed. (If you want to print the document without having WordStar read the merge-print commands embedded in the text, move the cursor to Interpret Merge Variables and press the space bar to remove the X.)

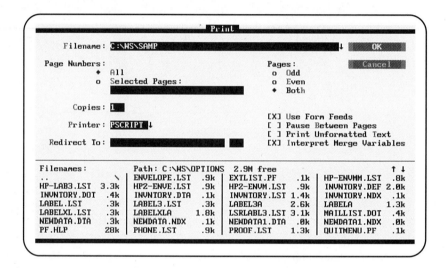

Fig. 14.22

Merge printing.

After you press Enter or click OK, WordStar begins printing your document file, merging it with the data found in the file you specified.

Troubleshooting

This section presents a few common problems encountered in merge printing. You also find suggested solutions to the problem.

My computer says it's printing but produces nothing.

Press Ctrl-P to see what's wrong with the print routine. After you press Ctrl-P, WordStar displays a message telling you that it doesn't understand a file name or a variable name or can't find your file. Make sure that you've entered the file name (in the .df line) and the variable names (in the .rv line) exactly as they should appear. If you're using a math variable and WordStar doesn't understand the equation, go back to the Set Variable to Math Result command to make sure that you've entered the equation correctly.

I get an error message saying that WordStar can't find my file.

Print from the directory in which your data file is stored, or type the full path to where your data file can be found after the .df command: *.df c:\ws\options\client.dta*, for example. This technique cuts down on the likelihood that WordStar will have trouble locating the data file.

Some variables get moved, so the wrong value appears in the wrong place.

If you haven't filled in all the variables on your data form and skipped them, WordStar—especially in nondocument data files—may move subsequent data items up in the document. To solve this problem, make sure that the number of fields in your .rv statement is the same as the number of fields in a record of your data file. If each record in your data file has 10 fields, the number of fields in your .rv lines must also be 10.

More than one document appears on a page.

Have you remembered to place a page break (.pa) at the end of the document? WordStar must encounter the page break command so that it knows to start over—on a fresh page—with another record from the data file.

The variables are printing as they are instead of substituting data.

After you choose the Print command and the Print dialog box appears, make sure that Interpret Merge Variables is checked. Otherwise, the document is printed with the variable names in place rather than the substituted data. Also be sure that the variable name you typed between the ampersands exactly matches (spelling, spacing, and so on) what appears in your .rv line.

Printing Mailing Labels

If you have ever typed mailing labels on a standard typewriter, you know that they can be a real headache to work with. MailList includes several print format files that make printing mailing labels easy for you. You create the data file, as indicated earlier in this chapter, to store all the information. Then, when you're ready to print, change to the OPTIONS subdirectory to display the different MailList print files.

Table 14.4 lists the various files you can use to print the data in the list format you want. All you need to do is to type your data file name after the .df command.

376

Table 14.4 Print Files for Label and Envelope Formatting

File Name	Description
ENVELOPE.LST	Prints a standard business-sized envelope with information you specify from WSLIST.DTA
HP-ENVMM.LST	Prints envelope on Hewlett-Packard printers
HP-LAB3.LST	Prints labels three across on Hewlett-Packard printers
HP2-ENVE.LST	Prints business envelope on HP LaserJet Series II or III printers
INVNTORY.LST	Prints an Inventory Proof Report
LABEL.LST	Prints 3½-by-1-inch labels
LABELXL.LST	Prints 5-by-3-inch labels
LABEL3.LST	Prints 3½-by-1-inch labels, three across
LSRLABL3.LST	Prints 3½-by-1-inch labels, three across, on a laser printer
PHONE.LST	Prints a phone directory, including client name and phone number
PROOF.LST	Prints a mailing list proof report, a hard copy report of all records in your mailing list data file
ROLODEX.LST	Prints 3½-by-4-inch Rolodex cards

These default printing files all have WSLIST.DTA entered in the first line as the data file to be used at print time. If you have created a different file, open the file as a nondocument (by pressing N when the opening screen is displayed), and change the .df line to specify the data file you plan to use. You then can print as usual, and WordStar and MailList work together to print the mailing labels, lists, reports, or envelopes you've chosen.

Chapter Summary

In this chapter, you've learned much about merge printing. Whether you enter and organize your data strictly from within WordStar or use the MailList utility to simplify the data-entry process, you should find many commands to help you produce the documents and labels you want. In the next chapter, you learn about sending and receiving WordStar files via modem and facsimile.

Using WordStar's Communication Features

The computer has made it possible for even the most remotely located computer user to link up with the outside world. Through
telephone lines, an entire world of information is available. By using a
modem and TelMerge—WordStar's communication software—you can
easily send and receive files to and from users in other offices. You can
also receive files from information services' vast collections of data and
from mail and message services.

In this chapter, you learn about the benefits of using a modem and are
given detailed instructions on how to use TelMerge. You also learn how
to prepare a fax file, which is a new feature with WordStar 7.0. Specifically, this chapter includes the following topics:

- Understanding modems
- Starting TelMerge
- Using the TelMerge Communications menu
- Placing a call
- Connecting with on-line services
- Sending a file
- Receiving a file

■ Ending a communications session

■ Creating a file for fax transmission

Understanding Modems

As was the case with the mouse, the modem was not used in the mainstream of personal computer applications when computers were first introduced into the home and office. Today, modems are extremely popular, linking users and businesses all over the world through telephone lines.

The term *modem* is short for *modulator/demodulator*, which refers to the process the modem uses to turn data into audio signals (modulate). The modem sends signals through the phone lines. Another modem receives the signals and changes the data from audio signals into an electronic form that a computer can use (demodulate).

The earliest modems were *acoustical* modems. They required that you place the handset of the phone into the cuplike receptacles of the modem, which then sent and received data through the phone lines. These modems, however, were sensitive to outside noise, which could produce a garbled file or end the transmission. More sophisticated and accurate modems soon replaced these early models.

Today's modems are either external or internal modems. An *external* modem is placed outside your computer and connected through an ordinary phone cord to both the system unit of your computer and the telephone jack. An *internal* modem is a modem built on a board that is placed inside your computer and plugged into the motherboard of the system. The board is equipped with a modem port, which enables you to plug the phone line directly into the port on the back of your system unit.

Many different modems are available, but any Hayes modem or Hayes-compatible modem is a sure bet for quality and for compatibility with most popular communications programs—including TelMerge.

What Can I Do with a Modem?

If you are new at using computers, you may have to stretch your imagination a bit to picture yourself using a modem. Initially, users are somewhat intimidated by telecommunications, even though the process is simple, and connecting to other computers and services is fun. Once you step into the communications area, however, you may find that going back is difficult.

In addition to the basic uses of sending and receiving files, modems give you access to an incredible range of information, from on-line library systems to airline reservation counters to message services to game clubs. The following paragraphs provide some idea of what you can accomplish with a modem.

Computer-to-computer communications. With the significant increase in the number of home offices, communications (the process of linking computers via phone lines) has become a new trend in personal computing. Imagine this scenario: You are working on a report that is to be presented at a corporate meeting on the 14th of the month. Two days before the meeting, you learn that you must travel to another state to solve a personnel problem. Because of communications, you can take your laptop computer and modem with you to finish the report and send the file back to your assistant at the home office. Your assistant can print and copy the report in time for the meeting.

Retrieving information from information services. A modem provides access to a world of information previously available only in the most up-to-date libraries. Through the use of *information services* like CompuServe, you have at your fingertips information on almost every subject. Information services are actually large mainframe computers. From an information service, you can learn many things. For example, you can

- Find out about cruises to Alaska
- Check up-to-date stock information
- "Talk" to users of your favorite software package
- Get advice on publishing your corporate newsletter
- Find out the weather in Tibet
- Play games on-line with users across the country
- Send and receive messages from clients or friends in another part of the world
- Find educational software for your kids
- Make airline reservations
- Read the *Wall Street Journal*
- Get the latest sports information

The list could go on and on. The TelMerge utility provides not one but several information services you can use from within WordStar.

Information Services Available in TelMerge

From within TelMerge, you can connect to the following information services: CompuServe, ITT Telex and TIMETRAN, Office Airline
Guides, RCA Telex and TELEXTRA, and EasyLink. Each information
service charges a subscription fee and either a monthly or per-
minute charge. To subscribe to a service, call the subscription
number of the service. A representative provides you with a tempo-
rary access code and enrolls you in the service. As you become
more familiar with information services, you can try other services,
too.

Electronic mail. An electronic mailbox is similar to an answering
machine, but the operation is performed with the use of computer technology. Mail services, such as MCI Mail or ONTYME Messaging Service,
enable you to receive and send electronic messages. Suppose, for example, that you are working on a project and you have a question about
a chart you are creating. You can leave a message on another user's
message system, and that person can answer you electronically. Unlike
answering a phone, the reader can read the electronic message when
convenient and return a message to you without interrupting your work.
With electronic mail systems, you are charged a subscription fee and a
per-minute or per-message rate.

Introducing TelMerge

TelMerge—a software program that has been with WordStar through
several upgrades—is WordStar's communications utility. As explained in
the last section, you can perform a variety of tasks if your system is
equipped with a modem and communications software. In this section,
you learn how to prepare for a TelMerge communications session and
then call a remote computer, send a file, receive a file, and end transmission.

What Do I Need To Use TelMerge?

Before you begin to use TelMerge, use the following checklist to ensure
that TelMerge is ready to run:

- Do you have a modem connected to your computer? (TelMerge
works with any Hayes-compatible modem.)

- Is the phone line connected from your computer to the phone jack? (Make sure that the lines are connected securely.)

- Did you install the TelMerge utility when you installed WordStar? (If not, exit WordStar, type *WINSTALL*, and use the Add or Remove a Feature option to add the TelMerge files.)

- Have you disabled call waiting if that feature is included with your phone service? (Call waiting disrupts data transmission if you receive a call while you're sending or receiving a file.)

- Have you removed other memory-resident programs from your computer's RAM? (Memory-resident programs, such as SideKick, may interfere with TelMerge as it sends and receives files. Disable all memory-resident programs before you use the program. Instructions for removing programs from memory can be found in the manual of the appropriate program.)

Additionally, if you plan to use the communications services listed on the TelMerge Communications menu, you must edit the TELMERGE.SYS file to include the phone numbers, IDs, and passwords needed to log onto the service. This process is explained in the next section.

Editing the TELMERGE.SYS File

The TELMERGE.SYS file, located in the OPTIONS subdirectory of WordStar, is a vital file that stores information about your modem and about the various services you use in TelMerge. To open TELMERGE.SYS, follow these steps:

1. From the opening screen, change to the OPTIONS subdirectory by pressing L (for changing the logged directory), and type *OPTIONS* (uppercase or lowercase letters) in the blank provided. Click OK or press Enter.

   The OPTIONS subdirectory is displayed.

2. Press N to open a nondocument file.

3. Type *TELMERGE.SYS* in the Filename text box and press Enter or click OK. The TELMERGE.SYS file appears on your screen (see fig. 15.1).

Now that you're in the TELMERGE.SYS file, you may want to take a few minutes to read the instructions, at the beginning of the document, on how to edit the file. You then can move to the section that contains the numbers and log-on sequences for connecting with information services by pressing Ctrl-F, typing *Service Station*, and pressing Enter. The screen shown in figure 15.2 appears.

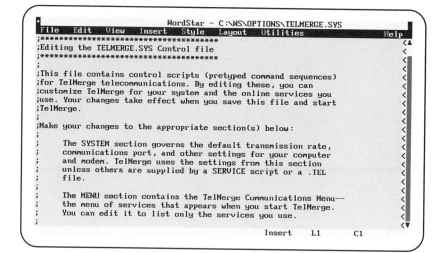

Fig. 15.1

The TELMERGE.SYS file in nondocument mode.

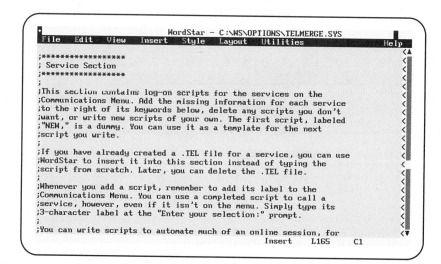

Fig. 15.2

Preparing to add numbers and log-on sequences to TELMERGE.SYS.

You can press Page Down a few times to bypass the instructions (you may want to read through them first) and arrive at the location where you enter information for the services. Figure 15.3 displays the settings for using MCI Mail. As you can see, the Label, Service, and Logfile entries have been made for you. You need to fill in the Number (phone number dialed to access the service), the user ID (your account number provided to you by the service), and your password (the password the service gives you at sign-up). Move the cursor to the line you want to add, and type the text as you type in any normal file.

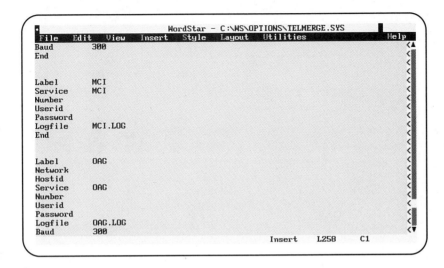

Fig. 15.3

Adding information to
TELMERGE.SYS.

When you are finished editing TELMERGE.SYS, press Ctrl-KD to save the
file and return to the opening screen.

Beginning a TelMerge Session

To start TelMerge, begin at the opening screen. Press A to open the Additional menu and T to select TelMerge. After a second, the Communications menu appears (see fig. 15.4).

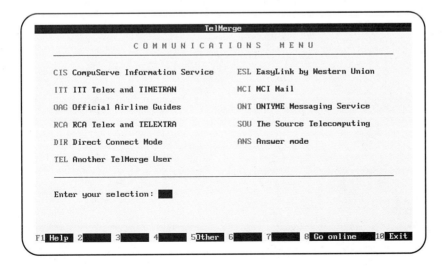

Fig. 15.4

The TelMerge
Communications
menu.

Service Directory

You may be wondering how can you get in touch with these services to sign up. The following list provides the addresses and phone numbers of the services listed on TelMerge's Communications menu:

Service	Address and Phone
CompuServe	CompuServe Information Service 5000 Arlington Centre Blvd. Columbus, OH 43220 (800)848-8990
ITT Telex	ITT World Communications and TIMETRAN 100 Plaza Drive Secaucus, NJ 07096 (800)922-0184
Official Airline Guide	Official Airline Guide 2000 Clearwater Drive Oak Brook, IL 60521 (800)323-4000
RCA Telex and TELEX	RCA Global Communications TRA201 Centennial Avenue Piscataway, NJ 08854 (800)526-3969
EasyLink by Western Union	Western Union Telegraph 4230 Altha Road Dallas, TX 75244 (800)527-5184
MCI Mail	MCI Mail 1150 17th St., N.W., 8th Floor Washington, DC 20036 (800)444-6245
ONTYME Messaging	ONTYME Marketing TYMSHARE Service 2560 North First Street San Jose, CA 95131 (800)435-8880

With the Communications menu, you can access a variety of services and functions. To the left of each service is a three-letter code you can use to select the item. At the bottom of the screen, the functions are presented: press F1 for help, F5 to select a service or number not shown on the menu, F8 to call the service of your choice, and F10 to exit TelMerge. Table 15.1 describes each option on the Communications menu.

Table 15.1 Options on the Communications Menu

Option	Enter	Description
CompuServe Information Service	CIS	Accesses an international on-line information service
ITT Telex and TIMETRAN	ITT	Enables you to telex information and provides an information service
Official Airline Guide	OAG	Enables you to access current airline schedules and rates
RCA Telex and TELEXTRA	RCA	Includes an information service as well as mail and electronic messaging services
Direct Connect Mode	DIR	Enables you to connect directly to another computer
Another TelMerge User	TEL	Connects you to another computer currently running TelMerge
EasyLink by Western	ESL	Enables you to send and receive Union electronic mail as well as access an information service
MCI Mail	MCI	Enables you to send and to receive electronic mail and log onto telex networks.
ONTYME Messaging Service	ONT	A worldwide messaging service
Answer Mode	ANS	Prepares your computer to receive an incoming call

Now you are ready to begin communicating with the service of your choice (assuming that you've entered the necessary information in the TELMERGE.SYS file). In the Enter Your Selection text box of the Communications menu, type the three-character code for the service you want. Press Enter. TelMerge then dials the service you selected.

If a problem connecting to the service develops, TelMerge stops processing and displays a message box alerting you to the problem. Check the numbers you've entered for the service in the TELMERG.SYS file and make sure that the phone lines are connected securely before trying again. (Refer to "Editing the TELMERGE.SYS File" in this chapter for more information.)

Understanding the TelMerge On-Line Screen

Once you've made your connection, TelMerge displays an on-line screen (see fig15.5). From this screen, you can perform the following tasks:

- Send your user ID
- Send your password
- Print information displayed on-screen
- Save the current screen of information
- Disconnect the transmission
- Send a file
- Receive a file

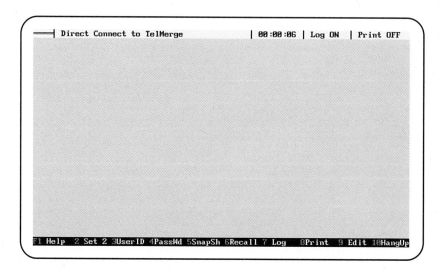

Fig. 15.5

The TelMerge on-line screen.

All these tasks are performed with the function keys shown at the bottom of the on-line screen. Although you see only one set of function keys (keys F1 through F10), two sets actually exist. You can display the second set by pressing F2. Table 15.2 lists the tasks you can perform with the function keys.

Table 15.2 On-Line Function Keys

Set	Key	Command	Description
1	F1	Help	Displays a help screen explaining the function of all keys
	F2	Set2	Displays the second set of function keys (used as a toggle; when the second set is displayed, pressing F2 returns you to the first set)
	F3	UserID	Looks up your UserID in the TELMERGE.SYS file and sends it to the service
	F4	Passwd	Looks up your password in the TELMERGE.SYS file and sends it to the service
	F5	SnapSh	Saves the current screen in the log file your computer stores in memory during the work session (you can save up to five screens in one session)
	F6	Recall	Enables you to display the screens you saved by pressing F5 (SnapSh)
	F7	Log	Acts as a toggle to turn the log on or off
	F8	Print	Enables you to print the current screen or to turn off printing
	F9	Edit	Enables you to exit TelMerge in order to edit a file but keeps the connection. You can return to the communications session by pressing F8.

continues

Table 15.2 Continued

Set	Key	Command	Description
	F10	HangUp	Terminates the connection and exits TelMerge
2	F1	ShoFil	Displays any file
	F2	Set1	Displays the first set of function keys. (a toggle; to return to set 2, press F2 again)
	F3	DOS	Without breaking the connection, enables you to exit to DOS (To return to the communications session, type *exit* and press Enter.)
	F4	Send	Enables you to send a WordStar or an ASCII file
	F5	XM Rec	Enables you to receive a file using the XMODEM protocol
	F6	XM Snd	Enables you to send a file using the XMODEM protocol
	F7	User1	Enables you to program your own functions
	F8	User2	Enables you to program your own functions
	F9	Break	Interrupts transmission with remote computer
	F10	HangUp	Terminates communication and exits TelMerge

Sending Files

When you're ready to send a file, assuming that you've logged onto the service or connected with the remote computer, follow these steps:

1. Press F2 to display the second set of function keys (see fig. 15.6).

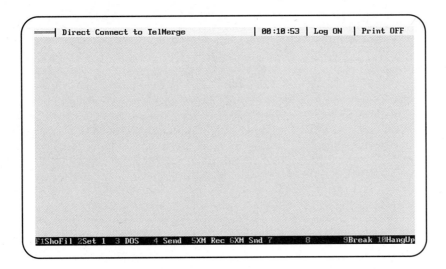

Fig. 15.6

The second set of
function keys.

2. Press F4. A pop-up box appears asking for the file you want to send
(see fig. 15.7). You can type the file name exactly as it appears in
the Filenames list on the opening screen, or you can use a wild-card
character in the file name.

```
═══╡ Direct Connect to TelMerge              │ 00:08:36 │ Log ON   │ Print OFF │
   ┌─────────────────────────────────────────────────────────┬──────────┐
   │ File to send (wild cards accepted): ▮                     │ Escape   │
   └─────────────────────────────────────────────────────────┴──────────┘
```

Fig. 15.7

Entering a file to send.

3. Press Enter to send the file.

Sending Files in XMODEM

You can choose to send a file by using the F6 function key in the
second set of keys on the on-line screen. This key enables you to
send the file in XMODEM protocol, a data-transmission format used
by most computers and information services. When you press F6
(XM Send), a dialog box appears asking for the name of the file to
send. Enter the file name and press Enter.

Receiving Files

When you are receiving files from a remote computer or from a communications service, you have two options in the way you capture the data. The first option, Snapsh, is available in the first set of function keys. SnapSh (F5) takes a snapshot of any data on the screen. The data is saved in a file, called a *log*, that you then can display and edit as necessary. You can press F5 up to five times, saving five screens of information in one work session. Using SnapSh is especially helpful when you are working with services that do not have a download capability (that is, they cannot send files or enable users to retrieve information in file form).

Printing Displayed Information

You also have the option of printing the information displayed on your screen. Pressing F8 toggles printing on so that you can get a hard copy of the information passing across your screen.

Another method of retrieving files is to press F5 when the second set of function keys is displayed. This key selects the XM Receive command. A dialog box appears asking you which file you want to receive (see fig. 15.8). Type the name of the file you want and press Enter. TelMerge then downloads the file and places it in the current directory.

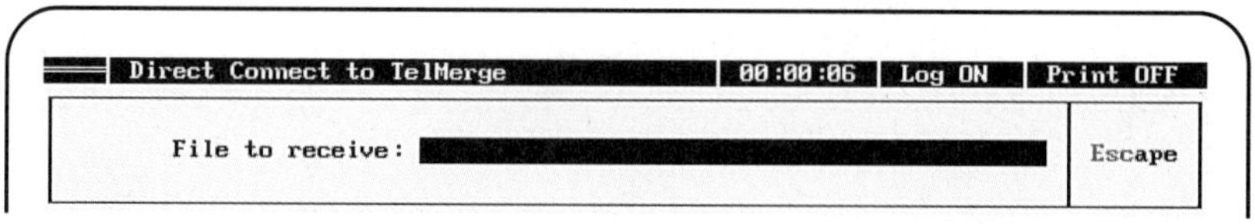

Fig. 15.8

Entering a file to receive.

```
┌────────────────────────────────────────────────────────────────────┐
│ ▆▆▆▆▆│ Direct Connect to TelMerge        │ 00:00:06 │ Log ON │ Print OFF │
│                                                                      │
│        File to receive : ▆▆▆▆▆▆▆▆▆▆▆▆▆▆▆▆▆▆▆▆▆▆▆│ Escape │
│                                                                      │
└────────────────────────────────────────────────────────────────────┘
```

Ending the Session

As you can see, you can spend hours—even days—exploring the various services and functions available with TelMerge. Whether you want to connect directly to another computer or to a mainframe information service, the process is simple and direct. Here's a review of the process:

1. Before you start TelMerge, enter the necessary information in the TELMERGE.SYS file (in the OPTIONS subdirectory).

2. Start TelMerge by pressing AT from the opening screen.

3. When the Communications menu appears, in the box provided, type the code of the feature you want to use.

4. Press Enter.

5. When the on-line screen appears, use the function keys to respond to prompts displayed by the service to which you are connected. (When the service prompts for your user ID, for example, press F3.)

6. Use the function key sets 1 and 2 to send, receive, display, print, and edit information.

When you're ready to end the communications session, simply press F10 to select the HangUp command. A pop-up box appears telling you the name of the file storing the information from the session and prompting you to press F1 to restart TelMerge or F10 to exit (see fig. 15.9). If you want to return to the TelMerge Communications menu, press F1. To return to the WordStar opening screen, press F10.

Name of file storing
information from
session

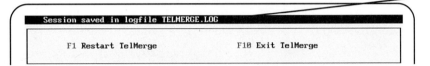

```
    Session saved in logfile TELMERGE.LOG


   F1 Restart TelMerge              F10 Exit TelMerge
```

Fig. 15.9

Exiting TelMerge.

Working with Fax Materials

Just when you start to get comfortable working with a piece of aging computer equipment, the industry feels compelled to throw a new device into the works—supposedly to make your life easier. Of course, you're grateful for the capability to work more proficiently, but any new instrument brings with it a new learning curve. One recent innovation is the fax machine.

In the last few years—and particularly in the last two—fax machines have found their way into offices throughout the country. They enable users to send with the speed of a phone call an exact replica of a document. Consider the implications. Now, instead of waiting for Federal Express to deliver new contracts for you to sign and return, you have to wait only for the contract to scroll out of your fax machine. You can sign the contract and feed it back through in seconds with your signature intact. No waiting. No delivery fees. And everything's legal. The fax machine is becoming a "must" for all companies—and individuals, for that matter—who deal with documents in a time-sensitive environment.

The developers of WordStar 7.0, aware of this growing need for documents that can be sent via a fax machine, added the capability to create fax-ready files. Now you can write your report (or your contract), save it in fax-ready form, and send it from the fax board in your computer. The process is easy and the time savings enormous. Before you get into the nuts and bolts of the process, however, the following section defines the function of a fax machine.

What Is a Fax?

With traditional fax machines, you insert the sheet you want to send, and the fax "reads" the sheet (like a scanner), changes what it "sees" to transmittable signals (like a modem), sends the data to the receiving fax, which then reconverts the signals (like a receiving modem) and prints the data (like a printer).

The early fax machines were stand-alone items. They looked a little like the old answering machines that had a receiver stuck on one end. Initially, the price for a fax machine was a bit out of reach for the personal computer user—often costing as much as the computer system itself.

Today, you can purchase fax boards that plug right into your system unit (similar to modem boards), enabling you to send fax files from your desktop. With WordStar 7.0, you have the capability to prepare fax files, which you can then send via a fax board to a fax machine in a remote office. Straight from your computer, you can send your files so that they are printed on another person's fax machine.

Preparing Fax Files

After you've created your document in WordStar, you can have the program convert the file to fax format. Follow these steps to convert a document to fax format:

1. Open the File menu and select the Fax command (see fig. 15.10). The Fax dialog box is displayed, as shown in figure 15.11.

Fig. 15.10

Choosing the Fax command.

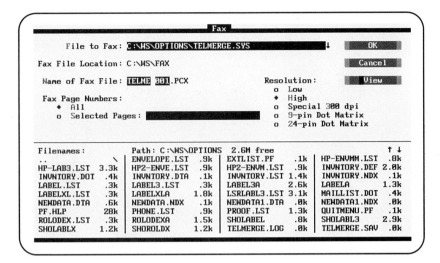

Fig. 15.11

The Fax dialog box.

2. In the File to Fax text box, type the name of the file you want to convert. (WordStar keeps a copy of the file in its original format and makes a copy in fax format and stores the fax format file in the C:\WS\FAX directory). Press Tab.

3. In the Name of Fax File text box, type the name you want to assign to the converted file. (Note that you cannot change the extension: WordStar automatically assigns the PCX extension to fax files.) Press Tab.

4. Select the pages you want to fax in the Fax Page Numbers area. You can choose All (the default), or you can choose Selected Pages and enter the numbers of the pages you want to fax. Remember to separate the page numbers with commas. Press Tab.

5. Choose the resolution of the fax output you want to produce. Select the setting you want by typing the highlighted letter or by clicking the setting button. The default, High Resolution, outputs the document in laser quality.

6. Click View if you want to see the document in fax format. This view is the way the document appears to the receiver. WordStar displays the document in preview mode (see fig. 15.12). To return to the Fax dialog box, press Esc.

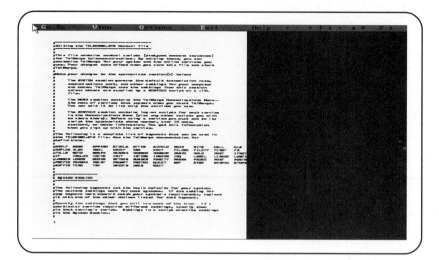

Fig. 15.12

Previewing the document to be sent via fax.

7. Click OK or press Enter. WordStar then returns you to preview mode momentarily and displays the message Building FAX file at the top of the screen (see fig. 15.13).

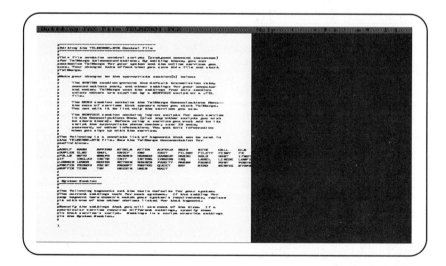

Fig. 15.13

Creating the fax file.

When WordStar finishes creating the file, you are returned to the opening screen. The file is stored in the FAX subdirectory. You now can use your fax software to send the file from the fax board in your computer to a remote fax.

Chapter Summary

In this chapter, you have learned how to link up with the outside world by using TelMerge, WordStar's communications utility, and the new fax capability of WordStar 7.0. Whether you are connecting to another computer running TelMerge or a massive information system halfway across the world, TelMerge turns your personal computer system into a limitless source of information.

And in keeping on the cutting edge of technology, the makers of WordStar 7.0 have added fax capability to enable you to produce fax-ready files—complete with text, graphics, and special items like footnotes, endnotes, and indexes—that you can send to a fax machine by using your computer's fax board and fax software.

In the next chapter, you learn about two additional WordStar features you can use when creating long documents: the indexing and table of contents features.

Using the Index and TOC Features

Although you have covered a wide range of WordStar 7.0 features so far in this book, you need to be introduced to two more capabilities: indexing and generating a table of contents.

Any time you work with long documents, you need to provide for your readers some method of finding specific items in the text. If you are writing a research project about Eastern religions, for example, your readers cannot know that Taoism is explained on page 23 unless you include an index or a table of contents (or both) so that they can find the sections they need.

In this chapter, you learn how to create an index and a table of contents from within WordStar. Specifically, you learn to perform the following tasks:

- Mark index entries in your document
- Add index entries
- Compile the index
- Edit the index
- Print the index
- Add the index to your document
- Mark items for the table of contents
- Compile the table of contents

- Edit the table of contents
- Print the table of contents
- Add the TOC to your document

Creating an Index

In this section, you learn how to create, edit, print, and incorporate an index into your long document. First, however, start with an overview of the index concept.

Reference books of all kinds include an index. In fact, almost every non-fiction book *should* include an index so that readers can skip straight to the topic they need to read about. Not only a service to the readers, an index can help you check the organization of your document and make sure that the document is put together logically.

Most indexes list nothing more than a topic and a page number, enabling you to find easily the page that has the information you need. Other indexes have subordinate topics—that is, subtopics of the main topic—that also may interest you. Indexes also often include cross-references, which serve as pointers to additional information readers may want to consult for related topics. Consider the following excerpt of an index:

> disks, 26
> > 3.5-inch, 36-377
> > 5.25-inch, 30-36
> > backup copies, 42-48
> > copying, 40-48
> > formatting, 50-53
> > > *see also density, 45*
> > > high-density, 50-51
> > > low-density, 52-53

In this example, the main category is *disks*, for which page 26 includes a basic discussion. The subordinate topics (from *3.5-inch* to *formatting*) provide more specialized information related to disks. The *formatting* subordinate topic also has subordinates of its own (*high-density* and *low-density*) and refers you to another page to find out more about *density*.

You can create indexes as simple or as complex as you want by using WordStar's index generator. The process consists of these basic steps:

1. Open the document you want to index.

2. Mark the entries you want to include in the index.

3. Save the document.

4. From the opening screen, press Alt-U to open the Utilities menu, and press I to choose Index.

5. Enter the name of the file in which you've entered index entries; then press Enter. WordStar compiles the index and places the index in a file with an IDX extension.

6. You now can open and edit the index file and incorporate the file into your original document.

In the next two sections, you learn the two different methods you can use to add index entries in your text. The first method enables you to type an index entry directly into the text. The second method enables you to mark text in the existing document to be compiled in the index.

Inserting Index Entries

First, you need to open the file you want to index. After the file is open on the edit screen, move the cursor to where you want to add an index entry. Then follow these steps:

1. Press Alt-I to open the Insert menu.

2. Press I to display the Index/TOC Entry options (see fig. 16.1).

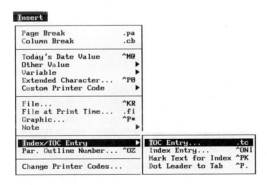

Fig. 16.1

The Index/TOC Entry options.

3. Choose the Index Entry command. The Index Entry dialog box appears (see fig. 16.2).

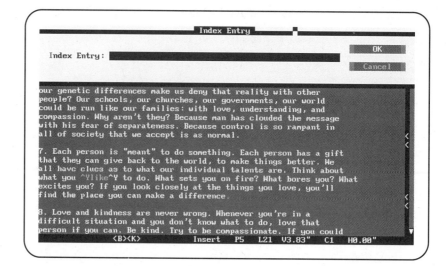

Fig. 16.2

The Index Entry dialog box.

Keying in on Speed

Notice that the quick-key combination for the Index Entry command is Ctrl-ONI. After you begin entering a number of index entries, using the quick key is much faster.

---

4. Type the first-level topic (for example, *families*). If you want to type a second-level (or subordinate) topic, type a comma and then the second-level topic—for example, *in society*. Your Index Entry dialog box now should resemble the one in figure 16.3.

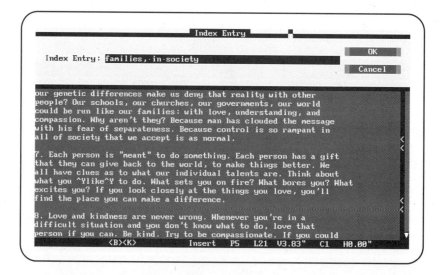

Fig. 16.3

Entering a first- and second-level topic.

5. Press Enter or click OK to finish the entry and return to your document.

After you return to the document, you see that WordStar has inserted a nonprintable index tag at the cursor (see fig. 16.4). WordStar truncates the words in the tag when you're looking at the document in the edit screen, but the entire word appears after you compile the index.

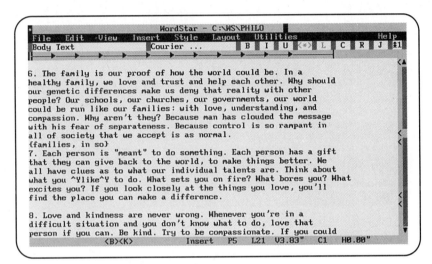

Fig. 16.4

The index tag inserted in the text.

You can continue through your document, inserting index entries as necessary. The following tips can help you fine-tune the look of the index you produce:

- If you are entering an index entry that you want to stand out, you can have WordStar boldface the page number by typing a plus sign in front of the text in the entry. After the Index Entry dialog box appears, type the plus sign before you type the entry text.

- You can add a reference to another topic by adding a minus sign (–) before the text. If you type the line *–families in recovery, see Counseling Techniques, Theory and Practice* in the Index Entry box, for example, readers don't see a page number for *families in recovery*, but they see the reference to other sections they can consult for more information.

Looking for Cross-References

Remember that the more complete your index, the more easily your readers can find what they want. You can think of indexing as a kind of puzzle or word game; thinking of all the different ways your readers may look something up is a challenge. With the entry you just created in the preceding example, for example, you may want to create other entries that help readers find the information under different entries. Besides *families, in society*, you may add the following entries:

    society, family influence in
    influences, of family on society
    government, compared to family
    society, family roles in
    families, compared to government

Remember that the comma separates the second-level entry from the first-level entry. But what do you do if you want to use a level that includes a comma, such as the following:

    families,
        ethnic, spiritual, and historic qualities, 34

In this case, you enclose the second level in quotation marks so that WordStar knows that this entire level stays together. Your entry in the Index Entry dialog box looks like the following:

        families, "ethnic, spiritual, and historic qualities"

The quotation marks do not appear in the compiled index. They're just an indication to WordStar that this entire phrase belongs together.

Marking Entries in Text

The other method of including index entries involves marking existing text. If you use headings in your documents, you may find that marking text is easier than typing an index entry. If your ideas are mixed together in the text, however, you may have a harder time finding in the text words that say exactly what you want to include in an index entry.

To mark text for inclusion in the index, follow these steps:

1. Move the cursor to the beginning of the phrase you want to mark for the index entry.

2. Press Alt-I to open the Insert menu.

3. Press I to choose Index/TOC Entry. The list of options appears.

4. Choose Mark Text for Index. (The quick-key combination for this command is Ctrl-PK.)

You are returned to the document. The symbol ^K appears at the cursor position to mark the beginning of the text for the index entry. To mark the end of the entry, move the cursor to the end point and press Ctrl-PK. Another ^K appears (see fig. 16.5). When you compile the index, the entry appears at the appropriate place in the document.

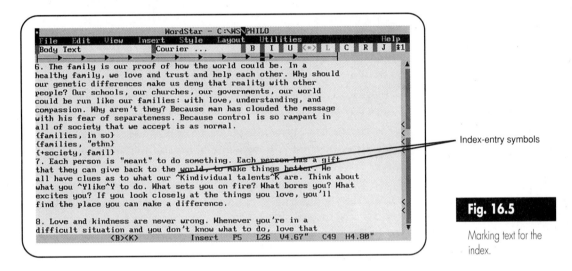

Index-entry symbols

Fig. 16.5

Marking text for the index.

Go through the rest of the document and insert or mark the index entries you want. After you finish, press Ctrl-KD to save the file.

Compiling the Index

After marking and inserting the necessary index entries, you're ready to compile the index. Follow these steps:

1. Return to the opening screen. (Save your file if you haven't done so already.)

2. Press U to open the Utilities menu.

3. Press I to choose Index. The Index dialog box appears (see fig. 16.6).

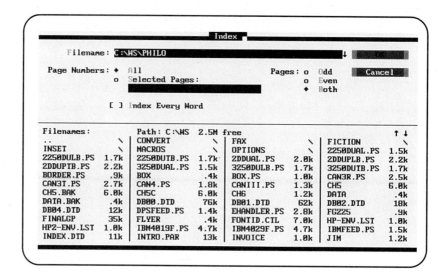

Fig. 16.6

The Index dialog box.

4. In the Filename text box, type the name of the file you want to index. Press Tab.

5. In the Page Numbers section, choose whether you want to index All or Selected Pages. (If you choose Selected Pages, type the page numbers in the text box.) Press Tab.

6. Because the Index Every Word check box is blank by default, the index includes only the entries you inserted or marked. If you want to index every word in the document, press I to move to this option, and press the space bar to place an X in the box. Press Tab.

7. Choose whether you want the index to be performed on Odd, Even, or Both (odd and even) pages. (Both is the default).

8. Click OK or press Enter.

WordStar displays a message, telling you that the file is being indexed. (You can press Ctrl-U to abandon the index.) WordStar generates the index and saves it in a file with the same name as the file you indexed, except with IDX as the extension. (If, for example, your original document file is named BOOK.TXT, the index generated by WordStar is named BOOK.IDX.) After the index is finished, WordStar returns you to the opening screen.

Viewing and Editing the Index

You now can look at the index. To see what you've created, follow these steps:

1. Press D to open the index file.

2. Choose the name of the index you just created from the Filenames list or type the file name. (The file ends with the extension IDX.)

3. Press Enter. The file then appears (see fig. 16.7).

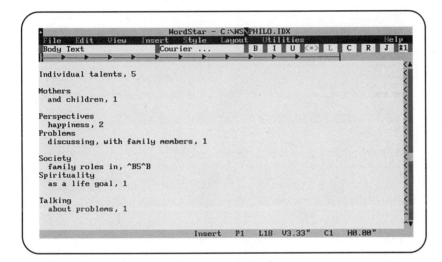

WordStar — C:\WS\PHILO.IDX

File   Edit   View   Insert   Style   Layout   Utilities   Help
Body Text   Courier ...   B   I   U «*» L   C   R   J   ±1

```
Individual talents, 5

Mothers
  and children, 1

Perspectives
  happiness, 2
Problems
  discussing, with family members, 1

Society
  family roles in, ^B5^B
Spirituality
  as a life goal, 1

Talking
  about problems, 1
```

Insert   P1   L18   V3.33"   C1   H0.00"

Fig. 16.7

The compiled index.

As you can see, in the compiled index, second-level entries are indented, entries beginning with the same letter are grouped together, and page numbers are in boldfaced type. You now can edit the file as necessary. You can add different type styles or fonts and make any other corrections you make on a normal file.

Printing the Index

Particularly if you are working with a long index, you may want to print a copy so that you can edit the index and compare entries. Printing is the same simple process, now that the index has been compiled into a file: press FP from the opening screen (or Ctrl-P from the edit screen), type the file name, and press Enter. The document then is printed as usual. For more details on printing, see Chapter 11.

Adding the Index to Your Document

You may find that including the index file in your WordStar document saves you a few steps. You can easily include the index in your document by positioning the cursor at the end of the document and pressing Ctrl-KR. The Insert File dialog box appears, asking you which file you want to insert into your document (see fig. 16.8). Type the name of the index file and press Enter. WordStar then places the index at the end of your document.

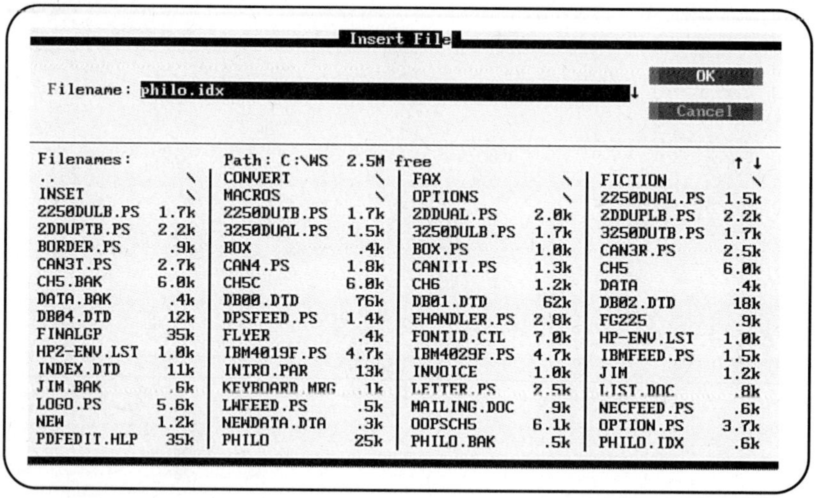

Fig. 16.8

Adding the index to your document.

Creating a Table of Contents

Generating a table of contents (TOC) may seem like a much simpler matter than generating an index, but the complexity depends on the length of your document. If you have created a 200-page dissertation, chances are that you have many headings which need to be included in a TOC.

Like indexing, TOC generation is an easy process in WordStar. The basic steps follow:

1. Open the document for which you want to generate the TOC.

2. Insert TOC markers into the text.

3. Save the file.

4. Use the TOC command on the Utilities menu on the opening screen to compile the TOC.

You then can view, edit, print, and add the TOC to your document as necessary. The following sections explain specifically how to create a table of contents for your document.

Marking TOC Entries

When you're creating a table of contents, you can go through the document and manually write down all the headings and page numbers you want included. A simpler method is to mark the entries you want to use in the TOC and have WordStar do the work for you.

Before you can mark TOC entries, you first must open the document you want to use. (If you're using a sample document, you may want to use the same document you used for the index generation.) Now, follow these steps:

1. Move the cursor to the point in the document where you want to add the TOC entry.

2. Press Alt-I to open the Insert menu.

3. Press I to choose the Index/TOC Entry command. A submenu appears (see fig. 16.9).

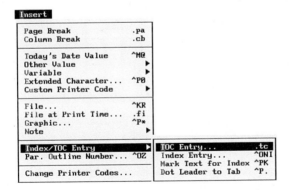

Fig. 16.9

Inserting a TOC entry.

4. Press Enter to choose TOC Entry. (Notice that the dot command for this option is `.tc`.) The Insert TOC Entry dialog box appears (see fig. 16.10).

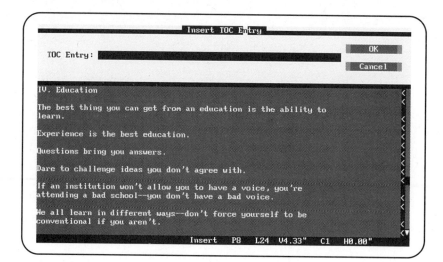

Fig. 16.10

The Insert TOC Entry dialog box.

5. Type the entry for the TOC in the TOC Entry text box.

6. Click OK or press Enter.

WordStar then returns you to the document. The program inserts the .tc command and displays the entry you typed. (Remember that dot commands do not print when you print the file.)

Insert TOC Entries Manually

You can type TOC entries directly into your text by using the .tc command. Position the cursor on the line where you want to add the entry, and then type *.tc* and the entry name. If you want to indent an entry so that it appears as a subheading beneath another heading, press the space bar after the .tc command. If you want to include dot leaders (the line of dots that leads to the page numbers in a compiled TOC), you can position the cursor at the end of the entry and press Ctrl-P(period).

Move through the document and insert the TOC entries as necessary. Figure 16.11 shows two sample TOC entries—one marked as a heading and one marked as a subheading. The TOC dot commands that appear in the text do not print; they serve only as commands during table of contents generation.

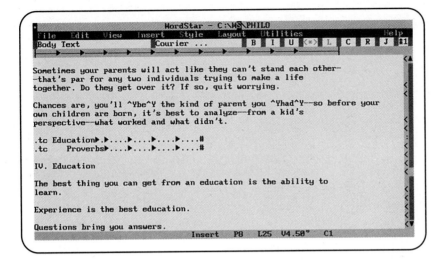

Fig. 16.11

Sample TOC entries.

After you finish marking the entries in your document, you're ready to compile the table of contents. Save the document by pressing Ctrl-KD.

Compiling the TOC

Similar to the process of compiling an index, compiling a table of contents is a straightforward process. To compile the TOC, follow these steps:

1. Display the opening screen.

2. Press U to open the Utilities menu.

3. Press T to choose TOC. The Table of Contents dialog box appears (see fig. 16.12).

4. In the Filename text box, type the name of the file you want to use. Press Tab to move to the Page Numbers option.

5. In the Page Numbers area, choose whether you want to include All pages in the TOC or Selected Pages. (If you choose Selected Pages, type the page numbers in the text box.) Press Tab.

6. Choose whether you want to generate the TOC for Odd, Even, or Both (odd and even) pages.

7. Click OK or press Enter to compile the TOC.

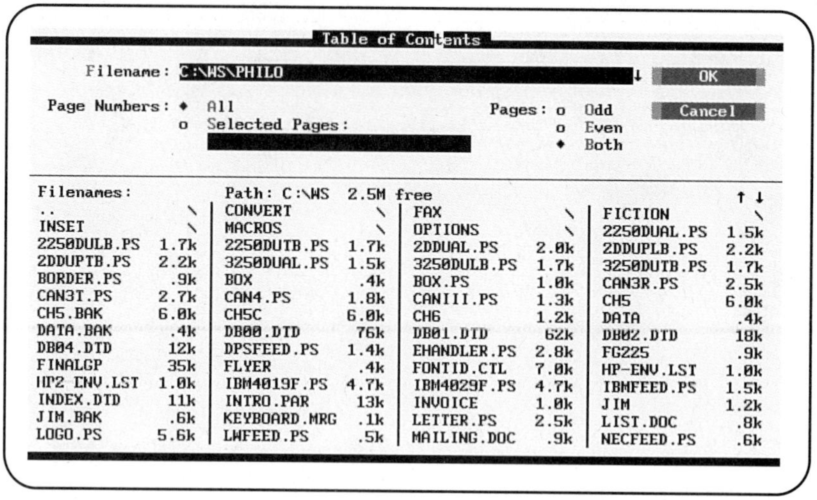

Fig. 16.12

The Table of Contents
dialog box.

WordStar displays a message, telling you that the table of contents is being generated. WordStar compiles the TOC and saves it in a file with a TOC extension. (A file named BOOK, for example, is given a TOC file named BOOK.TOC.) After the program finishes, you are returned to the opening screen.

Viewing and Editing the TOC

After you compile the TOC, you can view it by following these steps:

1. Press D to open a document.

2. Type the name of the table of contents file (the file name ends with a TOC extension), or choose the file from the Filenames list.

3. Press Enter or click OK.

The table of contents then appears. To see the table of contents the way it will print, you may want to press Ctrl-OP to preview the document (see fig. 16.13). Press Esc to return to the edit screen. You then can edit the table of contents as necessary.

Printing the TOC

You can print the TOC as a normal document by pressing FP from the opening screen (or Ctrl-KP from the edit screen), typing the file name, and pressing Enter.

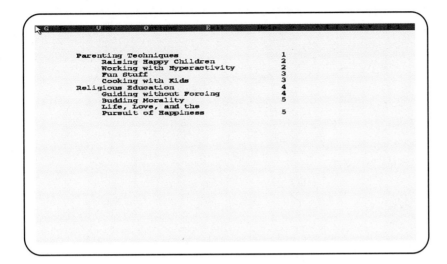

```
        Parenting Techniques                    1
            Raising Happy Children              2
            Working with Hyperactivity          2
            Fun Stuff                           3
            Cooking with Kids                   3
        Religious Education                     4
            Guiding without Forcing             4
            Budding Morality                    5
            Life, Love, and the
            Pursuit of Happiness                5
```

Fig. 16.13

Previewing the TOC file.

Adding the TOC to Your Document

As you did with the index you created earlier in this chapter, you may want to add the table of contents to the beginning of your document. Follow these steps:

1. Open the document into which you want to place the TOC.

2. Move the cursor to the point where you want to add the file.

3. Press Ctrl-KR. The Insert File dialog box appears.

4. Type the name of the TOC file and press Enter.

WordStar then inserts the table of contents at the cursor position.

Chapter Summary

In this chapter, you've learned much about two add-on utilities of WordStar 7.0: the indexing feature and the table of contents generator. As you've seen, both utilities are easy to use and can enhance your long documents greatly. The next chapter wraps up the book by providing you with several different samples of WordStar documents.

A WordStar Sampler

In this last chapter of the book, you get a bird's-eye view of the process involved in creating different kinds of documents. Many procedures that you've seen throughout the book are incorporated so that you can get an idea of how the many features of WordStar 7.0 work together.

This chapter includes information about the following sample documents:

- A business report
- A resume
- A newsletter
- An instructional manual

Keep in mind, however, that the instructions provided are just guidelines to get you started. For detailed steps, you need to see the chapters that discuss each feature.

A Sample Business Report

The first sample in this chapter is the 1992 Annual Report for Visionaries, Inc. To create this document, you use the following WordStar features:

- *Cover page.* On the report's cover page, the text is centered vertically (see fig. 17.1). First, you assign the Title paragraph style to the text; then you add four spaces between the first and second lines of text. Finally, move the cursor up to the beginning of the document, press Alt-L to open the Layout menu, press E to display the Special Effects options, and choose the Vertically Center Text on Page command. Be sure a page break (.pa) is in the line following the second line of text. (Choosing Center Text on page automatically inserts .pa.)

Fig. 17.1

The report cover page in preview mode.

■ *Header lines.* For the top of the document, you type header commands at the top of the document to enter three different header lines. Because the first header line is a line of hyphens, type *.h1 ----------*. The second line contains text (*.h2 Visionaries, Inc.*), and the third line sets off the text with another row of hyphens (*.h3 ----------*).

■ *Page numbers.* In the second header line, press Tab five times to move to the right side of the page, and then type *1992 Annual Report, pg. #* (see fig. 17.2). At print time, the header includes the page number.

■ *Offset margins.* So that you can bind the report, change the page offset to increase the inside margin. Open the Layout menu and choose the Page command; then enter *1.2* for the Odd Offset and Even Offset settings. WordStar places the page offset codes in the document.

Page offset commands

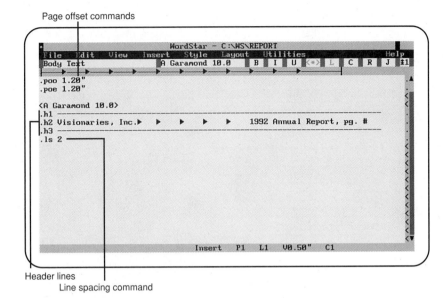

Fig. 17.2

The offset, header, and line-spacing codes.

Header lines

Line spacing command

- *Fonts and styles.* When you create a report like this one, you must decide whether to use the paragraph styles provided with WordStar, create your own paragraph styles, or enter the font and style settings as you go. For this example, use the Font option on the Style menu or click the Font box on the style bar to set the font at 10-point Garamond. The <A Garamond 10.0> command appears before the header lines, as in figure 17.2.

- *Double-spaced text.* You can choose to use double-spaced text by positioning the cursor before the text in the document and clicking the line-spacing button in the far right end of the style bar. WordStar inserts the code at the cursor position.

- *Table of contents.* To insert the table of contents on page 2 (shown in fig. 17.3), add the TOC entries at the appropriate points in the document (the TOC command is .tc), compile the table of contents by using the TOC command in the Utilities menu of the opening screen, and then press Ctrl-KR to import the TOC file into the report document.

- *Single-column, justified text.* Because single-column text is the default, you don't need to do anything to set the column number. To choose justified text, click the Justify button on the style bar. You also can display the Alignment and Spacing dialog box by pressing Ctrl-OS.

- *Imported graphics.* On the third page of the report, press Alt-I to open the Insert menu, press G to choose Graphic, and choose a PIX file from the displayed list at the bottom of the Insert File dialog box to import a graphic item. WordStar then inserts a graphics tag. To display the graphic, you must preview the document by pressing Ctrl-OP (see fig. 17.4).

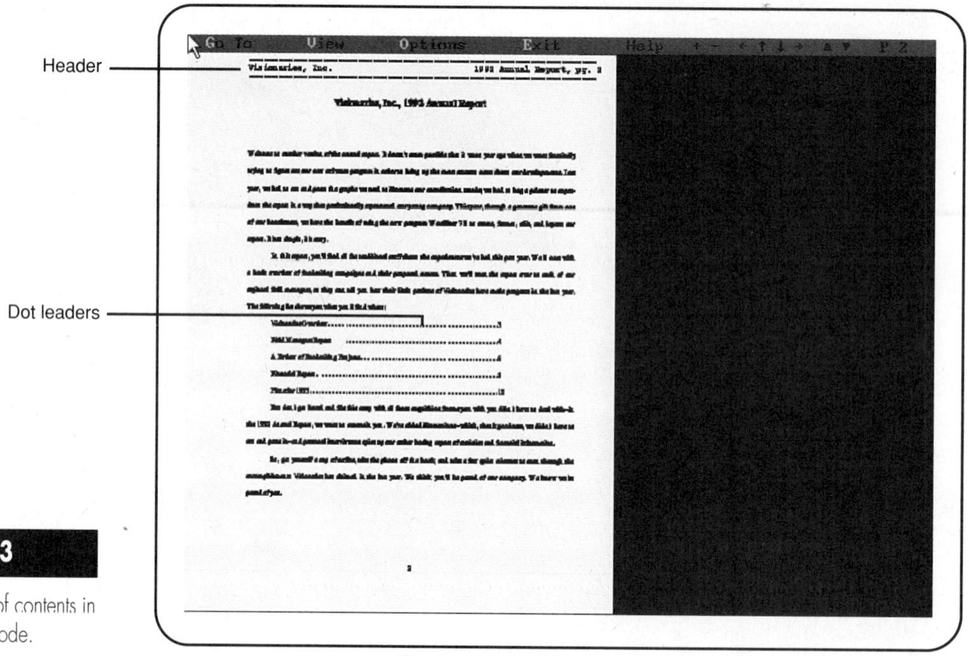

Header ——

Dot leaders ——

Fig. 17.3

The table of contents in preview mode.

- ■ *Calculator.* At the bottom of page 3, a set of numbers is just begging to be calculated (see fig. 17.4). To perform the calculation, press Ctrl-QM to use the calculator, or choose the Calculator option from the Utilities menu (see fig. 17.5).

- ■ *Footnotes and endnotes.* To add footnotes and endnotes, press Alt-I to open the Insert menu, press N to choose Note, choose the note type, and enter the text in the note window displayed at the bottom of the screen. After the text is entered, press Ctrl-KD to save the note file and place the footnote (or endnote) tag in the text.

- ■ *Index.* To add index entries to the report, press Ctrl-ONI to display the Index Entry dialog box, type the entries, and press Enter (see fig. 17.6). Then, use the Index command on the Utilities menu to compile the index, which you can incorporate into the document by pressing Ctrl-KR.

Header
lines

Footnote
marker

Imported
graphic

Calculations

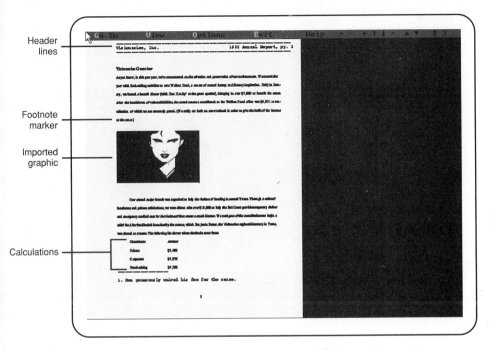

Fig. 17.4

Page 3 of the
document.

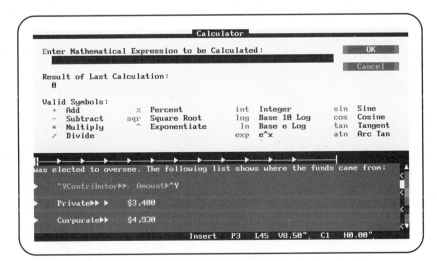

Fig. 17.5

The Calculator.

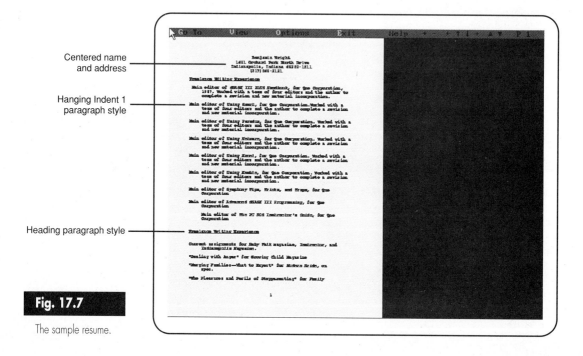

Fig. 17.6

The Index Entry dialog box.

A Resume

The resume example is a bit more straightforward (see fig. 17.7). The resume uses WordStar's default margins, and you can use WordStar's preset paragraph styles. By using the guidelines in the following paragraphs, you find out how to create this simple document.

Centered name and address ————

Hanging Indent 1 paragraph style ————

Heading paragraph style ————

Fig. 17.7

The sample resume.

- *Centered title or name.* The first four lines of the resume contain name and address information. Apply the Title paragraph style, and use 12-point New Century Schoolbook as the typeface and size.

- *Headings.* Set the style for the headings in the resume by using WordStar's default Heading paragraph style. Apply the Heading style to the text by positioning the cursor before the text, clicking the paragraph style box in the left side of the style bar, and choosing Heading from the displayed list.

- *Hanging indent style.* For the body of the resume, choose Hanging Indent 1 paragraph style by clicking the paragraph style setting (or pressing Ctrl-OFS) and choosing the style you want.

- *No page numbers.* For this resume, suppress automatic page numbering (which places the page number at the bottom of the page) by moving the cursor to the top of the document and typing *.op.*

A Newsletter

The newsletter incorporates some of the features from the report and some from the resume (see fig. 17.8). The following paragraphs describe the different settings used to create the two-column newsletter.

- *Graphic line.* You can create the dark lines above and below the banner by using the Alt-F1 macro several times to add a horizontal line across the page. After creating the top line, you mark the line and copy it after the banner.

- *Banner.* To create the banner, choose the Title paragraph style and 72-point Garamond for the font.

- *Table of contents.* You can add the table of contents by first adding the TOC entries at the appropriate points in the document (the TOC command is .tc), using the TOC command in the Utilities menu to compile the table of contents, and pressing Ctrl-KR to import the TOC file into the report document.

- *Two columns.* Select the columns by opening the Layout menu (Alt-L) and pressing O for Columns. In the Column Layout dialog box, enter the number of columns you want (for this example, enter *2*). WordStar changes the Space between Columns automatically, but you can enter your own setting.

- *Imported graphics.* In the second column, you can import a graphic item. Press Alt-I to open the Insert menu, press G to choose Graphic, and choose the PIX file from the displayed list at the bottom of the Insert File dialog box. WordStar then inserts a graphics tag. To display the graphic, you must preview the document by pressing Ctrl-OP.

Lines added with macro

Title paragraph style

Picture added with Inset

Page number

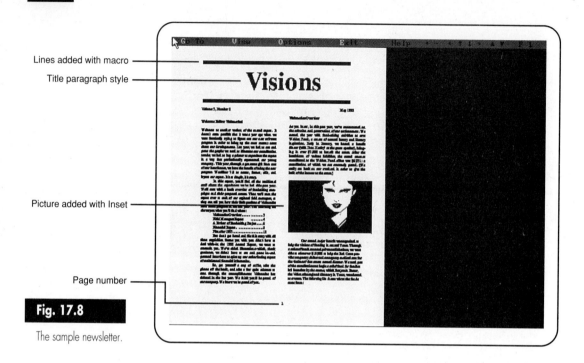

Fig. 17.8

The sample newsletter.

- ■ *Page numbers.* WordStar automatically enters the page numbers at the bottom of the page.

- ■ *Single-spaced, justified text.* The Body Text style contains the settings you need to align the text in single-spaced, justified format. You may need to change your Body Text paragraph style from flush-left to justified alignment, however, by pressing Ctrl-OFD to display the Define Paragraph Style dialog box and changing the necessary settings.

- ■ *Headlines.* You must decide whether to apply another paragraph style to the headings or to boldface them to make them stand out. Because of the size of the banner in this example, you should boldface the headlines. Position the cursor before the text you want to boldface and press Ctrl-PB; then move the cursor to the end of that text and press Ctrl-PB again.

An Instructional Manual

An instructional manual, as you may expect, is a long document in which you must use headers that include page numbers, a table of contents, and an index to help readers find the information they need. Figure 17.9 shows the title page of the sample instructional manual.

Title para-
graph style

Body
Text

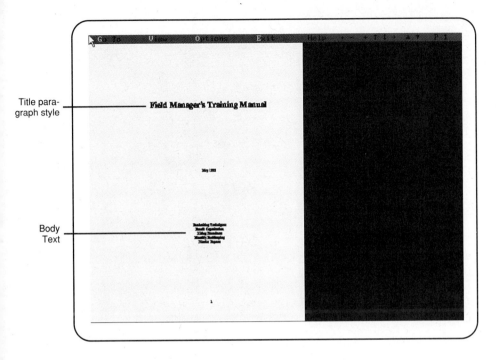

Fig. 17.9

The title page of the
instructional manual.

The following paragraphs give the general guidelines to create this example instructional manual.

■ *Offset margins.* Because the manual will be bound, you need to add extra space in the page offset settings on the Page dialog box. To display the Page dialog box, press Ctrl-OY. Then change the Odd Offset and Even Offset options to reflect the settings you want (for this example, 1.5 inches).

■ *Title page.* To create the title page, press Enter until the cursor is about one-third of the way down the page. Then choose the Title paragraph style and Garamond 24-point type before entering the manual's title. (The Title paragraph style centers the text as you type.) Then, to enter the rest of the text on the page, press Enter, choose the Body Text style, and type the additional text. At each line, press Ctrl-OC to center the text.

■ *Table of contents page.* Because this document is long, and particularly because the document is organized in an instructional format, a table of contents is a necessity. Page 2 of the document is the TOC page (see fig. 17.10). Use the Title paragraph style for the page heading (*Table of Contents*), and create TOC entries by inserting the .tc command at the appropriate points in the document. Then compile the TOC by using the TOC command on the Utilities menu. Finally, insert the TOC into the manual by pressing Ctrl-KR.

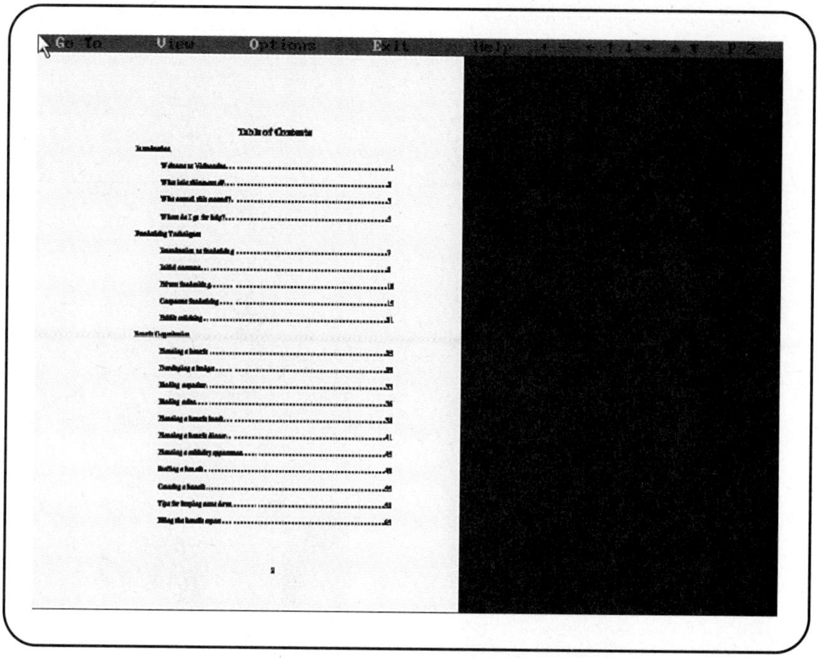

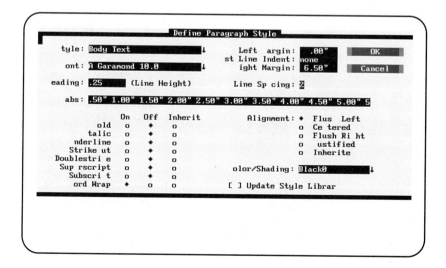

Fig. 17.10

The table of contents
page.

■ *Single-spaced text with greater leading.* For the body of the document, you must modify the Body Text paragraph style. To display the Define Paragraph Style dialog box, press Ctrl-OFD (see fig. 17.11). Change the Leading setting from .17 (the default) to .25. Also change the Alignment setting from Justified to Flush Left.

Fig. 17.11

The Define Paragraph
Style dialog box.

- *Paragraph indents.* In the Define Paragraph Style dialog box, also change the 1st Line Indent from none to .5 to cause all paragraphs assigned to the Body Text style to be indented .5 inch.

- *One-column layout.* Because one-column mode is the default setting, you don't need to make any changes for the instructional manual.

- *Different level headings.* Because different heading sizes and styles are used to show different heading levels in the document, use the Define Paragraph Styles option on the Style menu to create three different paragraph styles to show the different heading types:

Paragraph Style	Description
Heading1	16-point text, boldface
Heading2	14-point text, boldface
Heading3	12-point text, boldface italic

Figure 17.12 shows an example of page 3, which uses two different heading styles and the modified Body Text paragraph styles.

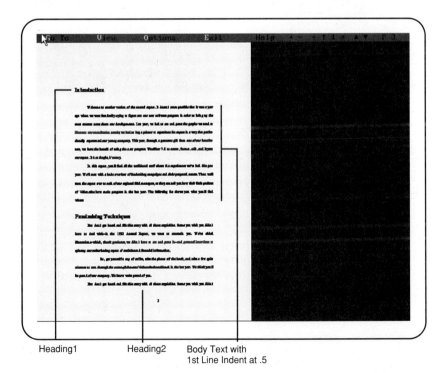

Fig. 17.12

Page 3 of the manual.

■ *Imported graphics.* On the fourth page, import a graphic item by pressing Alt-I to open the Insert menu, pressing G to choose Graphic, and selecting the PIX file from the displayed list. WordStar then inserts the graphics tag. To display the graphic, you must preview the document by pressing Ctrl-OP (see fig. 17.13).

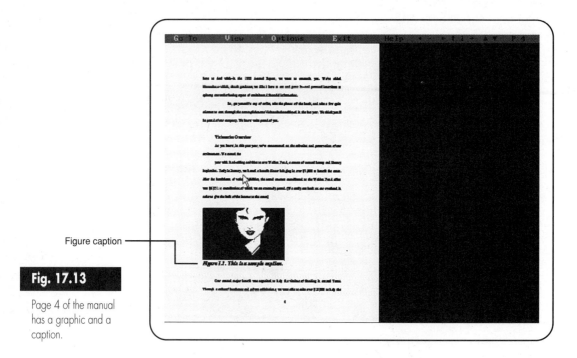

Figure caption

Fig. 17.13

Page 4 of the manual has a graphic and a caption.

■ *Figure captions.* In the Define Paragraph Style dialog box, you can define another paragraph style, Caption, to format the figure caption. The caption is set in 12-point boldfaced italic type. Set the 1st Line Indent to 0 so that the figure caption aligns with the picture (refer to fig. 17.13).

■ *Index.* You can add index entries by pressing Ctrl-ONI to display the Index Entry box, typing the entries, and pressing Enter. Use the Index command on the Utilities menu to compile the index, which you then can incorporate into the document by pressing Ctrl-KR.

Chapter Summary

This chapter concludes your trip through WordStar 7.0. Throughout this book, you've become familiar with many of WordStar's powerful features—features that cut a significant amount of time and effort from your routine typing tasks. Not only can you create a simple document in a fraction of the time required by manual typing, but with WordStar 7.0 you can produce high-quality, professional documents, complete with graphics, endnotes, footnotes, headers, footers...the list goes on.

You won't be a WordStar expert overnight; learning any software program takes a bit of trial-and-error and experimentation. Now that you've finished this book, however, you have all the tools you need to set your creativity loose and begin designing your own documents. Good luck, and—more important—have fun!

Installing WordStar 7.0

This appendix explains how you can install WordStar 7.0 on your computer and set up the program to work with the components of your computer system.

To use WordStar, your system must meet these minimum requirements:

- IBM or compatible
- Hard disk drive
- At least one floppy disk drive
- 512K memory (640K to run Page Preview)
- DOS 2.1 or later

The disks included in WordStar 7.0 are compressed; therefore, you must go through the installation process to install WordStar correctly. Do not try to copy the disks onto your hard drive without going through installation.

Making Backup Copies

Whenever you are preparing to install a new program, making a backup copy of the program is always a good idea, even though you're going to install the program on the hard disk of your computer. Creating a backup provides you with a safety net in case something happens to one of the disks during the installation process (which is extremely unlikely).

To make a backup copy of the program disks on a two-disk drive system, first start with a blank, formatted disk. Place one original program disk in the appropriate disk drive. Place the blank, formatted disk in the other disk drive. Then type the following command:

COPY A:*.* B:

This command tells DOS (your operating system) to copy all the information from the disk in drive A to the disk in drive B. (If you have your original disk in drive B and are copying to drive A, you reverse the drive names in the command line.) Press Enter. DOS copies the contents of the disk in drive A to the disk in drive B.

If you are using a system that has only one disk drive (besides the hard drive), DOS prompts you when to change disks so that the operating system can write the information to the blank disks.

Copy all your disks this way, and then put the originals away in a safe place. You can use your backup copies for the installation and subsequent changes that require the original disks.

Installing WordStar 7.0

Because WordStar 7.0's installation process is fully automated, all you must do is answer a few prompts and change disks when prompted. If at any time during installation you want to stop the process, you can press Esc to cancel. Be careful, though, because this action cancels the entire installation, and you must start over.

To start the installation, follow these steps:

1. Place Disk 1 in the disk drive.

2. Make sure that your computer is on and displaying the DOS prompt for the root directory (C:\, D:\, and so on).

3. Type the name of the disk drive in which Disk 1 is placed (*A:* or *B:*) and press Enter. The prompt changes to A:\ or B:\.

4. Type *WSSETUP* and press Enter. After a minute, the WSSETUP opening screen appears, as shown in figure A.1.

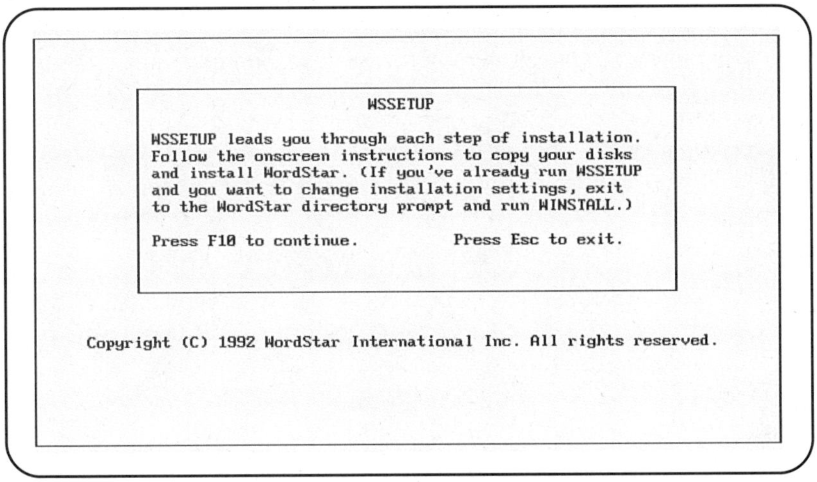

Fig. A.1

The WSSETUP
opening screen.

5. Press F10. Another screen appears, prompting you to type the serial number for your version of WordStar. (You can find your serial number on the registration card in your software package.)

6. Type the serial number and press F10. The Disk Drive Names screen appears, as shown in figure A.2.

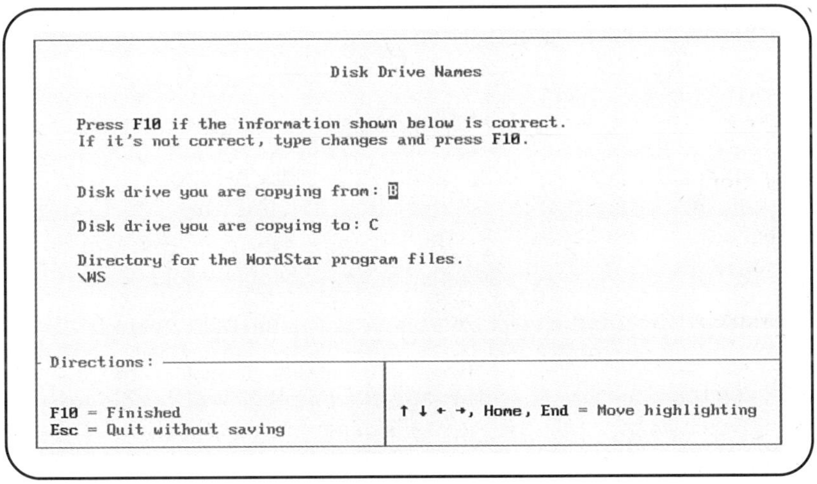

Fig. A.2

The Disk Drive Names
screen.

7. If the settings are correct, press F10.

   If you need to make changes—for example, if you want to change the Disk Drive You Are Copying To setting to D—use the arrow keys to move the cursor to the item you want to change and then type the correction. If you decide to install WordStar to the \WS directory or any other directory, WordStar creates that directory for you. When all settings are correct, press F10.

8. The Add or Remove a Feature screen appears, as shown in figure A.3.

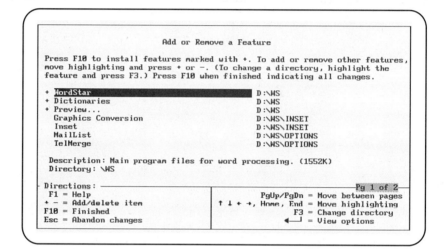

The Add or Remove a Feature screen.

The first three items—WordStar, Dictionaries, and Preview—are marked with plus signs (+) to indicate that when you press F10 to start the installation procedure, those features are copied to your hard disk. You can add as many features as your computer's disk space allows. To mark additional features, use the arrow keys to move the cursor to the feature you want, and press the + key. If you want to remove the selection of a feature, move the cursor to the feature and press the minus (–) key.

Notice that as you scroll through the list, the Description line changes to tell you how much disk space the feature needs and provides a brief explanation of what the feature is.

Not Done Yet

It's easy to miss, but another page of features appears after the initial Add or Remove a Feature screen. To move to the next page of features, press Page Down. You then can select or deselect the features as described in step 8.

9. After you choose all the features you want, press F10.

WordStar then begins copying the files to your hard disk, into the drive and directory you specified. The Add or Remove a Feature screen continues to be displayed, while WordStar lists across the bottom part of the screen the various files being copied (see fig. A.4).

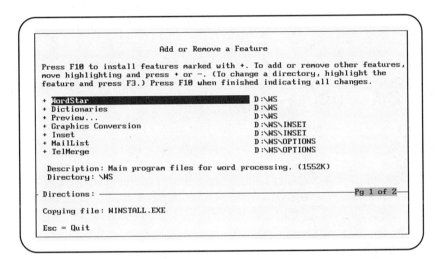

```
                    Add or Remove a Feature

Press F10 to install features marked with +. To add or remove other features,
move highlighting and press + or -. (To change a directory, highlight the
feature and press F3.) Press F10 when finished indicating all changes.

 + WordStar              D:\WS
 + Dictionaries          D:\WS
 + Preview...            D:\WS
 + Graphics Conversion   D:\WS\INSET
 + Inset                 D:\WS\INSET
 + MailList              D:\WS\OPTIONS
 + TelMerge              D:\WS\OPTIONS

 Description: Main program files for word processing. (1552K)
 Directory: \WS

- Directions: ─────────────────────────────────────Pg 1 of 2─

Copying file: WINSTALL.EXE

Esc = Quit
```

Fig. A.4

WordStar begins copying the files.

After WordStar copies all the files on the current disk, the program prompts you to insert another disk (see fig. A.5). Remove the current disk and insert the new disk. Press F10. WordStar again begins copying the necessary files.

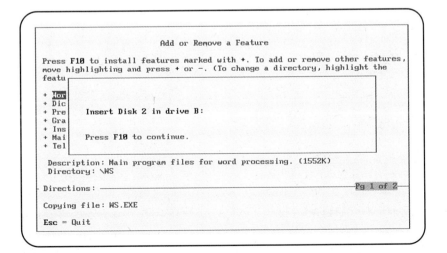

```
                    Add or Remove a Feature

Press F10 to install features marked with +. To add or remove other features,
move highlighting and press + or -. (To change a directory, highlight the
featu┌──────────────────────────────────────────────┐
 + Wor│                                                │
 + Dic│                                                │
 + Pre│    Insert Disk 2 in drive B:                   │
 + Gra│                                                │
 + Ins│                                                │
 + Mai│    Press F10 to continue.                      │
 + Tel│                                                │
      └──────────────────────────────────────────────┘
 Description: Main program files for word processing. (1552K)
 Directory: \WS

- Directions: ─────────────────────────────────────Pg 1 of 2─

Copying file: WS.EXE

Esc = Quit
```

Fig. A.5

WordStar prompts you to insert another disk.

As WordStar finishes installing each feature, the cursor moves down the list on the Add or Remove a Feature screen. WordStar replaces the plus symbol beside installed features with a small square symbol.

Continue following the prompts until WordStar displays the message Finished adding features. Remove your disk and press F10 to continue.

After you press F10, a small screen is displayed, saying that you will install your monitor for use with WordStar. You now have copied all the files to the hard disk.

Installing the Monitor

As the prompt requests, press F10 again. The Install a Monitor screen appears, listing different monitor types (see fig. A.6). WordStar suggests that if you are unsure what monitor type you have, select the first option, IBM PC or Compatible. To choose a different monitor, press the down-arrow key to move the cursor to the monitor you want and press Enter.

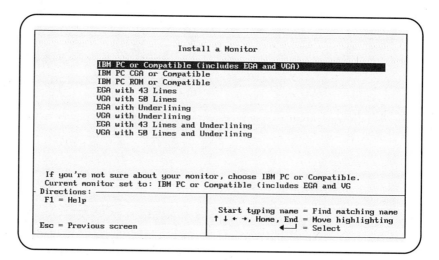

The Choose Default Colors screen appears, asking you to choose whether to use a standard color or monochrome or an alternate monochrome monitor (like the monitor that laptop computers use). Select your monitor's color capabilities and press Enter.

Another small screen appears, telling you that next you will install the printer. Press F10. At the prompt, reinsert Disk 1 into the disk drive and then press F10.

Installing the Printer

After a few seconds, the Installed Printer Menu appears (see fig. A.7). On this screen, WordStar wants you to enter the name for a PDF (printer description file), in which the program stores important information about your printer. This file is very important to WordStar; you cannot print your documents without a PDF for your printer. Because at this stage you are creating a new PDF, you can enter a name similar to the printer you are using (for example, you might enter *PSCRIPT* for a PostScript printer). You can give your printer any name you want. Type the name for the PDF and press Enter.

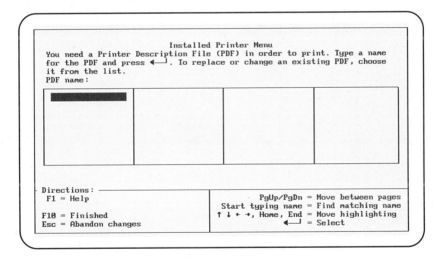

```
                        Installed Printer Menu
      You need a Printer Description File (PDF) in order to print. Type a name
      for the PDF and press ◄─┘. To replace or change an existing PDF, choose
      it from the list.
      PDF name :

      ┌─────────────┬───────────────┬───────────────┬───────────────┐
      │█████████████│               │               │               │
      │             │               │               │               │
      │             │               │               │               │
      │             │               │               │               │
      │             │               │               │               │
      └─────────────┴───────────────┴───────────────┴───────────────┘

      Directions :
        F1 = Help                          PgUp/PgDn = Move between pages
                                    Start typing name = Find matching name
        F10 = Finished              ↑ ↓ ← →, Home, End = Move highlighting
        Esc = Abandon changes                     ◄─┘ = Select
```

Fig. A.7

The Installed Printer Menu.

The next screen that appears lists the different types of printers you can choose from within WordStar (see fig. A.8). With the Printer Type Menu, you highlight the printer type you have and press Enter. A more detailed screen—called the Printer Selection Menu—appears, showing the variety of printers available within the type you have selected. Figure A.9 shows the Printer Selection Menu after PostScript Lasers was chosen from the Printer Type Menu.

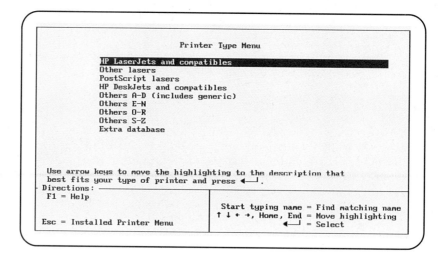

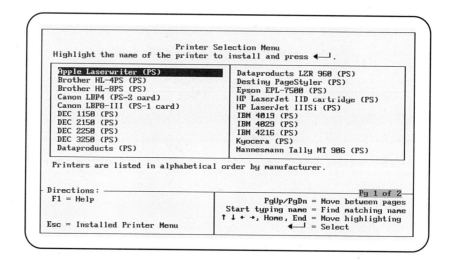

You can use the arrow keys or press the first letter of the printer type to
move to the name of the printer you want to select. (If you press the
character, the cursor moves directly to a printer beginning with that
letter.) Highlight the name of the printer you want and then press Enter.
If you don't see one that matches the type of printer you are using, check
your printer manual to see whether your printer emulates (or acts like)
other popular printers.

After you press Enter, WordStar displays a Please wait message for a
moment or two. Then the Additional Installation Menu appears
(see fig. A.10). You can change the printer adapter port (the default is
LPT1), install a sheet feeder, return to the Printer Information Menu, add
or delete fonts, or return to the Installed Printer Menu. Choose Return to

Installed Printer Menu to see your printer name listed. Press F10 to save
your selections.

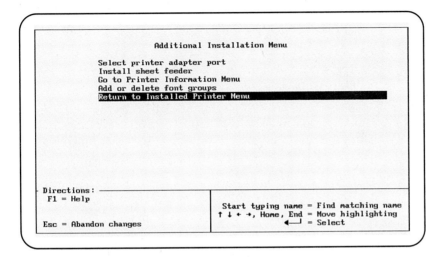

The Modify AUTOEXEC.BAT File dialog box then appears, asking
whether you want WordStar to add the WS (WordStar) directory to the
path in the AUTOEXEC.BAT file. (This file is an important one that your
computer reads each time it boots.) Type *Y* to select yes or *N* for no. If
you press Y, WordStar asks you to type the name of the drive from
which you boot.

The Installation Summary screen then appears, showing you the monitor
and printer you've chosen during installation (see fig. A.11).

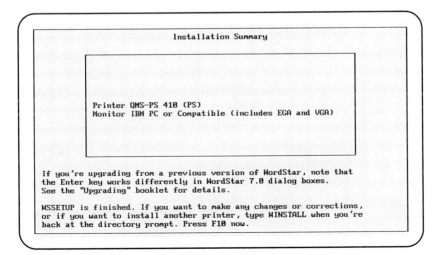

When you're ready to exit to DOS and try out your WordStar program, press F10. To start WordStar, type *WS* at the DOS prompt.

Using WINSTALL To Modify Installation

If you later want to add a printer or add or delete fonts (among other possible changes), you can go back into the installation settings by exiting to DOS and typing *WINSTALL*. You then see the WINSTALL main menu, which contains the following options:

- Install a Monitor
- Modify or Install a Printer
- Set Basic Editing Defaults
- Add or Remove a Feature
- Customize WordStar
- Add Fonts to Custom Database
- Save and Return to DOS

The only procedures in WINSTALL not shown in the basic installation procedure are the Set Basic Editing Defaults and Customize WordStar options. Chances are, as you start out with WordStar, you may want to leave the program defaults the way they are. As your experience with WordStar grows, however, you may want to tailor some of WordStar's features to better suit your individual needs.

For more information on using WINSTALL to customize WordStar, see your program documentation.

WordStar Troubleshooting Tips

This appendix lists common problems concerning printing, graphics, preview, and other features that may crop up as you work with WordStar. A suggested solution follows each problem.

The picture I imported came in looking squashed.

Depending on the program you were using when you captured the picture with Inset, you may need to resize the picture. Use the Inset Modify command to change the size and import the file again.

The headers are cut off at the top of the page.

Depending on the printer you are using, your printer may or may not need the line-feed command inserted automatically at the beginning of each document. The margins required by your printer type also may vary from the default margins. Try to solve the header problem by entering a larger top margin setting.

After I click OK to begin printing, WordStar beeps and displays Print Wait ***at the top of the screen.***

Your printer may be out of paper, or the printer cable may not be connected securely. Press Ctrl-KP to display the Printing dialog box; an error message may appear. If so, correct the error and try again. If no error message is displayed, check all connections and make sure that your printer has paper and is ready. Then press C to continue printing.

The message `Printer may not be ready` ***keeps appearing.***

Check all the physical connections and make sure that WordStar is sending the data to the correct port. You may also need to use WINSTALL to make sure that you've installed the correct printer. For more information, refer to Appendix A, in the section on installing the printer.

In preview mode, WordStar displays only part of the text in the document.

Your margin settings may be causing this problem. Check the page offset (by choosing the Page command from the Layout menu) and the margin settings for the document. If you're using columns, you may need to reformat the text before it all appears on the correct page in columnar form.

When I added a picture, some text disappeared.

WordStar doesn't automatically make room for the picture you insert; you must add the spaces by pressing Enter. Try positioning the cursor after the insert-graphic tag and pressing Enter several times. Then preview the document to see whether the text has come out from behind the picture.

I accidentally changed the help level to 0, and now I don't know how to display the menus again.

When you want to return to a different menu level, press Ctrl-JJ and type the number of the help level you want. (Pressing 4 at the opening screen displays the pull-down menu system.)

My printer will not print.

Make sure that the printer cable is connected securely to the back of the computer and to the printer itself. Also, make sure that the printer has paper and is on-line. If the document still will not print, make sure that you've selected the correct printer port. (You can see which printer port you selected by using the WINSTALL utility, described in Appendix A.)

Every once in a while, a line in my document will not print. WordStar just skips over that line as though it isn't even there.

You probably have accidentally inserted one of the command identifiers at the start of the line. If WordStar sees a period (.) at the beginning of a line, for example, the program thinks that the line is a comment line or a nonprinting command tag and skips the line when printing.

The page number isn't appearing at the bottom of document.

The automatic page number—placed in the footer of your document—appears only if you haven't added a footer of your own. If you've entered a new footer, you can include the page number by typing # in the footer line. The footer also can print only if your bottom margin is large enough. Therefore, try increasing your bottom margin (.mb).

I can't find the file I just created! (I know it's here somewhere. . .)

You probably are looking in the wrong directory. Double-click the directory you want in the Filenames section of the opening menu. You also may need to change to a different drive.

My dot-matrix printer starts to print and then prints a bunch of mysterious characters instead of my file.

Because your printer is initially printing the file correctly, the problem must be occurring as the printer gets overloaded with the flow of data WordStar is sending out. You can solve this problem by using the PRCHANGE program (discussed in Appendix A) to change the print speed.

When I use the Run DOS Command option on the File menu to load SideKick, my computer locks up.

The developers of WordStar recommend that you load any other memory-resident programs *before* you start WordStar. Doing otherwise may lead to unexpected results.

Everything in WordStar is set to be measured in inches, but I'm used to working with points and picas.

With WordStar, you can enter settings that require measurement several different ways: leave the default as inches (*.5"*), indicate points (*16p*), or use centimeters (*5c*). A complete list of units of measure accepted by WordStar can be found in the WordStar documentation.

Parts of my page are cut off when I print.

The problem may be two things: the document is too large to fit in your printer's memory, or you've created a document that extends beyond your printer's print margins. Try changing the margins on the page or removing one or two complex pictures to lessen the pull on your printer's memory.

When I try to preview my document, WordStar tells me I don't have enough memory space.

Have you been using Inset? Until you release Inset from memory, Inset occupies valuable RAM need by WordStar to load the preview utility. To remove Inset, exit from WordStar, change to the Inset directory, type *RI*, and press Enter. If you also have other memory-resident programs loaded, preview may be unable to run.

My printer is substituting Courier for the font I've selected.

For some reason, WordStar is not finding the font you specified when you worked with the document in the edit screen. Open the document and check the fonts and paragraph styles you've applied to the document. Then open the Fonts dialog box (by pressing Ctrl-P=) and make sure that the fonts you've chosen are available on your current printer. If you are using downloadable fonts, remember that you must download the fonts to the printer before you print; otherwise, WordStar does not know where to find the font information at print time.

I can't use landscape orientation for my documents.

Not all printers have the capability to print landscape pages. In landscape orientation, text is printed lengthwise on the page. Check your printer manual to see whether your printer has this capability.

I tried to import a picture but didn't find any PIX files.

You are not in the INSET subdirectory. To move to the INSET subdirectory, double-click INSET in the Filenames box on the opening screen.

I'm getting only half a page of output when I print my documents.

Check to make sure that you're not overloading your printer's memory. If you are working with a document that uses many fonts and includes special items, such as Inset graphics, your printer memory may not be large enough to support all the items in your document. You can create and print a test document (by copying the original and removing the Inset graphics) to see whether memory is the problem.

I created a macro and then tried to edit it as a nondocument. Now the macro won't work at all, and my computer locks up.

Although macros may *look* like nondocuments in WordStar, they actually contain codes that are part of the executable program lines. If you need to edit a macro, use only the Macro Create/Edit command.

The margins in my document are not printing the way I specified.

Some printers (especially laser printers) have built-in margins and do not print beyond a certain point on the page. The margins you specify are added to this nonprinting point on your pages; depending on the margins you set (and whether you've added Page Offset margins), the margins may be larger than you want. You can fix this problem by entering a smaller margin value or by changing the offset (available by choosing the Page command from the Layout menu) for your document.

When I try to load Inset, I get a message saying that the files are not found.

Perhaps when you installed WordStar, you didn't install the full version, which includes the Inset files. You can add the feature by exiting WordStar, typing *WINSTALL* at the prompt, and selecting the Add or Remove a Feature option from the displayed menu. You then can highlight the Inset feature and copy the files from your disks to your hard drive.

I just opened a document and added a header line. When I preview the document, nothing appears on the page.

Enter a few lines of text in the body portion of the document; then go back and view the document. The header should be in place.

Document Design Tips

This appendix presents an overview of various design suggestions scattered throughout *Using WordStar 7.0*. The suggestions are divided according to the type of document:

- Overall design tips
- Business letters
- Long documents
- Newsletters
- Fliers and brochures
- Business cards and stationery
- Business forms
- Training handouts

Overall Design Tips

Consider your audience.

Who will read your publication? Make sure that the style of the text and the artwork you choose are appropriate for the readers.

Think about your objectives.

What do you want to accomplish with this document? Are you telling clients about a new product that is going to be introduced? Think about the reaction you want from your readers.

Keep a folder of styles you like.

Whether you produce simple correspondence, brochures, fliers, menus, or newsletters, keep samples of published materials you like so that you can refer to them when you need ideas for creating your own publications. Remember not to copy exactly, though.

Business Letters

Determine the tone of your letter.

If you're writing to a client, a prospective employer, or someone else who may make decisions about you or your business based on the look of your letter, the tone and overall feeling of the letter are important. The typeface you choose affects the tone you send.

Choose the type of alignment that best suits the correspondence.

Different alignment types also convey different messages. The two most often used alignments are left alignment, in which the text is aligned along the left margin but ragged on the right, and justified, in which the text is aligned on both the left and right margins.

Decide whether you want to merge print the letter.

If you plan to use MailList to help you merge a mailing list of names and addresses with a form letter, you must enter variables for the changeable parts of your letter.

Consider using the Calculator.

Remember that you can use WordStar's built-in math features to help you calculate figures on your document. You can line up the numbers, table-style, and use the Calculator, available in the Utilities menu, to perform the calculations for you, without ever having to leave your document.

Whether you are printing on traditional 8 1/2-by-11 inch paper controls certain elements.

Depending on your printer's capabilities, you may be able to use different paper sizes and orientation. The orientation of your document refers to the way the text is printed on the page. With traditional *portrait orientation*, text is printed vertically on the 8 1/2-by-11-inch page; with *landscape orientation*, the text is printed horizontally, on a 11-by-8 1/2-inch page. (***Note:*** Not all printers support landscape orientation. Depending on the capabilities of your printer, this option may or may not be available to you.)

You can print envelopes from WordStar.

If you want to print the envelopes for your letters from within WordStar, you can do so by using the MailList utility. You can also use the Print from Keyboard command on the File menu.

Long Documents

Consider the tone when you choose a typeface.

In longer documents, your choice of typeface becomes more important. If your readers will be reviewing a large amount of text, choose a typeface that is easy to read.

Think about the margin settings for the page.

The left and right margins are important because—especially when readers look over pages and pages of text—narrow margins are tiring on the eyes. If your document is very long, move the right margin in more than you would in shorter documents, just to give the reader's eye a rest.

Think about the spacing you want to use for text.

Remember that readers get discouraged when too much text is crammed into too small a space. In some documents, such as college term papers, double-spacing enables reviewers to write comments easily between the lines.

Decide whether your document needs an index.

If you are covering various topics in your document, an index can provide readers with a way to find subjects they need to refer to. You can use WordStar's automatic index generator to create a simple or more detailed index for your document.

Decide whether you should use headers and footers.

Headers and footers give readers a reference point as they peruse your text. You may want to include your name or company name, department, page number, date, or other information that can help readers identify the document they are reading.

Think about whether the document requires a table of contents.

A table of contents is a kind of "reader service" item that can make a difference in the way readers feel about your document. If they can easily find the topics they need to read about, they will remember your document in a more favorable light.

Think about whether you want to include graphics.

Especially in text-intensive documents, graphics can provide a welcome break from page after page of words. With WordStar, you can import graphics by using the Inset program (available in the Utilities menu) to add special graphic touches to your document.

Be consistent with your design.

Keep the basic margin settings, text settings, and spacing the same from page to page. A little variety, for things such as tables and special design elements, can add to the design, but always remember to return to your original design so that your readers can follow the organization of your document.

Newsletters

Consider what type of design is appropriate for your audience.

If your publication is a serious medical document, for example, choosing a light, airy typeface and including humorous clip art might not fit the tone you are trying to convey.

Consider the length of the newsletter.

If you are planning a multipage newsletter, you need to think about the design of all pages. Do you want to repeat some of the same elements on every page (such as a logo or business name)? Do you want to keep the same column format on every page, or do you want to vary the layout from page to page?

Think about how many articles are involved.

Block out the number of articles you plan to use. Think about the approximate length of the articles and plan where you will place them in the newsletter. Sketching this design on paper is especially helpful if you have several articles that will continue on other pages of your publication. Planning also helps you fit everything together so that no text is left over and no gaping holes are left unfilled in your document.

Decide what type of banner your publication needs.

As you may know, a banner is found at the top of the publication. Typically, the banner includes the name of the publication. (Your company's name generally is placed in smaller type.) Are you designing the banner or does your company have a standard banner for all publications of this type? Again, consider your audience: think about the kind of type (light and friendly, or heavier and more serious) that you should use to communicate your tone. An appropriate, eye-catching banner can make a big impression on a first-time reader.

Determine what kind of graphics you should use.

As you know, WordStar 7.0 uses the Inset graphics integration program to add graphics to your documents. Is the art you want to use currently available in electronic form? Do you want to be able to convert charts you create in a popular spreadsheet program into a format that WordStar can use? (WordStar automatically converts graphics files to PIX files.) If the art is not available in computer form, do you need to leave space in your publication so that the art can be pasted in at print time?

Fliers and Brochures

Consider the kind of business you are promoting.

If you are advertising a service business, the text and graphics you choose for the flier or brochure should convey that idea. If you are promoting a product or advertising a sale at a local retail outlet, you may want to use Inset to bring in a picture that resembles the product or key products involved in your sale.

Determine what is most important about what you're trying to say.

A promotional piece (flier or brochure) is a "hit 'em fast" type of publication. Much communication power must rest on a few powerful words, and you need to choose your words carefully so that you convey the strongest message possible in a small number of words. Particularly in promotional materials, conciseness is important: don't use ten words to say something you can say in two.

Think of items you can use to grab readers' attention.

Because sales brochures are people-oriented, a friendly-yet-serious image is best for many businesses. You want the public to think you run a personable business but that you take your work seriously. The text and graphics you choose should reflect the image you want to convey.

Business Cards and Stationery

Design your cards, stationery, and other printed items consistently.

After you decide on a logo, use that logo on all your printed materials. The consistency of seeing the same logo and basic text layout (where you place the company name and address, for example) can help your readers identify your company.

Keep the design simple and memorable.

Especially with business cards, don't give in to the temptation to fill the card with too much information. Remember that you have only a limited amount of space and that unused space on small publications is just as important as the printed words.

Remember the basic function of your stationery.

You create stationery to accomplish two goals: to get your company name in front of people (otherwise you should use blank paper) and to correspond with your readers. Don't fill the stationery with unnecessary information.

Highlight the company name.

In your stationery and business cards, place the company name and logo in a strategic place so that the item draws the reader's eye. Remember that the use of white space is important—it helps guide readers to the item you want them to focus on.

Business Forms

Use the same company logo on all forms.

Again, using your logo consistently on all printed material helps customers build on their impression of you. Place the logo so that it is instantly recognizable, as soon as the customer opens the envelope.

Think about the number of columns you need and divide the space equally.

Whether you use one column or many, remember to divide the space evenly so that the columns are proportioned appropriately.

Organize the form into understandable sections.

Be careful not to cram all the information onto the form in an unorganized fashion.

Use only a few different typefaces.

Be consistent within the body of your business forms. Use one typeface for the column headings in your invoice, for example, and another for the company information. Remember that using too many different typefaces can give your publication a confusing look.

Training Handouts

Make your class objectives known.

Place the objectives—or goals—of your course in an easily identified spot on the handout. If you are designing a course that includes several different lessons, include only the objectives for the current lesson on the individual training handout.

Keep the handout brief, with only enough information to refresh the reader's memory when the handout is read later.

Remember that you don't need to restate the entire lesson in this backup material. Cover only the key points in your discussion so that the reader can recall important facts later.

You may want to include space for notes.

Depending on the nature of your course and whether you are pressed for space on the handout, you may want to add a section where students can write notes from your presentation.

Make the major points easy to find.

Use special styles to highlight the most important points on a page. You can use numbered steps, boldfaced type, or a picture such as an icon to draw the reader's eye to the most important items.

Quick Keys and Dot Commands

This appendix lists the quick-key combinations you can use to bypass the menu selections in help level 4 of WordStar 7.0. The second half of this appendix shows you the dot commands you can use to insert commands into your document.

Quick Keys

Table D.1 lists the keys for the commands in the menus on the opening screen. Table D.2 lists the same information for commands on the menus in the edit screen.

Table D.1 Opening Screen Quick Keys

Menu	Key	Command
File	FS	New
	FD	Open Document
	FN	Open Nondocument
	FP	Print
	FK	Print from Keyboard
	F\	Fax
	FO	Copy
	FY	Delete
	FE	Rename
	FC	Protect/Unprotect
	FL	Change Drive/Directory
	H[1]	Change Filename Display
	FR	Run DOS Command
	F?	Status
	FX	Exit WordStar
Utilities	UI	Index
	UT	TOC
	M[1]	Macros
Additional	AM	MailList
	AT	TelMerge
	AS	Star Exchange

[1] The menu must be opened before this command can be selected.

Table D.2 lists the keys in the menus on the editing screen. You may notice that some commands are not listed here. Not all commands have quick-key combinations—some have dot commands instead. (The next section lists the dot commands.)

Table D.2 Edit Screen Quick Keys

Menu	Key	Command
File	Ctrl-OK	Open/Switch
	Ctrl-KS	Save
	Ctrl-KT	Save As
	Ctrl-KD	Save and Close
	Ctrl-KP	Print
	Ctrl-K\	Fax
	Ctrl-P?	Change Printer
	Ctrl-KO	Copy
	Ctrl-KJ	Delete File
	Ctrl-KE	Rename File
	Ctrl-KL	Change Drive/Directory
	Ctrl-KF	Run DOS Command
	Ctrl-O?	Status
	Ctrl-KQX	Exit WordStar and Abandon Changes in Current Document
Edit	Ctrl-U	Undo
	Ctrl-KB	Mark Block Beginning
	Ctrl-KK	Mark Block End
	Ctrl-KV	Move Block
	Ctrl-KG	Move Block from Other Window
	Ctrl-KC	Copy Block
	Ctrl-KA	Copy Block from Other Window
	Ctrl-K[	Copy From Windows Clipboard
	Ctrl-K]	Copy To Windows Clipboard
	Ctrl-KW	Copy To Another File
	Ctrl-KY	Delete Block
	Ctrl-T	Delete Word
	Ctrl-Y	Delete Line
	Ctrl-Q-Del	Delete Line Left of Cursor
	Ctrl-QY	Delete Line Right of Cursor

continues

Table D.2 Continued

Menu	Key	Command
	Ctrl-QT	Delete To Character
	Ctrl-KU	Mark Previous Block
	Ctrl-QF	Find
	Ctrl-QA	Find and Replace
	Ctrl-L	Next Find
	Ctrl-QG	Go to Character
	Ctrl-QI	Go to Page
	Ctrl-OND	Edit Note
View	Ctrl-OP	Preview
	Ctrl-OD	Command Tags
	Ctrl-KH	Block Highlighting
	Ctrl-OK	Open/Switch Window
	Ctrl-OM	Change Window Size
	Ctrl-OB	Screen Settings
Insert	Ctrl-M@	Today's Date Value
	Ctrl-P0 (zero)	Extended Character
	Ctrl-KR	File
	Ctrl-P*	Graphic
	Ctrl-OZ	Par. Outline Number
Style	Ctrl-PB	Bold
	Ctrl-PY	Italic
	Ctrl-PS	Underline
	Ctrl-P=	Font
	Ctrl-OFS	Select Paragraph Style
	Ctrl-OFP	Return to Previous Style
	Ctrl-OFD	Define Paragraph Style
Layout	Ctrl-OC	Center Line
	Ctrl-O]	Right Align Line
	Ctrl-OL	Ruler Line
	Ctrl-OU	Columns

Menu	Key	Command
	Ctrl-OY	Page
	Ctrl-O#	Page Numbering
	Ctrl-OS	Alignment and Spacing
Utilities	Ctrl-QR	Spelling Check
	Ctrl-QL	Global
	Ctrl-QJ	Thesaurus
	Ctrl-P&	Inset
	Ctrl-QM	Calculator
	Ctrl-KM	Block Math
	Ctrl-K?	Word Count
	Ctrl-QQ	Repeat Next Keystroke

Dot Commands

This section lists the dot commands you can insert into your WordStar documents. In some cases, when you select a command from a pull-down menu (such as Headers from the Header/Footers menu), WordStar adds the dot command at the cursor position.

Forging out on your own to enter dot commands may be a bit technical for beginning users. If you want to enter your own dot commands, you may want to consult the documentation before doing so. Table D.3 lists the dot commands that WordStar uses.

Table D.3 WordStar Dot Commands

Dot Command	Description
.text	Specifies *text* as a nonprinting comment
.av	Asks for variable
.aw *on/off*	Word wrap
.bn	Sheet feeder bin control
.bp	Bidirectional printing

continues

Table D.3 Continued

Dot Command	Description
.cb	Column break
.cc #	Start new column
.co #, *m*	Print number of columns; # is number of columns, *m* is space between columns
.cp #	Conditional page break
.cs	Clears screen
.cv *n>x*	Changes note types
.cw *n*	Character width
.df *file name*	Data file
.dm *message*	Displays message
.e# *n*	Numbers endnote, where *n* = number to start endnote numbering with
.ei	Specifies end if
.el	Specifies else condition
.f# *n*	Numbers footnote
.f#d *n*	Numbers footnotes in a series
.f#p *n*	Restarts footnote numbers on each page
.f1	Footer line 1
.f2	Footer line 2
.f3	Footer line 3
.f4	Footer line 4
.f5	Footer line 5
.fi *file name*	Prints specified file
.fm*n*	Prints footer *n* lines below text
.fn*e/o*	Footer on even or odd pages
.fo	Same as footer line 1
.go *top/bottom*	In merge printing, moves to top or bottom of file
.h1	Header line 1
.h2	Header line 2

Dot Command	Description
.h3	Header line 3
.h4	Header line 4
.h5	Header line 5
.he	Same as header line 1
.hm*n*	Prints header *n* lines above text
.hy *on/off*	Turns hyphenation on/off
.if	Sets if condition
.ig *text*	Displays text as nonprinting comment
.ix *text*	Sets index entry
.kr *on/off*	Turns kerning on/off
.l# 0	Turns off line numbering
.l# d*n*	Use continuous line numbering (*n* = spacing; 1 for single, 2 for double)
.l# p*n*	Use line numbering, restart numbers on each page
.la	Changes language
.lh a	Line height to automatic
.lh *n*	Line height to *n* inches
.lm *n*	Left margin to *n* inches
.lq *on/off/dis*	Letter-quality on/off/discretionary
.ls *n*	Line spacing to *n* inches
.ma	Merge printing; math variable
.mb #	Bottom margin
.mt #	Top margin
.oc *on/off*	Centering on/off
.oj *on/off/r/c*	Justification on/off/right/center
.op	Page numbering on/off
.p# *n*	Paragraph numbering
.pa	Page break
.pc*n*	Print page numbers at column *n*
.pe	Print endnotes

continues

Table D.3 Continued

Dot Command	Description
.pf *on/off/dis*	Print formatting on/off/discretionary
.pg	Turns page numbering on/off
.pl *n*	Page length
.pm *n*	Start first line of paragraph
.pn *n*	Start page numbering
.po *n*	Page offset
.pr or=l	Sets landscape mode
.pr or=p	Sets portrait mode
.ps *on/off/dis*	Proportional spacing on/off/discretionary
.rm *n*	Right margin in *n* inches
.rp *n*	Print file *n* times
.rr	Adds ruler line
.rv	Read variables (merge printing)
.rv*	Read field/dBASE/spreadsheet variables for merge printing
.sb *on/off*	Suppress blank lines
.sr	Set super/subscript roll
.sv	Set variable
.tb	Set tabs
.tc	Table of contents entry
.uj *on/off/dis*	Microjustification on/off/discretionary
.ul *on/off*	Underline on/off
.xe	Redefines custom print control code Ctrl-PE
.xq	Redefines custom print control code Ctrl-PQ
.xr	Redefines custom print control code Ctrl-PR
.xw	Redefines custom print control code Ctrl-PW

Turning Your Document into a Finished Product

For most of your WordStar documents, you may not need to be concerned with professional publishing. Because of the quality of output available to you now that laser printers are the norm, you rarely—if ever—need to deal with that quick printing company around the corner.

If, however, you are responsible for having your documents copied, bound, or otherwise printed professionally, you must decide about paper weights, measurements, print quality, and a variety of other typographical issues. This appendix provides some information that may come in handy when you take your WordStar document into the printing store to have it professionally printed.

Many people feel "out of their element" after they walk into a print shop. They think that they don't know what questions to ask, what the "normal" choices are (paper weight and size, ink, and so on), or what price range to expect. If you are creating a newsletter for a small group or publishing pamphlets for a grass-roots organization, you may feel at even more of a disadvantage. Today, with the corporate world striving for more control of their published products, desktop publishing and final printing are not nearly as foreign as they once were.

Whether you feel threatened by this final step in the printing process or are more comfortable with printing decisions, this appendix tries to help you with basic printing questions. The best advice for working with professional printers, however, is to find a printer who is willing to advise you, who shows creative judgment you can trust, and who gives you a reasonable price. If you are satisfied with the quality, turn-around time, and cost, stay with that printer. Developing a business relationship with one printer is good business sense for anyone interested in creating professional documents in a timely manner, and this relationship works to your company's best interest in the future.

Preparing the Document for the Printer

Most of the time, after people finish a document, they don't want to look at it again. Part of the reason is that they're tired of reworking and revising the document; the other part is that they're afraid they may see something else they want to change.

Generally, when you consider yourself "finished" with a document, you should take one last, careful look. Make sure that the text breaks where you want it to, read the document over for grammatical and punctuation errors, and check your graphics to make sure that they printed correctly. If you have pasted down anything manually, make sure that the item is secure and neatly done (big wads of rubber cement don't look too professional). Finally, have all your pages together in the right order.

Understanding Typical Newsletter Format

More and more, businesses are going to a more polished, sophisticated newsletter style. Gone are the days of the typed-and-photocopied company newsletter. Now in-house publishing offices use eye-catching color, custom art, and laser- or typeset-quality type to create a dramatic effect for their publications.

These publications typically are four-page newsletters; a four-page newsletter is actually one sheet of a fairly heavy-stock paper printed front and back and folded in the middle. One-half of the last page is reserved for the mailing panel, to which mailing labels are affixed. The bulk mailing permit number and rate also may be printed in the top right corner of the panel. This kind of publication may have a print run from 2,000 to 4,000.

Although that kind of high-investment "typical" order may be the norm for the corporate world, many people still produce informational newsletters for nonprofit organizations, parent-teacher organizations, and businesses. This kind of business relies on WordStar's capabilities, making good use of the program's friendliness, flexibility, and wealth of features.

Choosing Paper

Depending on the publications you are creating, you need to take care in selecting the correct paper to meet your needs. Some questions with suggestions follow.

What paper weight do you want?

For newsletters, a 60-pound offset paper is best. The coarseness of the paper can stand up to printing on both sides. If you're on a low budget, you can use a 50-pound offset paper, but you run the risk of the ink's bleeding through when you print on both sides of the paper.

If you are producing a brochure for mailing, you should use a different kind of paper. You can choose from a flat finish, enamel (high gloss—which also strengthens the paper), text stock, or card stock. Text stock is a relatively lightweight paper that folds easily; card stock is heavier paper, used often for producing materials that include business-reply cards and similar items. Unless you are including a business-reply card that will be detached and mailed separately by the recipient, an enamel text stock is a good choice for a mailer. This stock folds neatly, doesn't need to be scored as card stock does, and costs less in postage. (The term *scored* refers to the process of cutting lines at the folds of the publication so that you can fold the heavy stock neatly.)

What size should the paper be?

For a typical four-page newsletter, professional printers most often use one 11-by-17-inch sheet. The sheet is folded in the center, giving you a "book" effect of having four pages.

If you have stayed within the default WordStar margins, your printer can print the pages on 11-by-17-inch paper. If you have changed the margins and extended the graphics to the edge of the page, or if you want a graphic image—like a rule or border—to bleed off the page, the printer must print the publication on a larger size paper and then cut the pages back to 11-by-17-inch size.

> **Larger Paper Size?**
>
> For documents other than the standard 8 1/2-by-11-inch size, keep in mind that the process may require cutting and/or printing on a larger or smaller size paper. (Naturally, the larger the paper size or the more work involved, the more you pay.)

If you are producing business cards, be sure to create the publication card at actual size: 2-by-3 1/2 inches. If the card is larger than standard business card size, the printer must photograph it, electronically reduce it, and print from the reduced copy. This process can detract from the readability of the card. Creating the card at the size you need is best; then you can print the card, take it in, and have the printer do the rest.

What color paper should I use?

From colors such as blue, pink, and yellow to more businesslike colors of gray, off-white, and white, you can choose the paper color that best suits your publication. Remember that you want a paper color to complement the ink color you use on the publication. If you're using red ink as part of a company logo, a publication on pink paper may make your readers cringe. Before you decide, ask the printer to see the color selection available.

Remember also that WordStar 7.0 can print in different colors that are supported by the printer. If you are printing on a color printer at the printing store, you can choose colors for your document before you save the file.

How much does the paper cost?

Several factors figure into the price of the paper you use: the weight, the size, the finish, and the quantity. Heavier paper costs more, but often is a necessity; and larger stock costs more than regular sizes.

Keep in mind that most printers offer a substantial price break for buying in quantity. If you are responsible for printing your organization's newsletter for 12 months, for example, and you expect to print at least 500 copies a month, you may want to buy all your paper for the year at one time. Most printers store the paper for you, giving you a significant price break on the paper as well.

Choosing Inks

Choosing the right quality and color of ink for your newsletter can add a professional look. Consider the following questions and ideas.

What color ink should I use?

As you may expect, black is the least expensive ink you can use. Most printers also have standard inks in several different colors. If you are trying to match a specific color or don't like the selection you have seen, you can request custom colors at a possible additional cost. For custom-color ink, you select the color from a chart (much like the paint scales at your local hardware store), and the printer mixes the color for you. Usually, an additional fee of $25 is charged for ink used for standard ink (the price may be more or less, depending on where you live), and an additional $10 to $15 is charged for custom colors.

Remember also that as technology evolves, color laser printers are making their way into printing stores. Call ahead to see whether the professional printer can laser print your documents in color. If so, you can set the colors you want within WordStar so that the document prints in color, enabling you to avoid expensive ink costs.

You can cut costs on printing in special ink and printing in quantities with one blow. Suppose that besides buying a mass amount of paper, you also want to print the company's name—in a custom royal blue ink—on the top of every page. The rest of the document will be done in black ink. In this instance, you can buy the paper in bulk and have the color printed for the whole amount at one time. This method keeps you from having to buy the paper and pay the specialized ink fee every month when you print the document. Then when you take the monthly document in to be printed, the cost is minimal.

Photocopying

Although your first thought may be that photocopying is less expensive, you need to consider the following ideas before you make your decision.

Is photocopying cheaper?

Depending on your project, the kind of audience you're reaching, and the quantity you want, photocopying is probably not your best bet. Although most people think, "I'll just take this flier down and run off 50 copies," the quality the customers get for the price they pay may be pretty poor.

Here again, think in terms of quantity. Is the flier you're producing a one-time, seasonal promotion that has a limited shelf life? Or can you use the flier several times throughout the year by circulating it to different client groups? If you can justify printing 100 or 150, have the printer reproduce the flier for you. The quality is much better, and the cost is still minimal: about $12 for 100 copies.

Understanding the Finer Points

This section contains a few pointers in addition to the basics covered in the preceding sections of this appendix.

Have the printer make suggestions.

The printer has worked with many clients, some of whom must have produced documents similar to yours. Rely on the printer's experience to tell you what paper, ink, envelope weight, and so on, works best for your particular project. Most printers keep samples of recent works so that you can feel the various paper weights, see the inks, and examine the layout.

Keep a folder of publications you like.

Identifying the styles that catch your eye is important; those styles also catch other readers' eyes. If you like the paper, the ink, or the size, keep the flier on file; then take the flier to the printer with you. The printer can make suggestions based on your likes and dislikes.

Ask questions.

If you don't understand something about the printing process or about your responsibilities in preparing the material, don't be afraid to ask. An informed customer is much easier for the printer to deal with than a customer who doesn't understand the process.

Get a guaranteed print date.

Most printers give you a target date or time by which they will have finished the publication. And reputable printers stick to that deadline. Bear in mind, however, that sometimes even in the best of situations, deadlines get bumped; if your chosen printing company misses by a little bit, don't write it off—unless the delays become a pattern.

Customizing WordStar

Throughout this book, examples and figures have been based on the default configuration of WordStar. (All settings, such as color selection, printer selection, drive designation, editing settings, and so on, have been left the way they were set up during WordStar's automatic installation process.) You can change many of WordStar's default settings to make the program conform more closely to your individual needs. A few changes you might want to make include the following:

- Changing the screen display of **boldface**, *italic*, or <u>underlined</u> text

- Selecting a different monitor

- Changing the size or speed of the cursor

- Turning on the type-ahead buffer (so that you can type faster than the screen can display the characters)

- Choosing different screen colors

This appendix provides an overview of the steps you can use to start the WINSTALL program and find the customization options you need and also provide you with enough familiarity with WINSTALL to make the changes just listed.

Starting WINSTALL

When you want to customize settings in WordStar, surprisingly, you don't start *in* WordStar. You begin at the DOS prompt. (If you're working in WordStar, save and close your file; then exit to the DOS prompt by pressing X when the opening screen is displayed.

When the DOS prompt (C:\WS or D:\WS) is displayed, type *WINSTALL* and press Enter. The WINSTALL main menu appears, as shown in figure F.1.

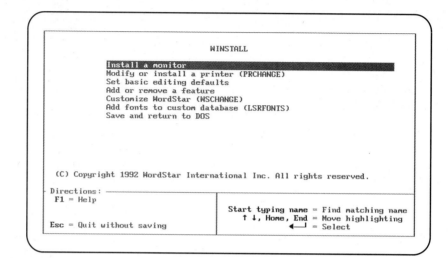

```
                              WINSTALL

                 Install a monitor
                 Modify or install a printer (PRCHANGE)
                 Set basic editing defaults
                 Add or remove a feature
                 Customize WordStar (WSCHANGE)
                 Add fonts to custom database (LSRFONTS)
                 Save and return to DOS




         (C) Copyright 1992 WordStar International Inc. All rights reserved.

   ┌ Directions: ─────────────────────┬───────────────────────────────────
   │   F1 = Help                       │
   │                                   │  Start typing name = Find matching name
   │                                   │     ↑ ↓, Home, End = Move highlighting
   │   Esc = Quit without saving       │          ◄─┘ = Select
```

Fig. F.1

The WINSTALL main menu.

Table F.1 summarizes the options on the WINSTALL main menu.

You've seen the screens behind many of these options before—when you installed WordStar for the first time. The Install a Monitor, Modify or Install a Printer, and Add or Remove a Feature screens are all displayed during basic installation. In the next section, you find out about changing basic program settings.

Changing Program Settings

To select an item from the WINSTALL main menu, use the arrow keys to highlight your choice and then press Enter. After you highlight Customize WordStar and press Enter, the screen shown in figure F.2 is displayed.

Table F.1 The WINSTALL Menu Options

Option	Description
Install a Monitor	Enables you to install a different monitor
Modify or Install a Printer (PRCHANGE)	Takes you through the steps for setting up a printer description file (PDF)
Set Basic Editing Defaults	Enables you to control the basic editing defaults (such as the default paragraph style, insert or typeover mode, and other editing settings)
Add or Remove a Feature	Enables you to add or remove individual program features from your installation of WordStar (such as Inset, TelMerge, and MailList)
Customize WordStar (WSCHANGE)	Provides you with a means to perform high-level (programming) changes within WordStar (recommended for experienced users only)
Add Fonts to Custom Database (LSRFONTS)	Enables you to create or change the database that stores laser printer fonts
Save and Return to DOS	Saves the WINSTALL changes and exits to the DOS prompt

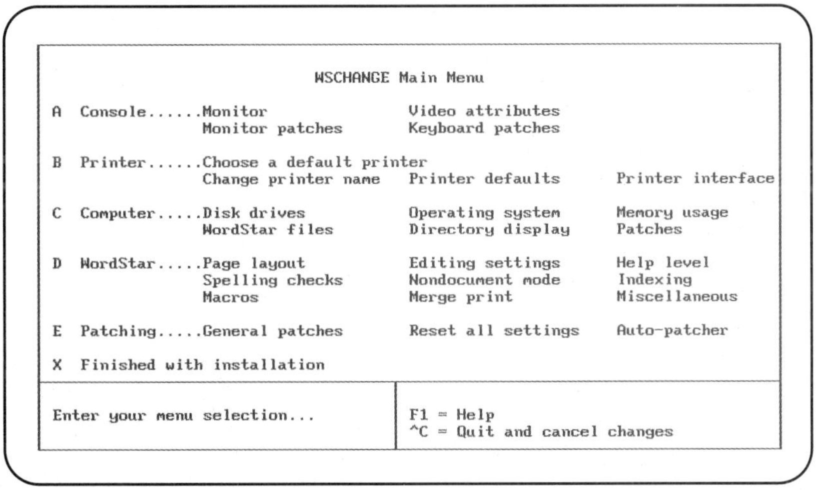

```
                        WSCHANGE Main Menu

A   Console......Monitor              Video attributes
                 Monitor patches      Keyboard patches

B   Printer......Choose a default printer
                 Change printer name   Printer defaults      Printer interface

C   Computer.....Disk drives          Operating system      Memory usage
                 WordStar files       Directory display     Patches

D   WordStar.....Page layout          Editing settings      Help level
                 Spelling checks      Nondocument mode      Indexing
                 Macros               Merge print           Miscellaneous

E   Patching.....General patches      Reset all settings    Auto-patcher

X   Finished with installation

Enter your menu selection...        F1 = Help
                                    ^C = Quit and cancel changes
```

Fig. F.2

The WSCHANGE Main Menu.

Table F.2 explains the options on the WSCHANGE Main Menu.

Table F.2 The WSCHANGE Main Menu Options

Option	Press	Description
Console	A	Enables you to change the colors on the screen, change the video display method, and modify screen size
Printer	B	Enables you to select the default printer you will use during your WordStar work sessions and to set printing defaults
Computer	C	Enables you to specify the disk drives in your system, change directory or file names, and customize the way WordStar uses memory
WordStar	D	Provides options for changing a variety of WordStar settings, including page layout, editing, spelling, indexing, and merge printing
Patching	E	Enables you to modify programming specifications for WordStar (not recommended for novice users)
Exit	X	Exits the WSCHANGE menu and returns you to the WINSTALL main menu

To select an item from the WSCHANGE menu, type the letter that corresponds to the option you want (for example, to select Console, press A). The secondary menu is displayed.

Follow the on-screen prompts to select the options you need. When in doubt, press F1 for help. When you're finished making changes, press X to return to the main menu.

Leaving WSCHANGE

If at any time you want to leave WSCHANGE without saving changes, press Ctrl-C to cancel all changes.

Changing Editing Defaults

The WINSTALL main menu also provides an option tailored specifically to changing editing defaults. After you select the Set Basic Editing Defaults option from the WINSTALL main menu, you are presented with the screen shown in figure F.3.

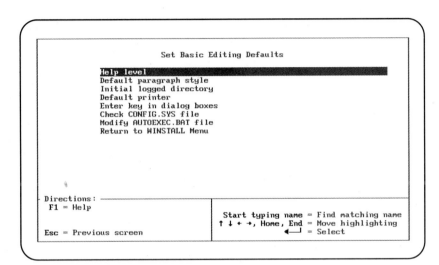

```
                    Set Basic Editing Defaults
              Help level
              Default paragraph style
              Initial logged directory
              Default printer
              Enter key in dialog boxes
              Check CONFIG.SYS file
              Modify AUTOEXEC.BAT file
              Return to WINSTALL Menu




  Directions:
    F1 = Help
                             Start typing name = Find matching name
                           ↑ ↓ ← →, Home, End = Move highlighting
                                         ◄─┘ = Select
    Esc = Previous screen
```

Fig. F.3

The Set Basic Editing Defaults screen.

To select an option, use the arrow keys to highlight the one you want and press Enter. Follow the prompts on the screen to make changes for the individual options. When you're finished making changes, press Esc (or whichever key is specified on that particular screen) to return to the Editing Defaults screen.

Table F.3 summarizes the editing default options.

Table F.3 The Set Basic Editing Defaults Options

Option	Description
Help Level	Enables you to set the default help level
Default Paragraph	Enables you to set tabs, margins, printing options, and fonts
Initial Logged Directory	Enables you to specify the drive or directory WordStar logs onto
Default Printer	Enables you to change the selected printer driver file (PDF) for all new documents
Enter Key in Dialog Boxes	Enables you to change the way the Enter key works in dialog boxes
Check CONFIG.SYS	Adds a statement to CONFIG.SYS
Modify AUTOEXEC.BAT File	Enables you to have WordStar modify the AUTOEXEC.BAT file

Exiting WINSTALL

When you're finished making changes in WINSTALL, return to the WINSTALL main menu. Then highlight the Save and Return to DOS option and press Enter. You are then returned to the DOS prompt.

Glossary

Alignment. A term used to describe how text is positioned within a column or on a page with respect to the left and right margins. In WordStar, you can choose text alignment by clicking an alignment button in the style bar row or by pressing Ctrl-OS to display the Alignment and Spacing dialog box.

ASCII. An acronym for American Standard Code for Information Interchange, the "common denominator" form of saving data. Most word processing programs can save data in ASCII format, which doesn't contain formatting or font specifications of any kind. WordStar then can import the ASCII files.

Bad break. An improperly hyphenated line break in which part of a word is wrapped to the next line or column.

Banner. The title that appears across the top of a newsletter or report.

Bit-mapped image. A picture created from a series of dots.

Bleed. A term (used in the phrase *bleed off the page*) that indicates a graphic element, such as a rule or box, that continues off the edge of the page.

Block. A marked or highlighted section of text. You must highlight a block of text before you can move, copy, or cut text.

Body text. The text of the document; also the name of a paragraph style included with WordStar 7.0.

Boot. The process of turning on the computer's power. See also *Cold boot* and *Warm boot*.

Brochure. A small, folded booklet or pamphlet.

Bullets. Dots or other characters used to set off items in a list.

Caption. A short legend or description used to explain a photo or illustration.

Callout. Text used to point out an element in a figure or in a shadow box to summarize concepts introduced in the text.

Clipboard. A storage area in Windows, that you can use to store the text block most recently cut, copied, or pasted, if you're running WordStar from within Windows.

Cold boot. The process of turning on the computer.

Color printer. A high-end laser printer that can print in four colors. (WordStar 7.0 supports color printing.)

Command tags. The WordStar codes inserted into your document to control formatting and style features. You can turn the display of command tags off (and on again) by pressing Ctrl-OD.

Crop marks. Lines on graphic images used to indicate to the printer where the image should be cropped (or cut).

Cursor. The flashing underscore that shows where characters are inserted when you begin typing. See also *Mouse cursor*.

Default. A command setting that a program uses unless you specify otherwise.

Desktop publishing. A computerized method of publishing printed materials.

Dialog box. A message box that provides additional options for the current operation.

Directory. An area on disk in which a specific group of files is stored.

Dot-matrix printer. A printer that creates characters and images by using patterns of dots.

Downloadable fonts. Fonts that are stored in your computer's memory and sent to the printer at print time. Also called *soft fonts*, these fonts are available for dot-matrix, inkjet, and laser printers.

dpi. Acronym for *dots per inch*, a measurement used to indicate the quality of text or graphics output produced in print.

Drag. An action in which you press and hold down the mouse button, move the mouse cursor to where you want it, and then release the button.

Draw-type picture. A drawing created based on extensive programming instructions; also known as an *object-oriented graphic*. The edges are clear and sharp, and you can resize, crop, and move such graphics without any loss of quality.

Edit screen. The screen on which you work with the WordStar document.

Elevator. The small box in the elevator bar that indicates your position on-screen.

Elevator bar. The vertical bar on the right side of the screen that has one arrow at each end and a small box between the arrows. You use this bar to scroll through your WordStar document by clicking the arrows or the gray sections of the bar.

Exporting. The process of saving a file in a format that other applications can use.

Fax. A data transmission and output device that scans information (or sends a file) to another facsimile or fax machine, which then prints the output. WordStar 7.0's FAX command enables you to convert WordStar files into a format that can be faxed.

Filenames list. A section at the bottom of WordStar's opening screen that lists the subdirectories of WS and the files in the current directory.

Font. A complete set of characters in a specific typeface, size, and style; for example, 12-point boldface Times Roman is one font, whereas 14-point boldface Times Roman is another font.

Footer. Lines of text that appear on the bottom of every page in a document.

Gutter. The white space between columns.

Header. Lines of text that appear at the top of every page of a document.

Highlight. Text or command displayed in reverse video. Before performing operations on text, you first must highlight the text.

Icon. A small graphical image used to help readers identify with a company by use of a logo or other symbol. Also, an on-screen symbol that represents a program, file, command, or other computer function.

Index. A WordStar command that compiles an index based on index entries added in a document.

Justified text. A text alignment setting in which text is aligned along the left and right margins.

Kerning. The process of reducing the amount of space between certain pairs of letters (such as *AV*, *VA*, and so forth) so that they look better in print. Kerning is used most often in headlines and titles.

Kilobyte. Approximately 1,024 bytes. Standard unit of measure for computer memory, abbreviated as K.

Landscape orientation. The mode in which the printer produces output lengthwise, parallel to the longer edge of a page.

Laser printer. A high-resolution printer that uses laser technology to produce print that rivals the output of electronic typesetting equipment.

Layout. The phase of putting all elements together to form a document.

Leading. The distance between lines of text, measured from the bottom of one line of text to the bottom of the following line of text. Also known as *line height*.

Left-justified text. An alignment setting in which the text aligns along only the left margin; also known as *ragged-right text*.

Letter quality. A term used loosely to describe the quality you can achieve from typewritten text. Dot-matrix printers often are described as being "letter quality" or "near letter quality."

Logo. A company's symbol or graphic image used on stationery, cards, invoices, and so forth.

Macro. A stored series of instructions that you can carry out by pressing a key combination. WordStar 7.0 is equipped with many different macros. You also can record your own macros or use WordStar 7.0's new powerful macro language to write the code for the macro.

Margin. The amount of white space reserved on a document in which text and graphics are not printed.

Megabyte. Approximately 1 million bytes. Abbreviated as M.

Menu bar. The bar across the top of the WordStar opening and edit screens, in which all the menu names are displayed.

Mini-save. The process in which you save an existing file quickly by pressing Ctrl-S.

Monospace. A term used to describe a font in which each character is given an equal amount of space.

Mouse. A small peripheral device used to point to and select menus, commands, and options. A mouse is optional with WordStar 7.0.

Mouse cursor. The on-screen rectangle that moves in accordance with the movement of the mouse; also called the *mouse pointer*.

Object-oriented graphic. See *Draw-type picture*.

On-line. For printers, a term that means the print head is positioned correctly and the paper has been inserted—the printer is ready to print. In communications, a term that means your computer has established connection with another computer or an information service.

Opening screen. The first screen of WordStar; shows the File, Utilities, and Additional menus and the Filenames list.

Orphan. A formatting error in which the first line of a paragraph appears alone at the bottom of a page or column.

Paragraph style. Preset formats that you can apply to your text. Paragraph styles include basic font, size, style, alignment, and tab information. You can use WordStar's preset styles or create your own.

Path. The drive and directory where WordStar can find or save files you specify.

PCL printer. A printer capable of printing high-quality text (300 dpi), that uses its internal fonts, font cartridges, or soft fonts to create characters. PCL stands for *printer control language*, which is used for defining a page, selecting fonts, and so on.

Pixel. A dot, the smallest element in bit-mapped graphics. Every character and image is composed of a pattern of pixels.

Point. A measurement of the height of a character, as in 12-point type; 72 points equal 1 inch.

Portrait orientation. The standard mode in which the printer produces output on an 8-by-11-1/2 page and prints across the narrow width of the page.

PostScript printer. A type of laser printer that uses a special page description language (called PostScript) to receive and print files. PostScript provides a wide range of fonts that you can scale to any size possible within the amount of RAM available in your printer and enables you to print high-resolution graphics.

Preview. A WordStar feature that enables you to see how your document will look in print. To activate preview, press Ctrl-OP.

Print head. The mechanism in a dot-matrix printer that forms characters by pressing pins against the printer ribbon and onto the page.

Print mode. A type of print quality provided by a printer. Most dot-matrix printers can print in more than one quality, or mode. Draft mode, for example, gives you a quick printout, but the quality is fairly poor. Near-letter-quality mode produces text with more clearly formed characters but takes longer to print. Compressed mode prints twice as many characters within the same amount of space used for draft or NLQ mode. (Not all printers support all modes.)

Printer cable. The cable that connects your computer to the printer.

Printer driver. The file that your computer uses to store printer-related information.

Printer memory. The amount of memory in your printer that stores external fonts and, in laser printers, stores fonts that are downloaded during a work session.

Printer port. The plug-like receptacle on the back of your computer into which you attach the printer cable.

Printer ribbon. The inked ribbon—like a typewriter ribbon—used in dot-matrix printers.

Pull-down menu. A menu you can display by using the mouse to "pull it down" or by pressing specified function keys.

Quick keys. Keystrokes displayed on WordStar's menus, showing you alternative ways to choose the options without using the pull-down menus.

RAM. An acronym for *random-access memory*. The memory where your computer stores active programs and open files.

Resolution. Used to refer to the quality (or lack of quality) in displayed characters or in printed output measured in dpi. Resolution measures the sharpness of an image on output devices, such as monitors and printers.

Ruler. A measuring feature across the top of the WordStar edit screen, that enables you to see left and right margins, tab stops, and text alignment.

Sans serif. A typeface without the small cross strokes that appear on the ends of characters.

Scanner. An input device similar to a photocopier that digitizes photographs and printed images into an electronically usable form.

Scroll. A term that describes the action of moving the screen display horizontally or vertically, enabling you to move to other sections of your document.

Serif. Small cross strokes across the ends of the characters.

Soft font. A font, packaged on disk, that is copied to the printer at print time. Also called *downloadable font*.

Sheet feeder. An add-on mechanism available for printers, that holds paper until needed and then sends separate sheets of paper to the printer. Also called *cut-sheet feeder*.

Spelling checker. A utility included with WordStar that checks the spelling of words in your documents.

Star Exchange. A utility provided with WordStar that enables you to translate files created in other programs into a format that WordStar can use.

Table of Contents. A command (on the Utilities menu) that generates a table of contents based on TOC entries you make in the document file.

Template. A document skeleton upon which you build the actual document. You can use templates to save time when you create similar documents or subsequent issues of a newsletter, for example.

Thesaurus. A built-in feature of WordStar that provides synonyms for words you specify.

Toner cartridge. The plug-in cartridge for laser printers, that stores a powderlike substance, known as *toner*, that places the text and graphics on the page.

Tractor feed. On a dot-matrix printer, a device built into the printer itself or an add-on mechanism that fits on the top of the printer above the paper feed slot. The tractor feed has "teeth" on which you place the punch holes of continuous paper so that the pages move smoothly through the printer without getting caught in the printer or shifting out of alignment.

Warm boot. The process of restarting the computer by pressing the reset button or by pressing Ctrl-Alt-Del.

White space. Blank space on a document, used to help give the reader's eye a rest and draw attention to important elements.

Wide-carriage printer. A dot-matrix printer that can print on double-width paper.

Widow. A formatting error in which the last line of a paragraph appears alone at the top of the next page or column.

Window. A second open editing screen displayed on part of the first open editing screen so that you can have two documents open at the same time. Use the Open/Switch command in the File menu to open and move between document windows.

Word wrap. An action in which WordStar automatically bumps words to the next line when the words you type pass the right margin.

WYSIWYG. An acronym for "what you see is what you get," used to describe programs that show on-screen what you will see when you print.

B

D

installing
  Inset, 300
  monitors, 432
  printers, 275-276, 433
  TelMerge utility, 380-381
  WordStar 7.0, 427-436
instructional manuals, creating, 420-424
internal fonts, 212
internal modems, 378
ITT Telex and TIMETRAN option, 385

J-K

justified text, 83, 217-218, 473

K (define highlighted word) quick key, 194
Keep Lines Together in Column
  command, 284
  dialog box, 284
Keep Lines Together on Page
  command, 283
  dialog box, 284
Keep Words Together on Line
  command, 283
kerning, 235, 248, 258, 474
keyboard shortcuts, see quick-key combinations
keyboards, 22, 25-26
  combinations, 25-27, 47, 73-74, 235
  editing, 72-81, 160-161
  IBM Enhanced, 24
  IBM PC AT, 24
  modes, 305
  printing from 290-292
  standard, 23
  text blocks, 164-165
key
  preview mode, 238
  special, 25
kilobytes, 474

L

L (cross-reference) quick key, 194
labels, printing, 375-376
landscape orientation, 119, 251, 474, 440
laser printers, 277-280, 474
Last Page command, 241
layout, 474
Layout menu, 59, 248, 454
leading, 259-260, 474
left alignment of text, 83, 217-218, 474
left margin, 253
letter-quality printing, 277, 474
letters
  alignment, 117
  creating, 444-445
  printing, 119
  spacing, 248
  see also kerning
levels of display, menus, 42
Line option, 175
line breaks, 471
Line Left of Cursor option, 175
Line Numbering
  command, 248
  dialog box, 268
Line Right of Cursor option, 175
line spacing
  button, 65-66
  editing, 208, 221-222
  setting, 200
lines
  blank, 252
  centering, 248
  command, 263
  ending, 259
  gluing, 283-284
  height, 248
  leading, 259-260
  numbers, 248, 267-268
  overprinting, 248, 282
  spacing, 84, 248

right alignment of text, 83, 217-218, 248
right margin, 253
root (\) directory, 96
ruler line, 231
Ruler Line
  command, 248
  dialog box, 253
ruler, 476
Run DOS Command option, 439

S

S (open file) quick key, 70
sans serif fonts, 120, 211, 476
Save and Close command, 331
Save As dialog box, 87
Save command, 87
Save Inset menu, 308
saving
  documents, 86-87
  files, 87, 102-104, 159
  macros, 328-330
  mini, 474
scalable fonts, 258, 280
Scan Range command, 243
scanner, 476
Screen Settings dialog box, 229
screen shots
  capturing, 307, 310-311
  editing, 311-312
  modifying, 311-312
screens
  edit, 49, 473
  Hardware Configuration Setup, 301
  on-line, TelMerge utility, 386-388
  opening, 92, 475
  preview, 236-238
scroll arrows, 45
scroll bar, 66
  displaying, 231
  mouse, 140-141

scrolling, 141, 148-149, 476
Select Paragraph Style
  command, 86, 151
  dialog box, 85
selecting
  color for monitor, 432
  commands, 37, 48-52
  data files, 350
  directories, 98-99
  drives, 99-100
  files, 107
  Find command options, 179-181
  help levels, 227-228
  inks, 462-463
  macros, 322-325
  paper size, 251-252, 461-462
  paragraph styles, 203-204
  printers, 284-285
  text, 75-76
  typeface, 120
  WINSTALL main menu items, 466
  WSCHANGE menu items, 468
semi-active keyboard mode, 305
sending
  files, 286-288, 388-389
  messages, electronic, 380
serif fonts, 120, 212, 477
Set Basic Editing Defaults options
  Check CONFIG.SYS, 470
  Default Paragraph, 470
  Default Printer, 470
  Enter Key in Dialog Boxes, 470
  Help Level, 470
  Initial Logged Directory, 470
  Modify AUTOEXEC.BAT File, 470
Set Marker command, 146
Set Variable command, 349
Set Variable to Math Result
  command, 374
  dialog box, 357

U-V

Free Catalog!

Mail us this registration form today, and we'll send you a free catalog featuring Que's complete line of best-selling books.

Name of Book _____

Name _____

Title _____

Phone ( ) _____

Company _____

Address _____

City _____

State _____ ZIP _____

Please check the appropriate answers:

1. Where did you buy your Que book?
   - ☐ Bookstore (name: _____)
   - ☐ Computer store (name: _____)
   - ☐ Catalog (name: _____)
   - ☐ Direct from Que
   - ☐ Other: _____

2. How many computer books do you buy a year?
   - ☐ 1 or less
   - ☐ 2-5
   - ☐ 6-10
   - ☐ More than 10

3. How many Que books do you own?
   - ☐ 1
   - ☐ 2-5
   - ☐ 6-10
   - ☐ More than 10

4. How long have you been using this software?
   - ☐ Less than 6 months
   - ☐ 6 months to 1 year
   - ☐ 1-3 years
   - ☐ More than 3 years

5. What influenced your purchase of this Que book?
   - ☐ Personal recommendation
   - ☐ Advertisement
   - ☐ In-store display
   - ☐ Price
   - ☐ Que catalog
   - ☐ Que mailing
   - ☐ Que's reputation
   - ☐ Other: _____

6. How would you rate the overall content of the book?
   - ☐ Very good
   - ☐ Good
   - ☐ Satisfactory
   - ☐ Poor

7. What do you like *best* about this Que book?
   _____
   _____

8. What do you like *least* about this Que book?
   _____
   _____

9. Did you buy this book with your personal funds?
   - ☐ Yes   ☐ No

10. Please feel free to list any other comments you may have about this Que book.
    _____
    _____
    _____

que

Order Your Que Books Today!

Name _____

Title _____

Company _____

City _____

State _____ ZIP _____

Phone No. ( ) _____

Method of Payment:

Check ☐ (Please enclose in envelope.)

Charge My: VISA ☐   MasterCard ☐

American Express ☐

Charge # _____

Expiration Date _____

Order No.	Title	Qty.	Price	Total

You can **FAX** your order to **1-317-573-2583**. Or call **1-800-428-5331, ext. ORDR** to order direct.

Please add $2.50 per title for shipping and handling.

Subtotal _____

Shipping & Handling _____

Total _____

que

BUSINESS REPLY MAIL

First Class Permit No. 9918   Indianapolis, IN

Postage will be paid by addressee

11711 N. College
Carmel, IN 46032

NO POSTAGE
NECESSARY
IF MAILED
IN THE
UNITED STATES

BUSINESS REPLY MAIL

First Class Permit No. 9918   Indianapolis, IN

Postage will be paid by addressee

11711 N. College
Carmel, IN 46032